LIBRARY OF

AND

MONEY · BANKING

HISTORY

THE HISTORY OF THE PUBLIC REVENUE
OF THE BRITISH EMPIRE

VOLUME II

THE
HISTORY
OF THE
PUBLIC REVENUE
OF THE
BRITISH EMPIRE

BY

SIR JOHN SINCLAIR

THE THIRD EDITION

[1803-1804]

IN THREE VOLUMES
VOLUME II

REPRINTS OF ECONOMIC CLASSICS

AUGUSTUS M. KELLEY · PUBLISHERS
NEW YORK · 1966

LIBRARY OF CONGRESS CATALOGUE CARD NUMBER

66 - 22636

HJ
2603
.S42
1966
V. 2

PRINTED IN THE UNITED STATES OF AMERICA
by SENTRY PRESS, NEW YORK, N. Y. 10019

THE

HISTORY

OF THE

PUBLIC REVENUE

OF THE

BRITISH EMPIRE.

CONTAINING

An Account of the public Income and Expenditure from the remoteſt Periods recorded in Hiſtory, to Michaelmas 1802. With a Review of the Financial Adminiſtration of the Right Honorable William Pitt.

———◆———

By Sir JOHN SINCLAIR, Baronet, M.P.

———◆———

IL N'Y A RIEN QUE LA SAGESSE, ET LA PRUDENCE DOIVENT PLUS REGLE, QUE CETTE PORTION QU'ON ÔTE, ET CETTE PORTION QU'ON LAISSE AUX SUJETS.

L'ESPRIT DES LOIX, l. xiii. c. 1.

THE THIRD EDITION.

VOL. II.

LONDON:

Printed by A. Strahan, Printers-Street,

FOR T. CADELL AND W. DAVIES, IN THE STRAND,
AND SOLD BY W. J. AND J. RICHARDSON, CORNHILL; W. CREECH,
EDINBURGH; AND J. ARCHER, DUBLIN.

1803.

ADVERTISEMENT

TO

THE SECOND VOLUME.

———

I REGRET much, that a feries of ill health, prevents me from completing at this time, the great plan I had fketched out, for laying before the public, the progrefs and prefent ftate of the finances of the Britifh empire; or even to do that juftice, which might other-wife have been expected, to the particular articles herein difcuffed. The work how-ever, as it is now printed, will, I truft, fur-nifh the reader with fome ufeful information, regarding the moft important branches of our financial hiftory*. The points remain-ing

---

* The Hiftory of the Revenue, as originally printed, is thus mentioned by a foreign author, who propofes giving a tranfla-tion of it into French.

Extract from a work intitled, " Effai fur le Credit Com-" mercial, et Profpectus de la Traduction de l'Hiftoire des " Finances de la Grande Bretagne, de Sir John Sinclair, M.P. " 2 vol. in quarto. Par J, H. Marniere. A Paris, an ix. " (1801.)"

" L'Hiftoire

ing for confideration are, 1. The prefent ftate of the national debt, with fome obfervations on the nature and real amount of the burden, and the means of difcharging it. 2. The revenue of Scotland. 3. The income, expenditure, and debt of Ireland. 4. The income and expenditure of the three kingdoms taken as one empire :—and 5. The national refources, including fome hints re-

---

"L'Hiftoire du Revenu Public, et du Credit de la Grande-
"Bretagne, par Sir John Sinclair, prefente le vafte tableau
"de toutes les opérations de finances que le gouvernement
"Anglois a faites depuis un fiecle dans le genre des emprunts,
"et dans celui des impofitions; et l'auteur en démontre les
"avantages ou les inconveniens, fans fe laiffer jamais égarer
"par des idées fyftematiques, ou des opinions de parti."—
Avertiffement, p. 3.

"Son ouvrage forme fans contredit le plus grand recueil
"de faits intéreffans fur les finances qui exifte en Europe."—
p. 111.

"L'Hiftoire du Revenu Public de la Grande-Bretagne, eft
"trop connue pour que je m'arrête a en faire l'eloge; je
"me contenterai de dire qu'elle donne le detail de toutes les
"opérations de finances, que la nation de l'Europe qui a fu
"procurer à l'etat le plus grand revenu et le plus grand credit,
"a faites depuis une fiecle ; et que l'auteur en montre les
"avantages ou les inconveniens par des obfervations dont
"la fageffe et la fagacité juftifient fa grande reputation."

The reader may eafily fuppofe, how anxious an author muft be, to complete and to render as perfect as poffible, any work that had the fmalleft pretenfions to fuch eulogiums.

garding

garding the political circumftances of the empire in general.

His obfervations on thefe important fubjects, the author will endeavour to complete, in the courfe of the enfuing year.

London, 10th *May* 1803.

CONTENTS

OF

THE SECOND VOLUME.

PART III.

APPENDIX.

THE

THE

HISTORY

OF THE

PUBLIC REVENUE

OF THE

BRITISH EMPIRE.

====

PART III.

CHAP. I.

Of the Progrefs of the national Income fince the Revolution.

AMONG the various political problems, which it would be not a little defirable to have fatisfactorily explained, there is none more curious in itfelf, or more truly interefting to this country, than a ftatement of the means, which have enabled it to bear its progreffive weight of taxes, but more particularly the heavy burdens to which it is now fubject.

National Income fince the Revolution.

National In-
come since the　ject. A century has scarcely elapsed, since a re-
Revolution.　venue of about two millions, was supposed to be
fully equal to its utmost ability ; nor since D'Avenant, the most intelligent writer of his time on
public questions, openly asserted, that the commerce and manufactures of England would sink
under a heavier load [a]. Whereas now, England,
alone, supplies the public treasury with above
thirty millions; and, till of late, any popular clamour that was heard, was more owing to the manner in which our taxes were laid on, than to the
quantum that was levied.

In endeavouring to account for this singular political phenomenon, it is natural to consider, as the
most efficient cause, the great addition that has
been made to the general wealth and capital of the
kingdom. The income of England, at the revolution, was usually calculated at forty-three millions.
On that sum the inhabitants of this country lived;
and, besides furnishing themselves with every article necessary for the sustenance and comfort of
life, supplied the public treasury with two millions
per annum. Whereas at present, in consequence
of the various improvements which have taken
place in *agriculture, manufactures,* and *commerce,*
the general revenue of the inhabitants of the whole
island, cannot be less than 150 millions, and hence
they are enabled to contribute a much greater sum
than heretofore, to the coffers of the public.

[a] D'Avenant's Works, vol. ii. p. 283.

Agriculture,

Agriculture, in particular, that beft and fureft *National Income fince the Revolution.* fource of national wealth, in no country perhaps of equal extent, has been carried to fuch perfection. By improvements in that art, not only the fields have been made more productive, but lands, formerly wafte and uncultivated, have been rendered fertile : nay, independently of other products of the earth, grain alone, to the value of nearly forty millions of pounds, has been fent to other countries. Indeed, during the fpace of only five years, from 1743 to 1749, no lefs a quantity than 3,768,440 quarters of corn of different kinds, the value of which, at the medium price of from forty to forty-five fhillings, could not be lefs than *eight millions*, were actually exported.

Formerly, England was obliged to fupply itfelf, with various important articles from other countries, and fent hardly any commodity, of confiderable value abroad, woollens alone excepted. But, fince the revolution, the cafe has been greatly altered : valuable manufactories of filk and cotton have been eftablifhed : with the affiftance of Ireland, it is now almoft able to fupply itfelf with the important article of linen ; and, inftead of importing, it actually exports glafs, paper, earthen-ware, and many other commodities, which formerly rendered the balance of trade, in particular with France, rather unfavourable to this country.

The general commerce of the nation, alfo, has been materially augmented. *Anno* 1697, the imports amounted to £. 3,482,586 10 s. 5 d. the ex-

ports

ports to £.3,525,906 18 s. 6 d. and the balance
in our favour only to £. 43,320 8 s. 1 d. Whereas
on 5th January 1800, the imports of Great Britain, for one year, amounted to £.29,945,808,
the exports to £. 35,990,000, and the balance to
£. 6,044,192. This is partly to be attributed, to the
increased induſtry and commercial exertions of the
nation, and partly to the great value and opulence of
our colonial poſſeſſions, which, notwithſtanding the
independence of North America, ſtill continue of immenſe importance. Our commerce and ſettlements
in the Eaſt, in particular, muſt be the means of
adding many millions to our national wealth.

At firſt ſight, it is natural to wonder, how 150
millions of annual income, can yield a public revenue of above thirty millions *per annum*, when forty-
three millions only produced two. But it ſhould be
conſidered, that it is from ſuperfluous wealth alone,
that a large revenue can be drawn. At the revolution, the people of England required the greater
part of their income, to purchaſe merely the ne-
ceſſaries and conveniencies of life : and four ſhillings in the pound, muſt be leſs felt, and leſs liable
to complaint, from the additional wealth that has
been acquired ſince, than one ſhilling in the pound,
taken from an income, that was little more than
ſufficient for the ſuſtenance of the people.

Beſides, the financial, like every other art, requires much experience before it can be brought
to perfection. The ingenuity of able men muſt be
exerciſed, to counteract the various artifices of
thoſe,

thofe, who may be defirous of evading the taxes to
which they are fubject; and in no country, can the
public revenue be brought to the higheft ftandard
of which it is capable, until many have made it the
fole, or at leaft the principal object of their ftudy
and attention; nor indeed until the people have
been accuftomed to taxes. For, however obnoxious they may be when originally impofed, yet,
in procefs of time, when they become familiar to
the public, they are paid with lefs reluctance, and
confequently become more productive. Hence,
if the general income of England had ftill remained at only forty-three millions *per annum*, a
much larger portion of that fum would probably
have been paid at prefent, than at firft could have
been expected.

The advantages refulting to a public revenue,
from an eafy circulation, and from credit being
fully eftablifhed in a country, from an abundance
of money, (whether paper or fpecie is of little
confequence, where paper is received by the
exchequer), and alfo from the eftablifhment of
public debts themfelves, have already been taken
notice of [b]. But there are two important circumftances, namely, the enormous fize of the capital,
and the luxurious manners of the people, which
have not as yet been confidered. Wherever great
multitudes are affembled together, there much
wealth muft be concentered; and the government

[b] See vol. i. p. 13, 14.

of

National In-
come fince the
Revolution.

of a country, finds it much lefs difficult, to draw a confiderable revenue from thofe who are immediately under its eye, and live contiguous to each other, than from fuch as refide at a diftance, and are fcattered over the whole face of the country. Nor is it perhaps an exaggerated calculation, that the inhabitants of London and its neighbourhood, in proportion to their number, pay as much again to the public, as thofe who dwell at a diftance from that metropolis ^c.

Laftly, the luxurious manner in which the inhabitants of this country live, is not a little favourable to an increafe of revenue. Where private economy reigns, no productive impoft can be laid, but on property alone. That refource, however, is very limited: for few can bear, that the public fhould fhare very largely in their wealth, or fhould openly demand too great a portion of their income. But in luxurious ages, a confiderable revenue may be raifed, without hurting the feelings of the people. Taxes on confumption become efficient and productive, and the confumer, confounding the duty and the price together, furnifhes,

^c The proportion paid by London and its neighbourhood, has been computed by fome writers to be much more confiderable. For inftance, it was afferted *anno* 1692, that Yorkfhire paid but 15 s. 8 d. the houfe; whereas Middlefex, abftracted from London, paid 21 s. and London itfelf £. 3 6 s. 8 d. and that the acre in Yorkfhire paid but 5¼ d. whilft that in Middlefex paid 5 s. 11 d. See Houghton's Collections on Hufbandry and Trade, vol. i. p. 84.

without

without relu&ance, to the public treafury, a fum, which by any other means could hardly have been exa&ed.

Thefe circumftances tend to elucidate, the afto-nifhing increafe of the revenue, within the laft century. Let us next give fome account of its progrefs fince the revolution, and fince the efta-blifhment of the funding fyftem, by which that Era is fo peculiarly diftinguifhed.

WILLIAM III.

The heavy debts and expences that were in-curred, during the reign of William III. unavoid-ably introduced not only a great variety of new taxes, but alfo confiderable additions to thofe du-ties that had formerly been laid on. It is not pro-pofed, however, to attempt, giving an account of every little minute regulation, that took place during the courfe of this reign. The curiofity of the reader, it is hoped, will be fufficiently gratified, by ftating the moft important particulars.

The permanent revenue arofe from the cuftoms, the excife, and a variety of mifcellaneous duties.

Many branches were added during this reign to 1. Cuftoms. the old fubfidy of tonnage and poundage. Duties were either impofed, or, after former grants were on the eve of expiring, were renewed, on the fol-lowing articles; namely, on wines and vinegar; on tobacco; on falt imported; on fpices and pictures;

on

National In-
come since the
Revolution.
on coals exported, or even carried coaft-ways; on muflins, whale fins; on French goods, foreign liquors imported; &c. By thefe means, during this reign, the fum of £. 13,296,833 was raifed, of net produce, befides all bounties drawbacks, and the expence of collection.

2. Excife.
Even the revenue of the Excife, though of a nature peculiarly obnoxious to the fpirit and principles of the Britifh conftitution, made no inconfiderable progrefs during the reign of William. Excifes on falt, on the diftillery, and on malt, fince known under the name of the malt-tax, were then firft introduced. This branch of the revenue yielded during the fame period £. 13,649,328.

3. Mifcellaneous taxes
and receipts.
The principal fources of revenue of a mifcellaneous nature, were, the land-tax, poll-taxes, the tax on marriages, births, burials, &c. hearth-money, the poft-office, and other fmaller branches.

Land-tax.
The circumftances of the country, at the acceffion of William to the throne, were fuch, that no tax could be depended upon as fufficiently productive, that was not impofed upon land, in the produce of which the wealth and income of England at that time principally confifted. That it might be rendered as efficient as poffible, new affeffments were taken of the property and income that each individual poffeffed. But the rate was far from being equal. Thofe who were attached to the principles eftablifhed at the revolution, were forward to fhew their zeal in favour of the new government, and gave in a fair ftatement of their real fituation;
whilft

whilft the fecret and avowed friends of the exiled *National In-*
family, the fordid and avaricious, gave in a very *come fince the Revolution.*
different account, eftimating their property at the
loweft rate at which it could be calculated. Hence
the affeffments, fince known under the name of land-
tax, were not in any refpect fo productive as they
ought to have been. The amount of this branch,
during the reign of that monarch, was £.19,174,059.

Though England, at the revolution, was in a *Poll-Taxes.*
ftate fufficiently flourifhing to bear a confiderable
load of taxes; yet fuch were the confequences of
an unfettled government, and of the factious fpirit
prevalent at that time, that the utmoft difficulty
was found in raifing the money neceffary for the reduction of Ireland, and for carrying on the war
againft France. Among the meafures adopted for
that purpofe, recourfe was had to poll-taxes; and
it may be proper to give, the following ftate, of the
laft fyftem of levying a revenue by that mode, that
has been attempted in this country.

	Quarterly Taxes.
	£. *s.* *d.*
Poll to be paid by all perfons, except the poor, in-cluding fuch as are not worth £. 50 -	0 1 0
All Perfons worth £. 300 reputed gentlemen	1 0 0
Tradefmen, fhopkeepers, &c. -	0 10 0
Perfons chargeable with finding a horfe for the mi-litia, for each horfe - - -	1 0 0
Perfons keeping a coach and horfes, who do not contribute a horfe to the militia -	1 0 0
Perfons keeping a hackney or ftage coach, for each coach - - - -	1 5 0
Peers of the realm, fpiritual or temporal -	1 0 0
Attorneys, proctors, and other officers of the civil and ecclefiaftical courts - •	1 0 0

Clergymen,

National In-
come since the
Revolution.

Clergymen, preachers, and teachers of any kind,
  enjoying *£.* 80 *per annum* - - *£.* 1 0 0
  All nonjurors in every cafe were to pay double.

Though, in so lax and factious a government as
that of England, poll-taxes could not be very rigoroufly levied; yet, at the rates above mentioned, they produce the fum of *£.* 2,557,649.

It cannot be doubted, that by a ftrict exaction
of the above rates, a much larger fum might have
been raifed : but the government was afraid to irri-
tate the people, by levying a tax fo generally obnoxious, in too harfh a manner.

Tax on mar-
riages,
births, bu-
rials, ba-
chelors, and
widowers.

Thofe taxes have ever been the moft approved
of, which operate as an ufeful regulation of police,
as well as a fource of revenue : and as in a political
view, it is of confiderable confequence, to know the
number of marriages, of births and burials, that
happen in a country, (becaufe thence the ftate of
its population may be pretty nearly calculated) ;
and as a tax on bachelors has been accounted an inducement to marriage, or at leaft a penalty upon
celibacy, the reader may be defirous of being informed, of the duties of that nature that were impofed during the reign of William.

BURIAL, BIRTH, and MARRIAGE RATES.

Degrees, Titles, &c.	Burials — The party's wife or widow. £ s d	Burials — Eldest son. £ s d	Burials — Younger children. £ s d	Births — Eldest son. £ s d	Births — Younger son. £ s d	Marriages — The party. £ s d	Marriages — Elder son. £ s d	Marriages — Younger son. £ s d
A Duke or Archbishop	50 4 0	30 4 0	25 4 0	30 2 0	25 2 0	50 2 0	30 2 6	25 2 6
A Marquis	40 4 0	25 4 0	20 4 0	25 2 0	20 2 0	40 2 0	25 2 6	20 2 6
An Earl	30 4 0	20 4 0	15 4 0	20 2 0	15 2 0	30 2 0	20 2 0	15 2 6
A Viscount	25 4 0	17 14 0	13 10 8	17 12 0	13 8 8	25 2 0	17 2 6	13 9 6
A Baron and Bishop	20 4 0	15 4 0	12 4 0	15 2 0	12 2 0	20 2 0	15 2 6	12 2 6
A Baronet or Knight of the Bath	15 4 0	5 4 0	1 4 0	5 2 0	1 1 0	15 2 0	5 2 6	1 2 6
A Knight, Bachelor, or Dean	10 4 0	5 4 0	1 4 0	5 2 0	1 1 0	10 2 0	5 2 6	1 2 6
The King's Serjeant at Law	20 4 0	1 4 0	1 4 0	1 2 0	1 2 0	20 2 0	1 2 6	1 2 6
Other Serjeants at Law	15 4 0	1 4 0	1 4 0	1 2 0	1 2 0	5 2 0	1 2 6	1 2 6
An Esquire	5 4 0	1 4 0	1 4 0	1 2 0	1 2 0	5 2 0	1 2 6	1 2 6
A Gentleman	1 4 0	1 4 0	1 4 0	1 2 0	1 2 0	5 2 0	1 2 6	1 2 6
Doctors of Divinity, Law, or Physic	5 4 0	1 4 0	1 4 0	1 2 0	1 2 0	5 2 0	1 2 6	1 2 6
Persons of £.50 per annum, or £.600 personal estate	1 4 0	0 14 0	0 14 0	0 12 0	0 12 0	0 12 0	0 12 0	0 12 0
Persons not otherwise charged	0 4 0	0 4 0	0 4 0	0 2 0	0 2 0	0 2 0	0 2 0	0 2 6

Each parifh was obliged to pay for the burials of the poor, and of their families; but the births or marriages of fuch perfons as received alms, were not liable to pay duty.

The annual taxes impofed on bachelors, above the age of twenty-five years, and upon fuch widowers as had no children, were as follows:

Degrees, Titles, &c.	The Party himfelf.			The Eideft Son.			The Younger Son.		
	£.	s.	d.	£.	s.	d.	£.	s.	d.
A Duke, &c. - -	12	11	0	7	11	0	6	5	0
A Marquis - -	10	1	0	6	6	0	5	1	0
An Earl - - -	7	11	0	5	1	0	3	16	0
A Vifcount - - -	6	6	0	4	8	6	3	7	8
A Baron - - -	5	1	0	3	16	0	3	1	0
A Baronet and Knight of the Bath -	3	16	0	1	6	0	1	6	0
A Knight Bachelor - -	2	11	0	1	6	0	0	6	0
The King's Serjeant at Law	5	1	0	0	6	0	0	6	0
Other Serjeants at Law -	3	16	0	0	6	0	0	6	0
Efquires - - -	1	6	0	0	6	0	0	6	0
Gentlemen - - -	0	6	0	0	6	0	0	6	0
Doctors of Divinity, Law, or Phyfic	1	6	0	0	6	0	0	6	0
Perfons of £. 50 per annum or £.600 perfonal eftate - -	0	6	0	0	3	6	0	3	6
Perfons not otherwife charged -	0	1	0	0	1	0	0	1	0

From this tax, all fellows, ftudents, and fcholars in the different univerfities of Great Britain and Ireland, and perfons receiving alms, were exempted. This and the preceding tax were originally impofed for five years from the 1ft May 1695, but were afterwards prolonged to the 1ft Auguft 1706. They produced, during the firft five years, £.258,094 or £.51,618 *per annum.* During the remaining period, they were exacted in fo carelefs a manner, that
only

National In-come since the Revolution.

only £. 17,422 16 s. 2½ d. was accounted for. Perhaps now, when we are a little more accuftomed to taxes, a fimilar plan might be enforced, and, with little alteration, might be contrived fo as to yield at leaft £. 100,000 *per annum.*

The remaining refources which this monarch enjoyed, arofe from hearth-money, from the poft-office, and from a variety of fmaller branches, together with the loans of a permanent nature, which he contrived to borrow, amounting in all to £. 9,745,300 10 s. 9 d. The total fum then received by William during the courfe of his reign was as follows :

Cuftoms - -	£. 13,296,833	14	6
Excife - - -	13,649,328	0	5¼
Land-taxes - -	19,174,059	8	3½
Polls - - -	2,557,642	7	7¼
Tax on marriages, births, &c. -	275,517	18	1
Various articles (including permanent loans)	9,745,300	10	9
Temporary loans unpaid -	13,348,680	5	10¼

£. 72,047,369 5 6¼

Towhich thereistobeadded £.80,138 18 s. 10¼ d. which remained in the exchequer, and in the hands of the feveral receivers, on 5th November 1688.

The income of England, *anno* 1701, the year preceding this monarch's death, was as follows :

Cuftoms

National In-	Cuftoms	-	£. 1,539,100
come fince the *Revolution.*	Excife - - -		986,004
	Poft-office, &c. - -		130,399
	Land-tax at 2s. in the pound - -		989,965
	Various fmall taxes - -		249,737

	£. 3,895,205
Income at the Revolution	2,001,855

Total additional revenue at the death of William	£. 1,893,350

During the courfe of this reign, it is well known that many taxes, fuch as the malt-tax, the tax on hawkers and pedlars, on hackney coaches, &c. were introduced. But as they are continued to the prefent hour, and as fome obfervations will be made on them in a fucceeding chapter, it feems unneceffary at prefent to enter into the fubject. It may be proper, however, to mention three modes of taxation which exifted at that time, and fhortly to ftate the reafons for which they were given up.

Tax on glafs and earthen wares.   By an act paffed *anno* 1695, certain duties were granted on glafs wares, and upon ftone and earthen bottles, &c.[d], and a new fet of commiffioners was appointed for collecting and managing the duty. *Anno* 1696, another act was paffed[e], by which the faid duties were continued *for ever*, and extended to all forts of wares or commodities made from earth or ftone. It has been afferted, that our neighbours in Holland, who were then our great rivals in thofe articles, fuggefted that tax. But an act was afterwards paffed, reciting, that the duties impofed were " vexatious and troublefome, and

[d] 6 & 7 William III. chap. 18.
[e] 7 & 8 William III. chap. 81.

very

very chargeable in the levying and collecting the *National Income since the Revolution.* and consequently abolishing those duties as destructive to that important manufacture. Only one-half of the duties on glass was repealed by that act. The following year, however, the remaining duties on glass were taken off, as being of small advantage to the crown, leffening the duty on coals, hindering the employment of the poor, and endangering the lofs of fo beneficial a manufacture to to the kingdom [g]. The neceffities of the public have fince occafioned the revival of this obnoxious and impolitic impoft.

By the great act of tonnage and poundage, paffed *anno* 1660, on the reftoration of Charles II. taxes were impofed upon the exportation of woollen manufactures, and on all corn, grain, bread, bifcuit, and meal, fent out of the kingdom. During the reign of William, the wretched policy of fuch regulations began to be difcovered; and a law was paffed *anno* 1700, by which the duties on the woollen manufactures were abolifhed, becaufe, in the words of the act, " the wealth and profperity " of the kingdom, doth in a great meafure depend " on the improvement of its woollen manufactures, " and the profitable trade carried on by the expor-" tation thereof [h]." Nay, fo much were the ideas of men altered in regard to matters of commerce and finance, that inftead of a duty being impofed upon the exportation of grain, a bounty was given

Abolition of the tax on woollen manufactures, and on corn exported.

[f] 9 & 10 William III. chap. 45.
[g] 10 & 11 William III. chap. 18.
[h] 11 & 12 William III. chap. 20.

National In-
come since the
Revolution.

when that article was fent out of the kingdom.
The intention of the legiflature was, to encourage
production, and to animate the farmer to induftry
and exertion, from the certainty of a market. The
propriety of the meafure has not a little been con-
troverted, and many plaufible arguments have been
urged againft it; but fince the bounty was firft
granted, it cannot be denied, that grain has been
more abundant than in any other era of our hiftory,
the price at any rate more equal, and lefs fluctuating
than formerly;—an advantage of the utmoft importance, and not too dearly purchafed by the
money that it has coft.

Tax on the
joint ftocks
of corpora-
tions.

A meafure was attempted during this reign,
which, had the minds of people been accuftomed
to it, and had it exifted at this time, might have
proved a moft important refource to the nation.
By an act paffed *anno* 1692 [i], a tax of £. 5 *per cent.*
was impofed upon every proprietor of India ftock,
according to the fhare and proportion thereof in
which he was interefted; 20 s. upon every fhare of
the joint ftock of the royal African company; and
£. 5 for every fhare in the joint ftock of the Hud-
fon's Bay company; to be paid quarterly, and deducted from the next dividends payable to the feveral perfons interefted therein. The tax was continued only for one year. It produced £. 43,219.
But the public creditors, whether incorporated or
otherwife, have fince taken care to have it fpecifically provided, that their annuities fhall be exempted from all taxes and duties whatfoever.

[i] 4 & 5 William III. chap. 15.

QUEEN ANNE.

The greater part of the reign of this princefs was paffed in carrying on an expenfive war againft the houfe of Bourbon ; and as the fame fyftem that was begun under the adminiftration of William, of borrowing money for the charges of war, and of impofing taxes merely to defray the intereft, was perfevered in ; it was on that account neceffary to make a variety of new laws and alterations every year in regard to the revenue, the detail of which would furnifh little inftruction or amufement to the reader. It is therefore propofed to ftate in this work only general obfervations.

The cuftoms during this reign, produced into the exchequer, the fum of £. 15,113,811. *The cuf-*
toms.

The revenue of excife yielded during the fame period £. 14,254,567. The produce of this branch greatly increafed, in confequence of a variety of duties impofed on a number of ufeful and neceffary articles; as candles, leather, foap, paper, ftarch, printed linens, &c. *Excifes.*

The land-tax, during this reign, was not a little productive, being generally kept up at the rate of 4 s. in the pound, and produced in all the fum of £. 21,285,909. *Land-tax.*

Without entering into the particular produce of the poft-office, &c. it may be fufficient to remark, that from Lady-day 1702 to Chriftmas 1715, the *Mifcella-*
neous taxes
and receipts.

smaller

National In-
come since the
Revolution. smaller branches of the revenue produced the total
sum of £. 5,261,346.

Loans.   It is difficult, at present, unless the records of the
treasury, and of the exchequer, were to be ransacked
for that special purpose, to give an exact account
of the money borrowed in the course of this reign.
It would appear, however, that including the loans
on temporary as well as perpetual taxes, the
amount may be stated at £. 59,853,154.

The following will then be the amount of the
sums received during the reign of Queen Anne:

Customs - -	£. 15,113,811
Excise - -	20,859,311
Land-tax - -	21,285,909
Miscellaneous taxes and receipts	5,261,346
	£. 62,520,377
Loans - - -	59,853,154
Total	£. 122,373,531

Tax on In-   This reign was distinguished by an attempt to
come.   lay a tax upon income. Resolutions were entered
into by the house of commons, that a duty of 50
per cent. should be laid upon the value of all stock
in trade, 25 *per cent.* upon all money at interest,
4 *s.* in the pound upon all annuities, pensions, and
yearly stipends; 5 *s.* in the pound upon all salaries,
fees, and perquisites of office; and 4 *s.* in the pound
upon persons exercising any profession whatsoever,
whether legal, medical, commercial, or ecclesi-
astical; and that all persons, the poor excepted,
                                             should

fhould pay within one year the fum of four fhillings. It was alfo voted, that a duty at the rate of one *per cent*. fhould be impofed upon the fhares of the capital ftock of all corporations or companies, to be continued for five years [m]. But the propofed tax on income was abandoned ; and a bill brought in for laying a duty upon buying, felling, or bargaining for fhares in joint ftocks, or corporations, was alfo dropped [n], the bank and Eaft India Company having petitioned againft it, as contrary to the public faith, and the acts by which they were eftablifhed. Another attempt of the fame kind, *anno* 1702, proved equally unfuccefsful [o]. Thus all idea of an equal pound rate, or a tax in a fair proportion to every man's yearly income, or the profits which he acquired from his eftate, bufinefs, or profeffion, was given up.

National Income fince the Revolution.

Some endeavours were made during this reign, to examine into the value of lands, and of all grants made by the crown fince the 13th of February 1688, with a view of refuming the fame, and of applying them to relieve the public neceffities, unlefs they were beftowed after due confideration. A bill for that purpofe was paffed by the commons, but rejected by the houfe of lords [p]. A refolution of the former, to lay a tax upon all grants from the crown fince the 6th February 1684 [q], of one-fifth

Refumption of crown grants.

[m] Comm. Journals, vol. xiii. p. 741. 743.
[n] Ibid. p. 834. 894. 896.   [o] Ibid. vol. xiv. p. 34.
[p] Hiftory of our National Debts, part ii. p. 130.
[q] Comm. Journals, vol. xv. p 78.

National Income since the Revolution.

part of the value of the grant at the time it was made, had been previously evaded; the leading men in both houses being too deeply interested in grants of that nature, to suffer such a bill to pass into a law.

Tax on white woollen broad cloths.

By a statute in the reign of Henry VIII. the exportation of white woollen broad cloths had been totally prohibited. Such a regulation, however, was supposed to be impolitic; and it was thought to be a sufficient encouragement to the dyers of this country, to impose a duty of five shillings *per* piece upon all white woollen broad cloths when exported [r].

Exportation of rock salt to Ireland.

Among the various advantages which Ireland enjoys, from the manner in which the two countries are at present connected, there is none of so singular a nature as the right which it possesses, of having rock salt exported from England duty free; whilst (with a few exceptions) if carried from one port to another in this country, it is liable to a considerable tax. But as so peculiar a privilege was owing to neglect, and not design, it is hoped that it will not be perpetuated. By an act passed *anno* 1710 [s], a duty of nine shillings *per* ton was imposed on all rock salt exported to Ireland for thirty-two years, from the 11th June 1711. Why it was not renewed when it came to expire, is not at present known; but justice to the people of Great Britain requires the revival of so equitable a regulation, or the ex-

[r] 6 Anne, cap. 9.   [s] 9 Anne, cap. 23. sect. 44.

tension

tenſion of the ſame privilege to the reſt of the kingdom.

The reign of Queen Anne is particularly cele-brated for the union which was ſo happily effected between the two kingdoms of England and Scotland. As before that event took place it was neceſſary to make a very minute inquiry into the revenues of both countries, we are thereby enabled to give a very accurate ſtatement of the income of England at that memorable æra, and of the different branches from which it was derived.

STATE of the REVENUE of ENGLAND at the UNION.
Civil Liſt Revenue.

The exciſe on beer (2 s. 6 d. per barrel) -	£. 286,178
Further ſubſidies of tonnage and poundage -	256,841
Poſt-office - - - -	101,101
Fines in the alienation office - -	4,804
Poſt fines - - - -	2,276
Wine licences - - - -	6,314
Sheriffs' proffers - - -	1,040
Compoſitions in the exchequer - -	13
Seizures of uncuſtomed and prohibited goods -	13,005
Revenue of the dutchy of Cornwall -	9,869
Revenue of the principality of Wales -	6,857
Rents of crown lands, fines, leaſes, &c. -	2,906
Total for the civil liſt	£. 691,204

Other TAXES:

Cuſtoms appropriated to Auguſt 1710 -	£. 345,704
Impoſitions on wine, vinegar, tobacco, ditto	373,485
Carried over	£. 719,189

Ad-

Brought forward	£.	719,189
Additional impositions	- -	39,645
Duties on coals and culm, appropriated to Sept. 1710		113,688
15 *per cent.* on muslins, &c. ditto	-	116,475
25 *per cent.* additional duty on French goods		10,794
5 *s. per* ton on French shipping	-	81
Plantation duties	- - -	877
4½ *per cent.* on Barbadoes and Leeward islands		6,459
The coinage duty	- -	7,350
Duty on whale fins and Scotch linen	-	10,939
⅓ additional tonnage and poundage for 98 years		81,745
¾ additional ditto for 4 years, from 1708	-	160,000
9 *d. per* barrel excise for 98 years	-	164,828
Another 9 *d. per* barrel to the bank	-	155,000
Another 9 *d. per* barrel for 99 years, from 1692		155,000
Duties on low wines, appropriated to June 1710		25,267
Rent of hackney coaches	- -	2,800
Licences to hawkers and pedlars	-	6,460
Stamp duty, partly to the East India Company, the rest appropriated to 1710	- -	89,110
1 *s. per* bushel on salt, appropriated to 1710	-	54,621
2 *s.* 4 *d. per* bushel on salt for the East India Company		128,038
The duty on windows appropriated to 1710		112,069
3,700 *l. per* week out of the excise	-	192,400
		2,352,836
The malt duty (often deficient)	-	650,000
The land tax	- - -	1,997,763
		5,000,599
Revenues of the civil list	- -	691,204
Total	£.	5,691,803

GEORGE I.

Little that is material occurs, in regard to the
progrefs of the revenue, during this monarch's reign,
which, on the whole, it was a period of great
tranquillity. The loans alfo were comparatively
fmall, amounting only to £. 2,832,093 of which
fum £. 141,093 might be charged with propricty
to Queen Anne's account, as it was appropriated
for the relief of the inhabitants of Nevis and St.
Chriftopher's, who had fuffered by an invafion of
the French, in the war ended by the peace of
Utrecht, and for whofe behoof a fum was voted by
parliament, for the purpofe of encouraging them to
refettle in thefe iflands.

The whole fum to be charged to the exchequer
of George the Firft will then be nearly as follows :

The cuftoms	-	-	£. 21,632,985
Excife	-	-	30,421,451
Stamps	-	-	1,675,609
Land Tax	-	-	18,470,022
Incidents	-	-	4,800,000
			77,000,067
Loans	-	-	2,832,093
			£. 79,832,160

Some financial events took place about this time,
which it may be proper to notice.

An act was paffed, *anno* 1721, abolifhing all
duties payable by law on the exportation of any
goods

National Income since the Revolution. goods or merchandize of the produce or manufacture of Great Britain, after the 25th March 1722, except on allum, lead, tin, coals, and fome other lefs important articles; and all forts of drugs and foreign goods ufed in dying, were permitted to be imported duty free [t]. As a farther encouragement alfo to the trade and navigation of the country, whale-fins and oil caught in the Greenland feas, or Davis's Straits, by Britifh fhips navigated according to law, were exempted from all duties upon importation [u]. But this encouragement proving infufficient, it was found neceffary, in the fucceeding reign, to promote fo ufeful a nurfery for our feamen, by a bounty.

Tax on papifts and nonjurors. By the annual land tax bill, the eftates of papifts and nonjurors are taxed double. But not fatisfied with impofing that burden, parliament, *anno* 1722, laid the additional fum of £. 100,000 upon their real and perfonal property; and to prevent the tax from being evaded, fpecific fums were affeffed upon each county, and upon fome of the cities of the kingdom. The tax notwithftanding produced only £. 96,000 [x].

Eftablifhment of two companies of infurance. The prodigality of minifters in the management of the civil lift revenue, during this reign, was fuch, that a great debt had been accumulated. In order to procure fome affiftance for difcharging it, without impofing any new aid for that purpofe, two companies called the Royal Exchange, and London

[t] 8 Geo. I. cap. 15. fect. 7, 8, 9, 10, 11.
[u] 10 Geo. I. cap. 16.   [x] 9 Geo. I. cap. 18.

Affurance

Affurance companies, were eftablifhed, agreed to *National Income fince the Revolution.* pay £. 300,000 for the ufe of his majefty. The fum, however, was found too great, and was afterwards reftricted to £. 150,000 each; " in tender " confideration of the great difficulties which the " faid companies laboured under [y]."

The public revenue at the time of this monarch's death produced, on a medium of four years, as follows:

Cuftoms - - -	£ 1,530,361
Excife, deducting 6 d. per bufhel on malt	1,927,354
Stamps - - -	132,665
Duty on houfes and windows -	131,011
Hackney coaches and chairs -	9,523
Hawkers and pedlars - -	8,055
6 d. per pound on places and penfions -	31,504
Firft-fruits and tenths - -	16,473
Poft-office - - -	75,545
Salt duty - - -	185,505
Small branches belonging to the civil lift	55,892
Taxes known under the name of the general fund	58,755

Total appropriated revenue -		4,162,643
Land-tax at 4 s. - £. 2,000,000		
Malt at 6 d. per bufhel - 750,000		
	2,750,000	
Deduct deficiencies in thefe taxes		
anno 1726	150,000	2,600,000
	Total	£. 6,762,643

[y] 7 Geo. I. ftat. 1. cap. 27.

GEORGE II.

Refined and fpeculative politicians, who are too apt to imagine that the counfels of princes are uniformly regulated by fome particular fyftem; and who hold it neceffary to give plaufible reafons for every hiftorical event, have endeavoured to account for the immenfe fums of money levied and expended during the reign of George II. by afferting that the court was fully impreffed with an idea, that nothing could curb the turbulent fpirit of the Englifh, or prevent another revolution, but engaging them in perpetual wars, and loading them with the heavieft taxes. It is difficult to pry into the fecret intentions of fovereigns, efpecially as their views muft often be altered by a change in the minifters they employ, and by a variety of other circumftances of fmaller importance. Nor is it to be denied that the difcharging the incumbrances of the nation does not feem to have been a very favourite meafure with this monarch, or his minifters. But if any political fyftem was invariably adhered to during this reign, the purport of it appears to have been to leave things as they were, and to check any attempt that might be made to innovation, or even inquiry.

The total fum to be accounted for during the reign of George II. is as follows :

Cuftoms	- - -	£. 49,838,854
Excife (including annual malt)		93,747,167
	Carried over	£. 143,586,021

Stamps

	Brought forward	£. 143,586,021
Stamps	- - -	4,377,957
Land-tax	- -	49,453,323
Miscellaneous taxes	- -	19,800,000
		217,217,301
	Loans -	59,132,472
	Total	£. 276,349,773

The abolition of a tax, is so uncommon a cir- *Salt-tax.* cumstance in the modern financial history of this country, that it merits particular attention whenever it has occurred. The duty upon salt had been long complained of as burdensome to the poor, injurious to many of our manufactures, and fatal to the progress of the British fisheries, so essential to our naval strength ; and such, it was imagined, was the flourishing state of the revenue at the commencement of this reign, that this duty might be safely dispensed with. Accordingly, by an act passed *anno* 1729 [z], both the customs and excise upon salt were abolished from Christmas 1730. But before the measure could operate beneficially to the nation, the abolished duties were revived [a]; at first only for three years, though since they have been rendered perpetual. Sir Robert Walpole, who was then chancellor of the exchequer, and who had moved the repeal, was not ashamed of acting the inconsistent part of proposing the revival. His object was to ingratiate himself, by that means, with the landed interest ; for it enabled him to re-

[z] 3 Geo. II. chap. xx.   [a] 5 Geo. II. chap. vi.

duce

duce the land-tax to one shilling in the pound.
But it may be asked in the words of an author,
who has given us an account of these transactions :
" Can we suppose that any man who is a friend to
" the fishery, or the naval power of this nation,
" will ever vote for continuing so pernicious a
" burden [b] ?"

When the salt-tax was revived, some very useful
regulations were proposed, to prevent its proving
so very pernicious as it had formerly been. In
particular it was suggested, that all salt employed in
victualling ships, in manuring land, in dressing and
curing leather, and in making glass and glass bottles,
should be exempted from duty. But such proposals were rejected : some favour was shewn to
the fisheries ; but such is the trouble with which
receiving drawbacks and bounties is attended, that
nothing but a total abolition of the duty once more,
or at least a commutation of it, in so far as respects
Scotland, can establish that most essential branch of
commerce to the extent to which it might be carried to the great advantage of this nation.

General ex-
cile.
The plan proposed by Sir Robert Walpole,
known under the name of the General Excise,
proves that minister's ability and skill in the revenue
department, had he chosen to exercise it. It was a
system, which, however ruinous it might be to the
smuggler, yet to the fair trader would have proved
infinitely beneficial. The public, it is true, would

[b] History of our National Debts, part iv. p. 50. also p. 38.
and 64.

thereby

thereby have loft the temporary ufe of the money, *National Income fince the Revolution.* which by the prefent laws muft be paid whenever goods are imported, and are drawn back upon exportation. But in return it would have enjoyed this advantage, that it could hardly have fuffered in the manner it has done, by frauds in the article of drawbacks. As to the plan infringing the liberties of the people, the clamours excited againft it on that head were in the higheft degree unjuft. The laws of the excife have fince been extended in a variety of inftances, without making the people flaves, as the nation was taught to believe would have been the cafe had the excife bill paffed. Nor is there any hardfhip in putting the dealer in excifeable commodities under fuch regulations, as may prevent private individuals from fraudulently enriching themfelves at the public expence.

It will fcarcely be credited by thofe who main- *Coach-tax.* tain the impracticability of levying fuch additional taxes upon the public, as might have kept down, if not totally extinguifhed the debts of the nation, that it was not until the year 1747 that a duty was laid upon coaches, belonging to private individuals, not let out to hire. Four pounds was the original tax [c], which has fince been increafed to £. 9 : 12 : 0. Even at that rate, it is not a little unequal : hackney coaches are now taxed at the rate of £. 26 *per ann.* In order that the proprietors, who are licenfed, may be enabled to pay that fum, and to acquire fufficient profit to themfelves, they are fuffered to

[c] 20 Geo. II. chap. x.

make

National In-
come fince the
Revolution.
make exorbitant charges on the public. Hence it
is evident, that fuch as are rich enough to keep
carriages of their own, pay proportionably an inferior rate to thofe who are obliged to hire carriages from others.

Anno 1759, the year preceding this monarch's
death, the public revenue produced the following
fums :

STATE of the PUBLIC REVENUE, *anno* 1759.

Cuftoms	-	£. 1,985,376
Excife (including annual malt)	-	3,887,349
Stamps	-	263,207
Incidents	-	650,000
		6,785,932

Land-tax at 4 s. given for - £. 2,000,000		
Deduct the deficiencies as *per*		
account 1760 -	262,392	
		1,737,608
Total	£.	8,523,540

GEORGE III.

From 1760 to 1789, though a fpace of only 28
years, fuch fums of money were paid into the public
treafury, as no former ftatefman would have believed, that this country could have furnifhed.
Nothing can more clearly demonftrate, the immenfe
wealth and refources of Great Britain ; and had any
confiderable portion of that money, inftead of being
wafted

wafted in war, been laid out in cultivating the arts *National In-*
of peace, the nation would perhaps have grown *come since the*
Revolution.
too rich and powerful; and indeed might have
already reached, that fplendid ftate of feeming
profperity, which is too apt to intoxicate a nation,
which is often accompanied with real weaknefs and
debility, and has not unfrequently proved, the bitter
fource of calamity and deftruction.

As it is propofed to give, in the third chapter of
this part of the work, a view of the prefent ftate
of our revenue, and the particulars of which it
confifts, it will be fufficient, at this time, to furnifh
the reader with an account of the money raifed by
taxes; from Michaelmas 1760, (about which time
our prefent fovereign mounted the throne), to
Michaelmas 1788.

The particulars of the revenue from 1788, to
the prefent time, will be given in a fubfequent
part of this publication.

PROGRESS of the REVENUE from Michaelmas 1760 to Michaelmas 1788 :

Anno				
1761		-	-	£. 8,800,000
1762		-	-	8,950,000
1763	Land-tax at 4s.		-	9,100,000
1764			-	9,250,000
1765	-	-	-	9,300,000
1766	-	-	-	9,350,000

Carried over   £. 54,750,000

Anno

*National In-
come fince the
Revolution.*

		Brought forward	£. 54,750,000
Anno 1767		- -	9,200,000
1768		- -	9,250,000
1769		- -	9,350,000
1770		- - -	9,500,000
1771	Land-tax at 3 *s.*	-	9,650,000
1772		- - -	9,850,000
1773		- - -	10,066,661
1774		- - -	10,285,673
1775		- - -	10,038,061
1776		- - -	10,265,405
1777		- - -	10,604,013
1778		- -	10,732,405
1779		- - -	11,192,141
1780		- - -	12,255,214
1781		- - -	12,454,936
1782	Land-tax at 4 *s.*	-	12,593,297
1783		- -	11,962,718
1784		- -	12,905,519
1785		- -	14,871,520
1786		- -	15,096,112
1787		- -	15,360,857
1788		- -	15,572,971

Total   £. 307,807,503

The loans during this reign have been equally diftinguifhed by the magnitude of their amount. The different periods at which they took place, and the fum borrowed or funded by each act, will appear from the following ftatement:

Sums borrowed or funded.

By 1 Geo. III. cap. 7.	-	- £. 12,000,000
1 Geo. III. cap. 20.	-	1,500,000
2 Geo. III. cap. 10.	-	12,000,000
3 Geo. III. cap. 9.	-	3,483,553

Carried over   £. 28,983,553

		Sums borrowed or funded.	National Income since the Revolution.
	Brought forward	£. 28,983,553	
By 3 Geo. III. cap. 12.	-	3,500,000	
4 Geo. III. cap. 25.	-	1,000,000	
5 Geo. III. cap. 23.	-	1,500,000	
6 Geo. III. cap. 39.	-	1,500,000	
7 Geo. III. cap. 24.	-	1,500,000	
8 Geo. III. cap. 31.	-	1,900,000	
16 Geo. III. cap. 34.	-	2,000,000	
17 Geo. III. cap. 46.	-	5,500,000	
18 Geo. III. cap. 22.	-	6,000,000	
19 Geo. III. cap. 18.	-	7,000,000	
20 Geo. III. cap. 16.	-	12,000,000	
21 Geo. III. cap. 14.	-	12,000,000	
22 Geo. III. cap. 8.	-	13,500,000	
23 Geo. III. cap. 35.	-	12,000,000	
24 Geo. III. cap. 10.	-	6,000,000	
24 Geo. III. cap. 39.	-	6,879,341	
25 Geo. III. cap. 33. and 71.		10,990,651	

£. 133,753,545

To which there is to be added :

1. From the Bank of England, by 4 Geo. III.
cap. 25.   -   -   £. 110,000
2. Various fums received from the Eaft India
Company for the territorial revenues and
otherwife, not included in cuftoms paid to
the exchequer   -   3,200,000
3. Difference between the unfunded debt and
other neceffary expences or claims, as that
debt ftood *annos* 1760 and 1788 [d]   -   5,170,273

Total   £. 142,233,818

[u] The difference between the unfunded debt, *anno* 1760, and *anno* 1788, is calculated as follows :

UNFUNDED

National In-
come fince the
Revolution.

Hence it will appear, that the fum paid into the exchequer of George the Third, free of all charges, and without including the cafual profits of a lottery, and other refources that might be mentioned, in the fpace only of 28 years, is as follows :

1. By taxes	-	-	£. 307,807,503
2. By loans, &c.	-	-	142,233,818

£. 450,041,321

Which is at the rate of £. 16,071,475 *per annum.*

The hiftory of our revenue, fince Michaelmas 1788, will be the fubject of future difcuffion.

It may now be proper to give an account, of the progrefs of the public revenue, and an abftract of the total fupply, from the 5th November 1688,

to

___

UNFUNDED DEBT *anno* 1788.

Exchequer bills	- - -	£. 5,500,000
Navy debt on 5th January 1789	- -	2,251,079
American loyalifts, extraordinaries of the army and navy, deficiencies of land and malt, and various other claims and expences not yet liquidated, fuppofed in all to amount to		3,000,000

£. 10,751,079

UNFUNDED DEBT *anno* 1760.

Navy Debt 13th September 1760	- £. 3,490,806	
Debt of the Ordnance (Suppofed)	- 590,000	
Exchequer bills - -	1,500,000	
		5,580,806

Difference   £. 5,170,273

to Michaelmas 1788, drawn up from the preceding ſtatements.

PROGRESS of the PUBLIC REVENUE
from the Revolution, to Michaelmas 1788.

Income of James II. -	£. 2,001,855
Increaſe during the reign of King William	1,893,350
Income of King William.	£. 3,895,205
Increaſe during the reign of Queen Anne	1,796,598
Income of England at the Union	£. 5,691,803
Increaſe during the reign of George I.	1,070,840
Income of George I. -	£. 6,672,643
Increaſe during the reign of George II.	1,759,897
Income of George II. -	£. 8,522,540
Increaſe during the firſt 28 years of the reign of George III. - -	7,050,431
State of the public revenue at Michael-mas 1788 -	£. 15,572,971

ABSTRACT of SUPPLIES ſince the Revolu-
tion, to Michaelmas 1788.

Supplies during the reign of King William	£. 72,047,369
Queen Anne	122,373,531
George I. -	79,832,160
George II. -	276,349,773
George III. from his acceſſion to Michaelmas 1788 -	450,041,321
Grand total	£. 1,000,644,154

Having

National In-
come since the
Revolution. Having thus accumulated, with as much accuracy as circumſtances would admit of, the various ſums which have paſſed into the exchequer of this country for the ſpace of about a century, I ſhall now proceed to explain, in what manner this nation has contrived, in the comparatively ſhort period of one hundred years, to expend above a thouſand millions of Engliſh money, equal to about 24,000,000,000 of French livres.

C H A P. II.

Of the Progreſs of the Public Expences ſince the
Revolution.

Public Ex-
pences ſince
the Revolu-
tion. IN private life, when an individual finds himſelf involved in pecuniary diſtreſſes, from the expences he has incurred, either by careleſſneſs or imprudence, the only mode of retrieving his affairs is, to examine into his paſt expenditure, to ſee what part of his income was properly laid out, and in what articles a ſaving may be practicable. After ſuch an inveſtigation, it will be much leſs difficult, to form a plan, ſuitable to his circumſtances in life, and conſiſtent with his real ſituation.

 The ſame ſyſtem, is the only mode, by which the embarraſſed ſtate of public affairs can be remedied ; by which miniſters can be taught wiſdom ; and nations, too prone to ruſh headlong into wars and other heedleſs expences, may learn to imbibe

the

the principles of moderation and peace. Wars sometimes are unavoidable; for no ftate ought tamely to bear repeated infults, or fuffer a proud and arrogant neighbour to lord over it. If a nation feems afraid of war, it only expofes itfelf to the incroachments of others, who, if fuccefsful in one unjuft demand, are thereby encouraged in attempting to make further claims. Too pacific a fyftem, therefore, whilft other ftates have either ambition or avarice in their councils, muft ever be dangerous. But the great leffon, which it is hoped the prefent inveftigation will imprefs on the mind of every Britifh citizen, is this, that however wars may tend to aggrandize the names, or to augment the fortunes of a few particular individuals ; and though it may be fometimes neceffary to check the ambitious defigns of other powers ; yet that no country can ever expect to be indemnified, by the conquefts it may acquire, for the money which muft neceffarily be expended, in the courfe of long and extenfive hoftilities, in addition to all the bloodfhed and calamities incident to fuch fcenes.

But war is not the only idle expence into which modern nations, and Great Britain in particular, have fallen. Even in time of peace, wanton and unneceffary charges are too often incurred. Not fatisfied with endeavouring to acquire extenfive territories by force of arms, a rage for acquifition, by the mode of colonization, has become prevalent ; and a nation flatters itfelf, to increafe its riches, population, and induftry, by fending a part

of

of its fubjects to cultivate and improve diftant
regions, inftead of improving and cultivating at
home. The revolt of our late colonies in America, and a ftatement of the expence occafioned by
their eftablifhment, will probably prevent fuch
ridiculous projects for the future.

In a former chapter, an account was given, of
the particular fums raifed during each reign,
fince the revolution, and of the total fums paid
into the exchequer fince that memorable era. It
is now propofed, to give a general view of the
manner in which that money was expended.——
By entering into minute inquiries, this work might
eafily be extended; but it would only have the
effect of rendering it lefs amufing, and more ob-
fcure and unintelligible.

WILLIAM III.

In the preceding chapter, it was ftated, that
the money received by the exchequer during this
reign, amounted to £. 72,047,369. The manner
in which this fum was expended is now to be
explained.

1. Civil lift.   No fpecific fum was allotted, at this period, for
the peculiar expences of the fovereign. Certain
taxes, however, were appropriated for that purpofe, amounting at an average to about £. 680,000
per annum; and the accompt that was made up of
the charges of the civil lift, during this reign, was
as follows:

STATE of the EXPENCES of the Civil Lift, *Public Expences since the Revolution.*
from 5th November 1688 to 25th March 1702 :

	£.	s.	d.
To the cofferer of the houfehold	1,300,130	2	2¾
To the treafurer of the chambers -	484,763	16	1½
To the treafurer of the chambers for the charges of the late queen's coffin, &c.	328	16	0
To the great wardrobe -	319,876	8	2¾
To the treafurer of the chambers for the late queen's mourning -	42,844	4	5
To the robes - -	57,128	2	2½
Ditto to the Lord Sydney upon account of clothes furnifhed King Charles II. when he was mafter of that office -	5,120	1	3
To the paymafter of the works -	474,050	15	1½
To do. on account of the late queen's funeral	4,000	0	0
To Mr. Roberts, paymafter of the works at Windfor, on account of works there, over and above what has been paid thereunto out of the revenues and honour of the caftle of Windfor - -	5,000	0	0
Gardens.—Upon account of making his majefty's gardens, over and above the gardeners' falaries payable by the treafurer of the chambers, until 1695 -	115,097	12	7½
On the contraƈt for £. 4,800 *per annum*, commencing from 1695	16,800	0	0
On the new allowance of £. 2,600 *per annum*, which commenced from Chriftmas 1700 -	1,900	0	0
Stables.—For buying horfes, for liveries, and extraordinaries -	235,965	15	3¾
Foreign minifters, for ordinaries and extraordinaries - - -	462,753	7	2½
Fees and falaries - -	858,056	16	9
Carried over £.	3,383,815	17	5½

Brought forward	£.3,383,815	17	5¼
Penfions and annuities - -	686,189	17	7
Queen-dowager - -	178,031	15	4
Late queen's treafurer - -	506,356	16	1¼
Ditto for French proteftants -	75,000	0	0
Prince and princefs of Denmark -	638,921	15	7½
Duke of Gloucefter on £. 1,500 *per annnm*	37,500	0	0
Band of gentlemen penfioners -	69,000	0	0
Secret fervices.—Secretaries of the treafury	616,323	7	2
Secretaries of ftate	76,963	19	6
To particular perfons by his majefty's warrants under his royal fign-manual	82,100	0	0
Privy purfe - -	483,555	0	0
Ditto for purchaf-⎱ To the Earl of Portland	24,571	5	4
ing fee-farm rents. ⎰ The Lord Somers at	33,600	0	0
Jewels - ? -	66,069	0	0
Plate - - -	102,843	13	8
Bounties paid at the exchequer to feveral perfons by his majefty's particular warrants in that behalf - -	226,823	19	1
Monfieur Fleury for goods taken from the French at Bourbon-fort, Hudfon's Bay, and given to the Hudfon's Bay Company, which, by the treaty of Ryfwick, were to be reftored - - -	7,086	17	0
Subfcribers of £. 2,000,000 for the Eaft India trade, an allowance of £.1 *per cent.*	20,000	0	0
The receivers of £. 2,000,000 in reward, and for charges in paffing their accounts	16,000,	0	0
To Mr. Stratford in part of £. 20,000 for cloth fent to Sweden - -	12,000	0	0
Earl of Ranelagh for Lord Fairfax £. 600; bounties for officers widows £. 1,670; for French officers £. 730; for liveries for Lumley's trumpeters £.393 : 3 : 0 ; and for court drums and fifes falary £. 240	3,634	3	0
Carried over	£. 8,346,417	0	1¼

Brought forward   £. 8,346,417   0   1¼

Contingents of divers natures ; *viz.* law charges ; liberates of the exchequer ; riding charges to meſſengers of the court ; and receipt of exchequer rewards and ex-traordinary charges to receivers of taxes, and to ſeveral others on ſundry occaſions ; ſurpluſes of accounts, printers' bills ; ſun-dry works and repairs by the ſurveyors of the woods, the private roads, and other particular officers ; his majeſty's ſubſcrip-tion of £ 10,000 to the bank of Enland ; a like ſum to the new Eaſt India Com-pany ; as alſo £. 3,000 for carrying on the trade ; bounties for apprehending highwaymen, traitors, and libellers ; mo-ney paid for purchaſing land to be laid into his majeſty's park at Windſor ; and many other accidental payments   -   534,089   1 10¾

Total   £. 8,880,506   2   9*

There is no reign, in which complaints were made, and to all appearance with ſo much juſtice, of neglect and inattention to the navy, as when William III, ſat upon the throne.   That monarch

* Another mode of ſtating this account is as follows :

Charges of the civil liſt from 5th November 1688

to Michaelmas 1689	£. 428,918	to Michaelmas 1696	£. 699,485
1690	644,145	1697	745,496
1691	657,092	1698	374,777
1692	631,988	1699	892,669
1693	696,968	1700	683,947
1694	682,436	1701	704,412
1695	764,739	to Lady-day 1702	293,919
		Total	£. 8,876,995

was

was a foldier and not a failor, which partly accounts,
for his having placed the direction of the naval department, in improper and unfkilful hands. The engagement off Beachy head, which happened foon
after the revolution, is the only conflict, in the courfe
of many years paft, that has in the leaft tarnifhed the
luftre of the Britifh flag. The lofs fuftained on that
occafion, is juftly attributed, to a very great inequality
of force between the two fleets, which was partly
owing to the negligence of the Englifh and Dutch
admiralties, and partly to the fuperior activity of
the French, by whom 30 fail were blocked up in
Plymouth harbour, and prevented from joining the
combined fleet until after the engagement. The
iffue was, that 78 fail defeated 56 ; and thus, the only
victory that a French admiral could ever boaft of
over a Britifh fleet, was gained without much real
honour or eclat. Nay, fuch was the negligence of our
naval rulers to the commerce of the kingdom, that
when the French fleet was unable to venture out of
its ports, the privateers of France, were fuffered to
range uncontrolled, preying upon our merchantmen, and enriching themfelves with plunder, to the
value of many millions fterling [e].

As the following fums were appropriated by
parliament for the naval department, its failure of
fuccefs, could not well be attributed to any deficiency of refources. The total fum iffued for
naval fervices was £. 19,822,141.

[e] It is calculated, that in three years, prizes to the value of
nine millions were taken by the privateers of France.

The

The naval peace eftablifhment, for the year 1698
amounted to £. 877,455. At the fame rate, the navy would have coft, during this reign, about £. 10,200,000. The difference, being £. 9,622,141, may be ftated as the extra naval expences during King William's wars.

The military expences, exclufive of thofe for Ireland, came to £. 18,166,051; and as nothing was allowed by parliament for the maintenance of guards and garrifons in time of peace, except £.300,000 a-year, that fum during William's reign, would have amounted only to £. 3,600,000; confequently the military charges of the war came to £. 14,566,051.

So low was the eftablifhment of the ordnance in time of peace, that *anno* 1698, only £. 50,000, and *anno* 1699, but £. 25,000 was voted for that fervice: £. 50,000 however may be called the peace eftablifhment for fupplying both the navy and army with military ftores. During the reign of William, this would amount to £. 600,000. But as the ordnance received in all £. 3,008,535, the war, it is evident, muft have produced an extra ex-pence of £. 2,408,535.

The armament fitted out by the Dutch, for bring-
ing William over into this country, occafioned a confiderable expence to the United Provinces, which England thought itfelf bound in gratitude to repay. For that purpofe £. 600,000 was voted by parliament. This probably was fully equal to

the

the real charges of the expedition, though the bill of cofts given in, came to £. 686,500.

It is hardly neceffary to inform the reader, that the eftablifhment of William's fovereignty over Ireland, met with a formidable refiftance in that kingdom; and it is a circumftance of which it may not be improper to remind our brethren in Ireland, at this time, that for the purpofe of eftablifhing the revolution there, the following fums were iffued from the exchequer of this country, namely:

To Mr. Harbord -	£. 1,073,288 12	7½
Mr. Henley - -	4,560 0	7½
Mr. Fox and Lord Conningfby	2,773,806 7	9¾
	£. 3,851,655 1	0¾

Befides naval expences, which were far from being inconfiderable.

The miferable ftate of the coin, and the charges neceffary to bring it to its proper ftandard, were fome of the greateft difficulties, that William and his minifters had to ftruggle with. The following fums were expended for that purpofe:

To the mint out of the coinage duty	£. 259,584 0	0
Deficiency on the recoinage (of which however £. 184,656 was repaid) -	2,599,797 14	10
New money in part of £. 1,122,584 old money recoined, paid the navy and army	84,963 0	0
To the commiffioners of excife in new money	56,988 0	0
Exchequer bills delivered for money *anno* 1695 - - -	158,589 0	0
Carried over £. 3,159,921 14	10	

To

Brought over £. 3,159,921 14 10   *Public Ex-*
To the treasurer of the navy, being old   *pences since*
  money new coined   - -   4,422 0 0   *the Revo-*
To the paymaster of the forces for £. 13,000   *lution.*
  in old hammered money   -   6,497 0 0

£. 3,170,840 14 10

In payment either of the capital, or of the in-   Interest of
terest of the various debts which the public at that   the public
time owed, the following sums were issued :   repayment
                                                of the prin-
                                              cipal.

Interest to several of the public creditors for
  temporary loans   -   £. 5,216,530
Interest to the bank of England   -   875,880
Annuities on the million act   -   1,079,809
Annuities on the tonnage act   - - 287,059
Annuities for 16 years   - - 1,049,776
To the malt lottery office, part of £. 1,200,000
  principal and interest   - - 760,142
To satisfy tallies on the excise and post-office   467,000
Interest to the East India Company   - 429,962
Expence of circulating exchequer bills   - 254,119
Money advanced to King William *anno* 1688   - 4,000
Principal money lent in the time of James II.   138,412
Debts due to the servants of King Charles II.   60,000
Interest of the bankers debt   - - 465

£. 10,619,555
Principal money repaid more than borrowed for
  several years   - - 3,341,903

£. 13,961,458

The remaining expences during this reign were   Miscella-
as follows :   neous ex-
                                                pences.

Redemption

Redemption of captives - -	£. 1,000
Privy purse of the late King James at the exchequer	200
To receivers of taxes in rewards for extraordinaries	5,466
To Patrick Hume, gentleman, to be paid as his majesty should direct - -	5,200
To rewards for bringing in plate to be coined	3,846
To the treasurer of Greenwich hospital -	19,500
To the commissioners for forfeited estates in Ireland	3,133
To the commissioners for stating the public accounts	3,500

£. 41,845

It now only remains, in order to give a distinct view of the state of the public expenditure during this reign, to furnish the reader with an abstract, first, of the total sum expended ; secondly, of the peace establishment ; and thirdly, of the charges of the war that was terminated by the treaty of Ryswick.

GENERAL VIEW of the EXPENCES of King William's reign.

The civil list - - -	£. 8,880,506
The navy - - -	19,822,141
The army - - -	18,166,051
The ordnance - - -	3,008,535
The Dutch-expences for the revolution -	600,000
Expences for the reduction of Ireland -	3,851,655
Charges of recoinage - -	3,170,840
Principal and interest of public debts -	13,961,458
Miscellaneous expences - -	41,845
Balance of account ending at Ladyday 1702, and various small sums • -	624,477

Total   £. 72,127,508*

* Instead of £. 72,047,369 as stated in p. 38, the total supplies in King William's reign amounted to £. 72,127,508 including £. 80,138 18s. 0¼d. which remained in the exchequer on 5th November 1688. See p. 13.

STATE of the PEACE ESTABLISHMENT.

The civil lift	-	-	£. 680,000
The navy	-	-	877,455
The army	-	-	300,000
The ordnance	-	-	50,000

£. 1,907,455

The charge of the war which William carried on againft Lewis XIV. amounted to the following fums :

Extra expences of the navy	-	£. 9,622,141
Ditto of the army	-	-	14,566,051
Ditto of the ordnance	-	2,408,535

26,596,727

Expences for the reduction of Ireland   3,851,655

£. 30,447,382

Thus it appears, that the extraordinary expences of the war, which lafted nearly ten years, amounted only to about thirty millions; and confequently did not much exceed three millions *per annum.*

But this expence, which was then confidered to be not a little burdenfome, was far from being entirely thrown away. The war, it is true, was neither fuccefsful, nor, (the battle off La Hogue excepted), attended with any brilliant confequences. Yet ftill it fhook the power of Louis, who affected to domineer over Europe, and rendered it eafier, in the following reign, to control,

and

and to reduce within proper bounds, the proud and
afpiring monarchy he governed: and it muft likewife be confidered, that this war was effentially neceffary, to protect, to extend, and to confirm the
liberties of Britain, which were in danger of falling
a facrifice, to religious bigotry, and civil defpotifm.

QUEEN ANNE.

It has often been remarked, notwithftanding all
the plaufible objections which have been urged
againft the government of women, that no two
periods in the hiftory of this country, fhine with
more diftinguifhed luftre, than thofe of Elizabeth
and Anne. During the reign of the former, this
ifland had the glory of humbling the too powerful
monarchy of Spain; and, during the government
of the latter, of checking the growth of the imperious houfe of Bourbon: and had not Anne been
unfortunately prevailed upon to change her minifters, and to difmifs the invincible Marlborough
from the command of her troops, it is more than
probable, that Europe would have had as little reafon to dread the future enterprifes of France, as of
Spain. Nor would the latter have been the only
example in modern Europe, of an extenfive monarchy reduced within proper limits, after vainly
attempting to tyrannife over its neighbours.

But though the reigns of the two queens refemble each other in fuccefs, yet with regard to the
charges

charges by which that fuccefs was acquired there is *Public Ex-*
no fimilitude.   The moderate expences of Queen *pences fince the Revo-*
Elizabeth have been already ftated, in a former *lution.*
part of this work ; and it is now propofed, to give
fome account of thofe, which took place, whilft
Anne fat upon the throne.

The fums received under the head of civil lift *Civil lift.*
revenues, amounted to £. 7,604,848, which, at
a medium, was about £. 586,900 *per annum.*   But
there was alfo voted, on 27th June 1712, the fum of
£. 500,000, to difcharge the debts due on account
of the civil government.

The general eftimate, of the whole expence of
the civil government, during this reign, was as
follows :

In the cofferer's office - -	£. 85,000
In the treafurer of the chamber's office -	30,000
In the great wardrobe - -	20,000
In the office of the robes -	3,000
In the office of the works - -	39,000
For buying coaches, horfes, liveries, &c. -	10,000
For ordinary entertainments, &c. and the extraordi-	
naries of the queen's foreign minifters -	75,000
Salaries payable to the exchequer .	80,196
Penfions and annuities - -	42,898
Annual penfions and bounties per warrants -	87,495
Secret fervices to the fecretaries of ftate -	6,000
Her majefty's fecret fervices - -	27.000
Privy purfe - - -	30,000
Jewels, plate, and prefents to foreign minifters	15,000
Contingencies - -	33,846

Total   £. 584,435[f]

[f] Commons Journals, vol. xviii. p. 84. In the fame journal there are pa -
ticular accounts of the different penfions and annuities that were granted during
this reign.

The

The civil lift revenues amounted to about £.700,000 a-year; but the queen devoted £.100,000 *per annum*, to the public fervice, for carrying on the war; and at her death, the debts of the civil lift came only to £.345,912, whereas fhe left funds belonging to her own revenues, amounting to £.379,448 [g].

How glorious foever victories and conquefts at land may be accounted, yet, to an ifland, great territorial acquifitions can never be of effential importance; whereas atchievements at fea, when properly improved, may be peculiarly ufeful. In that refpect, the reign of Queen Anne was not a little deficient. The chief, nay almoft the only exertions of the allies, feem to have been dedicated to armaments at land; and any ideas of deftroying the commerce and maritime ftrength of the enemy, were unfortunately unattended to, or abandoned.

The naval charges, at the fame time, during this reign, were not inconfiderable, amounting to £.23,484,574.

The peace eftablifhment, for the year 1714, came to £.765,700. At that rate, the naval eftimates, during Queen Anne's reign, would have amounted to £.9,571,250; and confequently, the war coft,

[g] Commons Journals, p. 113. It is faid, in a memorial at the bottom of this account, that £.150,000 was due to the French Proteftants; and £.42,000 was claimed for work carried on at Blenheim; but even with thefe additional demands, the receipts and iffues were very nearly equivalent to each other.

in

in addition to the ordinary eſtabliſhment, the ſum of £. 13,913,323.

The above ſum was far from being contemptible. But nothing can ever render a nation ſuccefsful at ſea, unlefs its maritime force is not only a great, but the principal objeſt of its attention. Naval ſtrength embraces ſo many objeſts, that it ſuffers by the ſmalleſt negleſt. If there is any failure in colleſting the ſtores neceſſary for building ſhips of war; if the ſhipwrights are not properly looked to; if the proviſions neceſſary for the ſuſtenance of the ſailors are not calculated for that purpoſe; if every care is not taken, to have the fleet manned by bold and able ſeamen; if its officers are not valiant and ſkilful in their profeſſion, and promoted according as they deſerve; if diſcipline is not maintained; and if the fleet is not directed to practicable ob_jeſts; but inſtead thereof, if its ſtrength is waſted in conflicting with the elements, and not with the enemy, it is in vain that money is given. Parliament may vote its millions, but to no purpoſe: a failure in any one of thoſe articles, is ſufficient to blaſt every hope of victory, and of that ſuccefs which might otherwiſe have been expected.

Many have affected to doubt, the capacity of the natives of this country, for military atchievements. Their valour, it is true, is univerſally acknowledged: but the ſea, it is ſaid, is their natural element; their experience in military operations is too confined, and without practice, no conſummate general can be formed. We muſt not, we are told, go ſo far back as the reigns of the Henrys and the

Edwards,

Edwards, becaufe the art of war was then in its in-
fancy, and their victories may be attributed, to mere
brutal force, and not to the fuperiority of their military
talents. Fortunately we can produce, in the perfon of the Duke of Marlborough, an example of
a Britifh fubject, equal to the greateft warriors of
antiquity, or of modern times, in genius and valour; a hero, who never befieged a town that he
did not gain, or fought a battle in which he did not
conquer. It was not, however, at a moderate expence that his conquefts were acquired, for the
military fervices, during Queen Anne's reign, came
to £. 32,975,331.

The peace eftablifhment, voted *anno* 1713, was
only 8,232 men, and two companies of invalids,
amounting to £. 386,427; and the forces in the
plantations, exclufive of Gibraltar and Minorca,
coft only £. 39,478, making in all but £. 425,905
per annum, which, in the fpace of twelve years, is
£. 5,140,860. Deducting this fum from the total
of the military charges, (thofe from Lady-day to
Michaelmas 1702 only excepted), there would remain £.27,104,691 for the extra expences of the war.

Half pay.   It was during this reign, that the charges of the
half-pay lift, both naval and military, and of
Chelfea and Greenwich hofpitals, began to be exorbitant. The original reafon affigned for granting
half-pay to the land officers, was becaufe a greater
arrear of pay was due to them, which could not immediately be provided for. It was alfo contended, that many officers had thrown themfelves
entirely out of other bufinefs, and had fpent a great
                                                    part

part of the prime of their lives in the fervice of *Public Ex-pences fince* their country. But *anno* 1713, when £. 17,000 *the Revolu-tion.* was voted for half-pay to naval officers, it was re- ftricted to thofe who had ferved *well* during the 27th May. war, and fhould be out of employment, both by fea and land, in time of peace [h].

Perhaps there could not, in a political light, be a better regulation. Every officer who claimed half-pay for his fervices in war, ought to prove, in the words of the above-mentioned vote of the houfe of commons, *that he has ferved his country well.* The very apprehenfion and terror of fuch an enquiry, might be productive of the beft of con- fequences; and the difgrace of not being thought entitled to the bounty of the public, might occa- fion the greateft exertions. Some difference ought alfo to be made, between thofe who have ferved long, and who have been but a fhort fpace of time in the army: for it is to be confidered, that the half-pay of the army and navy, is at prefent con- fiderably more than the whole peace eftablifhment of the army in the reign of William III. Nor is it a circumftance unworthy of attention, that, *anno* 1717, the demand for half-pay to land officers, amounted to £. 120,000, but upon a thorough en- quiry into the matter, it was reduced to £. 80,000.

The whole expence of the ordnance came to Ordnance. £. 2,100,676. The peace eftablifhment may be

[h] See Abftract of all the public Debts remaining due at Michaelmas 1722; by Archibald Hutchinfon, Efq. p. 25. Alfo Commons Journals, vol. xvii. p. 186 and 382.

ftated

Public Ex-
pences since
the Revolu-
tion.
stated at £. 58,000 *per annum*, or, in twelve years,
£. 696,000, consequently the extra expence of the
ordnance amounted to £. 1,404,676.

Transport
service.
The expence of conveying the troops, which at
this time made a separate article, amounted in all
to £. 796,220.

Sufferers of
Nevis and
St. Christo-
pher's.
Among the expences incurred in consequence of
Queen Anne's wars, may be included the sum of
£. 141,093 voted to the inhabitants of Nevis and
St. Christopher's, who had suffered by a French
invasion. Such, however, as did not resettle their
plantations, were not entitled to any share of the
bounty, and the debt was not fully liquidated till
the reign of George I.

Building
churches.
During this reign £. 480,000 was granted for repairing Westminster abbey, and building new
churches in the capital; and £. 2,500 was voted to
be remitted to Rotterdam, for a similar purpose.

Equivalent
to Scotland.
The adjusting the treaty of union between England and Scotland, was attended with this peculiar
difficulty, that the taxes of Scotland were small,
and its public debts were very inconsiderable.
Whereas England was subject to heavy taxes, and
its incumbrances were at that time accounted
enormous. To remove so fatal an obstacle, it was
agreed upon between the commissioners appointed
by both nations, that all distinctions between their
debts and taxes should be abolished, and that
Scotland should receive an equivalent, amounting
to £. 398,085 10 s. for the burdens to which it
was thus subjected. And to indemnify the city of
Carlisle,

Carlifle, and the Mufgrave family, whofe tolls *Public Ex-*
were taken away by the fixth article of the treaty, *the Revolu-*
the fum of £. 7,641 was granted by parliament. *tion.*

The coinage expences during this reign, were in Recoinage,
fome degree increafed, in confequence of that article of the union, by which it was declared, that
the fpecie of the two kingdoms fhould be the
fame in future. This branch of the public expenditure amounted in all to £. 81,934, of which
about £. 4,130 was laid out in the mint of Scotland[i].

No idea was then entertained, of the heavy Colonial ex-
charges with which our colonial fettlements would pences.
be attended. Indeed, fo far as can now be traced,
£. 37,100 is the whole that can properly be ftated
to the account of their civil eftablifhments. Nor were
the expences they occafioned, of a military nature, in
any refpect fo confiderable as they have fince proved.

A fingular article appears in the accounts of this Treaty with
reign, of £. 20,095 11 s. 7 d. paid to Francis Strat- Sweden.
ford, Efq. *for making good treaties with Sweden.*
The words may be interpreted in different ways ;
but their meaning probably is, that the fum was
paid, for the purpofe of fulfilling or making good,
the engagements we had come into with that
power, and not as a reward for having made a good
or a beneficial treaty.

Some charges of a mifcellaneous nature were Mifcella-
alfo incurred : £. 5,579 was paid to compenfate neous ex-
loffes fuftained by tumultuous and rebellious pro- pences.

[i] Commons Journal, vol. xvii. p. 8.

ceedings

ceedings ; £. 64,629 was granted to commiffioners for examining the public accounts, and for
ſtating the equivalent due to Scotland, &c.   The
whole might poffibly amount to about £. 200,000.

It could furniſh no uſeful information at this
time, to enter into any minute difcuffion, of the
various temporary loans which took place during
this reign, or any account of the intereſt paid on
the public debts of a more permanent nature,
which varied almoſt every year.   It may be fufficient to obſerve, that this important article of expenditure amounted in all to £. 52,184,527, of
which about £. 31,661,176, was laid out in re-
paying money borrowed upon the land and malt
taxes, and other temporary fecurities ; and the remainder, to wit, £. 22,523,351 was for intereſt
paid to the bank, and other permanent creditors.

The total expences during this reign were then
as follows :

The civil liſt - -	£. 7,604,848
The navy - -	23,484,574
The army - -	32,975,331
The ordnance - -	2,100,676
Tranſport ſervice - -	796,220
Building churches, &c. - -	482,500
Equivalent to Scotland - -	398,085
Recompence for tolls - -	7,641
Coinage expences - -	81,934
Expence of governments in the Weſt Indies _	37,100
Money ſent to Sweden - -	20,095
Various mifcellaneous ſervices - -	200,000
Carried over	£. 68,189,004

Brought over	£. 68,189,004	*Public Ex-pences since the Revolu-tion.*
Temporary loans repaid - -	31,661,176	
Interest of the permanent debts of the nation	22,523,351	

£. 122,373,531

The peace establishment may be thus stated:

The civil list - -	£. 700,000
The navy - -	765,700
The army - -	425,905
The ordnance - -	58,000
Miscellaneous services - -	16,000

£. 1,965,605

The expences of the war, terminated anno 1712, amounted to the following sums:

Extra expences of the navy -	£. 13,913,323
Ditto of the army -	27,104,691
Ditto of the ordnance -	1,404,676
Ditto of the transport service -	796,220
Sufferers of Nevis and St. Christopher's -	141,093

Total   £. 43,360,003[k]

As the war lasted for ten years, this amounts to £. 4,336,000 *per annum.*

[k] Two states of the expence of this war have been published, both of which make it more considerable. The commissioners of the public accounts appointed by the tory administration, who came into power about the close of Queen Anne's reign, calculate the whole expence at £. 65,853,799, and only deduct £. 12,930,461 for the peace establishment; and consequently estimate the expence at £. 52,023,388. See Chandler's Debates (Commons), vol v. p. 100. Even the whigs, in the view they printed *anno* 1712 of the taxes, funds, and public revenues of England, state the expence of the war at £. 48,513,773. But then they calculate the army at £. 350,000, and the navy at £. 120,000 *per annum,* which is by far too low an establishment.

Great

Great as the fum may appear, it was not entirely
wafted. It was an expence hardly to be avoided:
for, after Louis XIV. had thought proper to interfere in the internal government of this country, by
acknowledging a prince for its fovereign, whom
both the parliament and people of Great Britain had renounced, it was impoffible not to declare
war againft him. Befides, the nation received fome
recompence for the charges it was put to. It enjoyed the fatisfaction of repeated victories over the
enemy; and it acquired by the peace, the honourable, though not very lucrative, acquifitions of
Gibraltar and Minorca.

GEORGE I.

Since the reign of Queen Anne, the national accounts are far from being diftinguifhed for their regularity or precifion. No complete ftatement has
ever been made up, of the total income and expenditure of the country. Accounts are annually laid
before parliament, of the grants and fervices: but
they include only what is called the unappropriated
revenue. The appropriated taxes are perpetually
varying in their amount, and were, until lately
confolidated, a mafs of diforder and confufion;
and though the furpluffes and deficiencies were
ftated to parliament, yet it was difficult to difcover,
without a variety of calculations, what was the
total

total fum that was paid to, or expended by, the *Public Expences fince the Revolution.* exchequer each year. From fuch a chaos, it is eafy to perceive, that exactnefs cannot be expected; but, confidering the immenfe fums which have been expended fince the acceffion of the houfe of Brunfwick, it is not eafy to commit a miftake that can be of effential importance.

By an act paffed at the commencement of the *Civil lift.* reign of George I[1]. £. 700,000 a year was appropriated to the expences of his majefty's civil government; and £. 77,694 of unappropriated money, was directed to be applied, towards difcharging fuch extraordinary expences, as might be incurred at his acceffion to the throne. Nor was this all ; for different fums were afterwards voted by parliament in aid of the civil lift, The total of the money received on that account, during this reign, will be as follows :

1. £. 700,000 *per annum* for twelve years and
    a half   -   -   £. 8,750,000
2. Vote at the acceffion   -   -   77,694
3. By 7 Geo. I. chap. 27. in full of the fums
    to be paid by the two affurance companies   300,000
4. By 7 Geo. I. chap. 27. and 11 Geo. I.
    chap. 17. money borrowed for the ufe of
    the civil lift on the 6 *d per* pound deduction
    from penfions   -   -   1,000,000
5. Paid the Prince of Wales £. 40,000 *per
    annum* for twelve years and a half, and the
    Queen the fum of £. 6,250 out of the cuftoms   504,820

Total to the royal family   £. 10,632,514

[1] 1 Geo. I. feff. 2, chap. xii.

Confequently

Confequently the charges of the civil lift, and the whole eftablifhment of the royal family, came to about £. 850,000 *per annum.*

The fums granted for naval fervices, amounted to £. 12,923,851.

The ordinary of the navy was then about £. 740,000, which, multiplied by twelve and a half, amounts to £. 9,250,000 to which £. 370,000 may be added for incidental charges, making in all £. 9,620,000, and there would ftill remain, £. 3,303,851 for extra expences of the navy, in confequence of the hoftile operations which took place during this reign.

The military expences during the fame period, are eftimated at £. 13,842,467.

The peace eftablifhment of the army, including the forces in the plantations, the half pay, Chelfea hofpital, and other fervices, might be about £.900,000 *per annum,* amounting, during the fpace of twelve years and a half, to £. 11,250,000. This fum being deducted from the above total, leaves £. 2,592,467 as the extraordinary expences of a military nature, to which this country was put during the above period.

The peace eftablifhment of the ordnance, was about £. 73,000 *per annum;* which, multiplied by twelve and a half, produces £. 912,500. As £. 1,064,449 was voted for ordnance fervices, the extra expences may be ftated at £. 151,949.

The mifcellaneous expences were not very confiderable : £. 30,000 was voted for the expence of the

the mint; £. 23,935 as the damage incurred by burning two merchantmen from the Levant, in order to prevent infection; £. 11,659 to make up losses sustained by rebellious and riotouss proceedings in different parts of the country. Other particulars might be mentioned; but they cannot exceed in all £. 150,000.

The burden of the national debt, was greatly lessened during this reign, by lowering the rate of the interest paid to the public creditors. But still this article, including two millions discharged, and the usual deficiencies of the land-tax, amounted to about £. 41,218,879.

The whole expences of this reign, may be thus stated :

The civil list - -	£. 10,632,514
The navy - -	12,923,851
The army - -	13,842,467
The ordnance - -	1,064,449
Miscellaneous services - -	150,000
	38,613,281
Interest of the public debts, loans repaid, and land-tax deficiencies - -	41,218,879
Total £.	79,832,160

The peace establishment was as follows :

The civil list - -	£. 850,000
The navy - -	740,000
The army - -	900,000
The ordnance - - -	73,000
Miscellaneous services - -	20,000
Total £.	2,583,000

The

The inconfiderable warlike operations, which took place during this reign, coft the following fums :

Extra Expences of the navy	-	£. 3,303,851
Ditto of the army		2,592,467
Ditto of the ordnance	-	151,949
	Total	£. 6,048,267

GEORGE II.

The firft part of the government of this monarch, was diftinguifhed by every appearance of tranquillity, though not unaccompanied with a confiderable degree of rancour on the part of Spain, and of jealoufy on the part of France. During that whole period, the public expences were not very confiderable, and the nation was in fo profperous a ftate, that it was able, with any tolerable management, to have carried on a fuccefsful war. But fo prevalent was the fpirit of faction at the time, that it was not conquefts abroad, but victory in the cabinet, and in the fenate-houfe, to which our ftatefmen afpired. That fpirit prevailed not only in the firft, but in the fecond war in which this monarch was engaged: and both might have proved equally unfortunate, had not the nation at laft united as if it were one man; and at an expence till then unheard of, and unparalleled, convinced the enemy, what the refources of Great Britain were capable of effecting, when exerted to the utmoft.

By

By an act paffed at the commencement of the reign, the duties known under the name of the civil lift revenues, were continued during the life of the new fovereign[m]. It was at the fame time fpecifically provided, that if thofe revenues did not yield £. 800,000 *per annum,* the deficiency fhould be made up by the public; but that any furplus fhould belong to the crown. At firft they did not yield the income that was expected: for, *anno* 1728, £. 115,000 was granted on account of arrears in the civil lift revenue: and *anno* 1746, the fum of £. 456,773 additional for the fame purpofe. An account was laid before the houfe of commons, of that branch of the revenue, from Midfummer 1727 to ditto 1760, amounting to £. 26,784,715[n].

Public Expences fince the Revolution.

Civil lift.

---

[m] I Geo. II. chap. i.

[n] Commons Journals, vol. xxviii. p. 965, 9th December 1760. It is not printed in the Journals: but the following is an abftract of the account:

ABSTRACT of the CIVIL LIST Funds from Midfummer 1727 to Midfummer 1760.

Hereditary and temporary excife	£. 8,173,166	3	7¼
Subfidy of tonnage and poundage	9,599,267	19	10
By Act 1 Geo. II. from aggregate fund	3,960,000	1	0
By 4 Geo. II. from ditto -	61,647	1	0½
By 9 Geo. II. from ditto -	1,662,500	0	0
By 12 Geo. II. from ditto -	47,764	18	4
Revenue of poft-office -	1,191,613	17	9½
Fines of alienation-office -	102,480	13	1½
Poft fines - -	73,108	0	0
Wine licences -	216,870	17	4¼
Sheriffs' proffers - -	20,663	9	10
Carried over	£. 25,111,083	1	11¼

To this muſt be added, £. 247,543 granted by parliament, as portions with the princeſſes of the royal
family: and *anno* 1746°, £.25,000 *per annum* was ſettled on the Duke of Cumberland, for his important
ſervices in quelling the rebellion. Upon accumulating theſe different ſums, they may be calculated in
all at £. 27,382, 258, or £. 829,795 *per annum*.

The navy.
The ſums granted for naval ſervices, during this
reign, amounted to £. 71,424,171.

Such were the immenſe grants for naval ſervices.
But great as they may ſeem, they were not entirely
thrown away. In both the wars which took place,
during the reign of this monarch, our naval exertions were attended with ſucceſs. Twice was
the maritime power of the houſe of Bourbon almoſt
totally annihilated;—a circumſtance which this

Brought forward £.	25,111,083	1	11¼
Compoſitions in the exchequer -	218	8	6
Seizure of prohibited and unaccuſtomed			
goods - - -	876,127	13	1½
Rents of lands - -	44,136	19	11
Fines of Leaſes -	142,126	18	5
Sale of lands - -	9,293	16	8
	£. 26,182,981	17	6¾
By Act 2 Geo. II. cap. 18. out of the ſup-			
plies for the year 1729 -	115,000	0	0
By Act 20 Geo. II. cap. 36. out of the ſup-			
plies 1747 - -	456,733	16	3¾
Total £.	26,784,715	13	10½

° 19 Geo. II. cap. 29.

country

country can hardly too dearly purchafe, and to *Public Expences fince the Revolution.* fecure which no expence ought to be regretted.

The army during this reign coft £. 73,911,521.

The ordnance expences, in fo far as refpected The army. the land fervice, and the purchafing of ground for the The ordnance. purpofes of fortification, amounted to £.6,706,674.

Other expences were alfo incurred in confequence Other military expences. of the war. £.,5,000, included in the grants for 1739, was paid to Solomon Morrett and others for the lofs of the fhip Ifabella, taken by the Spaniards; £. 10,000 was voted to the town of Glafgow, which had been extorted from that city in the rebellion ; £. 13,869 was granted to the owners of the money and effects taken in the Spanifh fhip Anna Maria St. Felix, by grant *anno* 1756 ; making in all £. 28,869.

The money paid during this reign, for building Churches. churches, for repairing Weftminfter Abbey, and the churches of St. Margaret's and St. John's Weftminfter, came to £. 152,240.

For building Weftminfter Bridge, and opening Bridges. a way from thence to Charing Crofs, there was voted in all £. 216,500. Nay, the fum of £.45,000 was granted for rebuilding London Bridge, though, confidering the greatnefs of the thoroughfare, and the immenfe income enjoyed by the corporation of London, that work might have been executed without any public affiftance.

During this reign, a military road was formed Military roads. acrofs the ifland, from Newcaftle upon Tyne to Carlifle ; for which purpofe £. 24,000 was granted.

As

Public Ex-
pences since
the Revolu-
tion.
_____

As to the roads in the Highlands of Scotland, they were for many years included among the extraordinary expences of the army, and were not separately voted.

Harbours.

For finishing the harbour of Rye, there was granted £. 23,360 ; and the sum of £. 20,000 for Milford harbour in Wales.

Public re-
wards.

Sir Thomas Lombe, had, at a great hazard and expence, introduced into this country, the art of making fine organzine Italian filk, or thrown filk, out of raw filk, by an engine, which is erected in the town of Derby, and a model of which is preserved with great care and attention in the tower of London. As a reward for so important a discovery, the sum of £. 14,000 was given him by parliament. *Anno* 1738, £. 5,000 was alfo voted as a reward to Mrs. Stephens, for communicating to the public her remedy for the stone ; and *anno* 1755, £. 3,000 to Thomas Stephen, for difcovering the proper mode of making pot-afh.

Public mo-
nument.

Anno 1756, £. 3,000 was granted for the purpofe of erecting a monument to the memory of Captain Cornwall, who had died fighting gallantly in the fervice of his country. The public money could not be better expended. It was by fuch encouragements, that the free ftates of antiquity rofe to eminence and to glory. It is by fuch inducements, that individuals are beft animated to great and magnanimous exertions. To recompenfe military atchievements, by pecuniary rewards alone, or to make money the great object of gallant men, is in

the

the higheft degree impolitic ; for none are to be
accounted truly brave, or in great emergencies are to be depended upon, but fuch as are infpired by honour, and not by intereft, and who prefer fame to fortune.

At the union, the feudal fyftem exifted in full
force in the remoter parts of Scotland. In thofe wild and mountainous diftricts, the chieftains of the different clans, enjoyed almoft full power over the perfons and property of their vaffals. But fo tyran-nical a fyftem could not continue for ever. It was at length difcovered, that whilft it remained, no improvements could be expected in that part of the country. To break the power of thefe barons, parliament refolved to purchafe the rights and pri-vileges which they claimed; and £. 152,037 was granted for that purpofe. In a pecuniary view alone, perhaps the compenfation was adequate. But it is difficult to eftimate the ideal value, that might be attached to fuch important prerogatives, by perfons accuftomed to exercife them *.

The rebellion that broke out in Scotland, *anno*
1745, was principally fupported by perfons of def-perate fortunes, who expected to retrieve their affairs in the midft of buftle and confufion. The eftates of fuch as poffeffed landed property, were forfeited to the crown ; and parliament wifely de-termined, to appropriate the income they produced, to the purpofe of improving the Highlands and Iflands of North Britain. But fuch at the fame

---

* The author's father, got about £. 3000, for the heritable fheriffihip of the county of Caithnefs.

Public Ex-
pences since
the Revolu-
tion.

     time were the incumbrances due by their former poffeffors, that though they hardly yielded a clear rent of £. 8,000 *per annum*, government paid, *anno* 1759 and 1760, £. 72,410, and in the fucceeding reign £. 110,553 more, in order to difcharge the debts by which they were affected.

The mint.

     The extra expences of coinage, during this reign, in addition to the ordinary charges of £. 7,000 *per annum*, amounted to £. 31,364.

Horned cat-
tle.

     Among the many advantages which this country enjoys from its infular fituation, there is none more truly important, than the facility with which infectious diftempers, whether affecting the human fpecies, or their cattle, can be prevented. In Holland, above 500,000 cows, worth at leaft £. 10 each, have perifhed within the fpace of 20 years; and hence, in that fhort period of time, the States have loft above five millions by difeafes among their cattle [p]. The avarice of fome Englifh tanners, who brought over infected hides, introduced the difeafe into this country; and at different times, £. 208,123 was granted by parliament, to prevent fo fatal a diftemper from being extended.

Foundling
hofpital.

     During this reign, there was granted to the Foundling-hofpital, the fum of £. 128,277.

Lifbon
earthquake.

     Some nations of antiquity are juftly celebrated, for fending prefents to the ifland of Rhodes, when, by an earthquake, its renowned coloffus was thrown down, and other damage was fuftained. Great

---

    [p] This is a very moderate eftimate. I have heard the lofs calculated at forty millions fterling.

Britain

Britain difplayed equal, if not fuperior generofity, on a fimilar occafion ; for no fooner was intelligence received of the fatal earthquake at Lifbon, (which in 1755 almoft buried that proud metropolis in the earth), than the Britifh parliament unanimoufly voted £. 100,000 to relieve the unhappy fufferers ; —perhaps the only inftance, in modern times, of fuch extenfive liberality from one ftate to another.

Public Expences fince the Revolution.

As the expence of maintaining the Britifh forts on the coaft of Africa, and in full fatisfaction to the Royal African Company for their charter, lands, &c. £. 420,173 was voted during this reign.

African forts.

The charges which this country has been put to, on account of its fettlements in America, are hardly to be credited. As far back as the reign of James I. of England, the fum of £. 29,000 was raifed by lotteries, for the purpofe of eftablifhing the colony of Virginia [q] ;—a confiderable fum in thofe days, and which, if accumulated at compound intereft, fince the year 1620, would have paid no fmall fhare of the national debt. But, without going to fuch remote periods, it may juftly be afferted that the two laft wars, and all the enormous expences with which they were accompanied, may be traced to the fame fource. Even the war of 1739, partly originated from the clamours of the North Americans, and their refentment againft Spain, for attempting to prohibit the intercourfe they held with the colonies of that country. The

American expences.

[q] See Chalmer's Political Annals of the Britifh Colonies, vol, i. p. 32. and 41.

war

war of 1755, it can hardly be denied, was owing
to the anxiety of the inhabitants of Great Britain,
to protect their brethren in America from the in-
trigues of the French, and the attacks of Indian
favages. The war preceding the prefent, was
purely American, and would never have been
carried on, and fo anxioufly perfevered in, had it
not been imagined, that a great majority of the
people of that country, were defirous of preferving
a connexion with the parent ftate, and apprehended
the fatal confequences of which a feparation would
be productive. Nor was any expence ever fpared,
that could contribute to the good government,
that could promote the induftry, that could infure
the fafety, that could mitigate the misfortunes, or
could animate the exertions of the people of
that country, even for their own fecurity and
protection.

Anno 1729, the fum of £. 22,500 was voted
by parliament, to the proprietors of Carolina,
that the inhabitants of that province, inftead of
being oppreffed under an ariftocratical government, might enjoy all the bleffings of liberty and
of legal independence. And, *anno* 1741, when a
fire happened at Charleftown, £. 20,000 was
granted to be diftributed among the unhappy
fufferers.

The expences of Georgia, during this reign,
amounted to £. 117,110; and thofe of Nova
Scotia to £. 637,972.

By

By votes to the different provinces in America, *Public Expences since the Revolution.* to indemnify them for the expences they were put to in the expedition againſt Cape Breton, and to encourage them in the following war to exert themſelves with vigour in defence of his Majeſty's rights, and for their own ſecurity, there were granted, during this reign, the ſum of £. 899,842[r].

Theſe ſums joined together amount to £. 1,697,424.

The following are the only other miſcellaneous expences:

	£.	
1730. For the purchaſe of the wardenſhip of the Fleet priſon -	2,500	
1741. To the ſufferers by the failure of Mr. Henry Popple - -	8,716	
1754. For the office of marſhal of the Marſhalſea priſon - -	5,200	
For rebuilding the Marſhalſea priſon	7,800	
1759. To Dr. Long, for diſcharging a mortgage on an eſtate deviſed for the endowment of a profeſſorſhip at Cambridge	1,280	
	£. 25,496	

The mode of making good to his majeſty, money *Money paid pursuant to addresses.* voted purſuant to addreſſes from the commons, was firſt introduced in the year 1758. In this manner, £.31,000 was granted during this reign. It was principally intended for the expence of

---

[r] In this ſum is included a part of the expence of the garriſon of Cape Breton *anno* 1749.

printing

*Public Ex-
pences since
the Revolu-
tion.*
printing the journals of the houfe ;—a meafure of great public utility, and which has been the means of making known much material information. But this is a mode of voting money, which ought to be difcountenanced as much as poffible, if ever it is intended, that a real fpirit of economy fhould pervade our financial fyftem.

Intereft of
public debts,
&c.
It feems unneceffary to enter minutely, into the various fums paid during this reign, to the different public creditors, either in payment of the principal or intereft of their debts.   It may be fufficient to ftate, that they amounted in all to about £.93,347,134.

The total expenditure, during this reign, will then be as follows :

The civil lift - -	£. 27,280,000
The navy - -	71,424,171
The army -	73,911,521
The ordnance —	6,706,674
Other military expences -	28,869
Ecclefiaftical expences	152,240
Weftminfter Bridge -	216,500
London Bridge -	45,000
Military roads -	24,000
Making harbours - -	43,360
Public rewards -	22,000
Public monument to Captain Cornwall	3,000
Heritable jurifdictions in Scotland	152,037
The debts due on the Scotch forfeited eftates	72,410
Charges of the mint at £.7,000 *per annum* for	
33 years - -	231,000
Extra expences of the mint -	31,364
Horned cattle - -	208,123

Carried over   £.180,552,269

Brought over		£.	180,552,269
Foundling hofpital	-	-	182,277
Earthquake at Lifbon	-	-	100,000
African forts and fettlements	-	-	420,173
American Expences	-	-	1,697,424
Mifcellaneous expences	-	-	25,496
Money paid purfuant to addreffes		-	25,000

Public Expences fince the Revolution.

£. 183,002,639

Intereft of the public debts, and repayment
of the principal   -   -   93,347,134

Total   £. 276,349,773

The peace eftablifhment, towards the conclufion of this reign, may be thus ftated :

			Per annum.
The civil lift	-	-	£. 836,000
The navy	-	-	900,000
The army	-	-	900,000
The ordnance	-	-	80,000
Mifcellaneous expences	-	-	50,000

Total   £. 2,766,000

This reign is diftinguifhed by two wars. The firft began *anno* 1739, and was concluded by the peace of Aix la Chapelle *anno* 1748; the fecond began *anno* 1755, and was concluded by the treaty of Paris in February 1763. The expences of each war, it may be proper to ftate feparately.

Some account has already been given, of the firft war entered into during the reign of George II. It unqueftionably arofe from the turbulent fpirit of the

Expences of the war 1739.

the Englifh, who, tired of a long peace, engaged in hoftilities with Spain for very frivolous reafons. The trifling fum of one or two hundred thoufand pounds, was the original fubject of conteft. But the oppofition to the government at the time, knew well that the power and adminiftration of Sir Robert Walpole, could only be fhaken by fuch an event: And fuch was the clamour raifed by our merchants at home, and by our colonies in the Weft Indies and America, againft the treatment our fhips had received from the Spaniards, that, however cautioufly a nation ought to enter into war, little deliberation was made ufe of in commencing it upon that occafion. The difpute afterwards .became of a nature more general and extenfive.

In a former chapter, it was ftated, that the addition which this war made to the national debt amounted to £. 31,338,689. But this was far from being the total expence. The following fums may alfo be placed to the fame account:

1. Eight years land-tax at 4s. in the pound		£. 16,000,000
2. Ditto malt -	-	6,000,000
3. Taken out of the finking fund	-	7,800,000
		£. 29,800,000
Deduct eight years expence in time of peace		14,720,000
		£. 15,080,000
Add the debt contracted	-	31,338,689
Total expence of the war		£. 46,418,689*

* See the Prefent State of the Nation, printed *anno* 1748.

The

The war with Spain alone lasted about four years; and the extraordinary expences which it occasioned, may be estimated at £. 3,000,000 a-year. The remaining four years, of more general hostilities, cost about £. 8,500,000 *per annum*.

Public Expences since the Revolution.

It is natural for the reader to demand, what advantage did the country reap for so enormous an expence? and were the terms either lucrative, or honourable, on which the peace was concluded? The history of that war, and the manner in which it was terminated, are too well known to require any particular detail in this place. We had the honour, it is true, of supporting the house of Austria, when on the very brink of destruction; and it is to be hoped, that some time or other, we shall receive grateful returns for such generous assistance. We were fortunate enough to capture or to destroy, no inconsiderable part of the fleet of the house of Bourbon, which ought ever to be considered as an important object in the eyes of Britain. But as to any acquisitions, calculated to indemnify us for the expences we were put to, they are to be sought for in vain; and at the very instant when our enemies were reduced to the utmost necessity by famine, a peace was concluded, on such disadvantageous terms, that the ministers had not confidence sufficient to move for a vote of approbation in parliament.

The war concluded by the treaty of Paris, has this circumstance in its favour, that during the greater part of it, the nation was triumphant; and though

Expence of the war 1755.

though the peace by which it was terminated, was perhaps hardly adequate to the expectations of the public, yet it was the moſt lucrative treaty, in point of territorial acquiſition, that is recorded in the annals of this country. With regard to the charges of the war, they have been thus eſtimated: The ſupplies for the year 1753 (which was the laſt peace eſtabliſhment) amounted to £. 2,797,916. Every addition to that ſum, until the burden of the war was entirely ſettled, may be ſtated to its account. The ſums voted were as follows:

Voted anno 1754	£. 4,073,779	1761	£. 18,299,153
1755	7,229,117	1762	13,522,040
1756	8,350,325	1763	7,712,562
1757	10,486,457	1764	7,763,090
1758	12,749,860	1765	8,273,280
1759	12,503,564	1766	8,527,728
1760	19,616,119	1767	8,335,746

£. 150,442,820

Hence the total expence may be thus calculated:

Sums voted - -	£. 150,442,820
Peace eſtabliſhment for 14 years at £.2,797,916	39,170,824
Total charges of the war	£. 111,271,996

As it only laſted for ſeven years, the expence *per annum* amounted to £.15,895,999[t].

Great

[t] The extraordinary expence in France on account of this war has been ſtated as follows:

1756

Great as our fuccefs was, it was dearly purchafed at fuch a rate.

Nor are diftant and foreign acquifitions always of fuch utility as may at firft be imagined. The war now alluded to, was principally diftinguifhed by the acquifition of fome Weft Indian iflands, and by the refignation of the whole province of Canada by the French. But neither proved ferviceable to Great Britain. It is a fact which, however incredible it may appear, is beyond all doubt, that in order to procure a right to the foil of the iflands thus ceded to us by the French, namely, Grenada, Tobago, and St. Vincent's, no lefs a fum than three millions, was paid by Britifh fubjects to French proprietors, with which the remaining poffeffions of the French in that hemifphere were improved, and brought to that beneficial ftate of cultivation and produce, which they have fince boafted of. The finking of fo enormous a fum, was attended with very perni-cious confequences, in regard to our original pof-feffions in the Weft Indies, to our public and pri-

1756	£. 5,377,778
1757	6,044,444
1758	6,000,000
1759	8,652,924
1760	11,186,431
1761	5,364,034
1762	7,076,924
Total	£. 49,702,535

vate

vate credit, and to our circulation at home". As
to the acquifition of Canada, it was prophefied at
the time, that it would neceffarily occafion, what
we have li ed to fee, the independence of our colonies. When the retention of Canada was firft
propofed, that able ftatefman, the Duke de
Choifeul, declared, that he could not object to a
plan, which would neceffarily prove fo ruinous to
the enemies of France : for he wifely forefaw, that
our American colonies, when once relieved from
the terror of fuch a neighbour, when once freed
from all apprehenfion of being made fubject to
the houfe of Bourbon, would foon begin to confider Great Britain, as the only power of whom
they ought to be jealous.

Meditating on thefe events, who can avoid
breaking out into juft exclamations againft the
madnefs of war? The taxes which neceffarily
arife from extended and frequent hoftilities, every
warlike nation muft lay its account with : it muft
alfo put up with all thofe dreadful fcenes of mifery
and bloodfhed, which are their fure concomitants.
But a wife nation will alfo take into its confideration, the uncertainty of any recompence being
procured, for the expences that it muft fuftain ; and
that acquifitions which are at firft accounted of the
moft effential importance, may in the end prove
fatally deftructive.

ª It materially contributed to the failures *anno* 1772.

GEORGE III.

It is hardly poffible, to write the hiftory of our own times with fufficient impartiality. Notwithftanding the moft anxious defire, to give a fair reprefentation of the circumftances which have occurred, fome lurking prejudices, either adverfe or favourable to particular parties in the fcene, will in all probability appear, however cautioufly guarded againft. An author, at the fame time, cannot avoid making fome obfervations, on the character, the principles, and the conduct of individuals, when endeavouring to explain, the various facts which it is neceffary for him to bring forward. In general it may be remarked, that the hiftory of the prefent reign, in the page of fome future hiftorian, will form the fubject of a curious and important narration; and it will then probably be ftated, that a great and powerful empire, in confequence of internal divifions, was, at different periods, on the brink of falling from the higheft elevation of ftrength and power, into an abyfs of mifery and weaknefs; and thence it will become a curious fubject of political fpeculation, whether that corruption, which is inherent in a defpotic government, or that factious fpirit, which fo often prevails in a free ftate, is the moft unfortunate circumftance to a country.

The firft act that was paffed after the king's ac- *Civil lift.* ceffion to the crown, granted to his majefty the

ium

sum of £. 800,000 *per annum*, subject to the several annuities of £. 50,000 a-year to the Princess
Dowager of Wales, £. 15,000 to the Duke of
Cumberland, and £. 12,000 to the Princess Amelia.
This, in the space of twenty-eight years, amounts
to £. 22,400,000 but is far from being the total
sum laid out during this period in the expences of
the civil government ; for on 28th February 1769,
£. 513,511 was granted to discharge certain arrears
of the civil list, contracted prior to the 5th January 1769. And on the 16th April 1777, the
sum of £. 620,000 was again voted for a similar
purpose, together with an additional £. 100,000
per annum, to the income of the crown. £.120,000
was also given as the marriage portions of the princesses Augusta and Matilda. The annuity of
£. 25,000 to the late William Duke of Cumberland was continued during his life ; and annuities
out of the aggregate fund, at the rate of £. 8,000
each, were granted to their Royal Highnesses the
Dukes of York, Gloucester, and Cumberland, commencing 5th January 1767[x]. The following then, is
a pretty accurate statement, of the sums paid to the
royal family, by the public, during the present
reign, up to Michaelmas 1788.

The original civil list revenue of £. 800,000 *per*
  annum from the accession to Michaelmas 1788 £. 22,400,000
The additional £. 100,000 from 5th January
  1777 (12 years)   -   -   1,200,000

                       Carry over   £.23,600,000

[x] 7 Geo. III. cap. 19

                                      Civil

Brought over	£. 23,600,000	*Public Ex-*
Civil lift debts paid *anno* 1769 -	513,511	*pences since*
1777 -	620,000	*the Revolu-*
1784 - -	60,000	*tion.*
1786 - -	30,000	
Exchequer bills due on civil lift, paid off *anno* 1786 - - -	180,000	
Marriage portions - -	120,000	
Additional income to William Duke of Cumberland for five years - -	125,000	
To the Dukes of York, Gloucefter, and Cumberland, being the amount of the annuities paid to them out of the aggregate fund -	360,000	
For enabling his Majefty to make a feparate eftablifhment for his Royal Highnefs the Prince of Wales - - -	60,000	
For difcharging the debts of the Prince of Wales, and for the works at Carlton Houfe	181,000	
	£. 25,849,511	

This during the fpace of 28 years, amounts to £. 923,196 *per annum.*

But great as this fum may appear, it would not have proved fufficient, had not other additions been made to it[y], and had not fome attempts been made

[y] In Almon's Parliamentary Regifter, *anno* 1777, vol. vii. p. p. 57, there is an exaggerated account of the total of the royal income. It is there afferted, that exclufive of the additional votes above mentioned, it could not be lefs, *communibus annis*, than £. 1,400,000 a-year. The fum is thus made out:

Civil lift - - -	£. 800,000
Revenue of Hanover after paying all charges	100,000
Carried over	£. 900,000
	Ireland

made, to eſtabliſh a ſyſtem of economy, in this branch of the public expenditure. Indeed ſuch is the profuſion inherent in the very nature of courts, that nothing but fixed and unalterable rules, to be ſtedfaſtly and inviolably adhered to, and on no account to be departed from, can poſſibly prevent the income of the crown from being perpetually deficient.

Here it may be proper, to give ſome account, of the applications made to parliament, for paying the

	Brought over	£. 900,000
Ireland -	-	90,000
Wales -	-	10,000
Lancaſter	-	20,000
Cornwall	-	70,000
$4\frac{1}{2}$ *per cent.* duty in the Weſt Indies	-	50,000
Coal-pits of Louiſburg	-	12,000
Intereſt of the debts due to the late king	-	150,000
	Total	£. 1,302,000

The remainder is made up, from—the quit-rents in North America, which it is ſaid amounted before the war to £.15,000 *per annum*; — the $4\frac{1}{2}$ *per cent.* duty in North America, which produced about £. 50,000 *per annum*;—the money procured from the ſale of Somerſet Houſe, which is ſtated at £. 100,000;—and preſents from eaſtern princes, which are calculated at a million. But every one muſt perceive that theſe ſums are not a little exaggerated; and with ſome of them, the ſurplus revenue of Hanover in particular, this country has no connexion.—In the accounts produced to parliament (Ditto, p. 59.), it is acknowledged that there was received, between 5th January 1769 and 5th January 1777, from the dutchy of Cornwall, &c. the ſum of £. 205,422 18 *s.* $6\frac{1}{4}$ *d.* making in all about £. 25,677 *per annum.*

civil

civil lift debts, and of the various regulations which have been eftablifhed, in regard to that important department.

Public Expences fince the Revolution.

The firft application for public affiftance, to difcharge the debts of the civil lift, which took place *anno* 1769, met with fome oppofition, but was carried on a divifion by a confiderable majority [z].

But the next application, *anno* 1777, not only for a confiderable fum of money to pay arrears, but alfo for an additional income of £. 100,000, occafioned violent debates. The crown was as ufual fuccefsful in parliament; but the attempt was univerfally odious to the people, and excited a clamour, which rendered the government at the time not a little unpopular. In a fucceeding feffion, the table of the houfe of commons was covered with Petitions, praying for a reform in this branch of the national expenditure. On the 11th February 1780, Mr. Edmund Burke, in one of the moft fplendid orations ever delivered in a public affembly, introduced his bill for the better regulation of his majefty's civil eftablifhments; and on the 6th of April following, on the motion of Mr. Dunning, the houfe came to the following important refolutions:

1. That it is neceffary to declare, that the influence of the crown has increafed, is increafing, and ought to be diminifhed.

2. That it is competent for parliament to examine into, and to correct abufes, in the expendi-

---

[z] 248 voted in favour of the motion; 135 againft it; majority 113.

ture

ture of the civil lift revenues, as well as in every other branch of the public revenue, whenever it fhall appear expedient to the wifdom of parliament fo to do [a].

It was not however until the year 1782, that any effectual ftep was taken to reform thefe expences. By Mr. Burke's original fyftem, the annual favings were calculated at £. 75,343, without including the board of police in Scotland ; and it was ftated, that it would detach from the influence of the crown, nine members in the houfe of lords, and thirty in the houfe of commons. By the plan of 1782, the following favings were propofed :

	Annual Savings.
By abolifhing the office of third fecretary of ftate	£. 7,500
Board of trade　-　　-	12,600
Lords of police in Scotland　-　　-	6,600
Board of works　-　　-	7,462
Great wardrobe　-　　-	3,506
Jewel office　-　　-	2,000
Treafurer of the chamber　-　　-	3,000
Cofferer of the houfehold　-　　-	3,000
Board of green cloth　-　　-	8,000
Mafters of the harriers and of the ftag-hounds　-	3,000
The eftablifhment of the mint　-　　-	13,000
Paymafter of penfions　-　　-	2,700
Total　　£. 72,368 [b]	

But fchemes, however plaufible in theory, are difficult to reduce into practice. The favings actually carried into effect (by 22 Geo. III. cap. 82.)

[a] Commons Journals, vol. xxxvii. p. 763.
[b] *Ibid.* vol. xxxviii. p. 971.

were

were below even £. 50,000, and from that fum above £. 18,000 muſt be deducted for fome time, being the compenfation to which various perfons, whofe offices were fuppreſſed, were found to be intitled ; and the public has fince been under the neceſſity of difcharging the arrears, for which thofe very favings were appropriated.   The merit, however, of the honourable gentleman who brought forward the regulations contained in that act, ought not to be forgotten.   By his exertions, the payments of the civil liſt expences, have been arranged in a manner, which will probably prevent any material excefs in future.   Penfions, (except in certain cafes fpecified in the act), are reſtricted to a fum not exceeding £. 95,000 *per annum* ; and the conſtitution is protected from any riſk of injury, by the wife and falutary rules which are eſtabliſhed, refpecting the diſtribution of the fecret fervice money with which the crown is intruſted.   Thefe are material points, for which the thanks of the country are due to the citizen who achieved them.   In regard to other particulars in the bill, opinions may vary : for one, I do not hefitate to declare, that, in my judgment, the jealoufy of the crown, fo manifeſt in the act above alluded to, was carried too far. However much fecret corruption ought to be reprobated, the avowed influence refulting from the difpofal of employments, neceffary for the fplendour of the court, or the carrying on of the public bufinefs of the country, ought not to be too bounded. In political, as well as in other lotteries, there

ought

ought to be an adequate proportion of fmaller, as well as of greater prizes; and unlefs fome method is adopted, by an increafe of patronage, of attaching a greater number of individuals to the crown, than at prefent look up to it, from the places they enjoy, it is not difficult to forefee, that the government muft either become weak and fluctuating, or that the balance of the conftitution will be overturned, nay, the fpirit and morals of the people endangered, by too numerous and wealthy a peerage, which has already been increafing with too rapid ftrides, fince other means of influence were abolifhed [c].

This branch of the fubject may be concluded with the following abftract of the actual difburfements of his majefty's civil government, for the year 1785, being the lateft account that appears on the Journals; and by examining which, the reader will find the different particulars he may wifh to be acquainted with, fully detailed.

ABSTRACT of a particular ACCOUNT of the DISBURSEMENTS of the CIVIL LIST for the Year 1785.

First clafs.	The penfions and allowances to the royal family	£. 192,000
Second clafs.	The lord chancellor, judges, &c. -	32,955
	Carried over	£ 224,955

[c] This was originally written *anno* 1790, and has fince been amply verified, in fo far as regards the increafe of the peerage.

The

Brought over	£. 224,955	*Public Expences since the Revolution.*
The foreign minifters – –	75,543	
Approved bills for his majefty's fervice –	138,641	
The menial fervants of the houfehold –	89,799	*Third clafs.*
Penfions and compenfations for fuppreffed offices	125,757	*Fourth clafs.*
Various other falaries payable out of the civil lift	82,187	*Fifth clafs.*
The falaries of the board of treafury –	13,822	*Sixth clafs.*
Occafional payments – –	147,764	*Seventh clafs.*
		Eighth clafs.
	898,468	*Ninth clafs.*
To cancel exchequer bills for paying the arrears on the civil lift, but which were fince difcharged by parliament – –	50,000	
	£. 948,468[d]	

The real expences of the civil lift, thus amounted
to £. 898,468, and there is too much reafon to believe, that it will require attention and economy, to
confine the charges, in future, to the fum allotted
for that purpofe, namely, £. 900,000; particularly
confidering the increafing price of every article of
confumption, and other circumftances that might
be mentioned.

Only two other particulars remain, which it
feems neceffary to take notice of, as connected
with the income and expenditure of the royal family; namely, 1ft, That by 15 Geo. III. cap. 52.
Buckingham-houfe was fettled on her majefty, in
room of Somerfet-houfe, granted by a former act.
The original price of the queen's royal palace, as

[d] See Commons Journals, vol. xli. p. 639; and another account of the fame nature, vol. xliii. p. 328.

it

it has been since called, was £. 28,000. But from
Lady day 1762, to Christmas 1774, £. 72,627 was
expended in enlarging and improving it, making
in all £. 100,627 [e].   In the event of surviving the
king, her majesty will be entitled to an annuity of
£. 100,000 *per annum*, being £. 50,000 in addition
to her present allowance.

In regard to the settlements on the other branches
of the royal family; by 18 Geo. III. cap. 31.
£. 60,000 *per annum* is settled on his majesty's
sons, and £. 30,000 *per annum* on the princesses
of the family, payable on the king's demise ;
together with £. 8,000 *per annum* on the son, and
£. 4,000 *per annum* on the daughter of his royal
highness the duke of Gloucester, commencing at
his death [f].   These provisions are surely moderate,
but are equal perhaps to what a nation so loaded
and embarrassed as this is, can well afford.

The naval charges of this reign, to Michaelmas
1788, may be thus stated :

Anno 1761	£. 5,072,602	*Anno* 1766	£. 2,680,683
1762	5,688,012	1767	1,400,409
1763	1,975,661	1768	1,238,883
1764	2,053,200	1769	1,828,057
1765	2,886,876	1770.	1,580,467

Carried forward   £. 26,304,850

[e] Commons Journals, vol. xxxv. p. 320.

[f] By 25 Geo. III. cap. 53. an annuity of 9,000 *per annum,*
payable to the Duke of Gloucester during his life, is transferred
from the $4\frac{1}{2}$ *per cent.* Leeward Island duty, to the aggregate
fund

Anno

Brought forward 26,304,850 £.

Anno 1771	£.2,967,409	*Anno* 1780	£.6,777,632	
1772	1,813,164	1781	8,603,884	
1773	1,833,573	1782	7,095,228	
1774	2,052,917	1783	6,197,832	
1775	1,599,453	1784	3,086,269	
1776	3,092,967	1785	2,504,507	
1777	4,053,666	1786	2,381,526	
1778	4,779,151	1787	2,286,000	
1779	4,106,374	1788	2,236,000	

	93,872,402
Navy debt funded by 3 Geo. III. cap. 9.	3,483,553
Ditto funded by 5 Geo. III. cap. 29.	1,500,000
Ditto funded by 24 Geo. III. cap. 39 and	
25. ditto cap. 33 and 71 -	17,869,993
Total £.	116,725,948

Great as our naval exertions were, and powerful as the confederacy was, againſt which we had to contend, during the American war, yet ſo enormous an expence can hardly be juſtified. It is aſſerted, that two millions are perfectly ſufficient to build a very formidable fleet; and during the period above mentioned the contract price for building King's ſhips in the merchants' yards, was as follows:

	Rate.	Price *per* Ton.	No. of Tons.	Total Price.
Ships of	74 guns	£. 17 15	1650	£. 28,462
Ditto	64	16 16	1400	23,520
Frigates	36	11 5	700	7,875
Smaller ditto	16	9 11	300	2,850

At thoſe rates, the following number of ſhips might be conſtructed, for, comparatively ſpeaking, a very moderate ſum.

Fifty

Fifty fhips of 74 guns at	£. 28,462 each	£. 1,423,100
Twenty ditto 64	23,520	470,400
Twenty large frigates	7,875	157,500
Twenty fmall ditto	2,850	57,000

£. 2,108,000

As fhips of war might certainly be built for lefs money in the king's, than in the merchants' yards, it can hardly be doubted, that for two millions, feventy fhips of the line, and forty frigates, might have been conftructed.

The army.   The following fums were granted for military fervices :

Anno 1761	£. 8,344,030	*Anno* 1775	£. 1,597,051
1762	7,657,205	1776	3,500,366
1763	4,593,805	1777	3,797,632
1764	2,267,867	1778	4,833,666
1765	1,784,856	1779	6,013,082
1766	1,910 413	1780	6,589,080
1767	1,537,314	1781	7,723,912
1768	1,472,484	1782	7,645,237
1769	1,497,921	1783	5,577,474
1770	1,547,931	1784	3,153,191
1771	1,810,319	1785	1,689,169
1772	1,551,428	1786	1,594,115
1773	1,516,402	1787	1,831,069
1774	1,549,720	1788	1,979,020

Total   £. 96,565,762

Miferable indeed is the reflection, to what little purpofe fuch fums were given by the public. In the year 1704 the whole of the military and naval eftimates, amounted only to £. 4,647,140. Yet that

that year was diftinguifhed, by the victories of Blenheim, and of Malaga; and the campaign was carried on in Spain, in Portugal, in the Low Countries, on the Rhine, and on the Danube. Whereas the immenfe treafures which were voted during the American war, even for military fervices alone, were not attended with the confolation of one brilliant event by land, (the gallant defence of Gibraltar alone excepted) and far lefs with any important acquifition.

Public Expences fince the Revolution.

The whole expence of the ordnance, from the acceffion, to Michaelmas 1788, may be ftated at £. 17,079,011, without including fuch ordnance debentures as were funded, at the fame time with the debts of the navy.

The ordnance.

It is not propofed, to enter into any minute detail, of the various mifcellaneous expences, which occurred during this reign.   They amounted in all to £. 4,466,508.   At the fame time, it may be proper to make fome obfervations upon any branch of this expenditure, the nature, or the magnitude of which, more particularly entitles it to the public attention.

Mifcellaneous expences.

There is no branch of the national expence, at which a Britifh patriot is more apt to repine, than the money laid out, whether for the civil or military purpofes of our colonies in North America. To check that rage of colonization, which has coft this country fo much, it may be proper to give a ftatement of the fums granted to thofe provinces,

American expences.

vinces, in the courfe of this reign, together with
a general view of the whole expence of our
American colonies, fince the acceffion of the houfe
of Brunfwick.

The firft expences of this nature to be mentioned, are the fums which were granted to reim-
burfe thofe colonies, for raifing and maintaining
troops, in fact neceffary for their own defence, or
employed in the attainment of objects, (as the
conqueft of Canada,) which they had particularly
at heart. For this purpofe, the Britifh parliament
granted, during this reign, £. 472,676.

The furveys made of the coafts of America, (a
matter of more confequence to them than to us,)
coft £. 34,296.

For the fupport of their refpective civil governments, from Michaelmas 1760, to Michaelmas
1788, there was voted as follows:

	£.
For Nova Scotia	186,565
Georgia	77,303
Eaft Florida	105,450
Weft Florida	102,311
St. John's	32,550
New Brunfwick	22,356
Cape Breton	10,600
Newfoundland	2,365
	£. 539,500

One of the moft fplendid inftances of public
generofity, which the world has as yet exhibited,
is to be found in the conduct of the Britifh legiflature,

lature, at the conclusion of the American war: when, undifmayed by the lofs of thirteen provinces, and all the enormous debts and taxes of which the war was neceffarily productive, it did not hefitate to hold forth, hopes of compenfation to thofe, who had fuffered by their attachment to the mother-country, in the courfe of the conteft. After the reftoration, parliament had granted £. 60,000 to be diftributed among thofe unfortunate royalifts who had undergone a feries of diftrefs, during the civil wars by which the reign of Charles the Firft had been afflicted [s]. But inftead of voting, on the fame prudent principles, a fpecific fum for the pur-pofe, commiffioners were appointed, upon this oc-cafion, to make a general enquiry " into the loffes " and fervices of all fuch perfons who have fuf- " fered in their rights, properties, and poffeffions, " during the late unhappy diffenfions in America, " in confequence of their loyalty to his majefty, " and attachment to the Britifh government."

The reader will naturally be defirous, of having a fhort account of the progrefs of this expence, and a ftatement of what the whole amounts to.

The firft mention of any claim of this kind, is in the account laid before parliament, of the debts of the civil lift, as they ftood on the 5th of January 1777. It was there ftated, that £. 32,934 : 16 : 6 had been iffued for the relief and benefit of fundry American civil officers and

[s] Hiftory of the Revenue, part i. p. 132.

others,

others, who had fuffered for their attachment to his majefty's government. This fum, after a fhort debate, was ultimately made good by parliament [h].

Anno 1778, the fum increafed to £.56,680 : 2 : 6; and the fucceeding year to £.60,527 : 3 : 6, which Lord North, (then chancellor of the exchequer,) ftated, in the committee of fupply, was a grant that would probably diminifh for the future, as feveral Americans who had fled from Georgia, and were fupported here by the national generofity, had returned home, and confequently that any claims of that nature, could not be fo great after their departure.

During the fucceeding years, various grants were made by parliament, partly to American fufferers in general, and partly to thofe civil officers who had been driven from that country; the whole, from 1776 to 1789, amounting to £.720,873, in addition to the fums laid out under the direction of the commiffioners of enquiry.

The reports given in by the commiffioners are intitled to particular attention. They firft ftated the number of claims given in to be 2994; the grofs amount of the fums claimed for lofs of property £.7,261,358, and that £.90,236 of annual income was alleged to have been loft. But thefe claims, when examined, were confiderably reduced, and the following ftatement was drawn up by the commiffioners, difcriminating the various defcrip-

[h] Parliamentary Regifter, vol. vii. p. 356.

tions

tions of loyalifts, and the loffes of property, or of *Public Ex-*
income, fuftained by each :

	Number.	Property. £.	Income. £.
1. Loyalifts who have rendered fervices to Great Britain -	204	596,092	25,085
2. Loyalifts who had bore arms in the fervice of Great Britain	481	254,988	6,503
3. Loyalifts zealous and uniform	626	590,424	38,871
4. Loyal Britifh fubjects refident in Great Britain -	20	89,371	1,070
5. Loyalifts who took oaths to the American ftates, but afterwards joined the Britifh -	27	35,046	280
6. Loyalifts who bore arms for the American ftates, but afterwards joined the Britifh -	23	22,853	2,725
7. Loyalifts fuftaining loffes under the prohibitory act -	3	13,971	
8. Loyal Britifh proprietors	2	258,254	
9. Loyalifts now fubjects of the United States, but who have met with peculiar hardfhips -	25	26,549	970

CLAIMS difallowed and withdrawn :

	1. For want of proof of loyalty -	7
	2. Want of proof of lofs -	250
10.	3. Fraudulent -	12
	4. For debts only	10
	5. Withdrawn -	34
		313

| Total | 1,724 | 1,887,548 | 75,504 |

In

In addition to the above, it was stated, that
there were four loyal subjects, who have relief
provided for them by the treaty of peace, but
cannot procure it, whose claims amounted to
£. 45,363, and that the probable amount of future
claims would be £. 300,000.

It is farther to be observed, that commissioners
had been appointed, for the purpose of enquiring
into the losses of such persons, as had suffered in their
properties, in consequence of the cession of East
Florida to the king of Spain; which commissioners
reported, that they had received 268 different
claims, whose gross amount was £. 602,765 : 1 : 7,
upon examining 179 of which number, they found
the sum of £. 127,552 : 14 : 3 ought to be
allowed.

On the 6th of June 1788, this important subject
came under the consideration of parliament. After
some discussion, resolutions were come to by the
committee of supply on that day, in consequence of
which a bill was brought in, which has to a certain degree, ascertained the extent of those claims.
By the act 28 Geo. III. cap. 40. certificates bearing
an interest of 3½ *per cent.* were ordered to be
issued to various classes of loyalists, to the amount
of £. 1,228,239, and the claims of the East Florida
proprietors were admitted, to the amount of
£. 113,952 : 14 : 3. Certain allowances were also
made to those loyalists, whose losses of income had
been proved to the satisfaction of the commissioners. But this is far from winding up the account:
for

for the commissioners appointed to examine into *Public Ex-*
this business, have already received £.38,093:16:11. *pences since the Revolu-*
The East Florida commissioners £. 3,700. The *tion.*
fees at the exchequer, on the receipt of £.150,000,
paid to the loyalists *anno* 1785, and which was
reimbursed by the public out of the supplies 1786,
amounted to £. 3,750 : 14. Lands purchased at
the Bahama Islands and St. Vincent's, for the behoof of the loyalists, together with the expence of
surveying and settling new establishments for them
in Nova Scotia, and other parts of North America,
will probably require in all at least £. 250,000 [f].
and the estimate originally given in of the half-
pay of the American forces, was at the rate of
£. 60,000 *per annum*.

The following account, will then give some idea,
of the magnitude of this branch of our American
expenditure.

STATE of the probable Amount of the EX-
    PENCE resulting from the Compensation and
    Relief given to American Loyalists, and the
    Proprietors of East Florida :

1. Sums paid prior to, or since the appointment
    of the commissioners of enquiry, exclusive of
    the sums distributed under their direction   - £. 720,873
2. Loyalists certificates, by 28 Geo. III cap. 40.   1,228,239

                         Carried over   £. 1,949,112

[f] £. 50,000 was voted *anno* 1787, for victualling the loyalists
in their new settlements in Nova Scotia. See Parliamentary
Register, vol. xxii. p. 134.

                                 3. East

Brought forward £.	1,949,112
3. East Florida loyalist's certificates, by ditto -	113,952
4. Unliquidated claims (calculated at) -	300,000
5. Annual incomes of the loyalists, if reduced to £. 35,000, at ten years purchase -	350,000
6. The half-pay of American forces, (£.60,000 *per annum*) at eight years purchase -	480,000
7. The expence of the commissioners before their enquiry is concluded, will probably amount to	50,000
8. The East Florida commissioners -	3,750
9. Lands purchased for the loyalists in the West Indies, and expence attending their new settlements in Nova Scotia - -	250,000
10. Fees at the exchequer - -	2,750
	£. 3,500,564

Thus the whole cannot be calculated at less than three millions and a half.

It must yield no small degree of satisfaction, to every citizen of this country, to be able to produce so unparalleled an instance of national liberality and spirit; and the business being now in some measure concluded, the most penurious can hardly wish it undone, notwithstanding the expensive consequences of which it has been productive. It is to be hoped, however, that some caution will be exercised for the future, in giving way to similar claims. It will not be difficult, if any other rebellion should arise in the foreign possessions of Great Britain, to practise a thousand frauds upon the public, if such a principle is to be adopted in future. The timid and the wealthy, under the pretence of loyalty, will

naturally

naturally fly from the fcene of war, and fhelter *Public Expences fince the Revolution.* themfelves in a country, by which their property will be reftored, if it proves fuccefsful, or who will recompenfe them for their loffes, if otherwife. The leaders of the rebellion will engage with more fpirit in the caufe, from the hopes of confifcation and plunder; and enriched with the fpoils of thofe who have fled, will undergo any extremity fooner than relinquifh them : and thus Great Britain may fubject itfelf to an enormous expence, for the purpofe of rewarding the attachment of thofe, who never could be of any material fervice to it, whilft the war is rendered at the fame time more difficult to make up, and more inveterate.

The particulars above ftated, however, are far *Warlike expences in America.* from including the whole of our American expences. But the naval, military, and ordnance charges of the colonies cannot be accurately made up, in confequence of their being involved in the accounts of other fervices ; and in particular from the indiftinctnefs with which the extraordinaries of the army are laid before parliament. But it would be well worthy the attention of any really patriotic minifter, to have all obfcurity on this fubject removed, and an accurate ftatement drawn up, for the fatisfaction of the public, of the fum which each of our foreign poffeffions has coft us for this century paft. In the mean while, the following general view of our American expences, is fubmitted to the reader.

STATE of the EXPENCES of our American Colonies, from the Acceſſion of the Houſe of Brunſwick, to Michaelmas 1788:

1. For ſettling and ſecuring, and for defraying the expences of the civil governments of the American colonies   -   -   - £. 1,294,582

2. For compenſation and rewards to the ſaid colonies for exertions in their own defence, or for aſſiſting in warlike operations calculated for their own immediate advantage   1,372,518

3. For bounties granted on the importation of American commodities   -   -   1,609,345

4. To the proprietors of Carolina, for purchaſing their title to that province   -   -   22,500

5. To the ſufferers by the fire at Charles Town, *anno* 1740   -   -   -   20,000

6. Expence of American ſurveys   -   34,296

7. From 1714 to 1775, the money voted by parliament for the forces employed in defence of the colonies, amounts to   -   8,779,925 [g]

8. Ditto from 1775 to 1788 (both incluſive) at the rate of 100,000l. *per annum*   -   1,400,000

9. Extraordinary Expences of forts, garriſons, ordnance ſtores, preſents to Indians, &c.   10,500,000 [h]

10. Expences of fleets and naval ſtations, eſtabliſhed for the defence of America   -   12,000,000

11. Compenſation and relief to American loyaliſts   -   -   -   3,500,000

Total   £. 40,533,166

[g] See the Rights of Great Britain aſſerted againſt the Claims of America, written by Sir John Dalrymple *anno* 1776, who was the firſt that attempted to open the eyes of this country to the magnitude of its expences in America.

[h] In the Parliamentary Regiſter *anno* 1776-7, vol. vi. p. 80. there are eſtimates of the yearly expence in North America, in ſo far as reſpects merely the extraordinaries of the army, according to the uſual eſtimates prior to the late war, the total of which amounts to £. 57,122 : 2 : 8½ *per annum*. But the detail takes up 68 pages in 8vo.

Thus,

Thus, the whole expences we have been put to, in confequence of our poffeffing colonies on the continent of North America, may be eftimated at *forty millions* in addition to the charges of at leaft two wars, which coft us above 240 millions more, and which were entered into principally on their account.

Public Ex- pences fince the Revolu- tion.

It is the more neceffary to bring forward inquiries into this branch of our expenditure, as the rage for colonization has not as yet been driven from the councils of this country. We have loft New England ; but a New Wales has fince ftarted up. How many millions it may coft, may be the fubject of the calculations of fucceeding financiers, a century hence, unlefs by the exertions of fome able ftatefman, that fource of future wafte and extravagance is prevented.

Our colonies in the Weft Indies, are poffeffions attended with this advantage, that in addition to a very lucrative commerce, they have alfo in general yielded a revenue, adequate to their civil eftablifh- ments. Indeed, the following are the only fums in our public accounts, which can be ftated againft any part of our infular dominions in that quarter of the globe :

Weft India expences.

For the Bahama Iflands - -	£. 21,340
Bermuda - - - -	3,832
Chief juftice of Dominica - -	600
	£. 25,772

For affifting the colony of Barbadoes in rendering the harbour there more fafe and commodious,
£. 10,000 was granted.; and in the year 1781,
£. 120,000 was voted to relieve the inhabitants of
that ifland, and of Jamaica, who had fuffered by a
violent hurricane : £. 10,000 was alfo granted,
anno 1765, to Barbadoes, for the affiftance given
by that colony, to the forces under General Monk-
ton, fent againft Martinique.

The African forts, and the civil eftablifhment at
Senegambia, during this reign, have coft £.480,990.

Since 1777, a new fource of expence has appeared, which it is difficult to know how to remedy. Prior to the late war, it was ufual to tranfport to America, thofe unfortunate individuals, who
were convicted of fuch fmaller felonies as are too
frequent in a country, where, from the freedom or
the government, no ftrict police can be eftablifhed,
and where the morals of the people are apt to be
corrupted, by the temptations of a luxurious capital. The independence of the colonies, having
put an end to that mode of punifhment, it became
neceffary to adopt fome other fcheme, for the purpofe of endeavouring to reform, the unhappy defcription of perfons above alluded to, or at leaft to
protect the public from their depredations. Various
plans, with fuch views, were propofed to government. The one actually adopted has been, to
place them on board of hulks in the Thames, where
they may be of fome ufe in raifing ballaft for
fhipping; and fince their numbers became too
great

great for any employment of that kind, an attempt Public Ex-
pences since
the Revolu-
tion. has been made, to found a new empire, by sending them to the diſtant regions of New Holland. Would it not be in every reſpect more adviſable, to employ them in carrying on public works, and other improvements, in the remote and uncultivated diſtricts of our own country[1] ?

It is beyond the limits of a work of this kind, however, to enter into the diſcuſſion of ſo extenſive a ſubject. It is proper at the ſame time to remark, that even in a financial view, it is entitled to very ſerious attention. From 1776 to 1789, £. 220,873 was expended in maintaining the convicts on the Thames, a very large ſum has already been laid out in eſtabliſhing the colony of New South Wales. At the moſt moderate calculation, the puniſhment of petty felons, if the ſame meaſures are purſued, will coſt above £. 100,000 *per annum.* It is ſurely deſirable to ſave ſuch an expenditure as much as poſſible, or to lay it out to the beſt advantage.

It may be proper to take notice of the expences Somerſet
Houſe. which have been incurred in the new buildings at

[1] It appears, from the 28th Report of the Committee of Finánce, that the expence of the ſettlements at Botany Bay, for 12 years, ending in 1797, amounted to no leſs a ſum than £. 1,037,230, beſides about £. 30,000 *per annum* for the Hulks. The effects of ſuch an expenditure, in the northern parts of Scotland, in making roads, harbours, &c. and other improvements, would have been infinitely more advantageous.

Somerſet-

Somerſet Houſe, were it only for the purpoſe of
warning the public, againſt giving way to plans,
which, however moderate they may at firſt appear, yet in general turn out very different from
the original eſtimate. When theſe buildings were
propoſed to parliament *anno* 1775, it was ſtated,
that the expence would not exceed £. 135,700,
whilſt the repairs neceſſary at the ſeveral offices
propoſed to be removed, the rents paid annually
for the ſame, the value of the property and
buildings thereof, and the price of the ground at
Somerſet Houſe which would remain unoccupied,
might be calculated at £. 99,550, conſequently the
public might enjoy the ſatisfaction of poſſeſſing a
magnificent edifice, and the advantage of having
a number of public offices concentered together,
for about £. 36,150 [k], in addition to other charges
that muſt have been incurred.

It is unneceſſary to detail, the various ſums,
which have been paid at different times, ſince the
year 1775, on account of theſe buildings. It is
ſufficient to remark, that on the 19th February
1788, they amounted to £. 306,134. But the
whole coſt, including the ſum of £. 100,000 paid
to the crown, for purchaſing and repairing the
Queen's palace [l], will probably reach half a million, before the plan is completed. The buildings
are certainly uſeful, and perhaps were neceſſary.
They have given employment to the poor, and

[k] Commons, Journals, vol. xxxv. p. 321.
[l] By 15 Geo. 3. cap. 52.

they

they contribute to ornament the capital of the *Public Ex-*
country, which is rather deficient in such decora- *pences since the Revolu-*
tions.   But the sum they are likely to require is to *tion.*
be regretted, not only on account of its exceeding
the original estimate in so large a proportion, but
also as being expended for the accommodation of
offices, where less magnificence might have suf-
ficed, at a period when we were involved in so
many other enormous expences, and at a time
when the palaces of the sovereign, are far from
being distinguished by the splendour of their appearance.

For some years past, it has not been unusual to *Expence of*
appoint parliamentary commissioners, for the pur- *various com-*
pose of making various important inquiries of a *missions.*
public nature.   The expence attending these com-
missions has already amounted to the following
sums:

1. To the commissioners of public accounts	£. 57,400
2. Commissioners of American loyalists -	38,093
3. Commissioners of East Florida loyalists -	3,700
4. Commissioners for the woods and forests, and the land revenues of the crown - -	7,200
5. Commissioners for inquiring into fees -	1,603
6. Commissioners for discharging the national debt	2,061

£. 124,457

Whoever will take the trouble of perusing the
accurate and able reports drawn up by the first of
these boards, will not probably regret that part of
the above expenditure.   And perhaps more bene-

fit

fit is to be derived, by appointing occafional commiffioners for fpecific purpofes, than by forming
regular eftablifhments, which are too apt to lofe
fight of the purpofes for which they were inftituted.

Without entering into any particular detail of
the various other expences, of a mifcellaneous nature, which have occurred during this reign, it
may be fufficient to give the following fhort and
general abftract of the particulars of which they
confifted:

An ACCOUNT of various INCIDENTAL
EXPENCES, incurred in the courfe of the
prefent Reign, from Michaelmas 1760 to Michaelmas 1788.

Parliamentary Expences.

1. To make good to his majefty various fums iffued
   purfuant to addreffes   -   -   £. 336,172
2. For compiling indexes to the journals of the houfe   15,900
3. The expence of different Eaft India committees   2,806
4. Charges incurred by the fmuggling committee   230

                                                    £. 355,108

Public Profecutions.

1. Expences incurred in the profecution againft Sir
   Thomas Rumbold   -   -   -   £. 3,587
2. Trial of Mr. Haftings   -   -   8,058

                                                    £. 11,645

Commercial Expences.

1. To the Levant Company, to affift them in carrying
   on their trade   -   -   -   £. 75,000
2. Surveys of the weft coaft of Great Britain and Ireland, and the expence of engraving the fame   2,145
3. For making difcoveries to the South Pole   -   5,000
4. To Dr. Irvine for his method of making fea-water
   frefh and wholefome   -   -   5,000

£. 87,145

Public Rewards.

1. To David Hartley Efquire, towards enabling him
   to afcertain the practicability and utility of his
   method to fecure buildings and fhips from fire   £. 2,500
2. To various perfons for difcovering dyes ufeful to
   our manufactures   -   -   -   9,500
3. To Charles Dingley for erecting a public wind
   faw mill for manufacturing timber   -   2,000
4. To John Blake Efquire, to affift him in carrying on
   his fcheme for tranfporting fifh to London by land-
   carriage   -   -   -   2,500

£. 16,500

Compenfations.

1. Various compenfations to different individuals for
   fhips detained for the public ufe and the like   £. 16,521
2. In fatisfaction of loffes incurred in preventing the
   infectious diftemper among the horned cattle from
   fpreading   -   -   -   £. 4,074
3. Compenfation for damages fuftained by powder
   mills   -   -   -   5,000
4. To Dr. Peter Swinton for damage to his eftate at
   Chefter in the rebellion *anno* 1745   -   700

5. To

5. To Meffrs. Hodgfon and Company, being the account of excife duties overpaid by them   -   4,363

6. Compenfation to perfons who had fuftained damage in the riots in London *anno* 1780   -   31,206

£. 61,864

Public Roads, Harbours, Buildings, &c.

1. Scotch roads   -   -   -   £. 111,422
2. Repairing roads in Durham, and building the bridge at Coldftream   -   -   4,000
3. For making a road on Penmaenmawr in Wales   2,000
4. To the foundling hofpital   -   -   368,679
5. London Bridge   -   -   -   37,000
6. Rebuilding Newgate   -   -   -   30,000
7. Paving the ftreets of Weftminfter   -   -   20,800
8. Weftminfter Bridge   -   -   6,000
9. Making a commodious paffage to the Houfe of Commons   -   -   -   -   12,000
10. Catwater harbour at Plymouth   -   3,000
11. The Britifh mufeum   -   -   39,750

£. 634,651

Various Expences.

1. The extra expences of the mint   -   £. 573,089
2. Debts due on the forfeited eftates in Scotland   110,553
3. Lands purchafed for extending the fortifications at Portfmouth and at Plymouth   -   30,358
4. General James Murray (late governor of Minorca), to indemnify him againft the verdict obtained by James Sutherland, and the expences attending the fame   -   -   -   -   5,489

£. 719,489

There

There was received by the public creditors, in *Public Expences since the Revolution.* the course of this reign, up to Michaelmas 1788, in payment either of the principal or of the interest of their respective debts, to the amount of *Public Debts.* about £. 189,354,581.

The total expences of this reign until Michaelmas 1788, may be thus stated:

The civil lift	£. 25,849,511
The navy	116,725,948
The army	96,565,762
The ordnance	17,079,011
Miscellaneous expences	4,466,508
	£. 260,686,740
In payment of the principal and interest of the public debts	189,354,581
Total	£. 450,041,321

The peace establishment on an average of four years, ending 1770, was as follows:

Average of Navy	£. 1,573,422
Army	1,513,412
Ordnance	227,907
Miscellaneous services	108,231
Total	£. 3,422,972

The peace establishment being thus ascertained, it is evident that any expence exceeding that sum, from the commencement of the American war *anno* 1775, to this time, may be stated to its account.

The

The following fupplies (including votes of credit for feven years) were granted fince that period :

Anno 1775				£. 3,584,955
1776				8,187,480
1777				9,649,792
1778				11,585,409
1779				12,365,645
1780				5,749,199
1781				19,189,187
1782				17,709,055
1783				13,694,102
1784				7,154,568
1785				4,773,377
1786				5,038,344
1787				4,448,495
1788				4,943,883

The navy debt, funded *anno* 1784 and 1785, amounted to   -   -   -   17,869,993

The unfunded debt *anno* 1788 may be ftated at - -	£. 10,750,000	
Anno 1774 was only about -	3,000,000	
Difference		7,750,000

£. 163,693,484

By the mode purfued of giving the public creditors a great additional capital when any debts were funded, the public has incurred an artificial debt of about   -   -   23,400,000

£. 187,093,484

The peace eftablifhment, at the rate of £. 3,422,972 *per annum* for the fpace of 14 years, would amount to   -   -   47,921,608

There remains the expence of the American war, being   -   -   £. 139,171,876

When

When this ſtatement is conſidered, it is difficult to conceive how the war could have proved ſo un- ſucceſsful.   One would imagine, that it was hardly poſſible to contrive the means of waſting ſuch enormous ſums of money, to ſo little purpoſe. The naval victories of Rodney, and the gallant defence of Gibraltar, are almoſt the only circum- ſtances, that can afford us any conſolation, for ſuch a fruitleſs waſte of the national wealth.   But it was in vain to expect ſucceſs abroad, while a factious ſpirit triumphed at home, preying on the ſtamina of the country, and conſuming its vitals and its ſtrength [m].

Public Ex- pences ſince the Revolu- tion.

It may now be proper, to give ſome general ſtatements of the total of our public expences ſince the revolution, to Michaelmas 1788.

1. EXPENCES of the CIVIL LIST during the Reign of

William III.	-	-	£. 8,878,230
Queen Anne	-	-	7,604,848
George I.	-	-	10,632,514
George II.	-	-	27,382,258
George III. to Michaelmas 1788	-		25,849,511
			£. 80,347,361

[m] Juſtly it is obſerved by Shakeſpear,
————" O ! England, England !
" Thou little body with a mighty heart;
" What might'ſt thou do,
" Were all thy children kind and natural !"

2. NAVAL EXPENCES during the Reign of

William III.	-	-	-	£. 19,822,141
Queen Anne	-	-	-	23,484,574
George I.	-	-	-	12,923,851
George II.	-	-	-	71,424,171
George III. to Michaelmas 1788		-		116.725,948

£.244,380,685

3. MILITARY EXPENCES during the Reign of

William III.	-			£. 22,017,706
Queen Anne	-	-	-	32,975,331
George I.	-	-	-	13,842,467
George II.	-	-	-	74,911,701
George III. to Michaelmas 1788		-		96,565,762

£.240,312,967

4. ORDNANCE EXPENCES during the Reign of

William III.	-	-	-	£.3,008,535
Queen Anne	-	-	-	2,100,676
George I.	-	-	-	1,064,449
George II.	-	-	-	6,706,674
George III. to Michaelmas 1788		-		17,079,011

£. 29,959,345

5. MISCELLANEOUS EXPENCES during the Reign of

William III. (incidental expences)	£. 41,825	
Dutch expences, recoinage, &c.	4,389,991	
		£.4,431,816
Queen Anne (incidental expences)	£. 200,000	
Transport service, building churches, &c.	-	-	1,823,575	
		2,023,575

Carried forward,   £.6,455,391

			Brought over	£. 6,454,391	*Public Ex-*
George I.	-	-	-	150,000	*pences since*
George II.	-	-	-	3,651,404	*the Revolu- tion.*
George III. to Michaelmas 1788		-		4,466,508	

£. 14,723,303

6. INTEREST of the PUBLIC DEBTS, LOANS repaid, &c. during the Reign of

William III.	-	-	-	£. 13,971,458
Queen Anne	-		-	52,184,527
George I.	-	-	-	41,218,879
George II.	-	-	-	93,574,134
George III. to Michaelmas 1788			-	189,354,581

£. 390,276,579

7. GENERAL VIEW of the PUBLIC EX- PENCES from the Revolution to Michaelmas 1788.

The civil list	-		-	£. 80,347,361
The navy	-	-	-	244,380,685
The army	-	-	-	240,312,967
The ordnance	-	-	-	29,959,345
Miscellaneous expences		-	-	14,723,303

609,723,661

Principal discharged, and interest of the public debts paid, since the Revolution   -   390,276,579

Grand total   £. 1,000,000,240

8. PROGRESS of the PEACE ESTABLISH- MENT since the Revolution.

During the reign of King William	-	£. 1,907,455
Queen Anne	-	1,965,605
		George

During the reign of George I.   -   £. 2,583,000

George II.   -   2,766,000

George III. (*anno* 1770, including the civil lift)   4,322,972

Eftimate of the peace eftablifhment in future   4,937,274

The latter fum confifts of the following particulars:

Civil lift - • -	£.	900,000
Navy - - - -		1,800,000
Army • - •		1,600,000
Ordnance - - -		348,000
Militia - - -		91,000
Mifcellaneous fervices - -		74,274
Increafed plantation expences, and Heffian fubfidy		124,000

£. 4,937,274

But this eftimate is greatly exceeded every year, particularly under the heads of naval, military, and mifcellaneous fervices.

9. EXPENCES of War fince the Revolution.

Expences of war during the reign of William III. - -	£. 30,447,382
Queen Anne - • -	43,360,003
George I. - • -	6,048,267
Expence of the war begun *anno* 1739 -	46,418,689
Ditto of the war begun *anno* 1755 -	111,271,996
Ditto of the American war - -	139,171,876
Ditto of the Dutch armament [a] - -	311,385

Total   £. 377,029,598

It

[a] The merit of the revolution in Holland, which re-eftablifhed the Stadt-holder, was pretty generally attributed, in this country, to the wifdom and fpirit

It seems scarcely necessary, to remind the reader, *Public Expences since the Revolution.* that minute exactness, in accounts of such magnitude, is not to be looked for. But the above statements, it is believed, are sufficiently accurate, to give him a general view of the nature of the public expenditure for this century past.

It is impossible for any one to consider for a moment the preceding accounts, without demanding *Conclusion.* in what respects the nation is bettered, and what objects it has attained, in consequence of such enormous expences. True it is, that we retain some provinces in North America, some colonies in the West Indies, some settlements on the coast of Africa, the fortress of Gibraltar, and extensive possessions in the East. But these acquisitions,

spirit of *our* cabinet; and particular credit is taken, on account of the small sum, which our exertions on that occasion are supposed to have cost. But the Prussian minister (the Count de Hertzberg) tells us a different tale. We are informed by him in his Memoire " sur le vrai caractere d'une bonne histoire, et sur la seconde année du regne de Frederic Guillaume II. Roi de Prusse; lu dans l'assemblé publique de l'Academie des Sciences de Berlin le 21 Août 1788." " C'est ainsi que *Le Roi* a eu la gloire et la satisfaction, " d'avoir operé une des plus grandes revolutions, dans un etat voisin, en " quatre semaines de tems, sans grande effusion de sang, par des resolutions " promptes et vigoreuses, executées par la conduite sage et valeureuse du " Duc de Bronswic, de ses generaux, et d'un petit corps de troupes Prus- " siennes." Thus attributing the whole merit (in which he certainly went too far) to the Prussian government. With regard to the expence, when the Hessian subsidy of £. 36,093: 15 for four years, together with the sum of £. 100,000 *per annum* of additional establishment for protecting our West India islands, are considered, it will not appear so very insignificant. The subsidy amounts in all to £. 144,375, and the addition to our establishment is equal to the interest of £. 2,500,000 at 4 *per cent.* To this, the increased half-pay of the naval and military officers promoted upon the occasion, must be added. It is farther to be considered, that the manning of the fleet was almost universally defective, which greatly curtailed the expence of that department.

however

however great or valuable, can never compenſate for the waſte of treaſure and of blood, which has taken place, in conſequence of that ſyſtem of political conduct, which, ſince the Revolution, has been purſued.

The ſyſtem to which I allude, had two objects in view. Firſt, to check the power of the Houſe of Bourbon, which ſeemed to threaten Europe in general with ſubjection. Next, to acquire, to eſtabliſh, or to preſerve, colonial ſettlements for the purpoſes of commerce. As that ſyſtem has not proved very beneficial, it may be worth conſideration, whether by altering it either in whole or in part, by abandoning all jealouſy of France, and commencing a friendly intercourſe and connection with that country; or by emancipating our American and Weſt Indian colonies, we might not prevent ſuch enormous expences for the future, and be enabled, honourably to diſcharge the incumbrances we have already incurred.

The ſituation of France has lately been repreſented to the world, in a manner that is ſufficient to impreſs the ſtrongeſt ſentiments of jealouſy in the minds of its neighbours. We are told by a miniſter of that country, who had every acceſs to authentic information, that it boaſts twenty-ſix millions of inhabitants; that it poſſeſſes above ninety millions ſterling of circulating ſpecie; and that the balance of commerce in its favour, is about three millions *per annum.* Allowing for ſome exaggeration, it cannot be doubted that
France

France is poffeffed of fuch population, induftry, and wealth, as to render it not a little dangerous; and if it were to aim at new conquefts and frefh acqui-fitions, it is to be hoped that a formidable confede-racy would arife againft it, fufficient to check its progrefs, and control its power. But if, on the other hand, the court of France is fatisfied with the territories which it enjoys, and is determined to perfevere in a pacific fyftem; if the human and beneficent principles of a Necker, have funk deep into the minds, and made a lafting impreffion on the fovereign of that country and his minifters.; if the court of Verfailles, inftead of being the fatal fource of intrigue and of war, is anxious to prove itfelf the fpring of peace, and of happinefs to mankind; and if, as the prelude to that fyftem, it is defirous of entering into a clofe and intimate connection with the crown and people of Great Britain, undoubtedly there are terms on which fuch an intercourfe may be fafely concluded °.

As the firft ftep to remove that rancorous jea-loufy which fubfifts between the two countries, it would be neceffary to conclude a treaty of com-merce and alliance on terms mutually advanta-geous ᴾ. Such a treaty, founded upon liberal prin-ciples, would contribute to augment the wealth and

---

° Two able political authors, Monfieur de Calonne, and the famous Mirabeau, have inculcated the advantages of fuch a connection between France and England, with great ability.

ᴾ The reader will pleafe to remark that this was written *anno* 1785.

increaſe the proſperity of both ; and would ſoon
abate, if not totally remove the enmity that ſub-
ſiſts between them.

It ſhould be an indiſpenſible article of ſuch an
agreement, that the two contracting parties ſhould
guarantee to each other the poſſeſſions they now
enjoy, in whatever part of the world they may be
ſituated, and ſhould aſſiſt each other in defending
ſuch poſſeſſions, if attacked : and perhaps it ought
to be underſtood, that in future Great Britain was
to be the preponderating power in the Eaſt, and
France in the Weſt Indies.   Indeed were our India iſlands, (Jamaica alone excepted), exchanged
for the French poſſeſſions in the Eaſt, both nations
might find it for their advantage.

Laſtly, in order to remove all cauſe for jealouſy,
it might be proper to enter into diſtinct ſtipulations,
in regard to the fleets and armies they are recipro-
cally to maintain.   A ſuperior force by land, is
neceſſary for a continental power like France ; but
that it ſhould keep up an inferior navy, is an article that cannot be diſpenſed with.   Britain is not ſafe
in the neighbourhood of ſo warlike and ſo powerful a nation, if it is not miſtreſs of the ſeas ; and
unleſs France will aſſent to the juſtice of this principle, an intimate connection with that country
muſt be avoided, as dangerous in the extreme [q].

> [q] If the port of Cherburgh is not annihilated, and the navy
> of France reſtricted to forty, or fifty ſail of the line, and a pro-
> portional number of frigates, the friendſhip of that country is
> not to be depended upon.

Such

Such are the terms which ought to be kept in *Public Expences since the Revolution.*
view, whenever an alliance between the two coun-
tries, of a permanent nature, is propofed.

Every one muft perceive, from the preceding *2. General colonial emancipation.*
obfervations, that to enter into a fafe and intimate
connection with France, is a matter attended with
many difficulties; that many obftacles muft be removed, and many prejudices got the better of:
and as the greater part of our paft expences, has
been owing to our colonial poffeffions in the Weft
Indies, and in North America, which never yielded
a revenue to compenfate for the charges which they
have occafioned; and as a war might always be
carried on by this country, without much difficulty
or expence, unlefs it became burdenfome by providing for their protection, it is proper to confider,
if the preceding fyftem is found impracticable, whether it would not be politic, to propofe to the different nations of Europe, and to the new ftates of
North America, *a general colonial emancipation* [r].

Such a meafure, it is evident, would prevent
the enormous expences, to which, in the courfe of
future wars, this country will otherwife be fubject,
for the prefervation of its colonies. Perhaps the
very next war may fee thofe colonies torn from us;
and in the very act of lofing them, we may add
millions to our debts. Nay, if they are preferved,

[r] The author fuggefted this plan, in a little tract printed
anno 1783, intitled La Crife de l'Europe. It was publifhed in
the French language, to make it more generally known on the
continent.

they

they will coſt us more in the courſe of a ſingle war, than all the advantages to be drawn from them will ever compenſate.

But a ſaving of expence, is not the only circumſtance to be conſidered. If the French, the Portugueſe, and Spaniſh ſettlements, were emancipated, as well as ours, from the monopoliſing ſpirit, and reſtrictive regulations, of the countries to which they belong, an unbounded tide of wealth and commerce would flow into this country : our preſent burdens would then ſeem light and eaſy, and we ſhould be enabled to diſcharge, with little difficulty, no inconſiderable part of them.

Were this country convinced of the advantages of ſuch a meaſure, it would not be difficult, with any tolerable management, to form a confederacy, ſufficiently ſtrong to bring about ſuch an emancipation, with little hazard or expence.

The weakeſt and moſt unſkilful politicians muſt perceive, that ſince the Britiſh colonies have been ſucceſsful in throwing off the yoke of their mother country, it is to the higheſt degree dangerous, to ſuffer one family, united by the cloſeſt ties, or more properly ſpeaking, the one branch dependent on and ſubſervient to the other, to hold ſo preponderating a weight and influence in the American hemiſphere.

Neither could France nor Spain, with any degree of reaſon, complain, ſhould ſuch a ſyſtem be enforced by the united efforts of Europe. How can they juſtly object to the confirmation of South American

American and Weft Indian independence? they, *Public Ex-*
who fo liberally contributed their affiftance, to *pences fince*
enable the Britifh colonies to eftablifh themfelves *the Revolu-*
as fovereign ftates. The fame natural rights and *tion.*
privileges, which they fupported in one part of
America, every other diftrict, and every other in-
habitant of that continent, and of the iflands in its
neighbourhood, are equally entitled to; and if it
was not a generous fpirit for protecting the oppreffed, but a mean and contemptible jealoufy, or
a defire of avenging ancient injuries, by which
they were actuated, and which made them refolve
to take advantage of the difficulties in which a
neighbour was involved, with whom they were at
peace, for whom the greateft friendfhip was pro-
feffed, whofe poffeffions in thofe parts they have
guaranteed, and whom they were bound indeed not
to oppofe, but to affift: how can they imagine,
that the other nations of Europe, are not intitled
to adopt the fame line of conduct towards them,
for whom they have reafon to entertain a ftill
higher degree of jealoufy; from whom every one
of them has received, either in former, or in recent times, ftill greater and more fenfible injuries,
and whofe fubjects pant for freedom, and an exemption from their yoke?

Every art will undoubtedly be made ufe of, by
the partizans of the houfe of Bourbon, to prevent
any ideas of this nature, from being attended to by
the different powers of Europe. France, in particular, has long boafted of the dexterity, with
which

which she enters into the counsels of her neighbours, and renders their conduct subservient to her views. On this occasion, when a plan is proposed, that would at once put an end to the most valuable branch of her commerce, and the principal source of her wealth, every artifice will be used, to ridicule it as visionary, to pronounce it impracticable to execute, and to load it with a thousand other objections, which despairing ambition will invent.

With regard to Spain, it is much to be wondered at, that the indigation and resentment of Europe has not long, ere now, burst forth against that imperious country. The feelings of mankind must be callous indeed, to have suffered the most fertile and valuable provinces in the world, to be so long subjected to her stern and detestable domination. With what indignation ought not every nation to be filled, by the arrogant claims of a single monarchy, pretending to engross such an extent of empire, and to prohibit every other nation in Europe from approaching its shores! Had it not been for its oppressions and misgovernment, what myriads of new inhabitants might not have been flourishing at this time in those distant regions; and how much would not the enjoyments of Europe have been increased by an intercourse with them! It is full time therefore, that its tyrannical system of oppression should be abolished, and that its colonies should at last taste some share of liberty and good fortune.

But it is surely unnecessary to dwell longer upon this subject, or to point out the advantages which
Europe

Europe in general would receive, were fuch an *Public Ex-* important alteration to take place, in the fituation *pences fince the Revolu-* and circumftances of the moft fertile and valuable *tion.* provinces which the world contains. My breaft glows at the idea, that a time may poffibly foon arrive, when the fhips of Denmark, of Sweden, and of Ruffia, of Holland, of Auftria, of France itfelf, and of Great Britain, fhall no longer be debarred from failing to the coafts of Chili and of Peru, or be precluded by any proud monopolift, from exchanging the commodities of Europe for the riches of America ; and when every ftate, in proportion to the fertility of its foil, and to the induftry of its inhabitants, may be certain of procuring all the neceffaries and the conveniencies of life. With fuch a new and extenfive field opened to the exertions of mankind, what difcoveries might not be expected, what talents might not break forth ; to what a height would not every art and fcience be carried ? The mind of a philanthropift, muft be overpowered with the magnitude and importance of the ideas which prefent themfelves to his view ; when he can figure for a moment, mankind united together by mutual intereft, and bound by the ties of an unfettered commercial intercourfe, to promote the general happinefs of the fpecies '.

 ' This was originally written *anno* 1790, and it was thought proper to preferve it in this edition of the work. The obfervations which have occurred to the author, in confequence of the changes which the French revolution has introduced, will be the fubject of future difcuffion.

TO

TO THE READER.

*T*HUS *far had the work proceeded on the* 1*ſt of July* 1801, *when I found it neceſſary to ſtop its progreſs, both becauſe the expences of the late war could not then be aſcertained, and as buſineſs of conſiderable importance, (the improvement of ſeveral extenſive traÉts of country) rendered it neceſſary for me to viſit Scotland. Indiſpoſition prevented me from engaging in ſo laborious an attempt in the courſe of* 1802 : *but I truſted that every obſtacle to the completion of it would be removed in the following year, and with that view came to London towards the end of January* 1803. *Complaints, however, with which I have long been troubled, again returned ; upon looking over the materials colleÉted as a baſis for the work, I found that ſeveral important documents were miſſing ; the obtaining information and accounts from the different public offices, was attended with difficulty, (more owing at the ſame time, to the hurry of the different departments, during the ſitting of Parliament, than any unwillingneſs to furniſh them,) and in ſhort there were many inducements to relinquiſh the undertaking altogether ; but after fully deliberating on the ſubjeÉt it appeared to me on the whole better, to ſend an imperfeÉt work to the preſs than none at all, being fully*

perſuaded

*perfuaded that every candid reader would excufe de-
fects which in the circumftances of the cafe could
hardly be avoided, and which want of health rendered it impoffible to fupply. I trufted, at all events,
that the fubjoined review of the financial adminiftration of the late minifter, however haftily written,
might be of fome ufe. It would prove at any rate the
anxiety of the author, to be the inftrument of as much
public good, and the means of preventing as much
public mifchief, as lay in his power.*

London, 1ft March 1803.

CHAP.

C H A P. III.

Review of the Financial Adminiſtration of the Right Honourable William Pitt [a], *containing an Account of the Progreſs of the national Income and Expenditure, from Michaelmas* 1788, *to Michaelmas* 1802, *of the Sums borrowed during the late War, and the extraordinary Meaſures of Finance carried on during that Period.*

THE financial hiſtory of this country, for the ſpace of fourteen years prior to Michaelmas 1802, whether we conſider the immenſe ſums levied by various taxes,—the greatneſs of the public expenditure,—the magnitude of the loans borrowed,—or the variety of new meaſures which were brought forward, certainly contains more intereſting and extraordinary particulars, connected with queſtions of revenue, than ever occurred in the annals of any other country, during ſo ſhort a period. To enter into any minute detail, on ſubjects of ſo extenſive a nature, regarding which ſo many volumes have been already publiſhed, would render it neceſſary far to exceed the boundaries to which a work of this nature muſt be limited. I truſt the reader, therefore, will be ſatisfied with a general view, or

---

[a] Mr. Pitt's adminiſtration began *anno* 1783, but the progreſs of the income and expenditure of the country, till Michaelmas 1788, has been already ſtated in the former part of this work.

ſummary

fummary of the whole, divided into four great heads
or branches, namely, 1. The national income or
revenue raifed. 2. The loans borrowed. 3. The
expenditure : And, 4. The extraordinary operations of finance which took place during that period. For more minute information, the debates
in Parliament, and the numerous pamphlets which
have been publifhed refpecting thefe memorable
tranfactions, muft be confulted.

It is certainly difficult to write regarding matters
which have happened fo recently, and in which the
author himfelf bore fome part. It is the more
difficult, as it is impoffible not to admire the fplendid talents and fuperior powers of eloquence, by
which that minifter was diftinguifhed, who prefided
over the councils of this country during that event-
ful era [b], whilft at the fame time it may be neceffary,

[b] Some are inclined to think, that in the preceding edition of
this work, the obfervations made on the adminiftration of Mr.
Pitt were too fevere. The following is the opinion of an impartial foreigner regarding this point.

L'Hiftoire des Finances de la Grande-Bretagne par Sir John
Sinclair, m'a préfenté la réunion de tous ces avantages : elle en
offre un plus rare encore chez cette nation. La plupart des
Anglois qui out écrit fur la politique, dirigés par l'efprit de
parti, ont mis l'exageration des faits, et le fophifme, a la place
de l'exactitude et du raifonnement, et ont fouvent propagé des
erreurs dangereufes, au lieu d'enfeigner des vérités utiles. John
Sinclair ne merite prefque jamais ce reproche ; il eft ennemi du
principal miniftre, et cependant il le critique rarement, et ne le
critique qu'avec fageffe.

Effai fur le credit commercial, et profpectus de la traduction
de l'Hiftoire des Finances de la Grande, Bretagne de Sir John
Sinclair, Par J. H. M. à Paris, an 1801, p. 110.

in

in various refpects, to queftion the fyftem, and line of conduct he purfued. Complete impartiality and fair ftatement, however much it may be wifhed for by an author, cannot always be commanded, let his anxiety to attain them be ever fo great. But the moft likely means of doing juftice to all parties, doubtlefs is, on queftions of peculiar importance, to ftate the principal arguments which have been urged on both fides, and to leave the reader him-felf to draw the refult.

Without dwelling at greater length on general topics, we fhall now proceed to confider the par-ticular articles propofed to be treated of in this chapter.

SECT. I.

The national Income.

THIS general head of inquiry may be confidered under two branches; namely, 1. The produce of the old revenue; and, 2. The amount of the new taxes impofed during the late war. In regard to the nature and effects of thofe taxes, that fubject will be difcuffed in a fubfequent part of the work, when the prefent ftate of the national income, and the different articles of which it confifts, are ex-plained.

I. Pro-

I. Produce of the old taxes.

From an examination of the ftate of the finances of this country during the American war, there was reafon to believe, that no material defalcation had taken place in the permanent taxes of the country, even during that war, though it was unfortunately diftinguifhed by many difafters. Nor is this to be wondered at; for the very expences of war itfelf muft, to a certain extent, increafe the revenue, by increafing the income of numbers of individuals, who are thereby enabled to confume a greater variety and quantity of articles liable to taxation. If the fupplies were raifed within the year, this would not be the cafe, for the revenue of one individual would be diminifhed in proportion to the increafe of the other; but where the expences of war are defrayed by borrowing money, and in fact creating new capitals, and new incomes, the cafe is otherwife. When ten millions for inftance are raifed for the public fervice, at a high intereft, not only a new capital is in a great meafure formed, arifing from the profit of contractors, the pay given for labour that otherwife would not have exifted, &c.; but even where old capital is lent, from the increafe of intereft, the income of the lender is augmented; and the ten millions circulated amongft failors, foldiers, farmers, merchants, manufacturers, &c. not only furnifh them, but even thofe with whom they happen to have any dealing or connexion, with additional means of paying taxes to
the

the Exchequer, the effect of which, is fooner or later felt, throughout all the fources of revenue.

In the courfe of the late war however, the old taxes increafed in produce, not only in confequence of an increafed expenditure, but alfo from an unexampled feries of commercial and of general profperity. In former wars, it never was expected, that the trade and manufactures of the country could equal their extent in peace; but during the late war, various circumftances contributed to render Great Britain the emporium of Europe, and almoft of the univerfe. At home, the great increafe of population, (which recent inquiries have put beyond doubt,) enabled the country to have in pay, a greater number of feamen and of foldiers, than at any former period of our hiftory, and at the fame time there was no want of hands to carry on, to a greater extent than ever, agriculture, manufactures, and commerce [c]. Great Britain alfo acquired abroad many valuable poffeffions belonging to the French, the Dutch, and the Spaniards; by the greatnefs of its maritime power held the complete dominion of the fea; and whilft it poffeffed thefe advantages, the continent of Europe was convulfed with war, unable to direct its attention to commercial induftry, and had no other market but England from which it could procure the productions of both the Indies. It is not to be wondered at

[c] In this refpect, the improvements of machinery were of great ufe, enabling us to carry on more extenfive manufactures with fewer hands.

therefore,

therefore, that with fuch circumftances in its favour, the wealth and income of the nation fhould
increafe, and confequently that the old taxes fhould
become more productive.

It is alfo proper to obferve, that the minifter
anxioufly brought forward feveral judicious regulations, which materially tended to increafe the
amount of the revenue. The confolidation of the
cuftoms, the checks on fmuggling (which the war
itfelf contributed to render more efficacious), and
transferring the duties on wine and tobacco from
the cuftoms to the excife, all tended to enrich the
Exchequer, notwithftanding the enormous burdens
of additional taxation.

The following is a progreffive ftate of the net
produce of the old taxes from Michaelmas 1788
to Michaelmas 1802, eftimating the land tax at
£. 1,972,000, and the annual malt tax at £. 586,000
per annum [d].

Produce in the year ending Michaelmas

1789	-	-	-	£. 15,565,642
1790	-	-	-	15,985,068
1791	-	-	-	16,631,000
1792	-	-	-	17,382,435
1793	-	-	-	17,674,955
1794	-	-	-	17,193,171
1795	-	-	-	16,737,366
1796	-	-	-	16,286,647
1797	-	-	-	15,745,804
1798	-	-	-	15,820,848

[d] For the progrefs of thefe taxes during the preceding part
of this reign, fee p. 32.

fee p. 32.

Produce

Produce in the year ending Michaelmas

1799	-	-	-	£. 16,833,487
1800	-	-	-	18,144,504
1801	-	-	-	16,752,539
1802	-	-	-	15,779,682

Thefe taxes occafionally fell off, in confequence of the fcarcities with which the country was fometimes afflicted; but on the whole it is evident, that the average produce during thefe fourteen years, confiderably exceeded the average of the fourteen years immediately preceding.

II. Produce of the new permanent taxes.

The immenfe expences incurred during the late war, neceffarily occafioned an unexampled addition to the old taxes, to defray both the intereft of the money borrowed, and gradually to repay the principal, according to the provifions of a general law to that effect; and this independent of thofe extraordinary fources of revenue, as the income tax, &c. intended for the purpofe of raifing a part of the fupplies within the year, the nature and amount of which will be the fubject of future difcuffion and inquiry.

The following is an account of the produce of the new permanent taxes created fince the year 1793.

Produce anno 1794	-	-	-	£. 247,638
1795	-	-	-	547,524
1796	-	-	-	2,007,229
1797	-	-	-	2,923,121

Produce

Produce *anno* 1798	-	-	£. 4,697,392
1799	-	-	6,774,458
1800	-	-	8,205,290
1801	-	-	8,079,076
1802	-	-	9,187,287

It is a curious and interesting subject of inquiry to ascertain, how a nation, previously so heavily burdened, was capable of bearing such an additional load as the one above enumerated, of permanent taxes, besides the income tax.

1. It was certainly in a great measure owing to a circumstance already hinted at, namely, that the wealth of the country was rapidly increasing notwithstanding the pressure of a bloody and expensive war. Of this important event there cannot be a stronger evidence, than the variety and number of internal improvements, which were carried on during that period: and fortunately also, the progress of the revenue, even since the return of peace, is a sufficient proof that the wealth acquired was not of a fleeting or transitory nature.

2. The general alarm felt at the horrors resulting from the French Revolution, and the terror lest similar scenes might take place in this country, induced the people at large, and more especially those in the higher classes of society, to submit, without hesitation or reluctance, to any burden that might be imposed upon them. Whether that alarm was or was not carried to a height beyond what the circumstances of the case justified, and whether it was prudent for a free nation, to surrender its whole wealth to the discretion of one indi-

vidual

vidual or fet of men, are queftions which impartial pofterity will be better able to determine than can be done in thefe times; but however that difcuffion may terminate, the alarm that was propagated, certainly enabled the minifter to impofe a quantum of taxation, far beyond the contemplation of any of his predeceffors.

Laftly, the fkill of the late Chancellor of the Exchequer in impofing taxes [e], and carrying on the moft intricate operations of finance, cannot be queftioned. The authority alfo which he had acquired in the Houfe, the ability with which he propofed meafures in parliament, and the eloquence and dexterity in debate with which he defended them, enabled him to overcome financial difficulties from which moft other men would have fhrunk.

---

[e] The great object which the minifter muft have in view, when he propofes new taxes, is to raife a fum fufficient to defray the intereft, and gradually to redeem the capital of the loan of the year; but not to burden the nation to a greater extent than is really neceffary. This requires confiderable knowledge of finance, great information regarding the political circumftances of the country, and found political judgment. When it is known that taxes are to be impofed, the Chancellor of the Exchequer for the time being, is generally overwhelmed with fuch a multitude of projects of taxation, that it is often difficult to difcriminate the good from the bad, or rather the lefs exceptionable from thofe which are more fo, for there is hardly any tax that is not productive of fome difadvantages. The produce of taxes, of a nature entirely new, are the moft difficult to eftimate. Where they have been already tried, and are not too heavy, the amount of any additional duty, may be pretty nearly calculated. There is every reafon to believe, confidering

SECT. II.

Loans during the late War.

THERE is no political phenomenon that has ₁. Britifh loans. puzzled more either the theoretical politician, or the practical ftatefman to account for, than how Great Britain has been enabled to raife the enormous fums which it has obtained at different periods, more efpecially during the late war. I fhall endeavour therefore, previoufly to any ftatement of the money recently borrowed, briefly to explain, firft, the general foundations of the public credit enjoyed by this country, and fecondly, the actual fources whence the money it got was fupplied.

Such loans could not have been borrowed, unlefs there had been a great mafs of folid wealth in the country itfelf; for the money remitted from abroad, at any one period, was never very confiderable, though the total fum due to foreign creditors, may have gradually accumulated to a large amount.

Not only a great mafs of folid property is effential, but it is alfo neceffary to have a confiderable quantity of circulating wealth, which can eafily be tranfmitted from any part of the kingdom into the

considering the greatnefs of the fums borrowed during the late war, and the taxes neceffary in confequence thereof, that the produce of the different funds, were greater in point of amount, and came nearer to their original eftimate, than could poffibly have been expected.

Exchequer,

Exchequer, and thence fent wherever the public exigencies may require it : and it is of little confequence, whether the circulating medium confifts of paper or of fpecie, provided the paper is not difcredited, and that there is a fufficient quantity of coin or of bills of exchange, to anfwer for foreign expences.

It is alfo neceffary, that this circulating wealth, fhould be eafily acceffible, or in a great meafure be concentrated in a large metropolis. Indeed as the ftrength of a country depends fo much on its financial refources, which are moft available when a great mafs of circulating wealth is accumulated in the coffers of opulent individuals, conftituting what is called a moneyed intereft, and refiding contiguous to each other, it is evident that the power of a nation refts in a confiderable degree on the fize of its capital ; hence, as in ancient hiftory, the conteft properly was, between the cities of Rome and of Carthage, and not the countries they governed. So in modern times, the rivalfhip is not in fact between France and England, but between London and Paris, which places this country, in addition to its infular fituation, more on an equality with France, (notwithftanding the difparity in regard to population and extent of territory), than is commonly imagined.

The power of borrowing money, muft likewife depend on the belief, that there are refources fufficient to defray with punctuality and good faith, the intereft of the fums borrowed, and its credit muft

be

be ftill higher, if it can furnifh refources gradually to extinguifh the capital, fo as to prevent an inordinate accumulation of public debt.

In the laft place, it is alfo neceffary, that the form of its government fhould be calculated to preferve the rights and privileges, and to protect the property of its fubjects, and that the adminiftration at the time, fhould be entitled to the confidence of the public, either from their abilities, the refpectability of their private character, or their fuccefs.

We fhall next proceed to explain the actual funds or fources whence the money borrowed by the public may be fupplied.

1. Loans may fometimes be furnifhed, from money that has lain dormant or inactive, for want of proper means of employing it, and is called forth, by the high intereft, and other advantages arifing from lending money to the public, more efpecially, according to the modern fyftem of borrowing, by the fale of a certain quantity of 3 *per cent.* ftock, at a low price, which it is probable will afterwards rife confiderably in its value, on the reftoration of peace.

2. The fecond fource is, the transfer of capital from other objects, to that of public loans; for inftance, perfons of opulence may have it in view to build for themfelves new houfes, to purchafe pictures, furniture, and other expenfive articles, or to enter into various fpeculations in agriculture, manufactures, commerce, mining, &c. which plans may be given up, from the greater expence which

war

war muft neceffarily occafion in carrying on fuch undertakings, and from the profpect of employing their money to much advantage in public loans.

3. In every induftrious ftate, there is an annual accumulation of capital, from the induftry of the nation alone, which may neither lay dormant as in the firft cafe, nor be employed in domeftic improvements as in the fecond, but may be invefted in foreign fpeculations, or devoted to the purchafe of various articles of foreign produce. This fund alfo, in time of war, is naturally applied to domeftic public purpofes, and in particular to public loans.

4. In confequence of the many valuable colonies belonging to Great Britain, more efpecially in the Eaft and Weft Indies, confiderable fums are remitted to the mother country, which are generally invefted in the public funds, until the proprietors return home, and determine on fome other means of employing their wealth, for inftance, invefting it in land or otherwife. This fource was certainly extremely confiderable during the late war, more efpecially in confequence of the high prices which the Weft India productions fetched in the markets of Europe.

5. The accumulation of capital, from the expences of war itfelf, more efpecially when they are principally laid out at home, is unqueftionably one of the principal fources of future loans; and indeed the greater the loan is in one year, and the more the nation is impofed upon in its bargains, the greater is that refource during the enfuing year.

For

For example, if thirty millions are raifed by the public, of which twenty millions are paid to con-tractors for purchafing naval ftores, fupplying the army with ammunition or with bread, forage, &c. if thefe contractors contrive to make a profit of five millions, they are enabled to lend the whole of that fum to the public, deducting merely what is neceffary for their own fubfiftence. This fund is alfo increafed by the wealth of thofe, whofe in-come thefe contractors may have been the means of augmenting beyond their expenditure, and con-fequently who have additional capital to place in the funds [f].

6. Another great fource of public loans arifes from the favings of the intereft paid to the public creditors. It is generally underftood, that a large proportion of the public debt is due to individuals, who do not expend the intereft they receive, either living parfimonioufly, or having other funds arifing from commerce, &c. by which they are maintain-ed. Any furplus they can fpare, it is natural for them to reinveft in the public funds, more efpeci-ally in time of war, when the profit is fo confider-able. There is reafon to believe, that out of eighteen millions now annually paid to the public creditors on the debt funded and unfunded, a fum little fhort of one fifth part, is annually reinvefted in the funds, which increafes rapidly their value in time of peace, and is one of the moft important

[f] Another refource connected with war, is prize-money, whether acquired by the army, the navy, or private fhips of war.

refources

refources for obtaining money in time of war, which the public poffeffes.

7. Another refource arifes from money tranfmitted by foreigners to this country, and employed in our public loans. The amount however, at no period was fo confiderable as many have imagined, though foreigners were naturally defirous of having fome property in our funds, on account of the regularity with which the intereft was paid, the facility with which it could formerly be converted into fpecie, and the high credit which the Britifh government had fo long invariably maintained.

8. The laft refource is, from the furplus of the public revenue, or the intereft of any fund appropriated for the extinction of the national debt. The plan of borrowing, in time of war, from the commiffioners appointed to pay off the national debt, the money annually entrufted to them for that purpofe, was a part of the original fyftem when a finking fund was recently eftablifhed. But that regulation has fince been altered from the idea, that daily or weekly purchafes made by the public, tended to keep up the price of the ftocks, or at leaft had the effect of preventing any great depreciation. This is a queftion which nothing but experience can determine. It feems at firft fight an abfurd idea, to borrow with one hand, and to pay with the other. It is natural to fuppofe that the fmaller the loan, the better would the terms be, on which it could be procured. At any rate, though a certain fum might be of fervice in pre-

venting

venting too great a depreſſion of the ſtocks, ſay
a million per annum, or about £. 20,000 weekly,
yet beyond that amount it would be adviſeable to
direct the commiſſioners appointed for the redemption of the national debt when loans are neceſſary, to lend the whole of the fund entruſted to
them to the public, ſo as to diminiſh, to that extent, the loan of the year.

Such are the ſources whence public loans are in
general ſupplied, from the conſideration of which,
it will not be wondered at, that ſuch large ſums
could be procured by this country, more eſpecially
during the late war; and the following obſervations will explain, how the intereſt could alſo be
raiſed with equal facility.

For in the firſt place, the whole income of a
great and opulent nation may, to a certain extent,
be pledged for that purpoſe; and if done ſtep by
ſtep, which is always the caſe, where the intereſt,
and not the principal is demanded, the hardſhip
gradually increaſing, is leſs felt, and the ancient
poſſeſſors of the landed property of the kingdom,
are ruined, before they are aware of it.

In the ſecond place, the loan itſelf furniſhes a
new ſource of revenue. If the intereſt of the loan
requires a fund for inſtance of £. 1,600,000 per
annum, one fourth of that ſum, or £. 400,000 a
year, is paid either directly or indirectly into the
Exchequer, in conſequence of the various taxes on
conſumption, &c. to which public creditors reſid-
ing at home, are liable. The nation is in this caſe
like

like a private proprietor, who borrows £. 40,000
from his tenants, for which he agrees to pay them
£. 2000 a year, but who contrives at the fame
time to add £. 500 *per annum* to his rent-roll, to
be paid by the felf fame individuals.

It is certainly impoffible to fay, to what height
this fyftem may be carried, but there is every reafon to believe, that it might be continued for many
years, without any material public detriment.

In addition, however, to the fums borrowed for
the fervice of England, two new forts of loans for
the firft time appeared in our public accounts,
namely, loans for the ufe of his Imperial majefty
and for the fervice of Ireland. There was alfo a
confiderable difference between the unfunded debt
of 1793, and of 1803, which is a fum alfo to be
added to the loans of the late war.

2. Auftrian loans.   It had not been an unufual practice in former
wars, for the Britifh government to fubfidize fo-
reign powers, and when done with prudence, it is
the cheapeft way by which an opulent, can affift a
poorer country. For inftance, during the feven
years war, a fubfidy was granted to the king of
Pruffia of £. 600,000 *per annum*. If inftead of
money, we had fent men equivalent to that amount,
the aid would have been of little confequence, becaufe the expence of tranfportation, of feeding
them at fuch a diftance, of recruiting their number
from time to time, &c. would have been very
great, and perhaps our troops would not have cor-
dially agreed with the Pruffians, and could not have

been

been eafily marched to thofe places where their
fervices might be the moft ufeful. Whereas by
fending money to the Pruffian monarch, it might
be employed in the manner the moft likely, to be
ufeful to the common caufe, whether it was judged
beft to appropriate it to the paying of his troops,
purchafing arms, collecting provifions, fortifying
towns, obtaining intelligence regarding the motions of the enemy, &c. as the exigences of the
cafe might require. During the late war however,
the wants of the Emperor were fo great and urgent,
that no common fubfidy could anfwer his purpofe[g];
and according to fome, a fubfidy was not reckoned
perfectly confiftent with the imperial dignity. It
was therefore thought more expedient, that the
Chancellor of the Exchequer of Great Britain,
fhould raife money for the Emperor of Germany, in London, at the fame time with the Britifh
loans. It was natural to fuppofe, that there would
be lefs parliamentary difficulty in fending a large
fum of money to Vienna, under the name of a loan,
than that of a fubfidy. The ftrongeft affurances
were given that the money would be faithfully repaid[h]; but hitherto any engagement to that effect,
                                        whatever

[g] It is faid that the Emperor applied for a loan, a year before
it was granted, and that the difafters in Flanders would have
been prevented, had his requeft been earlier complied with.

[h] So ftrongly was the idea of repayment either believed, or
politically inculcated by the friends of the late adminiftration,
that in Mr. Rofe's pamphlet, p. 18. we find the following obfervation. " Nothing but a direct and flagrant breach of na-
                                        " tional

whatever may be the cafe in future, has not been complied with.

The following is the amount of Loans borrowed in Great Britain, for the fervice of his Imperial majefty, during the late war.

Year.	Sum raifed.			Capital created.			Interest.		
	£.	s.	d	£.	s.	d.	£.	s.	d.
1795	4,600,000	0	0	3,833,333	6	8	115,000	0	0
1796	1,620,000	0	0	3,669,300	0	0	110,079	0	0
	6,220,000	0	0	7,502,633	6	8	225,079	0	0
Annuity for twenty-five years on the firft loan							230,000	0	0
Management on ftock and annuity	-						5,963	13	8
Fund of 1 *per cent.* on the laft loan	-						36,693	0	0
Total annual charge	-						£. 497,735	13	8

It was alfo propofed to grant another loan to the Emperor *anno* 1797, but that plan was given up, when his Imperial majefty was reduced to the dreadful neceffity of fubmitting to the terms dictated to him by France.

3. Irifh loans.

It was during this war alfo, that a new practice was introduced, that of borrowing money in England, for the fervice of the Irifh government, of funding it in England, where the intereft was made

---

" tional faith, and the moft pofitive denial of juftice, in the
" ordinary diftribution of it at Vienna, can fix upon this coun-
" try ultimately, the charge incurred by the two imperial
" loans : the poffibility of fuch an event cannot be admitted
" till the fact be eftablifhed."

payable,

able, but under the exprefs ftipulation that the money fhould be remitted from Ireland for that purpofe. The loans neceffary for the fervice of Ireland had formerly been raifed at Dublin; but it was probably found, that in confequence of the heavy expences incurred during the late rebellion, that fyftem was no longer practicable to the extent that was neceffary, and the wealth of England furnifhed the only refource whence any additional fum could be obtained.

This plan evidently tends to make a confufion and intricacy in the public accounts of the two countries. It would be extremely defirable therefore, that both the capital of the debt, as well as the payment of the intereft, could be transferred to Ireland.

The amount of loans borrowed in Great Britain, for the fervice of Ireland, was as follows.

Year.	Sum raifed.	Capital created.	Intereſt, &c.
	£.	£.	£.
1797	1,500,000	2,925,000	126,775
1798	2,000,000	4,000,000	167,340
1799	3,000,000	5,250,000	212,314
1800	2,000,000	3,140,000	127,001
1801	2,500,000	4,393,750	188,000
1802	2,000,000	2,639,250[1]	106,125
	13,000,000	22,348,000	927,555

[1] In this loan, £. 139,250 confifts of what is called *deferred stock*, the intereft of which does not commence till the 5th of January 1808.

The

4. Unfund-
ed debt.

The nature of this debt, does not require to be explained to any perfon at all acquainted with the finances of this country. It confifts of fums borrowed on Exchequer bills, and other public fecurities, for paying the intereft of which, no particular tax has been impofed, *or fund provided*, hence it is known under the name of unfunded debt.

The amount of that debt, on the 5th January 1793, was £. 8,925,422. At Michaelmas 1802 it was at leaft nineteen millions and a half, making an addition, during the war, of £. 10,500,000, the annual intereft of which, ftating it only at three *per cent.*, cannot be eftimated at lefs than £.315,000 *per annum.*

We fhall now proceed to give a general view of the loans during the late war, deducting the Auftrian and Irifh loans, and adding the furplus of the unfunded debt, fo that the reader may be enabled to form an accurate idea of the whole debt incurred. It is proper at the fame time to obferve, that a part of that debt has been already paid, by the operation of the various finking funds appropriated for that purpofe ; and if the taxes impofed are found to produce the fums at which they were originally eftimated, the burdens of the late war, however grievous, will gradually melt away.

LOANS

LOANS during the late War.

Year when borrowed.	Sum borrowed, including the Amount of Navy and Exchequer Bills funded, also the Irish and Austrian Loans.	Stock created.	Annual Interest, Management, and 1 per cent. of Sinking Fund.	Rate of Interest on the Money borrowed.
	£.	£.	£.	£. s. d.
1793	4,500,000	6,250,000	252,812	4 3 4
1794	12,907,452	15,676,525	773,324	4 10 9
1795	19,490,646	25,609,897	1,227,415	4 15 8
1796	31,726,796	41,303,699	1,850,373	4 13 5½
1797	54,112,824	70,012,667	3,368,219	6 0 5½
1798	17,000,000	34,000,000	1,260,441	6 4 9
1799	18,500,000	32,699,250	1,132,207	5 8 8½
1800	20,500,000	32,185,000	1,089,933	4 14 2
1801	28,000,000	49,210,000	1,994,544	5 5 5
1802	25,000,000	44,328,637	1,552,927	3 18 3
	231,737,718	351,275,675	14,502,195	
Deduct the Austrian loans	6,222,000	7,502,633	497,735	
	225,515,718	343,773,042	14,004,460	
Deduct Irish loans	13,000 000	22,348,000	927,555	
	212,515,718	321,425,042	13,076,905	
Add surplus of unfunded debt	10,500,000	10,500,000	315,000	
Total during the war, after all deductions	223,015,718	331,925,042	13,391,905	

Note.

Mr. Morgan adds to the above capital the value of the long annuities, which, strictly speaking, may be right, but as there is evidently a great artificial capital in the amount of the stock created, it does not seem necessary to swell it more by such a conversion.

The

The fpecific terms on which thefe loans were raifed, were extremely various, the particulars of which cannot be detailed in a work of this nature. They are contained in the different acts which were paffed regarding them, and an hiftorical abftract of the particulars thereof, will be found in a fhort, but ufeful treatife, dedicated to that fpecial purpofe [k].

SECT. III.

Expenditure.

EVER fince the reign of king William (whofe income and expenditure was afcertained with uncommon minutenefs, and during whofe government particular attention was paid to matters of finance [l]), the public accounts of this country have had little pretenfion to accuracy or precifion. The receipts have been confufed by votes perpetually deficient, (as in the cafe of the annual taxes on land and malt), and the expences, by fums firft appropriated for one purpofe, and afterwards transferred to another, and various fums ftated as belonging to one fervice, which ought properly to

[k] See the terms of all the loans, by J. J. Gnellier, 2d edition, octavo, printed *anno* 1802.

[l] It will appear from a view of the income and expenditure of king William (which will be printed by way of appendix to this work), that the whole was accounted for to a fingle farthing.

have

have been placed to the account of a very different department. Much confusion also has of late years arisen, from votes of credit, anticipations of the revenue, funding bills of various descriptions, the intermixture of Austrian and Irish loans, discharging the civil lift debts, the payment of various sums in consequence of addresses from Parliament, and other sources of perplexity. In short, from these circumstances, joined to the magnitude of the sums received and expended, it was at last found necessary on the 10th of March 1797, to appoint a select committee, " with full power to form and di- " gest a plan for controlling the public expendi- " ture, and to report upon the best and most " practicable means of obtaining a diminution " thereof[m]." The mode of stating the public accounts has, by the measures recommended by that committee, been greatly improved. In regard to our expences for some years preceding that period, it would require the unceasing labour of an intelligent committee for several weeks, with full power over all the departments of the Exchequer, to draw up such an account as ought to be given of them. The reader therefore cannot expect any very accurate detail, but we shall endeavour briefly to state (with as much precision as the nature of the case, and the information that could be procured will admit of), the expences 1. of the civil lift; 2. of

[m] See Mr. Pitt's speech, 10th March 1797. Parliamentary Debates, vol. 2. p. 2.

the

the navy ; 3. of the army ; 4. of the ordnance ; 5. the miscellaneous expences; and lastly, the charges of the late war, including the sums expended in consequence thereof, both in Ireland and the East-Indies.

1. The civil list, and expenditure of the royal family.

The information regarding the income and expenditure of the royal family, during the above period, may be ascertained with more accuracy than any other branch of the present inquiry, a committee having been appointed to ascertain that particular point, whose report contains a variety of useful information upon the subject [n]. As this important document fills seventy-three pages folio, and contains a number of minute accounts and calculations, it cannot be particularly dwelt on. For our present purpose it is only necessary to state, 1. the sums which were actually expended in the civil list department for sixteen years, ending 5th January 1802 ; 2. the amount of the debt arising in consequence thereof; and, 3. it may be proper to give a general view of the personal income of the royal family.

---

[n] The editor of Debrett's Parliamentary Register (vol. 17. p. 546, and 547.) contends, that there is a material error in one part of this report, to the amount of about £. 200,000.

The

The following is an account of the charges of the Civil Lift, for fixteen years prior to 5th January 1802.

Glafs.	Annual Average of Expence.			Total in fixteen years.		
	£.	s.	d.	£.	s.	d.
1. Royal family	209,988	15	0	3,359,828	7	10¼
2. Great officers of ftate	33,279	10	0	532,472	0	1
3. Foreign minifters	80,526	0	2½	1,288,416	3	4½
4. Tradefmen's bills	174,697	13	11	2,795,163	2	3¾
5. Menial fervants of the houfehold	92,424	6	7½	1,478,789	5	8
6. Penfions	114,817	6	11	1,837,077	10	6
7. Salaries to various officers	76,013	18	2¼	1,216,222	17	0¾
8. Commiffioners of the Treafury	14,455	14	7½	231,191	13,	10¾
9. Occafional payments	203,964	6	0¼	3,263,428	16	4
Total -	1,000,167	9	6	16,002,679	17	0

Such were the real charges; we fhall next proceed to ftate the amount of the debt arifing in confequence thereof.

The total annual grant to defray the expences of his majefty's civil government, it is well known, is £. 900,000 *per annum*. The excefs confequently was at the rate of £. 100,167 : 9 : 6, which, in fixteen years, amounts to £. 1,602,679 : 15 : 0½. But the manner in which the fum actually voted by Parliament was made up, will appear from the following ftatement:

1. Excefs beyond the grants in fixteen years - - - £. 1,602,679 15 0½
2. Arrears of former civil lift debt - 192,500 0 0

Carry over - £. 1,795,179 15 0½

Brought over -	£. 1,795,179	15	0¼
5. Deduct various fums applied in aid of			
the civil lift - -	634,036	0	0
4. Deficiency on 5th January 1802	1,161,143	15	0¼
5. Deduct various balances remaining in			
the Exchequer, and fums payable by			
various perfons (fee Report, p. 58.)	265,174	8	10¼
	895,969	6	2
6. Add various fums advanced out of the			
civil lift, according to the particulars			
ftated in the Report, p. 50. -	94,084	0	0
	£. 990,053	6	2

Which was the fum actually voted by Parliament, (deducting fractions) though the manner in which it was afcertained, has not hitherto been explicitly ftated in any public document.

From an examination of the papers referred to them, it appeared to the committee, that the plan originally formed in 1786, for the expences of the civil lift, was calculated with an expectation of the duration of peace, and that the continuance of the war alone, through fo large a proportion of the time in queftion, fufficiently accounted for the greater part of the excefs. On the whole, though the debt actually incurred may be juftified, and confequently it was advifable to pay it, yet perfons accuftomed to fuch inveftigations, will naturally queftion the propriety of fuffering fo large a debt to accumulate, for fuch a number of years, without any communication to Parliament.

The income of the civil lift, by the experience
of

of fo many years, having proved inadequate, a committee was appointed, on the 16th of March 1803, to confider of the charges on that branch of the revenue, and to report the fame, together with their opinion thereupon to the Houfe; and as it has been found that a material deficiency has arifen for feveral years paft, the inquiry will probably terminate, in transferring fuch a number of articles from the civil lift, to the confolidated fund, as will enable a minifter, with any fhare of prudence and economy, in future to make the income and expenditure to quadrate.

On the fubject of the civil lift, it may be proper to add, that it would be extremely defirable to get rid of a number of trifling payments with which the accounts of that branch of our expenditure is at prefent encumbered [o]; and perhaps it might be expedient, even to diminifh the amount of the civil lift, and to pay the judges, the foreign minifters, &c. from other funds. Ignorant people fuppofe, becaufe £. 900,000 *per annum* is granted to the Crown, that all that fum is expended by the royal family, whereas the perfonal expences and allowances made to them, are extremely moderate, and cannot be objected to by any one who is at all aware of the advantages which neceffarily refult from the monarchical part of the conftitution [p].

The

[o] This might be done, by advancing a certain fum to the bank, on its undertaking to pay thofe allowances.

[p] A perfon attached to Jacobinical principles, difcuffing the fubject of government with one of very oppofite fentiments,

said

The following is a fhort ftatement of the allowances actually paid to all the branches of the royal family, not only from the civil lift, but from the confolidated fund whence the general expences of government are defrayed.

The PENSIONS and ALLOWANCES to the Royal Family.

From the Civil Lift.

			Annual Sum.
His Majefty's privy purfe	-	-	£. 60,000
The Queen	-	-	58,000
The Prince of Wales	-	-	60,000
Princefs Charlotte of Wales	-	6,000
Dutchefs Dowager of Cumberland	-	-	4,000

£. 188,000

From the Confolidated Fund.

Prince of Wales	-	-	£.65,000
Duke of Gloucefter	-	-	17,000

Carry over 82,000   £.188,000

---

faid to him, in ridicule of a monarchical government, " Why " the king will eat us up; he devours a million *per annum !*" " I deny that," faid the other, " for the whole royal family " do not coft the nation one third of the money. But if it " were a million *per annum,* and more, it is well beftowed, *for* " *the king prevents his fubjects from devouring one another.*" In fact, how can a country enjoy profperity to any great extent, without that fecurity and quiet, which generally accompanies hereditary monarchy ; and if in addition to the advantages arifing therefrom, rational liberty, and freedom from oppreffive taxation, can be obtained, the general happinefs of a nation muft be complete.

Brought

	Brought over £ 82,000	£.188,000
Duke of York - -	14,000	
Dutchefs of York - -	4,000	
Dukes of Clarence, Kent, Cumberland, Cambridge, and Suffex, £.12,000 each }	60,000	
		143,000
		£.331,000

The total expence of the civil lift, for fourteen years, ending 5th January 1802, at the average rate of £. 1,000,167, the eftimate of the committee, may be ftated at £. 14,002,338, in addition to any fums or annual grants paid out of the confolidated fund to the branches of the royal family.

2. Naval expences.

The glory acquired by the Britifh navy, during the late war, cannot be paralleled either in ancient or modern hiftory. The expences of that department at the fame time, have been fo confiderable, that Parliament has thought it advifable to appoint a fpecial commiffion for tne purpofe of inveftigating their nature and amount[p]. Until the report of that commiffion is communicated to the public, it is impoffible to form any juft idea of the extent of this branch of our expenditure, or whether the

p The author ftrongly recommended fuch a commiffion, in his Thoughts on the Naval Strength of the Britifh Empire, Part II. p. 108. Edit. 1795.

grants

grants of Parliament have in all inftances been fairly and judicioufly applied.   In the interim it may
be fufficient to lay before the reader, an account of
the fums annually voted for naval fervices for the
period to which this chapter relates.

STATE of the Naval Grants for fourteen years,
ending in 1802.

Year.		Sum.	Year.		Sum.
1789	-	£. 2,328,570	1797	-	13,033,673
1790	-	2,433,636	1798	-	13,449,388
1791	-	4,008,105	1799	-	13,642,000
1792	-	1,985,482	1800	-	13,619,079
1793	-	3,971,915	1801	-	15,857,037
1794	-	5,525,331	1802	-	13,833,573
1795	-	6,315,52			
1796	-	11,883,693			£. 121,907,305

Befides the above fums, the amount of various
navy and victualling bills feparately funded, and
that part of the ordnance expenditure, which
is appropriated for the naval fervice, might be
added.

In the courfe of the prefent war, in addition to
the ufual departments of the navy, a new inftitution was formed, under the name of the Tranfport
Board, the nature and advantages of which it may
be proper to explain, as there is a natural conftitutional jealoufy in this country againft all novel
eftablifhments.

The

The hiring of tranfports by one board, (a meafure Origin and ftrongly recommended by the commiffioners of inquiry in the year 1788), for the ufe of the other departments requiring tonnage, namely, the navy, victualling, and ordnance offices, together with the army, has prevented that competition in the engagement of fhipping, which had before exifted, and which during the prefent war, when tonnage on account of the immenfe extenfion of trade has been fcarce and dear beyond example, would moft undoubtedly have operated for that very reafon the more, to an additional enormous expenfe for this part of his majefty's fervice.

Tranfports, belonging to the feveral boards, have been known formerly to have remained unemployed, or to have fkulked in the execution or duty, for months, too much unnoticed, perhaps from the unavoidable circumftance of the preffure of other bufinefs on the feveral departments to which they belonged, and efpecially in the time of war. But if each of the three great boards, who, before the prefent arrangement, engaged tranfports, can be fuppofed to have permitted, on account of the employment of their chief attention to other duties, only one tranfport for each refpective department to be unneceffarily engaged, or mifemployed or unemployed; the hire of three fuch tranfports of the common fize would amount to above £. 8,000 *per annum*, and greatly exceed the expenfe of the tranfport eftablifhment, efpecially reduced,

Origin and advantages of the Tranfport Board.

reduced, as it now is, to three commiſſioners, ſince the ceſſation of the war. The ſaving, made by the board, on this head, by appropriating tranſports proportioned to their intended ſervices, by keeping them with every poſſible ſtrictneſs to their duty, and by diſcharging them immediately when they could be diſpenſed with, has been an article of the greateſt conſequence to the public purſe.

It was the practice, and perhaps the unavoidable one, of the boards, who formerly engaged tranſports, to devolve the examination of them, reſpecting ſize, fitneſs, &c. to inferior officers ſerving under them. None are now employed, who have not, over and above the ſuperintendence of the ſhipwright, officer, and an agent who is a commiſſioned officer in the navy, paſſed under the particular examination of one of the ſea-commiſſioners of the tranſport board, and approved by certificate under his hand. Very ſerious and expenſive abuſes are prevented by this meaſure.

For the conveyance of troops on ſhort ſervices, the officers commanding regiments, or detachments of regiments, were formerly accuſtomed to hire veſſels; but as theſe gentlemen could not be expected to know much of ſhipping, and particularly with reſpect to the two very important points of ſize and price; their engagements were generally attended with an extravagant charge, and often with

an

an unneceffary duration of hire by demurrages, through inadvertency or mifmanagement. Since the tranfport board has carried on the bufinefs, idle tonnage has been greatly avoided, many accommodations afforded to the troops, and heavy charges faved; all which could not have been effected, if left to the army; nor performed with equal advantages, if committed to other departments, embarraffed with duties of different kinds.

The tranfport board have alfo been engaged in the execution of frequent orders of a mifcellaneous kind, committed to them by the Lords of the Treafury, in the difcharge of which, and the other duties entrufted to their care, there is every reafon to believe that, by their probity and economy, they have faved their country feveral hundred thoufand pounds, or, in other words, more money, than the expenfe of the eftablifhment could amount to for a century.

It would appear too that the tranfport board has afforded no fmall convenience to the treafury, by the inveftigation of various memorials regarding naval matters, and in other refpects has been the means of faving great fums to the public, by enforcing fubordinate arrangements; by inveftigating the expenditure and return of ftores, by checking the times and places in which tranfports are employed; by mulcting defaults; by clofe examination of log-books and papers in tracing abufes;

abufes; by refifting falfe claims on various pre-
tences, which feamen only can detect; by rigidly
exacting mufters of complements; and by many
other articles of detail, too numerous to mention.

It is neceffary only to add, upon this head of the
tranfport-fervice, that the various duties above-
mentioned, muft be executed, either by one board,
or by feveral other departments: If by feveral departments, the difadvantages and expences would
be fuch as have been already confidered, and
would remain fuch probably without a remedy;
but, if by one board inftituted for the fole purpofe, the whole charge (as was before obferved)
may be comprized moft certainly within the expence of hiring of three tranfports at the utmoft,
with the advantage of precluding many expenfive
inconveniences and irregularities.

Charge of
prifoners of
war. About a year and a half after the inftitution of
the tranfport department, the care of prifoners of
war in health was taken from the commiffioners for
the fick and wounded, and confided to the tranfport
board. Two additional commiffioners were appointed, and the clerks, who had been formerly
employed on that duty, were removed to the
tranfport office.

Nothing detracting is meant againft the board for
fick and wounded feamen, confifting almoft entirely
of medical men, when it is obferved, that their habits
do not lead them to underftand the management
of feamen made prifoners, and to the engagement of
proper

proper veffels for cartels, &c. with an advantage equal to fea officers, who compofe the majority of the tranfport board, and who are accuftomed, from the nature of their profeffion, to underftand the methods of dealing with and managing, people of their own way of life, in preference to gentlemen of any other defcription. It may truly be faid, that much benefit, upon this ground alone, has arifen to the public from their employment.

There are alfo other benefits. By fixing upon fome principal depôts for the reception of prifon- ers, and by abolifhing twelve fmaller eftablifh- ments of the kind which appeared to be unnecef- fary, a faving was made, for the firft year, in fa- laries, rents, removals of prifoners, &c. of full £. 3000 *per annum*.

Six eftablifhments for prifoners in the Weft In- dies were alfo, by arrangements, rendered unnecef- fary and abolifhed, by which means the fum of £. 10,057 : 19 : 10 fterling *per annum* was faved in falaries, and the hire of prifons and prifon-fhips, and above £. 1000 more in extra charges.

Many other inferior expences have been fpared to government, through frequent vifits of the com- miffioners at the feveral depôts, in the correction of abufes, the reduction of unneceffary people, the in- ftitution of more minute and exact regulations, and many other circumftances of an inferior kind, which cannot be detailed without prolixity, but by which a great variety of charges have been either lopped off, or prevented to accumulate.

Only

Only one point more shall be added. The accounts for prisoners during the American war have not hitherto been liquidated: Those which have occurred for the last war, are in such a train of adjustment, that the home-business is already duly balanced, and, in a few months, the foreign will be completely brought up and settled.

These observations, certainly place in a very favourable point of view, the advantages of this institution.

3. Military expences.

The late war, though not so successful by land, as by sea, yet was distinguished by a number of important acquisitions, as Minorca, Malta, and Egypt, besides various valuable settlements belonging to the Dutch, the French, and the Spaniards, in Africa and both the Indies. Our greatest efforts, however, were naturally bent to the naval service, and we relied too much on the exertions of our allies for triumphs on the continent of Europe. It certainly would be desirable to ascertain, the circumstances which occasioned a disappointment in the expectations we were naturally led to entertain, of the success of so powerful a confederacy. It might have been occasioned by three causes, either want of force, or want of arrangement, or want of skill and honesty in carrying the plans against the common enemy into execution.

In regard to the first, when the confederacy against France was formed, there certainly was

force

force fufficient, if not to crufh the new republic, at leaft to keep it within its ancient limits.   As to the fecond point there feems to have been many unfortunate errors.   It was impoffible for fo many powers, remote from each other, to co-operate by means of negociations, carried on at each different court.   The Auftrian monarchy has found it ne-ceffary to diffolve the Aulic council of war, though fitting at Vienna, as a plan utterly incompatible with the management of a war; but during the late conteft, there was a fpecies of European council of war, the members of which fat at each of the ca-pitals of the confederacy, the confequence necef-farily was, that the plans were ill arranged, too late in being carried into execution, and almoft uni-formly difcovered by the enemy.   In the fubjoined note, a plan is mentioned, which, had it been adopted, would probably have given a different turn to the conteft on the continent [q].

As

[q] In March 1793, I drew up a paper to the following effect, which I tranfmitted to the Britifh cabinet. " Great Britain is more interefted in the prefent war than any other country in Europe. If it is unfortunate, the other powers will make peace with France, and leave England in the lurch. Then it will have to fight with a warlike and defperate enemy, who, from neceffity, muft carry on an offenfive war againft this country, by means of invafion. Great Britain therefore ought to en-deavour to unite all the powers now confederated together, in a joint and regular fyftem of attacking France; that the war may fpeedily be brought to a conclufion, and may not ultimately be pointed againft her alone, without any co-operation or affif-tance.

" But

As to ſkill in managing the war, and I am ſorry
to add, even honeſty in executing the plans re-
ſolved on, there is reaſon to believe, that the Auſ-

" But with that view it is abſolutely neceſſary, that there
ſhould be an executive cabinet council ſtationed at a centrical
place ; for the purpoſe of directing the execution of a regular
ſyſtem of attack, and that no time ſhould be loſt in adopting
that meaſure.

" A moment's conſideration muſt ſatisfy any one, that if there
is no concert among the confederates, or if it is eſſential, on all
occaſions, to ſend meſſengers to every Court in Europe, for
their opinion and conſent ; it muſt be impoſſible to expect ſucceſs againſt an active enemy, who takes its reſolutions one in-
ſtant, and executes them the next.

" It is therefore ſubmitted to the conſideration of the Britiſh
cabinet, whether it would not be a prudent meaſure, to propoſe
to the confederated powers, that each of them ſhould ſend a
confidential miniſter to ſome centrical ſpot, ſuch as Cologne,
Franckfort, &c. who ſhould always be within one or two days
march from the grand army, and who ſhould be inveſted with
unlimited powers of directing the operations of the armies, both
on the Rhine, and on the frontiers of Holland and Flanders.
That cabinet to be reſponſible for the activity of the troops,
and the general ſucceſs of the campaign. In ſuch a council,
Great Britain would neceſſarily have a conſiderable influence,
as it is only by its aſſiſtance that the confederates can expect
to make any real impreſſion upon France.

" At preſent, it is certain, that though the powers confederated againſt France, are, to all appearance, united together
in the ſame meaſures and ſyſtem, yet each unqueſtionably has
particular objects in view, fully as much as the ſucceſs of the
common cauſe ; nothing but ſuch a general cabinet, which will
baniſh petty views from their councils, will ever make them
enter into the war with that zeal and activity, which the importance of the intereſts they have at ſtake certainly requires.

" It

trian monarchy was not fo well ferved as it ought
to have been, and that many of the defeats and
loffes which it experienced, were occafioned, either
by the vileft mifmanagement, or the groffeft corruption.   Indeed when affertions to that effect
were fo generally circulated, it would have been
prudent for us, either to have infifted upon a change
of the generals appointed, or to have quitted an
ally, whofe fate, the confequence of its own imprudence, might eafily be forefeen.

The military expences during this period may
be ftated as follows.

ACCOUNT of MILITARY EXPENCES for
fourteen years, ending in 1802.

Year.		Sum.	Year.		Sum.
1789	-	£. 1,917,062	1797	-	£. 15,488,088
1790	-	1,809,574	1798	-	12,852,814
1791	-	2,062,548	1799	-	11,840,000
1792	-	1,819,460	1800	-	11,941,767
1793	-	3,993,715	1801	-	12,117,039
1794	-	6,641,060	1802	-	10,211,795
1795	-	11,610,008			
1796	-	11,911,899			£. 116,216,829

It has often occurred to me, that the nation was
in fome degree indemnified for the expences of the
late conteft, however enormous, by the experience

On the mi-
litary efta-
blifhment
during the
late war.

" It is fuppofed that the confederated armies may amount
to perhaps 200,000 men.   The force is great, *and fufficient for
every object in view.*   But unlefs they have provifions in abundance, able generals, and above all, unlefs they act in unifon,
they can do nothing effectual."

which

which it acquired in the art of war, and by the military fkill and fpirit which it was the means of fpreading from one end of the kingdom to the other. The extenfion of this military ardour does much credit to the zeal and talents of the war minifter at the time, (Lord Vifcount Melville), to whofe exertions it may in a great meafure be attributed. The fyftem he eftablifhed, I fhall endeavour briefly to explain, as it furnifhes a model, for any future period of fimilar danger and alarm.

When the fucceffes of France on the continent, had terrified all the powers of Europe, and there was reafon to imagine, that Great Britain would foon be obliged to contend, fingle handed, againft the new republic, it could hardly be doubted, that fuch a force *by land* was neceffary, to protect this country againft any rifk of invafion, as had never been requifite before. For however powerful we were at fea, yet a defcent was certainly not impracticable, and we had a defperate government at the moment to contend with, who regarded little what it did, and would not hefitate to fport with the lives of its fubjects, for even a remote chance of its fuccefs. In that critical emergency, a force was called forth, unparalleled in the hiftory of this country: It confifted of, 1. the regular army; 2. a militia; 3. fencibles; 4. volunteer corps receiving pay; and, 5. volunteers without pay, including that excellent inftitution, the yeomanry cavalry.

The

The regular army of Great Britain, exclusive of i. **Army.** Ireland, amounting, *anno* 1800, to about 105,000 men, certainly contained as large a proportion *of soldiers for life* as the population of this country could well admit of; and as to the idea of having the army filled with men enlisted for temporary service, nothing seems to me more ill judged. In almost all other professions, a person who enters into them, continues for life. What good reason then can be assigned, why the army should be an exception ? The public certainly cannot be benefited by having a raw recruit to pay a fresh bounty to, in room of a trained and veteran soldier, and in regard to the men, if after they become unfit for service, they are maintained at the public expence, during the remainder of their lives, they can have no just ground for complaint. Indeed, if another plan were adopted, and if soldiers were enlisted during a term of years, the state of this country might become in the highest degree alarming, if the period terminated in the midst of a war; or if in that case it could be prolonged till hostilities were concluded, yet an artful enemy might avail itself of that circumstance, by patching up a treacherous peace, and when all our veteran troops were disbanded, renewing unexpectedly the war. Such a system at least is perfectly inconsistent with any power having colonial possessions; for it would not be worth while to be at the expence of transporting soldiers to the East or West Indies, for the service of a year or two, and then to be under necessity

of

of bringing them back again ; and yet one half of every regiment might confift of perfons of that defcription. In fact, foldiers who enter into the regular army are, as it may be figuratively ftated, married to the drum, and no divorce ought to be admitted but in circumftances of a very peculiar nature. If there are any who wifh for temporary fervice, let them enter into the fencibles or the militia. And when we confider the nature of a military life, fo inconfiftent with the ties of marriage, with the rearing up, and education of children, and with returning to a life of ufeful induftry and labour, it is certainly not defirable to have a fingle individual of that defcription beyond what is really neceffary, or than the population of the country can eafily fpare.

2. Militia. A militia may be properly defined, *a body of men, collected from all the different diftricts in the kingdom, ferving by rotation, raifed merely for the internal defence of the country, and not fubjected, unlefs when actually embodied, to the duties of a foldier* [r].

The advantages atending fuch an inftitution are very great.

By eftablifhing a body of men who are never to be fent out of the kingdom, officers may acquire a certain degree of military knowledge and experience, who would never think of enlifting into a ftanding army, or would not choofe to run the rifk

---

[r] See Confiderations on Militias and Standing Armies, a tract written by the author *anno* 1782.

of

of being fent to contend with the frigid regions of Canada, or the fultry climes of Indoftan.

By collecting fuch a corps from every diftrict in the kingdom, military fpirit and fkill, is not confined to any particular fpot, but it is proportionally extended throughout every corner of the country.

Such foldiers alfo, not being totally dedicated to military objects, except in cafes of urgent neceffity, can never be accounted fuch a burden upon a nation, as ftanding forces neceffarily become in a period of long tranquillity.

It is by fuch a fyftem alone, that a wealthy and induftrious nation can keep up, for any length of time, a military fpirit; without which, of what avail is all the wealth and induftry it can amafs. They can only ferve to render a country more liable to the attacks of an enterprifing enemy, and perhaps more likely to fubmit to the invader.

Such are the general advantages attending the militia eftablifhment as it exifts at prefent; which I thought it neceffary fhortly to ftate, as fuggeftions have been thrown out that it would be politic to overturn the fyftem entirely, and to have an addition to the ftanding army in its ftead. I truft however that any attempt of that nature, will be defeated. If the militia is too numerous, diminifh the number, but do not deftroy the whole inftitution. If raifing men for that fervice, interferes with recruiting for the regular army, prevent fubftitutes as much as poffible, or allow a certain number of militiamen, annually to be recruited

into

into the line.   In regard to the difficulty of procuring officers, two modes might be fallen upon.
The firft is, that of having only two officers for
each company of 100 men, encreafing at the fame
time the pay of thofe who are retained.   It is
evident, that thofe whofe fervice is only of a temporary nature, require to be rather more amply
paid, than a body of men who are perpetually kept
in pay, and on this plan it might be done without
any additional expence to the public.   The other
mode occurred to a very refpectable country
gentleman, (Sir Cecil Wray), feveral years ago.
His idea was, that the gentlemen of the kingdom
fhould be divided into two claffes. 1. Thofe who
were poffeffed of eftates from £ 500 to £ 1000
per ann. and upwards, and 2. Thofe whofe incomes
were under either of thofe fums : that the former
fhould ballot for the higher commiffions, and the
latter for the inferior; and that all in their turn
fhould ferve in perfon for three years, or find
proper fubftitutes, or pay a certain fine, varying
according to circumftances, whether they were
fingle or married, &c.   This idea is well worthy
confideration, as the moft likely means of procuring
an effective body of officers, according to the true
principles of a conftitutional militia.

3. Fencibles.   By the old laws of Scotland, (whence the term
Fencible has been derived,) no poffible pains was
fpared to roufe and to maintain a military fpirit in
the kingdom.   Every individual was obliged, in
proportion to his rank and fortune, to have certain
kinds

kinds of arms in his poſſeſſion [s], and at certain
ſtated periods to produce them to the public [t];
it was alſo enacted, that on Sundays and other
holydays, every man ſhould be trained in the arts
and exerciſes of war, under the direction of an
able officer, called, *the Captain of the pariſh* [u];
a certain ſelect body of men under the name of
militia, which, in the reign of Charles the II.
amounting to 20,000 foot and 2,000 horſe, were
raiſed by certain proportions throughout the different counties, on principles ſomewhat ſimilar to
the preſent militia of England, and were ordered
always to be in readineſs for the public ſervice,
whenever it might be neceſſary: the remainder, in
the words of an old Act of Parliament, comprehended " *every man able of perſon to bear arms,*"
and being only intended for the defence of the
country, thence got the name of *Fencibles* [x].

[s] 9 Jac. I. c. 120, 121, &c.   11 Jac. III. c. 80.

[t] 2 Jac. I. c. 44.   3 Jac. I. c. 60, and many other acts in
the ſucceeding reigns.

[u] See 1 Jac. I. c. 18.   6 Jac. V. c. 91.   Sunday was then
included in the general term of Holyday.   This conſtant attention on the part of the legiſlature, accounts for the great
military ſpirit which prevailed in Scotland, and enabled the
Scotch ſoldiery, under the ſtandard of Guſtavus Adolphus, to
make ſo diſtinguiſhed a figure againſt the veterans of Germany.

[x] 6 Jac. V. c. 86. and 11 Act of the Convention of Eſtates
30th March 1689.   See alſo the famous act of Security which
poſſed Anno 1704, by which the whole proteſtant heritors, and
all the boroughs within the kingdom, were ordered, forthwith
to provide themſelves with fire arms, for all *the Fencible Men*
who are proteſtants, within their reſpective bounds, &c.

When

When a militia was eftablifhed in England, it is well known, that the meafure was confined to the Southern part of the kingdom, the policy or juftice of which, it is unneceffary now to dwell on, as the diftinction has happily been removed; but Scotland being thus left without any adequate defence, it was thought advifeable to raife fome regiments of men, under the name of Fencibles, to ferve in the room of a militia[x], and on the fame principle not to march out of Scotland. The number varied. During the war that ended *anno* 1760, there were two, the Argyle and the Sutherland: During the American War they were encreafed to four, and at the commencement of the prefent war feven battalions were raifed.

For reafons to be afterwards explained, I was always partial to that fort of fervice, and being convinced that it might be greatly extended, and rendered much more efficient, I propofed to raife a corps of Fencibles for the fervice of Great Britain, (which was the firft of that defcription) and foon after another battalion for the fervice of Ireland. The number of Fencible corps, both cavalry and infantry, were afterwards greatly augmented.

The advantages to be derived from fuch an eftablifhment, the reader will be able to appreciate, from a confideration of the following curfory obfervations.

Advantages of Fencible corps.   1. There are many men who will inlift for limited fervice, and for a limited time, (as the

[x] In the public accounts of 1760, &c. they are included in the militia eftimates.

duration

duration of a war), who will not engage for life, nor subject themselves to be sent to any climate however unwholesome. The number of men of this description may easily be ascertained, from a return of those who were lately disbanded as Fencibles, notwithstanding every inducement to enter into the line. Including both the old and the new Fencibles, the number will probably amount to above 10,000.

2. There are many gentlemen, who may be led on the spur of an occasion, to engage in the military line, for limited service in point of time and place, who are too old to enter into the army, and to pass through all the gradations of its different ranks, and who cannot be rapidly promoted without disgusting the officers of the regular forces, yet who may make excellent officers.

3. The militia of Great-Britain and Ireland, as now constituted, is certainly an admirable institution for national defence ; but in some respects it is surely in point of principle inferior to the Fencible system, where the men are all volunteers, instead of being ballotted, and where no qualification in point of property is required from the officers, which can never be considered as a proper test of military merit.

4. Having different descriptions of troops, often excites a very useful spirit of emulation. Fencible corps naturally wish to emulate the line, and the line to maintain a superiority. This circumstance, it is probable, contributed to that excellent state

of

of good order and difcipline which the Fencibles
in general, more efpecially thofe in Ireland, maintained during the late war.

5. It is contended that *difpofable troops*, as they
are called, are the only defcription of corps of
effential fervice to the public; and it is evident,
that the more difpofable an army is, it is the
better for general fervice. But if either owing to
a fcarcity of population, or to the temper and circumftances of the people, you cannot raife beyond
a certain number of men of that defcription, is it
not politic and prudent, to take the affiftance of
others, though their fervice fhould be of a more
limited nature, fince thus you would have a complete command over all your difpofable force, a
confiderable proportion of which muft otherwife
be retained for home defence. Befides, during the
late war, a body of men volunteered into the line,
from the Fencible fervice, without whofe aid, the
glorious expedition againft Egypt, could not have
been attempted, nor other enterprifes carried on.

6. Another argument in favour of the Fencible
fervice is, that on the whole it is rather cheaper
than the regular. The bounty given may be lefs,
there is no half pay attached to it, (though in
future no Fencible regiments will be raifed without
fome remuneration to the officers at the termina-
tion of the war), and being always at hand, there
is nothing to prevent an immediate reduction as
foon as peace is concluded, which might not be the
cafe, if the whole force of the country confifted of
regulars,

regulars, unlefs the youngeft regiments were always kept near home, in which cafe there would be little difference between them and Fencibles.

7. It is a great inducement to perfons of large property, more efpecially in the northern parts of Scotland, to keep up a great, and otherwife ufelefs population on their eftates, for the fatisfaction and credit of affifting government with great bodies of men in times of difficulty and danger, who may be inclined to follow a different fyftem, and materially to impair the military force of the country, if they have reafon to believe, that the fovereign and his minifters, do not confider the poffeffion of fuch a force of any material confequence to the nation.

The idea of eftablifhing Volunteer Corps originated during the late war, and in cafe an invafion had actually taken place, would have been found a moft important and ufeful eftablifhment; enabling the government to employ the whole regular and militia force then in the kingdom, againft the enemy, in confequence of its thus having a large body of men, trained to arms, capable of carrying on the more fubordinate operations of war.

4. Volunteers rece.ving pay.

The original fyftem by which volunteer corps were eftablifhed, was certainly, in fome refpects, defective, and is capable of feveral improvements: but on the whole it was an excellent idea, and it is a fortunate circumftance for the country that it was adopted.

Advantages of Volunteer corps.

1. It kept up a great body of men, trained to arms, at a very moderate expence.

2. It

2. It fpread a military fpirit, and military fkill, over the whole kingdom, from one end of it to the other.

3. It attached numbers to government, and kept down difaffection.

4. On many occafions fuch corps were of great fervice in preferving the police, and the quiet of the country.

5. In the northern parts of Scotland they tended much to prevent a fpirit of emigration, and fuch corps are the beft means of furnifhing thofe remote diftricts with fome military protection.

6. They enabled government to fend greater numbers of other troops out of the kingdom: without which Ireland could not have been pre-ferved, nor Egypt conquered.

Laftly, A large proportion of the pay of the Volunteers was fpent in purchafing articles liable to heavy duties, and which they would not other-wife have confumed. The exchequer therefore was repaid a confiderable fhare of the money ex-pended in their maintenance.

On thefe grounds, many intelligent individuals are anxious, that the volunteer corps fhould be eftablifhed on the following principles.

1. That they fhould ferve one day in the week in time of peace, and two days in time of war.

2. That they fhall be formed into companies of 60, and divided into three fquads. As in country places fuch corps muft confift of farmers and their fervants, it would be impoffible to call them all

away

away at once, particularly in feed time and harveft, unlefs in a cafe of the moft urgent neceffity : But one third of each company, under one of the officers, might eafily be fpared for garrifoning the forts, &c. then another fquad, and laftly the remaining third, in cafe of real danger.

Let us fuppofe that 60,000 men are kept up on this eftablifhment. During peace, the utmoft expence would not exceed 3 . per man, or 120,000l. per annum, of which at leaft one third would be repaid to the exchequer by taxes on their confumption : but if that were not the cafe, is the whole fum any objet, compared to the fatisfaction of having fo great and fo ufeful a force conftantly at command. As to the objection that thefe corps may interfere with the militia and the regular forces, it is eafily obviated, let them, if thought neceffary, be reftricted to married men, and let them be liable to be balloted for into the militia, and permitted voluntarily to inlift into the army, in which cafe they will be no impediment to the former, and may be a refource for recruiting the latter in any critical emergency[y].

Some refpectable individuals are of opinion, that in a free country like Great Britain, the whole nation ought to be armed. I am much inclined however to doubt the policy of that meafure ; for in the firft place, the training of large bodies of

5. Volunteers without pay.

---

[y] Perhaps alfo volunteer corps might be attached to regiments of militia, in cafes of emergency, and thus the militia might always be rapidly augmented.

men

men living contiguous to each other, in manufacturing towns, and still more in a luxurious
capital, might possibly be found a dangerous experiment, if the people imagined, that they had any
reason to be dissatisfied with their rulers, on account
of any partial stagnation of trade, or any temporary
scarcity of provisions, and still more, if their passions
were inflamed, and their principles subverted, by
the popular harangues of intriguing demagogues.
In the second place, such a plan, universally extended, might prove fatal to industry, as it would
be extremely difficult to make the same individual
an active soldier and an industrious mechanic; in
the third place, it is much better to make a distinction between those who voluntarily step forward,
are willing to be trained at their own expense, and
are ready to serve when necessary, from those who
would only act from compulsion; and in the last
place, when every individual is a soldier, from the
greatness of the number, the discipline must be
neglected, and many are obliged to appear, whose
personal defects tend to render the whole system
ridiculous.   Whereas when a few only are trained,
there is an audience as well as actors, and those
who do appear upon the military scene, are led by
emulation, to exert themselves to exhibit their
parts to the best advantage, and to display a military
superiority over their neighbours.

On these grounds, I have ever considered the
plan of establishing Volunteer corps, serving without
pay, and corps of Yeomanry cavalry, as infinitely
                                            preferable

preferable to the plan of arming the whole body of the people, which fome have recommended.

Such was the military fyftem adopted during the late war. The fubordinate regulations may in fome refpects be improved, but the general outline cannot be too much recommended to the attention of future minifters.

This is in a great meafure a new head of expen-Barrack de-diture fince the commencement of the prefent war. partment. Some barracks certainly had formerly exifted; but they were looked upon with a very jealous eye, and confidered by many as in the higheft degree unconftitutional. Various circumftances, however, which are fhortly explained in a pamphlet already alluded to[z], rendered it neceffary to extend the fyftem, and fortunately the plan has been found to anfwer even in an economical point of view. Indeed the faving by keeping men in barracks, on the great eftablifhment maintained for the internal defence of the country, during the greater part of the laft war, was extremely confiderable, amounting it is calculated to above 400,000l. per ann.

4 Ordnance Expenfes.

The charges of the Ordnance department exceeded all former calculations, as might well be expected from a war of fuch long continuance, and fo generally extended. The following is an abftract of the grants for that fervice, as voted by parliament.

[z] See Mr. Rofe's brief examination p. 57, and the table appendix, No. 5, annexed to that work.

NOTE

NOTE of SUMS voted for the Ordnance Department.

Year.		Sum.	Year.		Sum.
1789	-	£459,444	1797	-	£1,643,056
1790	-	455,872	1798	-	1,103,80
1791	-	594,678	1799	-	1,500,000
1792	-	422,001	1800	-	1,695,956
1793	-	783,75	1801	-	1,619,055
1794	-	1,345,008	1802	-	1,952,274
1795	-	2,321,010			
1796	-	1,954,635			17,310,375

The expenfes of the Ordnance are in general extremely unpopular, and indeed it is natural to fuppofe, that when once a country is fufficiently provided with artillery, and arms, it cannot require any great additional charge to keep up the ftock. It is to be obferved at the fame time, that a large proportion of the Ordnance expenditure, is for the fervice of the navy, where the confumption of powder and other articles muft be confiderable. In regard to plans of fortification, when they are brought forward by the Board of Ordnance, they cannot be too narrowly watched, as they have often proved a great and ufelefs fource of public extravagance.

5. Mifcellaneous Services.

It is propofed to give, firft, a general view of the fums granted for mifcellaneous fervices, and fecondly to make fome obfervations on fuch articles as may require any particular attention.

NOTE of SUMS voted under the head of
Miscellaneous Expenses.

Year.		Sum.	Year.		Sum.
1789	-	£756,309	1797	-	£3,294,443[a]
1790	-	500,518	1798	-	723,013
1791	-	691,294	1799	-	600 000
1792	-	574,950	1800	-	1,008,234
1793	-	723,830	1801	-	637,876
1794	-	741,696	1802	-	2,541,861
1795	-	1,467,750			———————
1796	-	3,490,289			18,152,143

Among the various miscellaneous expenses included in the above account, there are three of a
nature entirely new, namely, the sums granted to
the suffering Clergy and Laity of France, the
expenses of the Board of Agriculture, and the
annual grant to the Veterinary College, and two
of peculiar importance, as the expense of convicts,
and sums bestowed as public rewards, which it
may not be improper to distinguish from the rest,
and to give some explanation of them.

The Sums granted for the relief of the French
Emigrants were as follows:

1. French
Clergy and
Laity.

* Advances to the Emperor, and for the service of Ireland,
are deducted from the grants for miscellaneous services, of this
year.

NOTE

NOTE of SUMS granted by the Britiſh Parliament for the Relief of the ſuffering Clergy
and Laity of France.

Year.			Sum.
1794.	14th February.		27,692
1795.	23d February.	99,459	
Do.	14th May.	37,500	136,959
1796.	2d May.	129,350	
Do.	21ſt December.	140,090	269,440
1797.	25th April.	31,000	
Do.	26th June.	180,000	
Do.	23d November.	168,000	379,000
1798.	24th April.		12,677
1799.	————————		233,574
1800.	————————		302,798
1801.	————————		277,772
1802.	————————		173,535

£. 1,813,347[b].

It is certainly creditable to the generoſity and
munificence of the Britiſh nation, to have granted
ſuch large ſums to a number of unfortunate perſons,
with whom we had no particular connexion ; but
who were hurled by a dreadful revolution, from a
ſtate of comfort, and in many caſes of affluence, to
the fatal extremity of wanting the common ne-
ceſſaries of life in a foreign country.

2. Board of
Agricul-
ture.
The baſis of the proſperity and happineſs of a
country, muſt be founded on a thorough knowledge of its preſent ſtate, and the means of its
future improvement. It cannot be well governed,
unleſs thoſe who are entruſted with the adminiſtration of its affairs, are thoroughly acquainted with
its real circumſtances, nor can it be fertile and pro-

[b] In ſome of the latter years, the grants to the American
Loyaliſts are included.

ductive,

du[ctive, unlefs both the landlord and the farmer have eafy means of acquiring the knowledge neceffary for the management of an eftate, and the proper cultivation of the foil. Impreffed with thefe ideas, I ventured to propofe to the Britifh parliament, the eftablifhment of a board of agriculture and internal improvement, which was fortunately approved of by the Houfe, and having been recommended to the attention of the Crown, was ultimately eftablifhed.

The following are the fums which have been granted to that inftitution from its firft formation up to Michaelmas 1802.

NOTE of SUMS granted to the Board of Agriculture.

1793	•	£. 3000	1799	-	3000
1794	-	3000	1800	-	3000
1795	•	3000	1801	-	3000
1796	•	3000	1802	-	3000
1797	-	3000			
1798	-	3000			£. 30,000

It is evident that fo trifling an annual grant, is perfectly inconfiftent with the important objects for which the inftitution was formed, and the various meafures neceffary for their attainment.

In regard to the objects in view, it was intended, in the firft place to lay before government, the ftate of the country, without a knowledge of which, laws for promoting its improvement, however well intended, were not likely to be effectual, being deftitute of principle or fyftem; but when once know-

ledge

ledge is generally fpread, and a whole nation is fatisfied that certain regulations are neceffary for its
happinefs, a judicious fyftem of legiflation follows
of courfe.   It has often been remarked, that the
laws of fmall ftates, are in general wifer than thofe
of great empires.   The reafon is obvious, becaufe
the real fituation of a fmall, is better known than
that of a large community.   But if the circumftances of a large ftate, by means of general and
extenfive inquiries, are as well known as thofe of a
fmall one, the former can hardly fail to enjoy the
fame legiflative advantages with the latter.

In the fecond place, afcertaining the beft mode
of managing landed property, is a point of peculiar
importance.   The proprietors of land, are properly truftees for the public, whofe duty it is, to fee
that the territory of the country is not exhaufted
by improper treatment, produces all that it can for
the ufe and benefit of its inhabitants, and that the
perfons who cultivate the foil, live in a comfortable manner.   But how can that be expected, if
every queftion connected with the management of
landed property is not thoroughly difcuffed and
explained ?

In the third place, it is neceffary to afcertain the
true principles of cultivation; experiments have
been tried for ages, and knowledge has been accumulated, but they have never been hitherto reduced into a regular fyftem.   That indeed is not
to be wondered at, when it is ftated the immenfe
labour that is requifite to collect the neceffary information,

formation, and the variety of fubjects which ought to be difcuffed in fuch a work.

On the whole, the plan that was intended by the perfon who propofed the inftitution, was 1. to procure a feparate report from every county in the united kingdom. 2. To obtain diftinct communications from the moft intelligent individuals in the fcience of agriculture, regarding the particular points with which they were refpectively beft acquainted ; and, 3. on the bafis of the information thus collected, to draw up a general report, which would not only explain to the legiflature the ftate of the country, but would alfo point out to the landlord, the beft mode of managing his eftate, and to the farmer the beft means of cultivating his land, and in that refpect to become the future code or ftandard of a judicious fyftem of cultivation.

The allowing of fo fmall a pittance for fo important an object, (which at firft was very irregularly paid), and the deftroying its energy from perfonal or political refentment, is not only an unfortunate incident for this country, but a calamity to the human race; for what could be of more importance to mankind in general, than to have the principles of judicious cultivation, and the beft means of fecuring abundance of wholefome food, completely afcertained.   Notwithftanding the checks however which this inftitution received, it had already produced, even before the perfon who had inftituted it was deprived of the prefidency, the following important advantages.

1. It

On the ad-
vantages de-
rived from
the efta-
blifhment
of the board
of agricul-
ture.
1. It had excited a fpirit of inquiry, and of improvement in every part of the country.

2. It had made very confiderable progrefs in that great undertaking, the agricultural furvey of the kingdom.   When that is completed, it will then be enabled to draw up a general report, for the confideration of his majefty, and of both houfes of parliament, explaining not only the prefent ftate of the country, but the means of its further improvement.

3. It had fpread the knowledge of local practices, from one diftrict to another, where they were formerly unknown, and where they may be carried on to advantage.

4. It had collected much valuable information from foreign countries.

5. It had been the means of introducing beneficial laws into parliament; for inftance, the general bills of inclofure ; the act for regulating weights and meafures; and the repeal of the duty on oil cake ; and it had in contemplation to fuggeft others of great public importance ; as regulations for repealing the duty on bricks employed in draining, on falt ufed for agricultural purpofes, &c.

6. It had been the means of difcovering an article much wanted in this country, namely, the beft fpecies of millftone, which we have hitherto been obliged to import from France, but with which we fhall probably be able to fupply ourfelves in future.

7. It

7. It contributed effentially to fave the country from diftrefs, during the late years of fcarcity; 1. by afcertaining, and circulating information, refpecting the beft mode of feeding the poor; 2. by recommending a great extenfion of the culture of potatoes, and by promoting the planting them fo as to be ready earlier in the feafon than ufual; and 3. by inculcating the neceffity of fowing a greater quantity of wheat, in autumn 1795, which was attended with very happy effects in many parts of the kingdom.

8. It afcertained the beft mode of draining land, and a work has been publifhed, under its authority, which muft be the means of fpreading over the wholeifland, the knowledge of that valuable art.

9. It had propofed to afcertain, by experiment, the effects of all the different kinds of manures, on all the different forts of plants, which would have thrown more light on the fubject of agriculture than any meafure hitherto tried.

10. It had promoted, in a peculiar manner, the comforts of cottagers, and the means of bettering their condition.

Laftly, When the original prefident was removed, it was in a courfe of collecting and publifhing information, refpecting the proper management of grafs lands; the abolition of naked fallows, (an object, which if attained under the aufpices of the board, would make a very confiderable addition to the productions and wealth of the kingdom), the proper fyftem to be adopted in regard

regard to watering land; the moſt uſeful inſtruments of huſbandry; the beſt kinds of mills; the moſt profitable breeds of live ſtock; the advantages and diſadvantages of folding; the ſtate of the poor; in ſhort, every particular which in an agricultural point of view, could either promote the proſperity of the country, or the comforts of its inhabitants.

It is farther to be obſerved, that the board is a general depôt, for collecting and circulating uſeful information, both foreign and domeſtic; that any improvement, even in the moſt trifling article of management, when extended over a whole kingdom, muſt be attended with great national benefits; and that the effects of ſuch an inſtitution cannot be felt in the midſt of an expenſive war, to the ſame extent, that muſt neceſſarily be the caſe, when the capital of the country and the public attention, will be more directed to internal improvement, than can at preſent be expected.

Nor were thoſe advantages confined to Great Britain alone. It has alſo been the means of eſtabliſhing the cultivation of articles in the Eaſt Indies, which by the acknowledgment of the Eaſt India Company itſelf *is likely to be invaluable* [b], and indeed

[b] In proof of this aſſertion, ſee the following extract of a letter from the Honourable Eaſt India Company to the Marquis of Willeſley, dated 12th of March 1802. " We have peruſed " the proceedings of the board of ſuperintendance referred to " in your diſpatches, and we are much pleaſed to obſerve by " thoſe

indeed has excited such a general zeal for agriculture and a spirit of improvement, as cannot fail to be productive of the most important consequences in every quarter of the globe.

It is not to be wondered at, that I speak of this institution in such favourable terms, being inclined to attribute the greater part of the calamities experienced by this country, to the neglect paid to the suggestions of the board of agriculture. Had the recommendations of that institution been properly attended to, and acted upon with energy and spirit, the country would not have been afflicted with any of those scarcities which unfortunately took place; or at any rate they would never have been felt to the extent which the nation actually experienced. All the fatal consequence of those scarcities might thus have been prevented, namely, the heavy charge of additional pay to the army and to the navy, and the dreadful mutinies in the naval service, which were likely to have proved more ruinous to this country, than any circumstance that ever happened to it. The importation of grain also, occasioned the exportation of specie, or at least prevented the usual supply of bullion from being imported, hence the suspension of payments in cash

---

" those proceedings that the lucerne and Guinea-grass thrive
" in such a manner as to afford a reasonable prospect of their
" becoming an acquisition to the Bengal provinces that will
" prove invaluable." It was through the means of the president of the board of agriculture that these articles were sent to the East Indies.

at the bank, and all the confequences refulting therefrom: and if the grain we imported, in confequence of deficient cultivation, coft this country twenty millions (which is the fmalleft fum at which it can be eftimated), had we poffeffed fuch an addition to our circulating wealth, would not the commerce, the credit, and the revenue of the country been placed on a much higher foundation at the conclufion of the late war.

On this fubject I fhall only add, that whenever the board of agriculture is put on that refpectable footing to which it is fo well entitled, and is enabled to perform thofe public fervices for which it is fo peculiarly well calculated, that it cannot fail to prove the moft fortunate circumftance that could poffibly happen to the Britifh empire, if not to the fpecies at large.

Veterinary college.

The difeafes of horfes, and other domeftic animals, have only of late years been the fubject of fcientific inquiry, though every means by which the live ftock of the country could be preferved from difeafe, or cured when infected, is an object of infinite national importance. It is calculated that in the fpace of twenty years, the Dutch loft cattle, by thofe infectious diftempers which occafionally break out in Holland, to the amount of £. 5,000,000 fterling; and the value of the fheep which have been deftroyed in England, by the rot alone, (without touching on other difeafes), during the fpace of a century, is hardly to be eftimated. An inftitution having been formed, at the expence

of

of a number of private individuals, for eſtabliſhing the veterinary art in this country, it was ſurely a laudable meaſure in government, to give it ſome aid.   The following are the ſums granted for that purpoſe, and it were much to be wiſhed, that the public expenditure in general, were equally unexceptionable.

NOTE of SUMS granted for the Veterinary College.

1795	-	£. 1500	1800	-	1500
1796	-	1500	1801	-	1500
1797	-	1500	1802	-	1500
1798	-	1500			
1799	-	1500			£. 12,000

The expence of convicts, both at home, and in the new colony of South Wales, is an object, in every point of view, well entitled to the moſt ſerious attention of the Britiſh legiſlature.   An inquiry ought immediately to be inſtituted regarding that important ſubject, more eſpecially into the propriety of maintaining any longer the colony in South Wales, or at leaſt whether it is adviſeable to tranſport any additional convicts there, at an expenſe ſo enormous [c].   The meaſure of eſtabliſhing penitentiary houſes, according to the plan ſuggeſted by Mr. Bentham, is ſurely well calculated for a large proportion of thoſe who are condemned

[c] Mr. Jeremy Bentham, in two letters addreſſed to Lord Pelham, has given very ſatisfactory reaſons why any ſucceſs in the eſtabliſhment in South Wales can hardly be expected.

by

by the laws of their country to labour and confine-
ment. But why might not some of these unfortunate persons be employed in works of public
utility, in making new harbours, in opening new
communications, and rendering the most imper-
vious districts in the kingdom accessible to industry
and improvement. The same sums which have
been wasted in the settlement at Botany Bay, would
have rendered the northern districts of Scotland
one of the most valuable possessions belonging to
the British crown.

The following is a note of sums granted for convicts at home.

Year.		Sum.	Year.		Sum.
1789	-	£. 56,598	1798	-	£.36,863
1790	-	41,117	1793	-	72,914
1791	-	52,565	1800	-	40,353
1792	-	23,424	1801	-	45,317
1793	-	23 428	1802	-	31,024
1794	-	24,969			
1795	-	26,903			£.563,631
1796	-	20.757			
1797	-	67,399			

Public re-
wards.

In examining the nature of our public expenditure it is melancholy to think, how very inconfiderable a portion of the many millions we have laid
out, has hitherto been dedicated for the purpose of
rewarding merit, or promoting the industry and
improvement of the country. Some grants have
been voted for erecting monuments to the memory
of distinguished characters who have fallen in the
service of their country, and annuities have been
granted to those gallant heroes, who have distinguished

guished themselves during the late and former wars, but in the humbler walks of life, and for services of a civil or pacific nature, the only sums which appear in our public accounts of late years are the following:

1. To Mr. Elkington d for discovering his mode of draining land - -	£. 1000	0 0
2. To Dr. Jenner for promulgating his discoveries of the vaccine innoculation, by which a mild and efficacious mode of superseding that dreadful malady the small pox is established - -	10,000	0 0
3. To Mr. Greathead, boat builder, as a reward for his invention of the life boat, whereby many lives have already been saved, and great security is afforded to seamen and property in cases of shipwreck	1200	0 0
	£. 12,200	0 0 e

There is a pleasure in recording such instances of legislative attention to useful discoveries; the merit of Dr. Jenner however, far surpasses that of every other competitor for public reward. Indeed whilst many who have shone in power and

d The grant to Mr. Elkington was moved by the author in Parliament, and was not carried without considerable opposition. An ingenious agriculturist, (Dr. James Anderson), afterwards claimed the merit of the discovery, and certainly threw out, in one of his publications, a hint to that effect; but after making every possible inquiry for the purpose of ascertaining the fact, it appeared to me perfectly indisputable, that Mr. Elkington had carried the idea into practice, sometime before Dr. Anderson had recommended the theory, and consequently that the former was entitled to the whole reward.

e The sum of £. 1000 was also voted to John Davies, for his discovering the means of cleaning smutty wheat.

fplendour fhall be forgotten, he will juftly be celebrated, as one of the greateft benefactors to the human race, that any age or any country can boaft of.

On the ex-   It is impoffible yet to make up any accurate
pences of
the late war. ftatement of the expences, which the late war has
occafioned. It is evident that all the loans, and
any addition to the unfunded debt of the nation, is
in the firft place to be ftated to that account. The
extraordinary fources of revenue arifing from the
contribution tax, the income tax, &c. may be
placed to the fame head. The expences alfo incurred in Ireland, and in the Eaft Indies, ought to
be included. Without pretending therefore to any
accuracy, which from various circumftances cannot
at prefent be obtained, I fhall endeavour briefly to
fum up the expences of the late war, from the beft
information which it has been poffible for me to
collect.

STATE of the EXPENCES of the War ended by the Treaty of Amiens.

1. Amount of principal fums received for new
   ftock created   -   -   -   £. 215,015,718
2. Addition during the war to the unfunded debt
   of the nation   -   -   -   10,000,000
3. Extra contributions and refources (fuppofed)   22,000,000
4. Surpluffes of the confolidated fund   —   15,000,000

$\overline{\hphantom{aaaaaaaa}}$

£. 262,015,718

5. Auftrian loans if not repaid   -   -   6,222,000
6. Irifh loans funded in England   -   11,000,000
7. Additional Irifh expences (fuppofed)   -   12,000,000
8. Expences in the Eaft Indies (fuppofed)   10,000,000

$\overline{\hphantom{aaaaaaaa}}$

Total   -   £. 301,237,718

Such

Such are the expences occafioned by the late war, the policy and conduct of which have occa- fioned fo much difcuffion. The opinion which I have formed regarding it, I fhall endeavour fhortly to ftate with as much impartiality as poffible.

1. It certainly was impolitic, reducing the peace eftablifhment of this country fo low as it was in 1792, when from the ftate of France it was evi- dent, that all Europe was likely to get into a con- vulfed ftate. Had we been better armed at that tremendous crifis, the diforders of France would not have broken out as they did, or might eafily have been crufhed at the commencement.

2. The war perhaps might have been *evaded* for fome time longer, but could not poffibly have been *avoided*, after the rulers of France had refolved to fpread their revolutionary principles over Europe; and the danger of Great Britain would have been very great, if after the powers on the continent had been fubdued, France had bent all its military force againft this country, unarmed, inexperienced in war, and thinking of nothing but commerce: —to the commencement of the war therefore, I felt no hefitation in giving a moft hearty approbation.

3. The war, in fo far as regarded the naval de- partment, and hoftilities in the Eaft and Weft In- dies, together with the glorious campaign in Egypt, was certainly fuccefsfully conducted; but on the continent of Europe, the cafe was very dif- ferent, which I entirely attribute to the Britifh go- vernment not affuming that influence in the direc- tion

tion of the war, to which, on various accounts, it was so peculiarly well entitled. In fact, no confederacy can prosper, unless some particular power takes the lead. The combination against France, in the reign of Queen Anne, would not have succeeded, if the Duke of Marlborough had not been the soul of that confederacy, and directed the whole military operations against the enemy ; and if ever another coalition is formed against the power and ambition of France, Great Britain must be the active power to form and carry it on, must use its influence to prevail upon its allies to employ its best troops and ablest officers, must employ its wealth in procuring intelligence of the plans and intentions of the enemy, (the want of which occasioned the fatal overthrow at Marengo), must encourage, by honorary, and even pecuniary rewards, the officers of its allies to make every exertion in the common cause, (which they will soon find is more advantageous than any bribe they can expect from the enemy), and in fine must act a noble and disinterested part, proving to the world, that the war is carried on, not for purposes of ambition, but with a view of protecting its own independence, and asserting the liberties of Europe.

4. It is certain that the war might have been ended sooner, and much to the advantage of this country [f]. Even as late as the year 1796, France would

[f] Such was the ardour for war, that any person was stigmatised who ventured to inculcate peace ; of which the following verses in the Times of the 8th December 1798, may be cited as one proof, among many others.

Dialogue

would have agreed to the reſtoration of the Stad-
tholder, and the independence of Belgium.   The
rejection alſo of Bonaparte's firſt offer, in ſo
haughty a manner, was not very politic; for if the
government which he had then eſtabliſhed was
weak, the terms muſt neceſſarily have been better;
and if it was ſtrong, there was no riſk in conclud-
ing a peace.

5. The peace that was concluded at Amiens, if
it had been entered into with proper views by both
parties, was not perhaps materially inconſiſtent with
the relative ſituation of the two countries.   It is
unfortunate at the ſame time, that ſtipulations were
not entered into, for repreſſing any farther ſpirit of
aggrandiſement on the part of France, and for giving Europe ſome chance of enjoying a little quiet
and repoſe after ſo many years of calamity.

6. On the whole it is probable, that the miniſters
themſelves who conducted the late war, would in
many reſpects, alter their ſyſtem, if they had the
ſame ſcenes to react.   In matters of ſo extenſive
and complicated a nature, errors are unavoidable,

Dialogue between Alexander the Great and Parmeno.
The Macedon hero to Parmeno ſaid,
   Darius ten thouſand gold talents will give,
And his daughter Statira, that beautiful maid,
   If peace I will grant him, as long as I live.
Parmeno—Were I Alexander, to this I'd conſent.
Alexander—And were I but Parmeno, I would be content.
So if Sinclair were Pitt, for a peace he would ſue,
And if Pitt was but Sinclair, the ſame he might do.

even

even with the beſt intentions, and where the greateſt talents are employed.   It is of the utmoſt importance however, to review and to re-conſider ſuch events, as the moſt likely means of preventing ſimilar errors on future occaſions.   One point was certainly gained by the late war, that of preſerving this country from being overrun by the arms of France[g].   The other objeƐt, that of curbing the power of France, we completely failed in, and we have unfortunately ſeen it riſe to a degree of power, which, without being of any real advantage to itſelf, threatens at the ſame time Europe, and even the world, with ſubjeƐtion.   Our diſappointment in that reſpeƐt however, is in ſome degree compenſated, by our naval triumphs, the knowledge we have acquired of our internal means of defence, the military ſkill and ſpirit that has been ſpread from one end of the kingdom to the other, and the glorious campaign in Egypt, which it is impoſſible to refleƐt on, without a mixture of pride, admiration, and aſtoniſhment.

Such are the obſervations which have occurred to me, on the ſubjeƐt of the expenditure of this

[g] I do not give the miniſters any credit for preventing French principles from becoming predominant in this country; for in the firſt place they did but their duty, and in the ſecond place the French doƐtrines have never ſucceeded any where but where their arms have penetrated.   Indeed no eſtabliſhed government can poſſibly be overturned, but either by foreign arms, or the folly of its rulers.

country,

country, for fourteen years preceding Michaelmas
1802. It is certain that in confequence of the
meafures fuggefted by the Committee of Finance
originally appointed *anno* 1797, much more accurate information has been obtained, regarding
our financial fyftem, than was formerly known.
But the plan is ftill defective, and ought to be improved upon as much as poffible. It can hardly
be queftioned, that a nation which pays fo much,
is well entitled to know how its money is really
expended, and for that purpofe the public accounts
fhould be ftated in fuch a manner, as would make
them perfectly intelligible to every individual converfant in figures, or at leaft who had at all directed his attention to queftions of finance; but
with that view it would be neceffary, that the votes
of Parliament, fanctioned by the annual act of ap-
propriation, fhould never be violated; fuch public
accounts, as any fingle member might think neceffary, fhould be prefented, and no impediment
attempted to be thrown in the way of information and enquiry. Above all, the public accounts
fhould annually be referred to a committee of the
houfe, which any member might have the privilege
of attending, and the report of that committee,
fhould contain the moft accurate and diftinct ftatement that could poffibly be drawn up, of the public income and expenditure.

SECT.

SECT. IV.

Extraordinary Measures of Finance.

FROM the new scenes naturally to be expected, in the course of the great revolution that has taken place in the affairs of Europe, and the vicissitudes of a long and expensive war, some events of an extraordinary nature, connected with the Financial circumstances of the country, were to be looked for, but the wildest imagination could hardly have supposed, that they would have been either so numerous, or of so uncommon a nature, as will appear from the following general review of these transactions. The articles which I propose more particularly to allude to, are the following, namely, 1. The Loyalty Loan. 2. The Plans of raising the Supplies within the year. 3. The Aid and voluntary Contribution of 1798. 4. The Income Tax. 5. The Convoy Tax. 6. Taxes repealed or abandoned. 7. The Redemption of the Land Tax. 8. The System of Competition for Loans. 9. The Loan of Exchequer Bills, and other assistance given to the commercial and colonial interests. 10. The Bonding System. 11. The appointment of Financial Committees, and 12. The Suspension of Payments in Cash at the Bank of England; to which I propose to add some observations on the circulation and paper credit of

the

the country, and the means of eftablifhing them on the fureft and beft foundation.

There are few readers who will not begin with fome reluctance, the difcuffion of fo many important queftions. What then muft not the feelings of the author be, who undertakes to elucidate them, within the narrow limits of this publication?

The vaft accumulation of debt, beyond all former example, which had taken place towards the conclufion of the year 1796; the difficulties which were apprehended in raifing additional fupplies, the unlimited confidence which the great body of the people feemed to place in the minifter, and indeed the almoft *vizierial authority* he had acquired, induced him to bring forward a meafure, defcribed by his friends as being, " different from " former practice, but better adapted to the cir- " cumftances of the times." It was firft announced to the public in a letter, a copy of which, on account of the importance of the tranfaction, I have thought it proper to preferve in this work.

I. Loyalty Loan.

Copy of a letter from the Chancellor of the Exchequer, to the directors of the Bank of England.

Downing-Street, Wednefday,
30th November, 1796.

GENTLEMEN,

Under the prefent circumftances, it feems of peculiar importance, that a mode fhould be
adopted

adopted for providing for the fervice of the enfuing
year, without incurring fo heavy an annual charge,
and fo great an increafe of capital, as would attend
a loan, made in the accuftomed manner, at the
prefent price of the funds.   With this view it is in
contemplation to propofe to Parliament, that all
perfons poffeffed of a certain income, fhould be
required to lend a given proportion of it, fay one
fourth, to be repaid at the period, and on the
terms ftated in the inclofed memorandum.

There is great reafon to hope, that many perfons
poffeffed of confiderable incomes, both in the
capital and in the country, will be induced, without
waiting for the meafure being enforced, voluntarily
to contribute in a larger proportion than would
be required of them, but the extent of fuch a contribution, will in a great degree depend upon the
effect of examples, and particularly on the degree
of countenance which the meafure may receive
from the Bank.

I will requeft the favour of you to lay thefe confiderations before the court of directors, in the firft
inftance, and after, if they think fit, before the
court of proprietors, and to exprefs my earneft
hope, that from their great zeal for the public
fervice, and their fenfe of the importance of the
prefent crifis, they will not be difinclined to take
the lead in a meafure, which muft have the moft
beneficial effect on public credit, and the moft
evident

evident tendency to accelerate the reſtoration of peace, on ſecure, and honourable terms.

I have the honour to be, &c. &c.

(Signed)

W. PITT.

The Memorandum referred to in the letter, was to the following effect.

" Every ſubſcriber to receive for each £.100 a debenture of £.110 the intereſt of which is to be paid half yearly at 5 *per cent.*—And if he keeps this debenture till the expiration of four years, without aſſigning it, or one year after the ſigning of a definitive treaty of peace, he will then receive, at his option, either £.110 in money, or £.110 5 *per cents.* unredeemable for ſix years from this period, or the value of £110 in conſolidated 3 *per cents.* at 75 *per cent.*—If he keeps it three years in the ſame ſtate, he will receive £.109 5 *per cents* to be liquidated in the ſame manner at the end of four years, either in money or conſolidated 3 *per cents.* or to remain in 5 *per cents.* for the above term.— If he keeps it two years he will receive £.108 5 *per cents.* with the above privileges —If he keeps it one year, or upon making the full payments (the diſcount allowed upon which will be about 3 *per cent.*) he will receive £.107 5 *per cents.* as above, but the debentures will not be aſſignable after the ſecond payment.—They muſt after that period remain in the ſame hands till the full payments are made, either by anticipation or otherwiſe, when

they

they will be immediately made into ſtock and transferable like other funds at the Bank of England, but kept quite ſeparate from the preſent 5 *per cents.* You will obſerve it is the miniſters wiſh by this plan to give encouragement to thoſe who can keep the ſubſcription out of the market, to prevent it depreſſing the other Stocks."

The reception which this propoſal met with from intelligent perſons in the metropolis, and indeed the ſpecific principles on which it was founded, will be ſeen, from the following extract of a letter written from an eminent banking houſe in London, to their correſpondents in the country, dated 1ſt December, 1796.

" You may eaſily conceive, that many dif-
" ficulties muſt occur in every plan, for raiſing a
" ſum of eighteen or twenty millions, and Mr. Pitt
" ſeemed to have collected, from the various in-
" formation he had received, that it could not be
" obtained in the uſual way, without depreſſing the
" price of the other funds very materially, and
" that there might even be ſome apprehenſion of
" its not being negotiable at all.   He therefore
" has determined, to try whether the public ſpirit
" of the great incorporated bodies, and of the
" country at large, may not induce a voluntary
" ſubſcription to a loan, which, though not perhaps
" ſo beneficial as an inveſtment made in the other
" funds, would yet, under all the circumſtances,
" produce a very good immediate intereſt, and a
" certainty of conſiderable profit in a few years."

" We

" We were about to have fent this plan by
" yefterday's poft, when we found there was ftill
" another meeting, and it was not till late laft
" night, that fome of the laft alterations were made."

" To thofe who will not be induced to fub-
" fcribe by public fpirit, or led by a fenfe of their
" own intereft, to facrifice a part of their fortune
" to fecure the reft, he means to apply, by a tax at
" leaft equal to what may be fuppofed to be loft
" by the voluntary fubfcribers, and he expects a
" good example will be fet by men of high rank,
" and in high official fituations, as well as by the
" Bank of England, and other corporate bodies;
" and that fuch a fum will be raifed, as will make
" it very eafy to borrow what it may be fhort of
" the fum he wants, in fome other manner.   Mr.
" Pitt expects the fubfcription will fell at fome
" difcount, but flatters himfelf, the Country will
" think as he does, that a large voluntary contri-
" bution may be the means of extricating them
" from their prefent difficulties, by fhewing its
" enemies we are not without refource.   All muft
" agree, that whilft the war continues, money muft
" be had to carry it on with vigour, and the more
" unanimity and ftrength we fhew, the more
" willing our enemies will be to conclude peace on
" fair and permanent conditions."

These fuggeftions circulated in London, and
thence fpread from the moft refpectable quarters,
over the whole kingdom, and aided with all the
weight and influence which government could

furnifh, had, as might naturally be expected, a moft powerful effect.

Indeed the meafure was entered into by the public, with fuch fpirit and alacrity, that books being opened on the 1ft December, 1796, before twelve o'clock on Monday the 5th, the whole eighteen millions were fubfcribed : and fuch was the eagernefs of the nation, that double the amount might have been obtained. It was certainly an unfortunate circumftance that as large a fum was not raifed at once, and on the fame principle, as was found neceffary for the fervice of the year, more efpecially after the train had taken, and the fpirit of the country was roufed to carry through the meafure with eclat[h].

There would have been no difficulty, if the money fubfcribed exceeded the fum wanted, to have made a proportionable deduction from each fubfcription, which would have been rather a favour or a bonus to the fubfcribers than otherwife. The raifing of another loan, in the fame year, on different principles, " *and more conformable to for-* " *mer practice*," tended to depreciate the value of " *the Loyalty Loan*," as it was nicknamed at Change-Alley, and to expofe it to the contempt and ridicule of ftock jobbers, who greatly preferred the loan of £. 14,500,000 afterwards raifed for the

---

[h] It would have been better alfo, if the threat of *a forced loan* had been avoided, for fuch an idea ought not to have been brought forward, unlefs it had been required by the moft urgent neceffity.

fervice

fervice of the fame year. Nor is that to be wondered
at, as they had a greater additional capital, and at
the fame time a much higher intereft. It may be
worth while to compare the two loans together,
which will fully account for the unpopularity of
the loyalty loan, and the ftrong defire which the
monied intereft would naturally feel, to put an
end to that mode of raifing money.

Comparifon of the two loans raifed for the
fervice of the year 1797.

Loan.	Sum borrowed.	Capital created.	Rate of Intereft.		
1. The Loyalty Loan.	18,000,000	20,124,843	5	14	1
2. The 2d Loan.	14,500,600	28,275,000	6	6	10

From an infpection of this fhort table, it may
eafily be fuppofed, that the difcount on the Loyalty
Loan would foon become very confiderable, and
was more felt by the fubfcribers, as their brother
loan-mongers, in the fame year, were making money by their bargain. It is well known, that many
had fubfcribed to the firft loan, without funds adequate to pay their different inftalments, and confequently were under the neceffity of felling at any
price the article would fetch at the market. Many
perfons, of great political influence, were involved
in that unfortunate dilemma. In order to extricate
them from fo unpleafant a fituation, the chancellor
of the exchequer was prevailed upon to bring forward a propofition altogether unprecedented, namely, that of granting an additional bonus to thofe fubfcribers, and as a premium for their loyalty, voting
                                                    them

them a douceur which would have coft the public
about one million fterling.

The minifter was then at the zenith of his power
and influence, and every propofal he made, was fo
implicitly fanctioned by parliament, that, any oppofition to his will and pleafure was confidered as
fo much time and labour thrown away. It was
evident, however, that if this propofition were
affented to, befides the heavy immediate lofs which
the public muft have fuftained, it would have been
a fatal precedent for the future, and indeed would
have rendered all bargains for loans, in after times,
uncertain and precarious. I thought it incumbent
therefore upon a perfon, who had applied his mind
fo much to financial refearches, to oppofe by every
poffible effort, fo fatal an attempt, and by perfonal
or written applications prevailed on feveral members to attend, who protefted, at the time, that it
was perfectly ufelefs, but who could not refift the
importunity with which their prefence was requefted.   There were many objections to the
meafure, in confequence of its trenching on the
forms of the houfe.   For 1. it was altering an act
in the fame feffion, without authority being referved
for that purpofe in the original bill.   2. The
Committee of fupply having decided for the
fmaller fum in the original proceedings, the fame
committee could not add to that fum, and augment
the burdens of the country; and 3. it was alfo
contended, that conformably to the rules of the
houfe, all applications for money, for the benefit

of

of individuals, fhould originate in a petition from them, and that the confent or recommendation of the Crown, (the act of a refponfible minifter,) ought to be given upon the occafion. As the meafure was likely to go on, notwithftanding thefe objections in point of form, it was found neceffary to oppofe the principle; and after a long and defultory debate, when a divifion took place, to the aftonifhment of every one, the minifter found himfelf in a majority of only one, and the votes of one or two of thefe who voted with him, were objected to, as being interefted in the fuccefs of the application. After fuch an explicit declaration of the real fenfe of the Houfe, it was thought moft prudent not to perfevere in the attempt, and this example of fuccefsful oppofition, even in circumftances fo extremely unpromifing, it is hoped will prevent perfons engaged in a public caufe, when they are evidently in the right, from ever defpairing of fuccefs.

In a former part of this work, (vol. 1. p. 335.), fome obfervations will be found on the plan of raifing the fupplies within the year; and when in 1797 and 1798, it became fo difficult to procure money for the public fervice on the old fyftem, fuch a meafure came to be ferioufly confidered, not only by the minifter, but by the public at large. As in the event of another war, this expedient muft probably be reforted to, I think it proper to record, in this place, fome thoughts which occurred

2. Raifing the fupplies within the year.

red

red to me upon the fubject, when that idea was
more particularly under difcuffion.

The late minifter had certainly the merit of firft
attempting any meafure of the fort; but inftead of
raifing only a part of the fupplies within the year,
and borrowing the remainder, it feems to me infinitely better, by fome great and manly effort, to
endeavour to raife the whole without reforting to
a loan at all, unlefs with a view of adding to the
circulating medium in a manner to be afterwards
explained. For that purpofe, however, it is neceffary that there fhould be, 1. a fufficient quantum of general income or financial refources in the
nation, to afford the fum that may be required;
2. a fufficient quantity of circulating medium, to
carry through fo great an operation without inconvenience to commerce; 3. a perfect knowledge of
the ftate of the country, and the means the moft
likely to raife what may be wanted, without impofing any material hardfhip on any particular defcription of perfons; and, 4. that the nation fhould
have a complete confidence in its government at
the time.

Financial refources in the nation. As to the firft point, there can be no doubt of
the ability of the nation. Without entering how-
ever at prefent into minute calculations regarding
the national fund for taxation, which will be treated
of in another part of this work [1], it may be fufficient to remark, that the means which this country

[1] See the chapter on the national refources.

poffeffes

poffeffes for yielding a great additional revenue, is uncontrovertibly proved, by the aftonifhing fums which were paid by the public, for agricultural productions, during the late fcarcities, beyond what it had formerly expended on the very fame articles: and as this is a point of fuch great public importance, I have lately endeavoured, with the affiftance of a moft intelligent political arithmetician, (Mr. Arthur Young) to eftimate the amount, on the average of the late fcarcities, compared with former years of plenty.

The three principal articles to be taken into the eftimate are, wheat, barley, and oats; the prices of which, according as the feafon is productive or otherwife, may be thus ftated.

Grain.	Price in Years of Plenty per Bufhel.	Price in Years of Scarcity per Bufhel.
Wheat -	£.0 6 0	£.0 12 0
Barley -	0 3 0	0 6 0
Oats -	0 2 6	0 5 0

It is fuppofed that 9,000,000 of people in the kingdom, confume, at an average, one quarter of wheat each; 500,000, about nine bufhels of barley, and 2,500,000 about 25 bufhels of oats[k]. The difference will then be as follows.

[k] Oats is thus apparently the deareft grain to live on, but the reafon is, that thofe who are maintained on them feldom eat meat, which is not the cafe with thofe who live on wheaten bread.

Grain.

Grain.	No. of Confumers.	Quantity confumed.	Price in plentiful Seafons.	Price in Times of Scarcity.	Difference.
			£.	£.	£.
Wheat	9,000,000	9,000,000	21,600,000	43,200,000	21,600,000
Barley	500,000	562,500	675,000	1,350,000	675,000
Oats	2,500,000	7,812,500	7,812,500	15,625,000	7,812,500
	12,000,000	17,375,000	30,087,500	60,075,000	30,087,500

Enormous as the difference is, namely, £. 30,087,500, it can only be accounted about one half of the fum actually paid by the nation. There is to be added, the additional price of barley confumed in malt liquors, (in times of fcarcity the diftilleries were ftopped), the additional price of oats confumed by horfes, the additional price of beans, and other kinds of pulfe, the additional price of butcher meat, the additional price of milk, of butter, of cheefe, of tallow, of hides, of hay and corn, and other articles confumed by cattle and horfes. In fhort, the total cannot be eftimated at lefs than from fifty to fixty millions fterling.

The whole of the fum, whatever it may amount to, is, in fact, a fpecies of extraordinary tax, the produce of which does not go into the Exchequer, but into the pockets of individuals. It proves, however, what the nation could afford to pay, if, by promoting agricultural improvements, the price of provifions could be kept within reafonable bounds. For can it be doubted, that if from fifty to fixty millions can thus be raifed on agricultural productions alone, in times of fcarcity, if provifions were cheap, and if the fame articles could be purchafed at half the prices, that the public would

be

be enabled to pay into the Exchequer, a large proportion of the sum it saved.

The proposed plan however, could not be attempted with the certainty of success, unless there was a considerable addition to the circulating medium of the country; for otherwise such large sums might occasionally be locked up in the treasury, and all its subordinate departments, as might greatly check commerce and industry. Such an augmentation might be effected in two ways; 1. by issuing Exchequer bills for small sums, as was done with similar views, in the reign of king William during the great recoinage[1], and increasing our paper currency by other means; or, 2. by calling in, and coining, the silver plate of the kingdom.

In

Abundance of circulating wealth necessary.

---

[1] An ingenious author, in a paper intitled, " Two letters describing a method of increasing the quantity of circulating money upon a new and solid principle," printed *anno* 1799, has suggested *stock notes*, or converting fifty millions of the stocks into transferable paper, as a plan entitled to consideration. It was not however a new idea, for some loans in France had been established on the same principle; and in May 1796, I had previously suggested the following plan, in a letter to the minister, of which the following is an extract,

" I have long thought that a part of the stocks might unite the advantages of funded, and of unfunded debt, and of paper currency.

" One set of men prefer permanent stock, but the demand is bounded in that as in other things, and if you increase it beyond the real demand, the value is greatly depreciated.

" Another set prefer transferable securities of all the various descriptions known in this country. There also the demand is limited, and at present the market is overstocked. Transferring

In regard to the latter, it is probably a refource of greater importance than is commonly imagined. The opulent claffes in the community certainly enjoy incomes to the amount of 100 millions *per annum*, and if each of them have, on an average,

---

ring from the one, to the other, unlefs there is really a demand for permanent ftock, will not remedy our prefent pecuniary difficulties, becaufe the circulating medium, the thing wanted, is not increafed.

" But if you convert transferable fecurities, or permanent ftock, into a circulating medium, the objeċt is at once obtained, greatly to the advantage of the public.

" Let us fuppofe for inftance an addition of five millions to the 3 *per cents.* with an option to the creditor to take out his principal in ftate notes, bearing an intereft of 3 *per cent.*, and at any time to replace it in 3 *per cent.* ftock, there are united the advantages of permanent ftock, transferable fecurities, and paper currency.

" Thefe notes would differ from bank notes as they could not be converted into fpecie, and on that account are entitled to intereft. £. 10 at 3 *per cent.* would be fixpence *per* month, which could be eafily calculated.

" Such notes would bring the whole money of the country into circulation, as nobody would keep £. 10 in money in his coffers, if he could get fuch good fecurity bearing intereft.

" Forgeries would be immediately deteċted, (by proper notes indeed might be rendered almoft impoffible), as the notes would be brought to certain public offices half yearly to receive the intereft.

" The imperial loan might thus be raifed both at home and abroad, for the emperor could eafily raife one half of it abroad on thefe notes, which would obviate the objeċtions to the loan in this country, and prevent foreigners concerned in the loan, from being under the neceffity of employing agents here and giving them a commiffion."

plate

plate equal in value to the tenth part of their incomes refpectively, that would amount to ten millions in all: but fuppofe it were only five millions, including the plate of corporations, &c. the fum itfelf would not only be of moment as a loan, (the only one that ought to be negociated), but it would be of ftill greater fervice when coined, from its augmenting the circulating medium, and thus increafing the induftry, and augmenting the revenue of the country.

That the plate would readily be given in, if the public exigencies required it, cannot be doubted. Every individual would fee that it would be much more prudent, in a period of real difficulty, to coin our plate, in order to keep danger at a diftance, than to preferve it in its prefent form, which could only ferve as an additional ftimulus to the enemy, to make every poffible exertion to overcome the difficulties of invafion, for the purpofe of getting over to plunder it.

The only material objeftion to the calling in of the plate is, that the owner thereby lofes the expence of the manufafture, or the *fafhion*[m] as it is called.   But this objeftion is eafily obviated; for if the owners of plate get in lieu thereof, 3 *per cent.* ftock, at a war price, fay from 50 to 55, let the ftock be kept till peace is concluded, and the difference of price will enable the old proprietor to replace his plate, not only without lofs, but manu-

---

[m] A corruption of the French word *Façon,* or workmanfhip.

faftured

factured in the completeft manner, and modelled
in the moft elegant form.

It is alfo proper to obferve, that a large filver
coinage is effential for this country in another
point of view, namely, that filver and not gold is
the metallic medium we ought to encourage. Before the ufe of paper this might not be the cafe,
for, in a commercial nation, it is extremely defirable to have the medium of circulation as portable
as poffible, and confequently it was right to prefer
gold to filver; but now, when all large payments
are made in paper, it would be better to have our
metallic wealth in filver, in order to check the
poffibility of converting our paper circulation too
eafily into money, on every groundlefs public apprehenfion.   A thoufand pounds fterling in gold,
is conveyed away and concealed without much
difficulty; but the conveyance or concealment of
a thoufand pounds in fhillings, could not be fo eafily managed.

Knowledge
of the ftate
of the
country.   The next requifite effential for fo great an operation would be, a perfect knowledge of the ftate
of the country, and the means the moft likely to
raife fo large a fum without public clamour or diftrefs.   For though there may be refources fufficient for that purpofe, yet it may be extremely
difficult to reconcile the minds of the people to fo
heavy and unufual a burden, and it will require
great judgment to impofe it.   And as it feemed
to me impoffible that even the treafury, with all its
means of inveftigation, could obtain the information

mation that was really neceffary, I was thence induced, in February 1798, to fuggeft to his majefty's
minifters, the appointment of a board, by act of
parliament, confifting of feven or any other number of commiffioners that might be thought moft
advifable, for the exprefs purpofe of afcertaining
the beft mode of raifing the fupplies within the
year; fuch commiffioners to be invefted with full
powers to make the neceffary inquiries, to act
without falaries, and to confift of men in whom the
public at large was likely to place peculiar confidence. The appointment of fuch a board would
have convinced the enemy, that we were taking
every means in our power, to obtain refources for
continuing the war, fhould their ambition or info-
lence render it neceffary ".

But even the efforts of fuch a commiffion, however well conftituted, would have been in vain,
unlefs the nation was fatisfied that the minifters of

Confidence
in Govern-
ment.

ª I had even propofed at one time to have taken the fenfe
of the Houfe on the two following motions, namely, 1. That
it is the opinion of this Houfe, that it would be expedient to
appoint commiffioners, for the purpofe of afcertaining the beft
mode of raifing the fupplies within the year, during the farther
continuance of the prefent war; and, 2. That it is the opinion
of this Houfe that the faid commiffioners be farther empowered
to afcertain the beft means of reducing the public expences
both civil and military.

But there was fo fmall a profpect of fucceeding in either,
that I was induced to lay them afide; at the fame time, in the
courfe of fome future war, fome fuch meafures will probably
be found neceffary.

the

the crown were also entitled to the confidence of the people, and were pursuing measures likely to promote the real interests of the country. Such a plan could not be attempted, unless public economy were enforced in all the departments of the state, and unless what was liberally given was wisely expended. I cannot however entertain a doubt, by pursuing such measures as these, when any future exigency may require it, that the supplies may be raised within the year. Let us now proceed to consider the plans which were actually attempted during the late war, with a view of partly carrying such a principle into effect, namely, first by the assessed tax bill in 1798, and afterwards by the tax on income.

3. The aid and contribution tax of 1798.
The little success which had attended the loyalty loan in 1797, rendered it necessary to try some new plan of raising the supplies for the service of the ensuing year; and on the whole the minister thought it most advisable, to obtain a considerable part of the money wanted within the year, by increasing the assessed taxes, by voluntary contributions, and by a tax on imports and exports; and to procure the remainder, by a loan in the usual way.

The nature of his plan will appear from the following statement.

To be raised by the assessed taxes -	£. 4,500,000
To be raised by voluntary contributions	1,500,000
Carry over -	£. 6,000,000

Brought over	£. 6,000,000
To be raiſed by a tax on imports and exports	1,500,000
	£. 7,500,000
Loan, (excluſive of two millions for Ireland)	15,000,000
Total -	£. 22,500,000

But of the fifteen millions borrowed, it was propoſed that eight millions ſhould be repaid by continuing the aſſeſſed taxes, &c. until that could be
accompliſhed[o]; conſequently there remained only
ſeven millions to be provided for by permanent
taxes that year.

The propriety of multiplying the aſſeſſed taxes,
is thus defended by an advocate for the late miniſter.   " Notwithſtanding the various proviſions
" which had been made for the gradual and ſpeedy
" relief of the kingdom from the burdens unavoid-
" ably impoſed upon it, the funds, by the accu-
" mulation of new loans, were brought to a ſtate
" of depreſſion which made it expedient to raiſe a
" conſiderable proportion of the war ſupply within
" the year; the wiſdom of the Legiſlature, and
" the ſpirit of the people, inſtantly combined in a
" vigorous effort for this purpoſe; thus not only
" oppoſing to the enemy the moſt animated exer-
" tions for our own ſecurity, but looking with diſ-
" intereſted magnanimity to the eaſe and happineſs
" of poſterity."

o In fact the plan was ſimilar to the meaſures adopted in the
reign of king William, when taxes were impoſed to repay the
money borrowed in the ſpace of two or three years.

" When

" When the means of carrying into effect this
" plan was under deliberation in the preceding
" year, a tax on capital appeared to be utterly im-
" practicable ; it was demonftrated in the debate
" in the Houfe of Commons, that the affiftance of
" a lawyer and a mathematician would have been
" neceffary in almoft every cafe of real, and in
" many of perfonal, property ; and, if that diffi-
" culty could have been got over, that the whole
" of the interefts in reverfionary eftates (probably
" in value more than half the landed property in
" the kingdom), muft of neceffity have efcaped ;
" in other inftances the groffeft inequalities muft
" have occurred. A direct tax on income was
" next adverted to ; but it was then thought liable
" to many objections. ·Recourfe was therefore
" had to the meafure of a charge varying accord-
" ing to the amount of the affeffed taxes paid by
" perfons in different fituations, as likely to afford,
" though not a certain, yet a tolerably fair crite-
" rion of the income of individuals, to which their
" expenditure was fuppofed in general to be pro-
" portioned."

" Under this mode, the produce was nearly as
" confiderable as the calculation ftated in the
" Houfe of Commons ; and it was more owing to
" the evafions practifed to efcape the tax, than to
" the inefficacy of its principle that it was not
" more fo[p]."

The

The objections made to this measure, both in and out of Parliament were extremely numerous. The following are the most important, extracted from the speech of an intelligent member of the house, (John Nichols, Esq.) delivered on the 3d of January, 1798, and afterwards printed. 1. That the tax is unequal in the manner in which it affects the different classes of society. 2. That it is also unequal in the manner in which it affects different individuals of the same class. 3. That it will compel the higher orders of the middle class to lessen their expences, by which the employment of the artisan will be destroyed. 4. That the revenue arising from taxes on consumption will be rendered less productive, and 5. That if income is made the standard of taxation, Parliament must consent to the means necessary for investigating income, which is not consistent either with the principles of a commercial nation, or with those of civil liberty, or even with domestic happiness.

The assessed taxes, being a species of forced requisition, was extremely unpopular in every part of the kingdom; and the public feeling was so hostile to the attempt, that the minister was obliged to give way, and to modify the plan so as greatly to diminish the produce at which it had been originally estimated. But to the credit of the nation let it be recorded, that what it unwillingly yielded to power, it readily supplied from public zeal. In the words of a political author already quoted, " the voluntary contributions of in-
" dividuals poured into the public coffers by all
" ranks and conditions in the country, vying with
                                            " each

" each other, abundantly compenfated for the de-
" ficiency ; the fovereign and the royal family
" giving very large proportions of their difpofable
" income ; the nobility, gentry, merchants, manu-
" facturers, yeomanry, peafantry, and domeftics,
" coming forward with liberality and chearfulnefs ;
" and even the gallant feamen, foldiers, and
" militia, in addition to their perfonal fervices for
" the national defence, contributed alfo largely to
" it from their pay [q]." Nothing can be more fatisfactory than to narrate fuch an inftance of real
patriotifm. Indeed to the credit of Britifh fubjects
in our colonies abroad, and even in the dominions
of foreign powers, it is to be added, that very large
contributions were fent by them, to aid their native
country in the critical fituation in which it was then
placed.

When the plan of multiplying the affeffed taxes
was firft brought forward, I had refolved to give it
every oppofition in my power, as trenching on the
funding fyftem, to which I had always been peculiarly partial : but a circumftance occurred at the
moment, which induced me to alter that intention.

Great Britain was then juftly confidered as the
only power in Europe, capable of refifting the
efforts of France. The government of that
country therefore, had determined to bend all its
energy, not only to humble the power, but even to
conquer thefe kingdoms ; and openly announced
their intentions, in a proclamation which was publifhed in the Englifh newfpapers, on the very

[q] See brief Examination, &c. p. 28.

morning

morning of that day in which I had propofed to
begin a feries of attacks againft the financial operations of the minifter; inftead of which the circumftance above alluded to, induced me to ftate to
the Houfe, " that having feen the proclamation of
" the French Directory, the object of which was
" to explain to all Europe its intention of invading
" this country, as being the beft mode of bringing
" the conteft to a conclufion ; of eftablifhing what
" they called the freedom of the feas, which was
" tantamount to the deftruction of our naval
" power; and to make England pay the expence
" of the conteft, or in other words to make this
" country tributary to the French; under fuch cir-
" cumftances, I felt it incumbent upon me, as a
" member of that houfe, and a well-wifher to the
" country, not to prefs any thing that might tend
" to fhew there exifted at the time, any difference
" in that houfe regarding the raifing of the fup-
" plies neceffary to carry on the conteft, and
" fhould therefore decline taking the meafures in
" oppofition to the propofed tax, which I had in-
" tended." The Houfe in general feemed to
receive this facrifice at the fhrine of public fpirit,
with much approbation, and any indications of a
contrary difpofition, were amply recompenfed, by
the applaufe which that line of conduct met with,
both at home and on the continent [r].

Before

---

[r] A number of letters were fent to the author upon this occafion, from perfons with whom he had no acquaintance, ap-
proving

Before this subject is dismissed, it may be proper to remark, that if ever the necessities of the times should render a forced loan necessary, the assessed taxes would furnish a criterion sufficiently accurate for levying the sums that might be requisite, and such a loan should only affect the more opulent classes of the community; for there is a material distinction between a contribution by way of loan, and a contribution by way of tax. A contribution by way of loan, is a capital sum that can only be advanced by the opulent. If the taxes to be imposed for paying the interest of that loan, were also to be exacted from the opulent only, it would be absurd to talk of repayment; but the taxes would also be paid by the middling and poorer orders of the community, and consequently those who furnished the capital to such a general contribution, would, in process of time, be in a great measure indemnified, by those who could not conveniently contribute to the principal, though they might to the payment of the interest. In the event of such a loan, if any persons liable to the contribution, could not afford to furnish the whole of the principal, they might dispose of a part, which would sell at a price conformable to the value of stocks at the time, and the general credit of the country.

---

proving of his conduct; and the celebrated Mallet du Pan, then on the continent, informed a confidential correspondent, in England, that the circumstance made an impression abroad, extremely favorable to the interests of this country.

Instead

Inſtead however of a forced loan, to which there are ſo many objections, let us conſider whether a plan might not be formed, by which the nation would be induced to pay the ſum that might be required, without reluctance, in conſideration of the advantages that might be derived from it, not only in a public, but in a private point of view; and this I am perſuaded might be effected by the eſtabliſhment of a general tontine. The nature of that plan I ſhall endeavour briefly to explain under three heads, namely, 1. The contributions to be paid; 2. The advantages to be granted; and 3. The fund whence theſe are to be provided for.

The eagerneſs with which perſons of all ranks, even the humbleſt, enter into benefit ſocieties, and other inſtitutions for the relief of ſickneſs and old age, or the advantage of widows and children, notwithſtanding the riſk they run of being defrauded by thoſe to whom their funds are entruſted, ſufficiently prove the little difficulty that would be found in eſtabliſhing a general ſyſtem for that purpoſe, by which the public expences might be defrayed in time of war, and the debt of the nation might be rapidly diminiſhed, and the improvement of the country greatly promoted, during peace.

Plan of the Contributions for a General Tontine.

When the aſſeſſed tax bill was under conſideration, an account was laid before parliament, of the perſons liable to the duties on windows and inhabited houſes, of which the following is a copy:

	No. of Houses.		No. of Houses.
Houses liable to } 3s. *per ann.*	246,527	Brought over	566,213
From 3s. to 6s. -	19,679	From 9l. to 10l. -	5,060
—— 6s. to 10s. -	26,342	—— 10l. to. 12l. 10s.	6,767
—— 10s. to 15s. -	43,367	—— 12l. 10s. to 15l.	3,387
—— 15s. to 1l. -	43,280	—— 15l. to 17l. 10s.	1,907
—— 1l. to 1l. 5s. -	26,557	—— 17l. 10s. to 20l.	1,155
—— 1l. 5s. to 1l. 10s.	21,974	—— 20l. to 25l. -	1,182
—— 1l. 10s. to 1l. 15s.	17,826	—— 25l. to 30l. -	580
—— 1l. 15s. to 2l.	14,989	—— 30l. to 35l. -	320
—— 2l. to 2l. 5s.	13,628	—— 35l. to 40l. -	187
—— 2l. 5. to 2l. 10s.	10,156	—— 40l. to 45l. -	131
—— 2l. 10s. to 2l. 15s.	6,203	—— 45l. to 50l. -	94
—— 2l. 15s. to 3l.	8,966	—— 50l. to 60l. -	84
—— 3l. to 3l. 10s.	12,955	—— 60l. to 70l. -	60
—— 3l. 10s. to 4l.	10,515	—— 70l. to 80l. -	29
—— 4l. to 4l. 10s.	10,297	—— 80l. to 90l. -	16
—— 4l. 10s. to 5l.	8,047	—— 90l. to 100l. -	9
—— 5l. to 6l. -	9,487	—— 100l. to 150l. -	15
—— 6l. to 7l. -	7,943	—— 150l. to 200l. -	2
—— 7l. to 8l. -	7,613	—— 200l. to 250l. -	1
—— 8l. to 9l. -	5,862	—— 250l. to 350l. -	1
	————— 566,213	Total	587,200

In order to exemplify the nature of the proposed plan, we shall suppose that each person is charged, in proportion to the house he inhabits, a certain sum to be paid weekly as a contribution to the proposed tontine, and to entitle him to the advantages to be derived therefrom. The sums that ought to be charged, and the relative proportions thereof, may be altered as may be thought most expedient, after the plan has been more thoroughly digested. At present it is only necessary fary to remark, that it is propofed to have two forts of contributors, the firft confifting of thofe liable to the houfe tax, the fecond, of thofe who are exempted from that burden, but who would cheerfully pay a fmall weekly contribution, in confideration of the benefits to which they would be intitled.

PLAN of a GENERAL TONTINE.

1ft Clafs.

Perfons liable to the Tax on Houfes.

No. of Perfons contributing.	Propofed Weekly Contribution.		Annual Contribution.		Total.	
	s.	d.	l.	s.	l.	s.
378,195	2	6	6	10	2,359,936	16
76,346	3	0	7	16	595,498	16
38,953	4	0	10	8	405,111	4
12,955	5	0	13	0	168,155	
10,515	6	0	15	12	164,034	
10,297	7	0	18	4	187,405	8
8,047	8	0	20	16	167,377	12
9,487	9	0	23	8	221,995	16
7,943	10	0	26	0	206,518	
7,613	11	0	28	12	217,731	16
5,862	12	0	31	4	182,894	8
5,060	13	0	33	16	176,028	0
6,767	15	0	39	0	263,913	0
3,387	20	0	52	0	176,124	0
1,907	25	0	65	0	123,955	0
1,155	30	0	78	0	90,090	0
1,182	35	0	91	0	107,562	0
580	40	0	104	0	60,320	0
320	45	0	117	0	37,440	0
187	50	0	130	0	24,310	0
131	60	0	156	0	20,436	0
94	70	0	182	0	17,108	0
586,983			Carried over		5,973,944	16

No.

No. of Perfons contributing.	Propofed Weekly Contributions.		Annual Contribution.		Total.	
	s.	d.	l.	s.	l.	s.
586,983					5,973,944	16
84	80	0	208	0	17,472	0
60	90	0	234	0	14,040	0
29	100	0	260	0	7,540	0
16	200	0	520	0	8,320	0
9	300	0	780	0	7,020	0
15	400	0	1040	0	15,600	0
2	500	0	1300	0	2,600	0
1	600	0	1560	0	1,560	0
1	700	0	1820	0	1,820	0
587,200					£.6,049,916	16

2d Clafs.

Perfons exempted from the Tax on Houfes.

	s.	d.	l.	s.	l.	s.
600,000	2	0	5	4	3,120,000	0
500,000	1	6	3	18	1,930,000	0
1,000,000	1	0	2	12	2,600,000	0
400,000	0	9	1	19	780,000	0
300,000	0	6	1	6	390,000	0
2,800,000					£. 8,820,000	0

The following then would be the amount of this contribution.

Clafs.	No. of Contributors.	Total Sum.	
Firft Clafs.	587,000	£.6,049,916	16
Second Clafs.	2,800,000	8,820,000	0
Total.	3,387,000	14,869,916	16

It is evident, that by this plan, about £.14,000,000 might be obtained; and if the finking fund,

fund, now amounting to more than fix millions, were added, it would make a total of twenty millions, which might be raifed within the year, and which would be fufficient to carry on a naval war, conducted with any degree of prudence and economy.

In regard to the advantages to which the con- *Advantages to be granted to the contributors.* tributors to fuch a general tontine may be entitled, it is evident that they ought to be of as diverfified a nature as poffible, leaving it to every one to enter into that clafs or divifion for which he may entertain any peculiar predilection. For inftance, fome may wifh that the money they pay fhould accumulate for their own benefit when they become old; others that it fhould furnifh an annuity for their wives in cafe of furvivency : others for their children, when they come of age; and fo forth. In fhort, tables might be conftructed, *that would take in almoft every poffible cafe,* by means of which the plan would become a popular meafure, nor would the burthen of it be much felt, if provifions were kept at a reafonable rate, and if the circulation of the country was abundant.

It cannot be doubted, that the Sinking Fund, *Fund for payment.* which now yields fix millions per annum, would be a refource much more than fufficient for all the demands to which the Contributors would be entitled for a long period of time; and if no additional loans were to take place, and if the income arifing from the general tontine, were afterwards to be applied, in time of peace, to the diminution of

the

the debt, the public creditors could not object to
the meafure, and the redemption of the debt
would go on at leaft as rapidly as ever. The propofed Tontine therefore, and this plan of employing
the finking fund, could not be oppofed by the
warmeft friend to that redemption.

This plan has hitherto been only confidered in a
financial point of view, but in other refpects it
might alfo be attended with great public advantages ; for if fuch a meafure were carried into
effect, the whole nation would in a manner be
combined into one friendly or amicable affociation,
in the prefervation of which the whole community
would be interefted ; whilft every individual of
that community would have a part of his income,
accumulated in the manner the moft gratifying to
his own feelings, or the moft likely to be of
fervice to himfelf, or his deareft connexions.

4. Income Tax.   The plan of adding to the Affeffed Taxes
being found extremely unpopular, and not having
anfwered in other refpects the expectations formed
of its fuccefs, it was thought neceffary to try fome
other fyftem, and the celebrated tax on Income was
brought forward.   The friend and advocate of the
minifter, has thus explained the general principles
on which that meafure was founded.   " The in-
" equality, however, of the affeffment, (exclufive
" of that occafioned by evafion,) and ftill more of
" the contributions, was evident ; but the principle
" of raifing a large part of the fupply within the
" year was eftablifhed, and a meafure was effected,
                                          " which

" which had been frequently contemplated by
" theorifts in political economy with all that par-
" tiality to which its effects, in various points of
" view, feemed reafonably to entitle it; but they
" had fcarcely ventured to hope for its actual
" adoption in a country already burdened fo heavily
" as ours, where it might be fuppofed fatal to the
" popularity of the minifter who fhould propofe it,
" and adverfe to the immediate interefts of the
" people whom it was to affect.   It *has been*
" adopted however, ftill more effectually by the
" tax on Income, and it is no lefs flattering to the
" national pride, than it is promifing to the national
" fecurity and welfare, to confider that the good
" fenfe, the forefight, and the refolution of the
" people have kept pace with, and in fome degree
" anticipated the ideas of Government on the
" fubject.   The principle, the general propofition
" was recommended by the country.   The queftion
" of the beft mode of carrying into effect was left
" for the talents of the minifter to propofe to par-
" liament, where it was difcuffed, matured, and
" completed '."

As this obnoxious burden was repealed, by the
fucceffor of the minifter who propofed it, either
with the concurrence, or at leaft without any oppofition on the part of his predeceffor; and as in
all probability it will never again be revived, it does
not feem neceffary to enter into any detail of the
various debates, and other proceedings, which took

' Brief Examination, &c. p. 28.

place

place in parliament, regarding this celebrated financial tranfaction; but having ftated very fully to the
houfe, my fentiments upon the fubject, I hope the
reader will excufe me, for recording, in this publication, the opinions which I then urged, more
efpecially as I have ftill no reafon to call in
queftion their juftnefs or policy. The principal
debate regarding the Income tax took place on the
14th December, 1798, on which occafion the
author delivered himfelf in the following terms.

" Mr. Speaker,

" I arife to oppofe the motion made by the Right Honourable
Gentleman, (Mr. Pitt,) for taking into our further confideration the bill which he has propofed, from the full conviction,
that the prefent is fo exceptionable a meafure, that it is impoffible, by the efforts of any Committee whatever, to make it
entitled to the approbation of the Houfe; and I am induced
thus early to take the liberty of addreffing myfelf to you,
becaufe I think that it is a duty peculiarly incumbent upon
thofe, who have directed their attention to financial inquiries,
to prevent, by every poffible exertion, the paffing of fuch a
bill into a law. I fhall endeavour, however, with as much
brevity as the importance of the queftion will admit of, to explain what has occurred to me on this interefting fubject."
" The Houfe is fully aware, that for raifing thofe extraordinary fupplies which are neceffary to defray the expences of
war, one, of four meafures, has been ufually adopted. In fome
countries, a treafure has been accumulated for that purpofe in
time of peace: in others the neceffary fupplies have been
raifed within the year: according to a third plan, the fums
wanted have been levied by compulfive loans, of which there
was lately an inftance under the directorial tyranny of France:
the laft plan, is that of raifing money by means of voluntary
loans, or through the medium of what is called *the funding
fyftem*;

syftem; a mode of raifing money which fome gentlemen are inclined to reprobate, becaufe they only contemplate its defects, but which I have ever confidered, as the climax of financial invention, the greateft of all political difcoveries, the moft valuable mine that ever a nation was poffeffed of, and, in a peculiar manner, the fource of the ftrength, the profperity, and the happinefs of this country. Indeed, Sir, (without tiring the Houfe by a ftatement of the variety of arguments that might be urged in its favour, with which I am perfuaded that every individual who now hears me, muft be already familiarly acquainted,) it may be fufficient to remark, that if we had attempted to carry on our wars on any other plan, in confequence of the inability of the fubject to bear the preffure of additional taxes, either thofe wars muft have been in the higheft degree unfuccefsful, from the want of funds to carry them on, or the people would have been driven, by oppreffion and defpair, into a ftate of infurrection ; nor could we have preferved, as we have hitherto been fortunately enabled to do, amidft all the calamities of war, that beft fource of public profperity, the means of induftry and of reproduction.''

" But, we are told, that we have funded too much already ; that the price of ftocks is low ; that money cannot be borrowed in large fums, except on very difadvantageous terms : that we ought to hufband the funding fyftem ; that we muft pay a falvage for the protection of our property ; and, above all, that we are now under the neceffity of reforting to a new financial expedient, namely, that of borrowing a part, and of raifing the remainder of the extraordinary fupplies by taxes within the year.''

" There can hardly be, in my opinion, a more erroneous idea. If the funding fyftem is at all to be abandoned, inftead of purfuing this miferable expedient, the refult of irrefolution and timidity, we ought manfully to refolve to raife, not the half, but the whole fupplies within the year. By following the plan that is propofed, we fhall neither enjoy the advantages of the one fyftem, nor of the other, whilft we muft feel the difadvantages of both.''

" If all the taxes were raifed within the year, the money of the kingdom would not be collected in the metropolis, for the

purpofes of a loan ; fo that there would be a greater quantity
of wealth in the country, applicable to the payment of the extraordinary taxes to be impofed ; whereas, if we have both a
loan in London, and extraordinary contributions in the country,
it is abfurd to imagine, that the circulating wealth of the nation
will be equally divided : hence, there muft be either a deficiency
of money in the country, to pay the taxes, or a want of money
in the capital, to furnifh the loan."

" It is next contended, that the new fyftem has already anfwered in practice ; and to it, we are told, ought to be attributed, the prefent flourifhing ftate of our public credit, and
what is called the high price of ftocks. There never were
more groundlefs affertions. During the American war, the
loweft price that the funds ever reached, was in February
1782, when the 3 *per cents.* were never lower than 53⅛, though
no artificial means were made ufe of to buoy them up by means
of weekly purchafes. When the bargain for the loan was concluded in April laft, the 3 *per cent.* confols were above 48 ; they
are now at 54. Is it poffible to fuppofe therefore, that this
plan has at all materially contributed to increafe the price of
ftocks ? The difference is 6 *per cent.* Can no other caufe be
affigned for that rife, but the meafure now under contemplation ?
Is nothing, for inftance, to be attributed to the land-tax redemption bill, which, I am informed, has partially fucceeded
in particular diftricts, and the beneficial confequences of which
we hear fo much on other occafions ?—nothing to the aftonifhing increafe of our commercial wealth, and the improvement of our agricultural refources ; and nothing to our naval
victories ; to which, indeed, more than to the financial meafures
of the Right Honourable Gentleman, (Mr. Pitt,) our prefent
profperous fituation ought to be afcribed ? In fhort, four caufes
are affigned for this rife of 6 *per cent.* as fuits beft the convenience of the minifter. Let us give each of them a fair proportion, namely, 1½ *per cent.* Let us fuppofe that we have occafion for twenty-five millions this year, and that we borrow
the whole, inftead of raifing a part, on the new principle,
within the year, the difference, at the rate of 1½ *per cent.* is but
375,000*l.* and for that paltry and miferable fum, the whole

nation

nation is to be fubjected to the grievous oppreffion of this in. tolerable meafure."

" Let us admit, however, for the fake of argument, that it is wife and politic, to raife a part of the fupplies within the year, and that it has been found beneficial in practice ; it next becomes a matter of queftion, whether the affeffed tax bill of laft year, is not as fair a mode of raifing that contribution, as the new fyftem that is fuggefted ? And after all the arguments ufed in favour of that bill, and the ftrong language in which it was fupported in both Houfes, it is a circumftance hardly to be credited, that it fhould now be propofed to repeal that plan, and to fubftitute another in its ftead.   If the members of this Houfe in particular, were to recollect the many ftrong declara- tions which were made in its favour, from authorities they are in general accuftomed to liften to, with peculiar attention and re- fpect, they would probably hefitate, in regard to the adoption of a new fyftem, for raifing any part of the fupplies within the year."

" Indeed the queftion is, whether it is not better to have fome criterion, than none at all ? By having a criterion, you ftand fome chance of preventing evafion, and, above all, you render a harfh inquifitorial difclofure of property unneceffary : but if you have none, unlefs the moft oppreffive and tyrannical fyftem is purfued, the whole income you can expect to derive from the meafure, will depend on the voluntary zeal, and, un- fortunately, the lax morality, of the great body of the people, who have already fhown, what may be expected from them, when you appeal to their confciences on the fubject of taxation."

" But if a new plan muft be adopted, and if property, inftead of expenditure, muft be attacked, it becomes a matter of nice difcuffion, whether the extraordinary contribution fhould be raifed by a tax on capital, or a tax on income, or by blending the two together, which, though the moft complicated, yet being unqueftionably the jufteft, ought to be preferred. What I mean is, that every man fhould pay inftead of 10 *per cent.* on his income, ½ *per cent.* on his capital, and 5 *per cent.* on his in- come, by which perfons who had no capital, would be greatly relieved,

relieved, and thofe who were poffeffed of confiderable property, would pay more in proportion to their opulence, than under the fyftem that is propofed."

" Almoft the only objection to this plan is, the difficulty of afcertaining the value of a man's capital.   But is it not the fame in regard to his income, unlefs it arifes from fome fixed and regular ftipend, and is liable to no uncertainty of deduction ? Let us confider this important part of the fubject, in the three great lines, of a landed income, of a commercial income, and of a profeffional income."

" A landed income may be fuppofed the moft certain and permanent, and in fome particular inftances it may be fo ; but, in general, a perfon of landed property, after deducting every public tax or impofition to which he is liable, is fubject to a variety of burdens.   In the firft place, he is frequently under the neceffity of being at very heavy legal expences for preferving his property, and he is clearly entitled to deduct thofe expences, as it is propofed that the public fhall avail itfelf of that part of his income, by taxing the gentlemen of the law.   In the fecond place, he is under the neceffity of fpending money in the improvement of his eftates, as in draining, fencing, building, &c. And in the third place, any perfon of landed property is fubject to a variety of deductions in confequence of the rank he holds in the ftate : he is obliged to act as fheriff, as juftice of the peace, and other public fituations, without any recompence or emolument whatfoever ; and if any plan is in agitation, for building a bridge, for making a turnpike road, or forming a canal, which may ultimately prove of material confequence to the neighbourhood, a gentleman of landed property, muft fubfcribe to all fuch meafures, unlefs it is intended to check by law the progrefs of public improvement."

" It is ftill more difficult to afcertain the income of the commercial individual, whofe capital and income, indeed, are in fact fo intimately combined together, that it is impoffible to feparate them.   The income of a commercial man, alfo, depends upon a variety of circumftances befides his capital ; it depends on the fituation in which he happens to be placed, the connexions which he has formed or inherited, the talents which he employs

in

in his bufinefs, and the induftry with which he profecutes it.
Are we to tax fituation ? That was given up in the cafe of the
famous fhop-tax. Are we to tax the advantage derived from
connexion ? It would be the firft time that any individual ever
paid any demand to the Exchequer, for having a number of
friends, and probably deferving them. Are we to tax talents ?
It would be a ftrange circumftance in finance, to impofe burdens
upon thofe, by whofe ingenuity new arts were difcovered, or
the old ones improved; who contribute fo effentially to enrich
the nation, and who are juftly accounted the fureft fource of its
commercial profperity. Or, above all, are we to tax induftry ?
If fo, the man that is idle and profligate will pay nothing ;
whereas the fober and induftrious will be burdened in proportion
to their exertions."

" Let us next confider how profeffional men can afcertain
their incomes. To what a variety of cafualties are they not
expofed ? They may be difabled by ficknefs ? they may be
injured by ill-founded perfonal, or even political prejudices
entertained againft them ; or their profits may be impaired by
public calamity and diftrefs. Indeed, many of them muft be
ruined by this bill, which muft diminifh, in various inftances,
their profeffional bufinefs ; and all of them will be entitled to
the deduction of a full third of their clear income, which every
prudent profeffional man does ufually deduct, to form a provifion
for himfelf in his old age, and a capital for his family at his
death."

" Thefe circumftances prove, that it is as difficult to eftimate
income, as to afcertain the value of capital, and are ftrongly in
favour of that blended fyftem, which feems to be the only juft
principle, on which fuch a tax or contribution as this can be
impofed."

" Indeed, how is it poffible to demand, at the fame rate,
from a perfon who has an income without a capital, and from
one who has both income and capital ?—One perfon, for inftance, draws his fubfiftence from an income of 600l. a year,
from the profeffion of the law ; at 10 *per cent.* he is charged
with 60l. to the Exchequer, which he muft deduct from his income. Another perfon has 20,000l. of 3 *per cent.* confolidated
annuities,

annuities, producing him 600 *l.*   At 10 *per cent.* he will only
pay 60 *l.* alfo, though, by felling only about 120 *l.* of his 3
per cents, according to the price of the ftocks, he pays his tax,
and only lofes about 3 *l.* 12 *s. per annum* of his income.   Where
then is that boafted equality which is faid to be fo much in favour of this plan, and which renders it fo infinitely fuperior to
every other ?"

    " On thefe grounds, I cannot help thinking, that if the
meafure is at all to be adopted, it ought to be altered, on the
principle which I have now taken the liberty of recommending,
namely, that of laying the tax, partly on capital, and partly
on income."

    " Let us now, Sir, proceed to confider, the fpecific plan
that is fubmitted to our confideration, in the prefent bill."

    " The Houfe muft ftill recollect, the elaborate fpeech, in
which the Right Hon. Gentleman laid before us, a general
view of the income, fuppofed to be enjoyed, by all the various
claffes of the community.   In fome points I may differ with him;
and when I heard the Honourable Gentleman, expreffing himfelf with fo much doubt, refpecting various particulars, and
refting on the antiquated notions of Davenant, and the gueffes
of modern authorities, I could not help wifhing, that the
Honourable Gentleman had given more affiftance to an inftitution I had the honour of fuggefting; I mean, Sir, the Board
of Agriculture, by whom all thefe points, had it been properly
fupported, would have been, before this time, fully afcertained.   It has ever been a favourite opinion with me, that no
country could be well governed, unlefs its real fituation was
thoroughly known—" *Ad confilium de republica dandum, caput
eft, noffe rempublicam.*"   Indeed, had not the progrefs of that
inftitution been checked, by thofe who were regardlefs of the
interefts of the country they governed, provided they could
gratify their own perfonal fpleen and refentment, we fhould
now have been debating, not on loofe calculations, and uncertain data, but on a general report on the ftate of the country,
founded on authentic information, which it would have been
in my power, before this time, to have laid upon the table of
this Houfe."

                                                " But

" But let us suppose, that the calculations of the Honourable Gentleman, if not perfectly just, yet are sufficiently accurate for the purposes of discussion ; and that the various classes of the community, which he has enumerated, have an income of one hundred millions per annum ; yet I question much, whether they really can afford to pay, any thing like so large a sum as ten millions, in the course of one year, in addition to the thirty millions (including the expence of the collection) which they already yield to the Exchequer."

" The persons who will be subjected to this new tax on income, may be divided into three classes."

" The first consists of those who already save a part of their income, and who, by this act, will be obliged, however reluctantly, to part with a portion of those savings which they were anxious to lay up. It is the principal object of this bill, to get at this description of individuals. But I do not think that this resource is any thing like so considerable as Gentlemen imagine. If we suppose that there are 3000 persons, who enjoy, at an average, 1000 l. each (which in these luxurious times, will include, I am persuaded, all the misers in the kingdom), the total income they possess, will not exceed 3,000,000l. *per annum*, and the tax will not produce above 300,000l.

" Another description of persons, are those who formerly lived up to the full extent of their income, or perhaps beyond it, but who will now begin to save, and to reduce their establishments, in order to pay this new contribution. I am afraid this class will be a very numerous one, and that to the full amount they are compelled to pay to this tax on income, we shall lose in the excise and customs, and other branches of the revenue."

" The only remaining class, consists of those who will continue to live as formerly. Perhaps, indeed, they cannot retrench, owing to the largeness of their family, their professional situations, and various other circumstances. Having neither saved the money before, nor being able to save it now, they must either deduct it from their capital (if they have any), or borrow it where they can find it."

" And

" And this leads me again to allude, to the great difadvantage of blending the two fyftems together, namely, that of borrowing money for the public fervice, and of raifing the fupplies
within the year. The confequence of a public loan is, that all
the money of the kingdom, not only flocks into the metropolis,
but alfo into the hands of a particular fet of individuals who job
in the funds. What follows? It is evident that any private
perfon cannot borrow money almoft on any terms. Whereas,
if there were no loan, the circulating wealth of the kingdom,
would be fpread over the whole furface of the country; the
loan-mongers of London, would be glad to lend their money
on refpectable private fecurities, and lefs difficulty would be
found, in raifing the whole of the fupplies within the year, than
the proportion which it is propofed, by this bill, fhould be
levied."

" We fhall fuppofe, however, that the nation is able to pay
the propofed tax of 10 *per cent.* on income; yet, when I confider the various objections which may be urged againft it, fome
of which go to the very root of the meafure, and others, which,
though they affect only particular branches of it, yet are almoft
of equal moment,—I can fcarcely think that the Houfe will be
difpofed to pafs fuch a bill into a law."

" The radical objections are three; namely, that the meafure in queftion will promote emigration, will diminifh the produce of the old taxes, and will raife the price of all the neceffaries
of life."

" There is no circumftance, fo likely to be apprehended
from this meafure, as the emigration of the induftrious claffes
of the community. If, in addition to all the ufual taxes to
which the people of the country are fubjected, nnd which are
in general reckoned tolerably oppreffive, perfons are alfo made
liable to a compulfive difclofure of property, which has ever
been accounted fo odious and vexatious a meafure, and alfo to
have that property feverely taxed, it muft induce great multitudes of individuals, to defert a country, where they are fubjected to fuch grievous oppreffion, and to find out fome quiet
afylum, where they may efcape fuch rapacity. If fuch a circumftance were to take place, and it is evidently not impoffible,
nor

nor in my opinion, improbable, it would be the fource of infinite mifchief to this country. If the ingenious mechanic, the
induftrious artifan, the adventurous manufacturer, the hardy
feaman, the intelligent merchant, and the fkilful hufbandman,
oppreffed by financial exactions, are driven from this formerly
happy ifland, what will become of the boafted power and opulence of the Britifh nation ? Some are already gone, and others
are perhaps preparing to follow their footfteps. The paffing of
fuch a law as this, muft confirm any refolution they have taken,
and may banifh for ever from this country, fome of the moft
valuable fubjects it can at prefent boaft of."

   " Another material objection is, that it will occafion a very
fatal reduction in the produce of the old taxes. Many luxurious gratifications, which furnifh an ample revenue to the Exchequer, muft be curtailed or abandoned. Many people are
already confidering, whether they ought, or ought not to re-
plenifh their pipes and fnuff-boxes, on which depends a branch
of revenue (that on tobacco), yielding to the amount of
700,000*l. per annum*. Other articles muft fuffer in proportion.
If the national income, as ftated by the Right Honourable Gentleman (Mr. Pitt), is one hundred millions, we pay about thirty
millions of that fum to the Exchequer at prefent ; for which
fome allowance ought to have been made in his ftatements :
and if we are reduced to the private expenditure of fixty inftead
of feventy millions, there muft be a confiderable defalcation
from the thirty millions formerly paid : and if the fpirit of
economy is once introduced into the eftablifhments of private
families, which I think is likely to be the refult of fo violent a
meafure, that *cold economy* may continue ; in which cafe we fhall
lofe a permanent for a temporary advantage ; and thofe taxes,
on the produce of which depend the payment of our public
creditors, and the fubfiftence of our fleets and armies, may become inadequate to the purpofe. This is a point, in which
many perfons who now hear me, are deeply interefted, who are
thinking little at prefent, how much they are perfonally concerned in thefe difcuffions."

   " A third radical objection is, the effect that this tax will
have, in raifing the price of all the neceffaries of life ; infomuch,
                                                            that

that the middling and lower orders of the community will find it difficult to fubfift under it.   Several articles of general confumption, as falt, fugar, coals, &c. are already exorbitantly high, and muft become ftill more fo.   Indeed, if we feverely tax thofe who raife or produce the neceffaries of life, and thofe who deal in them, it is evident, that they will endeavour to throw the load off their own fhoulders, and will contrive to make the unfortunate confumer, pay tenfold, for the taxes to which they themfelves are fubjected."

" I fhall now proceed, to ftate fome objections of a lefs important nature, becaufe they are capable of being removed ; but which, at the fame time, unlefs they can be obviated, ought to prove fatal to the meafure."

" The firft point I fhall touch upon, under this head, relates to the taxing of the funds, which muft alarm every one, attached to the old financial fyftem and doctrines of this country, in oppofition to the new political dogmas, which, in thefe days, are fo boldly inculcated.   By the laws, as they now ftand, the interefts or dividends paid to the public creditors, are protected againft all charges and taxes whatfoever ; but, for the firft time, they are now introduced into the budget of the Chancellor of the Exchequer."

" It is faid, that there is no direct tax upon the funds ; that we do not intercept the money, as it goes into the pocket of the creditor ; but that we only put our hands into his pocket afterwards, and inform him, whether he confents or not, he muft, *at his peril*, (the words of the precept of the commiffioners are, ' thereof fail not at your peril') deliver over to us, a tenth part of that fum of money, which we affured him, when he lent the principal, was to be exempted from all taxes and charges whatfoever.   What a miferable evafion ! Indeed, if this principle of indirect and involuntary taxation, is once admitted in regard to the funds, there is no faying to what height it may be carried.   What is the remedy ? The remedy is an eafy one, and has been practifed on all occafions, when the principal or the intereft of the public creditor has been affected—let books be opened for receiving the names of all the creditors, who affent to this new mode of holding their property, and let it go no

farther

farther than to the perfons who fubfcribe.. I truft that a very large majority of the creditors, if not the whole of them, would agree to the propofal, and voluntarily fubject themfelves..to the new tax. At any rate, no confideration whatever, ought, in my opinion, to induce this Houfe, to countenance any paltry evafion, by which its folemn faith, pledged to the public creditors, can, to the fmalleft poffible extent, be violated."

" The next point I wifh to allude to, can alfo be remedied in the committee on the bill. It relates to the idea of taxing perfons refiding in this country, for the property which they poffefs in other parts of his Majefty's dominions ; for inftance, in Ireland and the Weft Indies. This feems to me unjuft in its principle ; and, fo far as my information reaches, without example in the financial hiftory of this, or of any other country. Both, in Ireland and in the Weft Indies, there are feparate legiflatures, who enjoy the privilege of impofing taxes, on the property of thofe who are fubject to their refpective jurifdictions ;— a privilege which they exercife to a confiderable extent. Taxing property in other places, by the authority of the Britifh Parliament, is reviving the old and exploded doctrines, which laid the foundation of the unfortunate war with America. But, Sir, I doubt, firft, the right, and, fecondly, the policy of this meafure. In regard to the right, taxes are defcribed to be ' a portion which each fubject contributes of his property, in order to fecure the remainder.' If this definition is a juft one, and it is Judge Blackftone's, we have no right to take the produce of the property of Ireland, except to defend Ireland ; nor the produce of the property of Jamaica, except to defend Jamaica. In regard to the impolicy of the attempt, it is, if poffible, ftill clearer. The effect of impofing fo heavy a burden upon perfons refiding here, with their property elfewhere, muft be, not only to drive them out of this country, but alfo to prevent others from coming into it ; in which cafe, we fhall not only lofe the propofed exaction, but alfo the taxes which they pay in various other ways ; and alfo, all the advantages we derive, from the circulation of from five to fix millions per annum."

" The only other point I wifh to touch upon at prefent, relates to the new inquifitorial power about to be eftablifhed."

" That

" That some regulations are neceſſary, in order to prevent evaſion, can hardly be queſtioned ; but that they ſhould be ſo very ſtrict, or rather ſo boldly tyrannical, as thoſe which are pointed out in this bill, ſeems to me completely inadmiſſible. To tempt a man to perjury, and to ſubject him, at the ſame time, to an inquiſitorial power, in order to make him condemn himſelf, is the height of cruelty and injuſtice. For my part, I think it infinitely preferable, that we ſhould loſe ſome money, than run the riſk of eſtabliſhing principles, abhorrent to that free conſtitution which this country has hitherto boaſted of. This is a part of the ſubject, however, which will require to be diſ-cuſſed, with peculiar anxiety, in a future ſtage of our pro-ceedings."

" But, Sir, it may be ſaid, that this is certainly a harſh mea-ſure, and liable to endleſs objections; at the ſame time, What can be done ? Some great meaſure of finance is now eſſential for the public ſafety, and if you oppoſe this meaſure, you ought to ſuggeſt ſomething elſe that may anſwer in its room."

" I cannot poſſibly ſubſcribe to that doctrine. No Member of the Houſe, is bound to do more, than to deliver his ſentiments on public meaſures, as they are reſpectively brought forward. No private individual, can have acceſs to that minute informa-tion, without which it is impoſſible to judge, whether a meaſure can be prejudicial to the public intereſt, or otherwiſe. But if there is any doubt regarding the beſt mode of raiſing the ſup-plies, let a ſelect Committee of the Houſe be appointed for the inveſtigation of that ſubject, armed with authority to ſend for perſons, papers, and records. The Houſe and the Public may be aſſured, if a proper ſelect Committee were appointed, that all the financial difficulties we are involved in would be removed ; and ſurely, ſince we had out-of-door committees, gravely deliberating on the beſt mode of levying taxes, and who have favoured us with their public declarations on the ſub-ject of finance, there can hardly be any well-grounded objection to the meaſure I have ſuggeſted ; and I hope, from the geſtures of the Right Honourable Gentleman (Mr. Pitt), that he ap-proves of, and will ſupport the idea."

" It

" It will naturally be expected, that on such an occasion, I
should again take the liberty of recommending to the attention
of the House, that most valuable of all resources, I mean
economy.   We are told by a celebrated statesman of antiquity,
whose orations the Right Honourable Gentleman has so frequently perused, and so closely imitates, I mean Cicero, " *opti-*
" *mum, & in privatis familiis, & in republica vectigal est, par-*
" *simonium:*" and I am perfectly satisfied, there would be no
difficulty, instead either of borrowing the sum in question, or
raising it by means of an extraordinary and harsh contribution, to save a large proportion of it, by a rigorous spirit of
retrenchment, in all our establishments both of income and expenditure."

" With a view of ascertaining the disposition of the House
towards economical arrangements, I thought it advisable, to
embrace the happy opportunity, which our late glorious naval
successes had furnished, of suggesting a very moderate reduction in our favourite service of the navy; because I was fully
persuaded, that, if it could be introduced there, it would not be
difficult to extend it afterwards, to all our other establishments.
I knew well it would be an unpopular suggestion, but I could
not hesitate, from any apprehension of that sort, to recommend
a measure, which seemed to me so necessary and so useful to the
public ; and which, if the war should continue much longer,
must, sooner or later, be adopted."

" Indeed, in my opinion, nothing could raise more the
character of the nation abroad, or give more satisfaction to the
people at home, than our enforcing a system of economy.   It
is well known, that in private life that individual is alone independent and respectable, who, without being too parsi-
monious, is yet attentive to his expenditure.   The same is the
case with nations.   In regard to the people at home, the minister may suppose, as they have submitted quietly to so many
burdens, that they will continue patient under more : he may
find himself mistaken.   By a profuse expenditure of the public
money he may secure the cry of those, who are preying on the
vitals of the public, and perhaps, for the moment, the assistance
of corrupt and profligate men ; but he will soon lose, what

every

every wife minifter would prize above all other acquifitions, the fatisfaction of his own mind, the confidence of a generous Sovereign, and the fupport of a great country."

" I fhall now, Sir, ftate fome additional confiderations to the Houfe, which feem to me decifively hoftile to the meafure in queftion."

" The firft is, the great tendency that the paffing of fuch a bill will have, towards perpetuating the war, and promoting public profufion. As foon as it is afcertained, that ten millions of additional revenue can be raifed upon the public, it will be confidered as a fund for borrowing, and at 5 *per cent.* would pay the intereft of two hundred millions of money. What a temptation to continue the war, when perhaps peace might be obtained on reafonable terms, and to carry it on with the moft unbounded extravagance and profufion !"

" Befides, Sir, is it poffible to imagine, if this tax is once impofed, that we fhall ever get rid of it ? Whilft the war continues, it is certain we cannot; and if peace were to be proclaimed to morrow, it is at leaft queftionable, whether fuch an addition to the public revenue, would not be neceffary, from the enormous peace eftablifhment, which the circumftances of the times may occafion, at leaft in the opinion of thofe, with whom cold economy is no particular favourite. And indeed, if it fhould not be found neceffary on account of our peace eftablifhment, fuch an addition to the public revenue, will be extremely convenient, to affift in difcharging the national debt, as a commutation for other taxes, or on fome fuch fimilar pretence."

" It is further neceffary to obferve, that this bill lays a foundation for endlefs vexatious exactions. The minifter now very moderately requires only a tenth part of our income ; but he eftablifhes a principle, that the Government of this country is entitled to demand a certain part of the income of each individual, and is alfo entitled, to enforce that compulfive requifition, by the ftricteft and harfheft regulations. Formerly, Sir, our principal taxes, arifing from confumption, and not extending to many of the real comforts and neceffaries of life, were in a manner voluntary. The exchequer was enriched, and

and the people were happy; and the profusion of Government was fortunately checked by the conviction, that, if the taxes were carried beyond a certain length, the produce, instead of increasing, would diminish. But, Sir, if this bill passes, the whole property of the country will in future lie at the mercy of the Minister; and though he now proposes to exact but a tenth part, what is to hinder him next year, from demanding a fifth, or even a third of our respective incomes?—Allow me to ask, how long it can be expected, that either the wealth or the industry of the people can hold out, under even the apprehension and terror of such exactions."

" Such, Sir, are the objections which have occurred to me, against this fatal measure, one, to which the attention of the House, and of the public at large, cannot be too earnestly and anxiously directed. The only answer likely to be given to these objections, and indeed the only arguments that can be urged in support of the measure itself, are those philippics against the French Directory, with which the Right Honourable Gentleman, and his friends, are accustomed to interlard their orations, and by which they endeavour to inflame the passions, and to perplex the understandings of a partial auditory. Permit me, however, to take the liberty of asking, What have such declamations to do with the present question? I detest the ambitious projects of the French Directory, as much as that Honourable Gentleman or his friends, and will go as great lengths to resist them. —But because the French Directory are ambitious, must the people of England be oppressed, and must we on that account give way, and submit, even without a struggle, to such a mischievous project as the one now under consideration; a project, Sir, which could only have been occasioned by the most unbounded profusion, could only have originated in the harshest tyrannical principles, and must either terminate, in the disgrace and ruin of the bold projector, or the destruction of the nation?"

" I have thus, Sir, stated at some length, but not longer than the importance of the question demands, my sentiments regarding it; and I earnestly intreat, that the Members of this

House, divesting themselves of partiality for one individual, and of prejudice against others, will consider the subject itself dispassionately, as one on which depends the future happiness of this country. Let them resolve, instead of taking a measure at this moment blindly upon trust, because it happens to be introduced by a favourite Minister, let them resolve, on the present occasion, to see with their own eyes, to hear with their own ears, and to be directed by their own judgment. Let them be assured, if they suffer this bill to pass, that it will be an event, which they themselves will severely repent of, when it will unfortunately be too late, and which their posterity will have just cause to lament, as one of the greatest calamities that could possibly have befallen that country they were doomed to inherit. Let them also be assured, if such a bill as this meets with their approbation, that the British House of Commons, will no longer be considered as that respectable Senate, whose conduct has formerly been looked up to, with admiration and respect, not only in this country, but in every other, where any vestige of liberty, or freedom of opinion exists; but that it will be accounted, a degraded chamber of commerce and finance, calculated solely for the purpose, of registering the edicts of a Minister, without knowledge of their contents, or conviction of their utility."

The minister having determined to carry through the plan, all opposition was fruitless, and in order to reconcile the minds of the nation to so heavy and so obnoxious a burden, a paper was written by a person connected with Government, who has defended the tax with considerable ability, and endeavoured to refute the various objections which have been urged against it. The impartiality of an historian renders it incumbent upon me, to state the observations of this ingenious writer, leaving the reader to form his own opinion, after having

thus

thus had the arguments both for and againft the meafure laid before him.

" Under the exifting circumftances, a tax upon all income has appeared to the parliament of the country to be the moft equal and practicable mode of raifing the neceffary fupplies: that it is practicable, no perfon has denied; that it is equal, has indeed by a few perfons been difputed. We do not mean to contend, that to this as well as to every other work of man, many very plaufible objections may not be ftated; we do not mean to contend, that in particular cafes it will not bear heavily on individuals, much more fo certainly than could be wifhed. The hardfhip in thefe cafes, however, arifes from the neceffity of raifing the money, and not from the mode in which it is propofed to raife it; for we venture to affirm, that this fyftem is, even upon the face of it, infinitely more equal than any which has ever been adopted, and that, in the progrefs of the bill, relief has been given in every cafe in which it was poffible to afford it, without affecting the fuccefs of the meafure.

" The firft objection that has been ftated to the bill, is, the injuftice of taxing different forts of income in the fame propor- tion and by the fame rule; for that there is a great difference between fixed incomes, uncertain and fluctuating incomes, fuch as incomes from trade or profeffions, incomes for life, and in- comes for years.

" That there is a difference between thefe various incomes no perfon can deny: this difference the bill finds, and certainly does not propofe to remedy; but, by taxing them all in the fame proportion, it leaves the different forts of income in the fame relative ftate in which it found them. Can any reafon be ftated why the favings and accumulations of fome fhould not contribute their proportionate fhare, as well as the expenditure of others? This is a meafure by which we tax ourfelves largely in the prefent year, to diminifh the permanent burden upon ourfelves and our pofterity. Thefe accumulations and favings, when they come into expenditure (which in the courfe of a few years *muft* be the cafe), will partake equally in the benefit of the meafure, and is it not juft therefore that they fhould contribute

tribute their fhare towards the fuccefs of it. The individual
who fpends his whole income, in fupporting a certain fituation
in life, is as important a character (though not more fo) in
the general ftate of fociety, as he who faves or accumulates.
From him you take a part of his expenditure, from the other
a part of his favings and accumulations. The real confequence or vanity of the former, is affected in as great a degree
by a diminution of his expenditure, as the fame qualities are in
the latter, by diminifhing his means of accumulation. Their
relative fituation in fociety, their advantages or difadvantages,
remain in that cafe precifely the fame. The increafing part of
the community can certainly contribute their proportion with
lefs prefent inconvenience or diftrefs to themfelves; but this
advantage is balanced by the confideration, that the growth of
their property is in fome degree retarded.

" But it is urged, that it is not juft to tax incomes for life,
or for years, in the fame proportion in which you tax perpetual
incomes. This objection is founded on a miftake of the whole
principle of the bill. The only advantage which the individual, whofe income is perpetual, poffeffes over the annuitant is,
that he has it in his power to fell or mortgage a part of his
property for the purpofe of paying the tax. Now the object
of this bill is, to raife out of the *income of the year* a certain part
of the fupplies, without impofing any burden upon pofterity;
and if individuals fhould burden a part of their property with a
view of paying this tax, in proportion as that fhould take place,
we fhould incur all the inconveniences of funding : for where
is the difference (fuppofing it to be in the fame extent) between the public, in their collective capacity, borrowing the
money by loan, and mortgaging it on their pofterity, and a
number of individuals borrowing the money on their private
eftates, and mortgaging it on their defcendants? But fuppofing
no part of the property to be fold, the only juftifiable grounds
upon which you could tax the poffeffor of perpetual property
in a greater proportion than the life annuitant is, that he muft
be fuppofed to have an intereft in his eftate after his death.
If this is the cafe, he muft be confidered, on the o her hand,
as fubject likewife to the burdens of the eftate after his deceafe.

I 6

If therefore it fhould be neceffary, from time to time, in periods of national emergency, to have recourfe to this meafure,
the property in which we muft fuppofe him interefted will, in
all thofe cafes, be fubject to the tax.   And would it not be unjuft, to tax thofe interefts in a greater proportion at prefent,
which, if we confider them only as life-interefts, ftand exactly
upon the fame footing as the life-annuities; and, if they are
perpetual interefts, are expofed to the tax in all future ages,
whenever it may be thought neceffary to adopt it?

" The next objection, which has been ftated to the meafure, is, the injuftice of taxing different rates of income in the
fame proportion; that perfons of large income cannot only afford to pay more, but even a greater proportion of their incomes, than thofe who poffefs fmall ones; and that there ought
to be, therefore, *a rifing fcale* applied to incomes of different
amount.

" The object of this bill is not to regulate incomes, but to
tax them; and if you take from different incomes the fame
proportion, you leave them of courfe exactly in the relative
ftate in which you found them.   The principle, on which the
objection is founded, might carry you the length of levelling
all property, and of not taxing moderate or fmall incomes at
all, till great ones were reduced to the fame level; a principle
deftructive of all idea of property, of all induftry and exertion
amongft mankind, and of the peace and well being of civil
fociety.

" But let us inquire how far the effect of this propofition
would be charitable and humane.—A perfon of two or three
hundred pounds a year is called upon for the tenth of his income: the tax may bear heavily upon him individually, but
he has, proportionably, few perfons dependent upon him who
will fuffer its confequence; he keeps few fervants, and employs
few tradefmen, &c. &c.; but in proportion as you rife in the
fcale of income, the number of dependent perfons increafe.
If, then, you tax thofe who are poffeffed of large property, in
a greater proportion than thofe who are only in moderate circumftances, you muft confider that, in taxing them, you are indirectly taxing all thofe who depend upon that property, and
live

live from the expenditure of it. The confequence would be, that, whilft in one way you are pretending to relieve the middle and induftrious claffes of the community, you are bearing at leaft equally hard upon them in another; fo that a rifing fcale of taxation is not only inconfiftent with every principle of property, but would not produce any of the beneficial confequences, or afford the relief it propofed to beftow.

" Thefe principles of the bill are not *new*; they are thofe on which the legiflature has always acted. In the land-tax, in the poor-rates, in county rates, &c., did we ever hear of a rifing fcale of taxation? Yet, if it was fair in this inftance, would it not have been equally juft in all thofe? In thefe inftances, did we ever hear of any diftinction between tenants in fee-fimple, tenants for life, and tenants for years? The tax has, in all thefe cafes, been taken in the fame proportion, out of the produce of the land in the year, without any confideration of the amount of the property, or the nature of the tenure [t]."

But thefe arguments, however plaufible, would not fatisfy the public. As foon as the war had terminated, there feemed to be an univerfal anxiety to get rid of fuch a burden. Petitions were preparing from all quarters of the kingdom, infifting on its repeal, and the new minifter, not knowing what might be the effect of attempting to retain it in force, very prudently yielded to the ftorm, reverted again to the principles of the funding fyftem [u], and abandoned this new and detefted financial fpeculation.

[t] See Review of the arguments advanced in the Houfe of Commons, in fupport of the bill, &c. impofing certain duties upon income. Printed for J. Wright, *an.* 1799.

[u] By converting the ftock charged on the income tax, amounting to £.56,445,000 into an annuity of £.1,713,016 13*s.* 4*d. per annum*, exclufive of £. 25,621 10*s.* for management.

The

The hiftory of this tax cannot be ftated better, 5. Convoy Tax. than in the words of an intelligent author, who has already been occafionally quoted in the courfe of this work.

" During the feffion of 1798, another meafure was adopted, for raifing, during the war, a confiderable fum within the year, of fufficient importance to be noticed here, both as a regulation of public policy and an expedient of finance ; we mean the Convoy-Tax, a fmall per centage on the value of goods exported and imported, with fome exceptions, and a fmall tonnage duty on all fhips arriving at or failing from any port in Great Britain. Our fuperiority at fea was decided, and complete protection had been afforded to every branch of our trade by convoys, to the perfect fatisfaction of the merchants; but their adventurous fpirit induced them frequently to fend their fhips to various parts of the world for an early market, without waiting for protection, from whence it too often happened that valuable cargoes were captured; and, what was of more importance, a number of Britifh feamen were fhut up and rigoroufly treated in the gaols of our implacable enemy ; a reftraint was therefore impofed on that practice in future, unlefs licenfes fhould be obtained from the Admiralty. The chearfulnefs with which this was acquiefced in by the merchants and manufacturers, exhibited another inftance of their zeal and public fpirit; for, although in fome cafes the tax is lefs than the infurance faved by its operations, a fmall advance

advance of capital became neceffary, and it was impoffible entirely to avoid all inconveniences refpecting the fhipping the goods."

" As a meafure of public policy, accompanied
as it is with the regulation above alluded to, it has
the effect at once of giving fafety to our trade, by
protecting it from the depredations of the enemy
(almoft the only fpecies of warfare left to their
exertions), and of depriving them of refources to
an immenfe amount, which they derived from the
prizes carried into their ports. As a meafure of
revenue, it combines eafe of collection with fecurity from fraud, arifing from the fmallnefs of the
duty, compared with the value of the merchandize
on which its levied. In almoft every cafe where
it was conceived it could be felt as a burden, exceptions were admitted."

" During the fhort time fince the tax took place,
in July 1798, its produce has been fuch as to afford
a moft fatisfactory proof, of the highly profperous
fituation of the commerce and navigation of the
country. The money paid to the cuftoms, in the
half year ending January 5, 1799, amounts to
639,000l [x]. which is confiderably under the actual
produce of the period. In a commercial view, it

[x] In this fum are not included either the duties due by the
Eaft India Company, on their imports, (which are not paid till
after their fales,) or the duties which are bonded by the ex-
porters :—and the largeft Weft India fleet of the year arrived a
few days before the act took place, the whole property in which
efcaped the tax.

has

has alfo been attended with the very advantageous effect of afcertaining, (contrary to inceffant declamations on the fubject,) that the real value of our exports exceeds, in the proportion of at leaft 70 per cent. the former eftimates of them."

Nothing but the peculiar circumftances attending the late conteft, when we poffeffed in a manner all the commerce of the univerfe, could have juftified fuch an impofition.   Nor is there any reafon to believe, that it was productive of any mifchievous confequences *during the war*.   But the tax having been quietly fubmitted to whilft hoftilities lafted, the Minifter was thence led to imagine, that, to a certain extent, it might be continued as a permanent fource of revenue.   In vain was it reprefented by the proprietors of Britifh fhipping, " that they had offered no oppofition to the ton-" nage duty, under the convoy act, *as a war tax*, " becaufe they found fufficient employment in the " government and merchant fervice, and could " then obtain freights that left them a reafonable " reward for their induftry ; but now, the ftate of " fhipping is materially altered ; they have little " trade, and what remains, is not worth accept-" ance ; befides, they have now to contend with " many competitors, fince the greateft part of " Europe is under the dominion or influence of " France, who under the fpecious principle of the " liberty of the feas, will ufe every means in its " power, to undermine our ftrength, by fupplant-" ing us in our trade as carriers."   Thefe remon-
ftrances

strances have not yet been abandoned ; but hitherto the ship owners have not been able to convince the Chancellor of the Exchequer, of the impolicy and the injurious tendency of the duty in question.

6. Taxes repealed or abandoned. When the immense variety of taxes, which the late Minister brought forward, during the course of his long administration, is considered, it cannot possibly be wondered at, that some of them should be found extremely exceptionable, and consequently were either repealed, or abandoned, after having been proposed to Parliament. Some memorials regarding the principal propositions of that description, it may be proper to preserve in this work, as a beacon to future ministers.

1. Tax on coals at the pit. This improvident and dangerous tax, was suggested by Mr. Pitt, at the commencement of his ministerial career. It was included in the budget he had brought forward on the 30th June 1784. He then proposed to lay a duty of three shillings *per* chaldron, or two shillings *per* ton, on all coals sold either by measure or weight. In order to prevent its being felt by the manufacturers, on whom, in many cases, this tax would not only have been extremely oppressive, but even ruinous, the idea was thrown out, of granting them certain drawbacks, according to the extent of the coals they consumed. But the tax was generally reprobated, and after all, being calculated to produce only at the rate of £.150,000 *per annum*, it was prudently given up, and on the 21st of July following, other sources of revenue were substituted in its room.

It

2. Shop tax.

It is natural for landed gentlemen, to be prejudiced in favour of any tax, that feems to affect merely the mercantile, manufacturing, or monied interefts; and hence the fhop tax was not unpopular with perfons of that defcription. Whether a tax upon fhopkeepers, by means of a moderate licenfe, might not have been impofed, is a different queftion, but to think of affefling a tax, not according to the *rent received*, but to the *rent paid* by the fhopkeeper, or taxing, (as has been well obferved,) not the chance of profit, but the certainty of lofs, namely, the perpetual and unavoidable burden payable for a fhop and houfe, was highly cruel and oppreffive.

The following reafons, drawn up by the committee of fhopkeepers in the metropolis, certainly materially contributed to the repeal:

" 1. That the effence of taxation lies in every man bearing his proportion of the burthens of the ftate according to his abilities. 2. That the fhop-tax is unjuft and partial in the extreme, becaufe it will fall upon one particular defcription of men; while others in far more opulent fituations, will not contribute one farthing towards it. 3. That the retail trader, already pays out of all manner of proportion to the exigencies of the ftate, and far, very far, beyond every other defcription of men, whofe incomes are infinitely greater. 4. That as retail traders are compelled to feek houfes in public fituations, the rents are extremely high, and as many taxes are collected by a pound rate calculated from

the

the rent, the retailer is confequently affeffed much heavier than perfons living in houfes not fo fituated, whether in or out of trade.   5. That the retail trader may very fairly be confidered to pay a very heavy fhop tax already, becaufe houfes in public fituations, produce twice the rent they would do, were they fituated in private ftreets, and as the house tax, and many other taxes collected by pound rate, being calculated from the rent, confequently, the retailer contributes more to thefe taxes, than any other defcription of men.   6. That the receipt tax is a very heavy impoft upon the retail trader, becaufe he is frequently obliged to furnifh his cuftomer with a receipt free of expence.   7. That from our experience we are warranted to fay, that neither the houfe or receipt tax have or ever can be laid on the commodity, nor is it poffible, in our apprehenfion, that any tax impofed perfonally upon traders can ever fall upon the confumer.   And, 8. That as it is impoffible the retailer can ever lay the intended tax upon fhops on the articles he fells, he will be compelled to pay this impoft out of his profits, and that fuch a mode of taxation we conceive to be unequal and unjuft."

3. Clock and watch tax.

The tax impofed by Mr. Pitt on clocks and watches, was productive of fuch ruinous confequences[r], that I truft it will never be tried by any other

---

[r] There are twenty different perfons employed in the making of every watch, all of whom ferve regular apprenticefhips to each branch; and there are ten different branches in clockmaking.

other Chancellor of the Exchequer, and if it is, that
he will fail in the attempt.   The minifter, unfortunately, could not be prevailed upon to repeal this
obnoxious duty, until it was too late, after it had
done confiderable mifchief.   In the memorial from
the committee of clock and watch makers, by
whofe efforts the repeal was at laft obtained, it is
ftated, that in lefs than a year from the commencement of the tax, a diminution exceeding one half
of the general manufacture of clocks and watches
throughout the kingdom, as well as of the various
branches of trade connected therewith, had taken
place even in that fhort period of time ; by which
means thoufands of deferving men were deprived of
employment and fupport, and induced to emigrate,
carrying with them the choiceft fecrets of the
trade, confequently depriving our manufacturers of
that unrivalled fuperiority in foreign markets which
they had hitherto enjoyed, a circumftance the more
to be regretted, as the manufacture is of great national importance, employed many thoufands of
workmen, by the ingenious operation of whofe
manual labour merely, the original value of materials, chiefly Britifh, was fo much increafed, that
the detriment which the lofs of this trade would

---

making. In both, there were many ingenious mechanics, to
whom the public were indebted for feveral valuable inventions,
who were driven out of work by the tax, and fome of them
being compelled to emigrate, would of courfe inftruct other nations in their different arts.

occafion

occasion to the commercial interest of these kingdoms, could hardly be estimated.

The tax on inland navigation, proposed by Mr. Pitt in 1797, fortunately never passed into a law: If it had, it is impossible to foresee the extent of mischievous consequences of which it must have been productive. On that occasion, I felt it my duty to draw up a paper, shortly representing how injurious, in various respects, it must prove to the public interest, a copy of which I subjoin, as I have some reason to believe, that it materially contributed to prevent this obnoxious imposition.

Observations on the Canal Tax, transmitted to Mr. Pitt in June, 1797.

It is impossible too highly to appreciate the advantages of canals. In fact, a nation can neither be rich nor populous without them. Neither China nor Holland, for instance, could furnish produce sufficient to feed the horses that would be necessary to convey, *by means of roads*, the goods which are carried by their canals and inland navigations, were the whole country dedicated to that single object; nor could either of them have ever reached the population or opulence they have attained, without their assistance.—Any check therefore to so essential a source of public prosperity is certainly to be avoided.

In other countries, every encouragement has been given to canals. In Spain they are made at the public expence.—Lewis XIVth gave assistance from the public revenues to the formation of the famous

famous Languedoc canal, and made it the property of the perfon who formed it, and his pofterity for ever: and in Holland, where they have taxed every thing, even corn ground at the mill, garden ftuff, and butcher's meat, yet they have always confidered a tax upon canals as much more exceptionable than even thefe heavy and unpopular impofts.

The Chancellor of the Exchequer, has, with great propriety, frequently ftated in his budget, the fums annually laid out in making canals, as a proof of the increafing wealth and profperity of the country. But the very idea of a tax, will prevent any material addition to the number of canal bills already paft. Moft of the canals have been made by the exertions of fpeculators, who are accuftomed to lay out a part of their capital in that line, and felling their fhares in the ftock of one canal, as foon as an opportunity occurs, are thus enabled to engage in another. But if they are to be taxed, there is an end to all fuch fpeculations, at leaft in this country, and they will go to America or to France, where many plans of the fame kind are in contemplation.—Is it worth while, therefore, to run even the fmalleft rifk of checking fuch ufeful fpeculations, and lofing fuch valuable fubjects, for fo trifling an addition to the public revenue as £. 90,000 a year.—Indeed there is no fet of men, who ought to be more cautioufly dealt with, than perfons of an enterprifing and fpeculative turn, poffeffed of *perfonal property only*.

—An

—An emigration to another country is nothing to them, and yet they are, upon the whole, from the nature of their property, and their enterprifing fpirit, peculiarly ufeful to any country where they refide. But, however enterprifing they may be, it cannot be fuppofed, that they will lay out their money in a way that will make it liable to be taxed in this country, whenever it exceeds the legal intereft, when in other countries, or in other fpeculations, even in this country, lefs ufeful to the public, they might fecure to themfelves all the profits to be derived from employing it.

There is hardly any canal, that either directly or indirectly does not augment confiderably the public revenue. If a canal, for inftance, by the frefh fupplies of manure it furnifhes, only adds a thoufand acres to the land cultivated for barley, is not the Exchequer thereby enriched by the taxes on malt and beer; many other refults of a fimilar nature might be pointed out; and if by any tax, fuch fources of profperity are diminifhed, would it not be exactly the ftory in the fable, " *of killing the hen that lays the golden eggs.*"

It does not feem fair, that the tax fhould effect the proprietors of canals, whenever they fhould divide 5 *per cent.*—The fact is, that £. 10 *per cent.* is little enough intereft for a commercial fpeculation. But whatever the fair intereft may be, it ought, in ftrict juftice, to be calculated from the commencement of the fpeculation, and though a canal may pay 10 *per cent.* at one time, yet it may

not

not have paid 3 *per cent.* from the commencement;
nay, after having paid 5 *per cent.*, and confequently
become liable to the tax, it may be again reduced
to 3 *per cent.* by the diminution of the commerce
which it had enjoyed.   It would be very unfair
therefore, to tax canals at all, unlefs the public
guaranteed their future dividends at 5 *per cent.*

There are other points of view alfo, in which
the fubject might be confidered, not very favourable
to the propofed tax.

For inflance, it would be eafy to evade it, by
laying out any furplus, above £.4:19 *per cent.*,
in falaries to the officers, or in improving the navigation itfelf, either of which the proprietors of the
canal would prefer, to paying any fhare of their
profits to the Exchequer.

Befides, in fome of the canal bills it is enacted,
that when the income exceeds a certain fum, the
rate of tonnage fhall be reduced, which is much
more equitable than that of paying the furplus to
the Exchequer, as all canals, though in general
advantageous, are attended with fome local inconveniencies; property is deftroyed and inconvenient-
ly divided, many trefpaffes are committed both by
the bargemen and their horfes, and the only compenfation for fuch difadvantages, is as cheap
conveyance of goods, as the circumftances of the
cafe will admit of.

Laftly, the only fair mode, by which the public
could avail itfelf of the profit to be derived from
canals, would be, to purchafe that fpecies of property

perty from thofe to whom it belongs at prefent, and to carry it on like the poft-office, or any fimilar fpeculation. In that cafe, the whole country *might be put exactly upon the fame footing.* Whereas a tax, like the one propofed, muft be partial, bearing hard upon one fet of men, whilft another, in the fame predicament, would be totally exempted. Such a circumftance would occafion a degree of difcontent, that cannot be too cautioufly avoided.

It certainly does credit to any minifter, to repeal or to abandon injudicious meafures of finance, more efpecially where there is any rifk of their diminifhing the productive induftry of a country ; for when the mifchief is once done, it is not always poffible to repair the evil. Nor is the direct injury alone to be confidered, the indirect and circuitous confequences are ftill more to be apprehended. By injudicious financial oppreffions, an imprudent government may not only impoverifh itfelf, but, by the expulfion of active and ufeful men, may enrich a rival and an enemy.

In the courfe of Mr. Pitt's adminiftration, fome other taxes were repealed or abandoned ; but the above are the moft important, and I truft, at the fame time, the leaft likely to meet with the fanction of any future minifter.

7. Sale and redemption of the land tax, and fimilar plan regarding tythes.   The idea of felling the land tax, has long been in contemplation. Several years ago, the author received a letter from a moft refpectable member of the Houfe, (Wm. Lygon Efquire, M. P. for
Worcefterfhire),

Worcefterfhire), of which the following is the fubftance :—" That an idea was then getting abroad,
" that the land-tax, at its prefent rate, might be
" offered to the refpective landholders, at from 20
" to 30 years purchafe. That the money thus
" raifed, might be applied in aid of the annual mil-
" lion for redeeming the national debt.   That any
" inconveniences which might be ftated to arife,
" might be obviated, were a committee to be ap-
" pointed for the fpecial purpofe of confidering the
" plan.   That the decreafing rate of the intereft of
" money at that time, appeared to make the period
" when that letter was written, (September 4,
" 1792), particularly favourable for fuch an at-
" tempt ; and that if I confidered the plan as likely
" to be of fervice to the public, and would have no
" objection to make a motion in the houfe regard-
" ing it, the writer of the letter would take every
" opportunity that might occur, of confulting the
" general fenfe of the people in his neighbourhood
" on the fubject, and of promoting the meafure as
" much as lay in his power."

Notwithftanding the refpect to which the opinion of fo intelligent a member of the Houfe was
juftly intitled, I could not approve of the fuggeftion, for reafons which will afterwards be fubmitted
to the Reader's confideration ; and it is probable
that fuch a plan would never have been ferioufly
thought of, had not an ingenious and plaufible
fcheme been drawn up by a gentleman converfant
in financial inquiries, which tended to prove, that

redeem-

redeeming the land-tax might not only produce some immediate advantage, but might also prove highly beneficial, by raifing the price of the funds, and fupporting the public credit of the country.

Induced by fuch expectations, and perhaps with ulterior views of ftill greater moment, (namely, that of extending the fame fyftem to tythes,) the minifter at laft brought forward the idea in parliament. Nothing but the complete controul which he had acquired in all legiflative proceedings, could have given him the fmalleft chance of fuccefs in carrying through fuch a meafure; and I am perfuaded, that had he forefeen the infinite trouble of which it was productive, the various acts which it was neceffary to pafs regarding it, the little progrefs that would be made, notwithftanding every exertion that government could employ in its behalf, and that it would not be in his power to extend it afterwards to tythes, he would not probably have perfevered in the attempt.

In every point of view, whether financial or conftitutional, it feemed to me effentially neceffary to give the plan as much oppofition as poffible, and felt it my duty therefore, to addrefs the Houfe of Commons upon the fubject to the following purport[z].

   " Mr. Speaker,

" I delayed troubling the Houfe with any obfervations which may have occurred to me, on the plan to which our attention is

---

[z] This fpeech was delivered in the debate on the 9th of May 1798.

once

once more directed, until this stage of our proceedings, because my objections lay, not to any particular branch of the resolutions which were originally proposed by the Right Honourable Gentleman (Mr. Pitt), but to the general scope and principle of the system : and I now arise to state those observations to the House, in the full conviction, that they will not only sufficiently justify the vote which I shall give this night, but also that they may contribute to awaken the attention of this House and of the public, to the danger of such a bill passing into a law, which, after all the consideration I have been able to bestow upon it, even in its present state of maturity, as ripened in the bill now before us, and brought to all the perfection of which it is probably capable, seems to be *at least* as exceptionable as any measure that, to the best of my recollection, was ever suggested, either by the present, or by any former minister of this country."

" Before I proceed, however, to state the reasons which have induced me to oppose this bill, I think that it may not be improper to submit to your consideration, and that of the House in general, an objection of a preliminary nature, namely, to the legality of our proceedings. It is well known that we have already voted a land-tax of 4 *s.* in the pound, *and no more*, for the service of the year 1798, and that an act has passed for carrying that measure into effect. We have therefore precluded ourselves, by the indisputable law of Parliament regarding the form of our proceedings, from again discussing the subject of a land-tax during the present session, unless we have reserved power for that purpose. The House has been accustomed to reserve such a power in two ways, namely ; first, a power to repeal the whole ; or, secondly, any part of an act. Of the first we have an example, in the 37th Geo. III. c. 4. § 60., the words of which are as follow : " Provided always and be it enacted, that " *this act* may be altered, varied, or repealed, by any act or " acts to be made in this present session of Parliament." The clause in the Land-tax bill of this year is, however, of a very different nature, and is conceived in the following terms : " Provided always and be it further enacted by the authority
" afore-

" aforefaid, *that any part of this act* may be altered, varied, or
" repealed, by any act or acts to be made in this prefent feffion
" of Parliament." Such a claufe, I underftand, was introduced into the annual Land-tax Bill fome years ago, with a
view of enabling Parliament to alter, to vary, or to repeal, any
of thofe local regulations with which the act abounds, that
might be found oppreffive, but it never could be intended to
fanction a plan like the prefent; the object of which is, to overturn, not any particular part, but the whole tenor and principle of the act; and, indeed, by making the prefent land-tax
perpetual, to render any future act, on the fame bafis, perfectly
unneceffary. It was in confequence of this claufe alone, that
we were juftified in permitting a bill to be introduced by an Honourable Gentleman, (Mr. Wilberforce Bird) regarding the
Land-tax Commiffioners. The object of that act is very properly declared in the title of the bill to be, " to alter and amend
" *fo much* of an act paffed in the prefent feffion of Parliament
" (namely, the Land-tax Act,) as relates to the qualification
" of the Commiffioners." Whereas this is a bill, not for altering any part of the Land-tax Act, which is all we are juftified in doing, but for making perpetual a tax, which by an act
paffed this very feffion, is only granted for one year and no
more. It overturns at the fame time a fyftem, that has been uniformly acted upon for above a century, and in which the exiftence and authority of this Houfe were fuppofed to have been
deeply implicated."

" I thought it neceffary to call your attention to this preliminary objection, from the full conviction, that if we once fuffer
the forms of the Houfe to be violated, we are not likely long
to enjoy the effence and fubftantial benefits of this Conftitution.
My objections; however, go, not only to the form of our proceedings, but to the principle of the bill itfelf. In regard to
the firft point, namely, the forms of the Houfe, if we wifh to
preferve the appearance of any refpect for them, we muft neceffarily defer the farther confideration of this bill until another
feffion of Parliament: but if we have any regard *for the real
interefts of this country,* I hope to make it appear, in the courfe

of

of what I am now about to obferve, that we ought never to fuffer fuch a bill as this to be again difcuffed within thefe walls."

" The firft objection that muft ftrike at once every indivi-dual, is the one founded on that important principle of this Conftitution, and which has long been confidered as effential to the exiftence and authority of this Houfe, namely, that the taxes on land and malt, which are the fureft and moft produc-tive branches of the revenue, inftead of being permanently granted to the crown, " for fupporting," in the words of the act, " His Majefty's Government," fhall be annually voted. But we are told, that though it is propofed to make the land-tax perpetual, yet that other taxes, even to a larger amount, (though that, by the by, has not been proved,) which are now perpetual, are to have their nature altered, and are to be fub-jected to the annual vote of Parliament; and certain duties on malt, fugar, tobacco, and fnuff, are appropriated, by this bill, for that purpofe. There is certainly fome plaufibility in the idea. At the fame time the Houfe will advert to this, that the produce of all taxes on confumption muft be fluctuating, and muft ever depend on a variety of circumftances which it is not in the power of parliament to controul: for inftance, prejudice, caprice, or paffion, might, in the fpace of a few weeks, annihi-late the revenue arifing from tobacco and fnuff: whereas the land-tax muft be paid, as long as the territory of the country remains productive. It is impoffible, therefore, to liften to this fophiftical anfwer to a plain and, indeed, unanfwerable objec-tion. The Right Honourable Gentleman propofes, that the pillars of this Conftitution, and the exiftence and authority of this Houfe, fhall reft upon fuch frail foundations as the con-tents of a fnuff box or of a pipe of tobacco. I wifh, on the other hand, to fee them remain on their old territorial bafis, and that the value of a certain portion of the produce of the country fhall be annually voted by the reprefentatives of the people for the maintenance of our fleets and armies, and the other expences of the crown; and that, unlefs fuch a grant is made, that the whole frame and fabric of our government fhall

be

be unhinged. The firſt is a meaſure that may ſuit the narrow
mind of a mere financier, who can think of nothing but taxation. The ſecond, which has been ſanctioned with the approbation of the greateſt ſtateſmen that ever ſat within theſe walls,
forms a check, which I hope this Houſe will not raſhly hazard
or abandon."

"My next objection is of a legal nature, namely, on the
effect that ſuch an act muſt have upon the landed property of
the country, and the endleſs confuſion and litigation it muſt occaſion, both in pariſhes regarding apportioning the land-tax,
and among individuals. On the firſt point there can be no
doubt: With reſpect to the ſecond, nothing can be more deſirable for a landed proprietor than to avoid law-ſuits, and to
have every thing connected with the title deeds of his eſtate as
clear and diſtinct as poſſible. But how is that to be the caſe if
theſe reſolutions ſhould paſs into a law. The land-tax, when
purchaſed or redeemed, is ſometimes to be a real eſtate, ſometimes
a perſonal eſtate, and ſometimes to be converted from a perſonal
to a real eſtate. Is it poſſible for this Houſe to countenance
ſuch confuſion; and before we ſuffer ſuch a bill to proceed one
ſtep farther, ought we not to hear what the Attorney General
for England, the Lord Advocate for Scotland, and other great
luminaries of the law, conſider may be the effect of ſuch a ſyſtem on the landed property of the two kingdoms ? The gentlemen of the long robe, though extremely numerous in the
Houſe, (for this is far from being a *parliamentum indoctum,*) have
in general preſerved a cautious ſilence upon this ſubject, which
was matter of aſtoniſhment to me, till I began to conſider how
much ſuch a bill muſt benefit the profeſſion, as we may trace
in it the foundation of at leaſt ten thouſand law-ſuits, one in
each pariſh, being a very moderate calculation ; and thus no
inconſiderable ſhare of the remnant of free property, which the
landed intereſt will be ſuffered to retain in their poſſeſſion, will
be abſorbed. Let us take, for inſtance, the clauſe for ſelling a
part of an eſtate for the purpoſe of redeeming the land-tax :
1. Any part of the manor is to be ſold, with the exception of the
manſion-houſe. If not ſold by public auction, how is it to be

ascertained

afcertained whether the price was a fair one ? Here is an abundant fource of litigation, more efpecially as there is no regulation as to the expences attending the fales, nor the purchafing
of the 3 *per cent.* ftock. 2. The furplus money is to be placed
in the Bank of England, in Government or other public fecurities, and then to be re-invefted in land for the like ufes, trufts,
intents, and purpofes, as the eftate originally fold. In the
courfe of fuch tranfactions, who does not fee a plentiful fource
of litigation, infinite trouble, and endlefs expence ? The right
honourable gentleman who brought in this bill was bred to the
bar, and having fome compaffion for his old affociates, whofe
profeffional profits have been fo much impaired by the prefent
unfortunate war, it is natural for him to embrace this opportunity of throwing fome crumbs from his plentiful table, and
of beftowing a million on Weftminfter-hall, which is the fmalleft fum that will accrue to it if fuch a bill paffes into a law ;
but thofe who have any regard for the landed intereft will ad-
vife them to remain as they are. At prefent they have nothing
to do but to pay their annual land tax to the collector; but if
they involve themfelves *in all the legal labyrinths of redemption,*
it is impoffible to fay when they will get out of them : they
may be affured, not without furrendering a confiderable part
of their property, to thofe profeffional friends who will undertake to extricate them "
" The next objection that occurs to me is of a financial nature. We all know that the land tax, as it is now impofed, is
extremely unequal : it is the object, however, of the prefent
bill to perpetuate that inequality. Indeed the land tax is not
only unequal, but has ever been confidered as a very exceptionable impoft, and one that ought only to be had recourfe to
in the moft preffing and urgent neceffity. In a famous debate,
anno 1732 [a], on the fubject of reducing it to one fhilling in the
pound, we are told, that a former Chancellor of the Exchequer,
(Sir Robert Walpole,) whofe language was then received with
repeated *hearems* and tumults of applaufe, thus expreffed him-

See Torbuck's Debates, vol. x. p. 149 and 187.

self: " As to the manner of raising taxes upon the people, it
" is a certain maxim that that tax, which is the most equal and
" the most general, is the most just and the least burdensome.
" When every man contributes a small share, a great sum may
" be raised for the public service, without any man being sen-
" sible what he pays; whereas a small sum, raised upon a
" few, lies heavy upon each particular man, and is the more
" grievous in that it is unjust. The landholders bear but a
" small proportion to the people of this, or of any other na-
" tion, yet no man contributes any the least share to this tax
" but he that is possessed of a land estate; and yet this tax has
" been continued without intermission for above these forty
" years—*it has continued so long and lain so heavy, that I may*
" *venture to say, many a landed gentleman in this kingdom has*
" *thereby been utterly ruined and undone :*" and at the conclusion
of the debate he added, " the land tax is the most unequal, the
" most grievous, and the most oppressive tax, that ever was
" raised in this country. It is a tax which never ought to be
" raised *but in times of the most extreme necessity.* The best
" judges, the truest patriots in all countries, have been of opi-
" nion, that of all taxes, that upon immoveable goods, that
" upon lands and houses, *ought to be the last resource.*"

" Such were the sentiments of a former Chancellor of the
Exchequer, in consequence of which he proposed reducing the
land tax to one shilling in the pound. His successor, who now
holds that office, follows a very different system, and endeavours to ingratiate himself with the landed interest by different
means and on different principles. For instance, he is the first
Chancellor of the Exchequer that ever attempted to keep the
land tax at its highest rate in time of peace, as well as in time
of war; that ever ventured to propose rendering that tax perpetual; and who not only insists on perpetuating the present
unequal land tax at its highest rate, but also who *threatens* the
landed interest with an unlimited addition to so heavy a burden. The additional tax, the foundation of which is so evidently laid in this bill, may at first be low, call it one shilling,
or even sixpence in the pound; but if the principle is once admitted, it will soon be found the readiest resource in all emergencies.

gencies. We are told, that freehold in office is a better tenure than a freehold eftate, and that taxes upon land furnifh a fecurity fo infinitely preferable to every other, that by converting excife duties into taxes upon land, the public may gain onefifth additional revenue. Can there be a ftronger temptation to throw as heavy a load as poffible upon land, and to exempt freehold in office from taxation ? Does not the principle of this meafure go to prove, that if £. 400,000 can be gained by perpetuating the land tax of two millions, that a million would be gained by laying five millions upon land, two millions by laying ten millions, and that by laying twenty millions four millions would be the profit of the Exchequer ? Here is a means of acquiring a great revenue, the practicability of which, *if this plan fucceeds*, cannot be queftioned, and which, if practicable, the neceffities of an extravagant government may foon render indifpenfable."

" The next objection that ftruck my mind was one of a political nature, but which I am happy to find is taken away by the amended bill, and therefore it is unneceffary to dwell much upon it. We all know, that by the union between England and Scotland, the proportion of land tax between the two countries is for ever afcertained. The one is to raife at the rate of nearly two millions, and the other about £. 48,000 *per annum*, or in that ratio, for any greater or leffer fum. People are apt to fay, that the burden is extremely unequal. It is a part, however, of an indiffoluble bargain between the two countries, which cannot now be altered. Befides, it can be proved, that the inequality is altogether owing to the fuperior agricultural legiflation and police of Scotland. Let the Englifh pafs a general bill for inclofure, let them modify tithes fo as to prevent their being a bar to improvement, let them reftrain the poor rates within moderate bounds, let them abolifh any obnoxious remnants of the feudal fyftem, and let the tenants have proper leafes of their farms, and the land of England will foon be as cheaply taxed as that in Scotland. It is owing to the circumftances above alluded to that the rents of Scotland have proportionably increafed more, under all the difadvantages of inferior foil, of an inferior climate, of an inferior capital, and of

inferior

inferior markets. Give England the same legal advantages which Scotland at present happily possesses, and its agricultural prosperity would increase in such a ratio, that the land tax it is now subject to would be to the full as low in England as in Scotland, and there would exist, on that account, no jealousy between the two kingdoms. It is unnecessary, however, to dwell on an objection which has been already happily adverted to and removed [c]."

" Another objection arises from a clause in the amended bill, respecting which the right honourable gentleman had preserved, as long as possible, a cautious and prudent silence. I had remarked from the beginning, that he had never explained the nature of the commissioners whom he had proposed to intrust with the authority of selling the land tax ; but the clause he has introduced (see p. 46.) is so exceptionable, that though it might be amended in a Committee, I think it proper to take this opportunity of alluding to it. The Commissioners are to be nominated by the Crown, and are to receive at the rate of threepence in the pound on the amount of the land tax sold by them ; that might extend, or be construed to extend, to an one-eightieth part of the £.40,000,000 proposed to be raised by the sale of the land tax, or no less a sum than £.500,000. But that would be too absurd. An one-eightieth part, however, of the two millions, or £.25,000, is an object which will require particular attention, should the bill be recommitted, and is an expence which ought certainly to be avoided."

" But the objection which strikes my mind the most forcibly, is one of an agricultural nature, and it seems to me sufficient of itself to overturn the whole system. The object of the measure is, *to tempt* the country gentleman to lay out any money he may have in his possession, or any sum he can borrow, or can procure, by a sale of part of his estate, or mortgaging the whole of it, in purchasing his land tax. Can there be a more destructive policy, either for the individual, or for the public ? If a landed proprietor has any money to spare, the proper mode for him to lay it out is, in the improvement of his estate ; in that way he may gain, instead of 5, from 7 to 15, or even

* The clause, however, was after taken out of the bill.

20 *per cent.* for his money, and by his improvements the public profperity is, in various refpeĉts, infinitely augmented. Population is increafed, abundance of provifions is fecured, important additions made to the revenue, nay, the great objeĉt of the bill itfelf, an increafed price of ftock, ultimately fecured. All hopes of that fort, however, will be annihilated, at leaft for fome time, if this meafure fucceeds ; and if it does not fucceed, are we not holding up delufive hopes to the country ? As to the idea of the proprietor borrowing money, or felling a part of his eftate to obtain it, I am perfuaded that neither of thofe plans can be much relifhed by the landed intereft. If money can be obtained in either way, let it be expended on improvement ; if borrowed at 5 *per cent.*, no advantage can be obtained from the tranfaĉtion ; if under 5 *per cent.*, the money will probably be called up when it becomes fcarcer and more valuable, and the proprietor will find himfelf involved in the greateft pecuniary difficulties. Selling a part of an eftate is feldom eligible; it can only be thought of when there are detached fpots, and in the cafe of fettled eftates, is attended with peculiar, indeed unfurmountable difficulties, and almoft endlefs expence and litigation."

" On the fubjeĉt of improvement, it may not be improper briefly to ftate the various meafures which have been adopted in different countries for its encouragement or otherwife, and by contrafting the one with the other we fhall be able more clearly to fee the *hideoufnefs* of the prefent meafure in its real colours."

" The beft mode of encouraging improvements, is the one adopted by Frederic the Great, King of Pruffia, who expended about two millions of German crowns, or three hundred thoufand pounds fterling *per annum*, in promoting the improvement of his country, and the general comfort of its inhabitants. We are told in particular, that he expended confiderable fums of money in promoting, even by premiums, the abolition of commons, and the inclofure of lands. What a contraft between fuch a wife policy and the praĉtice of this country, where the proprietors are not fuffered to inclofe and cultivate their own land, when they are ready and willing to do fo, without being

previoufly

previoufly fubjected to a heavy expence; and inftead of grants to encourage them, they are required to pay confiderable fums for a permiffion to begin their improvements! No wonder, therefore, that we were lately under the neceffity of laying out, in public bounties, no lefs a fum than £. 570,000 to encourage the importation of foreign grain, partly from thofe very deferts which the immortal Frederic, by his fuperior policy, brought into a ftate of cultivation. But he wifely confidered expence laid out for promoting improvement to be like manure fpread upon the ground, which fecured a more abundant harveft, and inftead of impoverifhing himfelf by that liberal policy, the refult was, that though originally mafter of a country, naturally barren, and without the advantages of extenfive commerce or valuable manufactures, yet he raifed it, by his genius and talents, and by his unceafing attention to its internal improvements, to be one of the moft powerful countries in Europe; and though he maintained a numerous army of 200,000 men, and fpared no expence in collecting great magazines of provifions, a formidable artillery, and all the other implements of war, yet he left behind him a treafure, *in fpecie,* of twelve millions fterling."

" The fecond mode of encouraging improvement, is a meafure which has been juftified by experience in fome countries, and which 1 hope will, fome time or other, be adopted here, namely, that of lending money to proprietors of land at a low intereft for the purpofe of enabling them to improve it. This is a fyftem that cannot be too ftrongly recommended to the attention of any government that is wealthy enough to attempt it."

" The third fyftem is the one that has hitherto been adopted in this country, by which a tax on land has, indeed, been impofed, varying in point of amount from 1*s.* to 4*s.* in the pound, but always levying a proportionable fum from the fame diftrict. This is an indirect encouragement to improvement; for the rate being once fixed, any additional value to an eftate, in confequence of expenfive improvements, goes, with the exception of tithes, into the pocket of the proprietor; and this
circumftance

circumſtance has certainly materially contributed to the improvement of this country."

" The next ſtep, to commence the progreſs of *diſcouragement*, is the one which the right honourable gentleman has in contemplation, and points out in this bill, namely, that of levying an equal land tax over the whole kingdom, varying according to the alteration of income, or annual value of an eſtate. It is evident that this muſt be an almoſt inſurmountable check to every ſpecies of agricultural enterpriſe; for in the face of ſuch a burden, who will venture to lay out his money for the purpoſes of improvement ?"

" But the ſummit of political abſurdity, if the improvement of a country ſhould be conſidered as an object worthy of conſideration, is the meaſure now under our diſcuſſion, by which, inſtead of granting money to the landed proprietor, or lending him ſums at low intereſt, for promoting agricultural exertion, or impoſing no additional burden on improvement, but giving the whole benefit of it to the proprietor, it is propoſed to take from him all the capital he has, or all the money he can procure, by any means, for the purpoſe of redeeming his land tax. A more effectual way of diſcouraging improvement could hardly be contrived. If it ſucceeds according to the intentions of the propoſer, forty millions ſterling would be paid by the landed intereſt for getting rid of this tax. Inſtead of that miſerable mode of laying out ſuch a ſum of money, let us conſider for a moment what would be the benefit of laying out forty millions on improving the territory of the country. The effect of ſuch an event would be not only making this country the garden of Europe, but alſo adding ſo much to its revenue and general proſperity, that we need not be apprehenſive of wanting financial reſources, or that our public credit could poſſibly be impaired. In fact, the difference between the two ſyſtems is ſhortly this : The right honourable gentleman wiſhes to ſupport the funded at the expence of the landed intereſt; whereas I wiſh to promote the improvement of the country without taking away any thing from the funds, perfectly ſatisfied that, when the country proſpers, no apprehenſion need to be entertained

tained that the funded intereft will not thence derive the moft effential benefits."

" I fhall next proceed to confider the arguments which have been made ufe of in favour of this meafure, namely, that it may add from £.200,000 to £.400,000 *per annum* to the revenue, and may take 80,000,000 of 3 *per cent.* ftock out of the market."

" In regard to thefe fuppofed advantages, they entirely depend upon the poffibilty of carrying the meafure into effect; whereas I confider the plan not only highly exceptionable, for the reafons I have already affigned, but, on its prefent footing, (for the plan might be greatly improved,) perfectly impracticable in itfelf, were it liable to no objection."

" There are but five defcriptions of perfons who are likely to purchafe the land tax, namely, the landed proprietor himfelf, public bodies and truftees, wealthy individuals in London, or their foreign correfpondents, monied perfons in the country, and opulent farmers."

" As to the firft, it is on all hands admitted, that in confequence of various circumftances, on which it is unneceffary now to dwell, there are few if any landed proprietors who are in a fituation to purchafe their own land tax. Public bodies, or truftees acting for others, will hardly venture on fuch a fpeculation. Monied men in London, and ftill more the foreign capitalifts with whom they correfpond, are not fo infenfible to their own interefts as to take 5 *per cent.* when they can get 6, on fecurity equally good, and infinitely more convenient, from the eafinefs of transfer, the regular payment of the intereft, and the certainty with which it can be fold. In regard to monied men in the country, they are now as converfant in the ftocks as the citizens of London themfelves, and will not be eafily tempted to give them up on terms fo difadvantageous; befides, taking up the money in the country would have the effect of diminifhing the manufacturing capital, and confequently the commercial profperity of every part of the kingdom, which, in fact, according to a homely expreffion, would be killing the hen that lays the golden eggs. In regard to the former, two or three years ago confiderable fums were in the poffeffion of

that

that body of men, but from the low price of grain, and the importation of fuch enormous quantities from foreign countries, their profits and their wealth have been confiderably diminifhed : befides it would rather be an awkward circumftance for a proprietor to pay a tax on his own tenants ; it would occafion fuch a jealoufy between the two orders as would necefsarily be productive of many unpleafant confequences. On thefe grounds I think the meafure fo extremely impracticable that no material advantage, as it now ftands, can be expected from it.''

" Thefe, Sir, are fome of the principal obfervations which have occurred to me on this important queftion, and which I have endeavoured to condenfe as much as I could, not wifhing to prevent the Houfe from hearing other gentlemen as early as poffible, who may be defirous of ftating their fentiments on fo interefting a topic ; and, on the whole, confidering the extent and magnitude of this fubject, can the Houfe ferioufly determine to hurry fuch a meafure through in the courfe of the prefent feffion ?   The bill is now brought to all the perfection of which probably it is capable.   Let it be circulated, in that ftate over the whole kingdom   If the meafure fhould then meet with general concurrence, let it be paffed early in the courfe of next feffion.   The plan cannot poffibly make any progrefs till the 25th of March next, becaufe it is univerfally acknowledged that very few proprietors, indeed, can purchafe their land tax ; and till then, no other party can interfere.   Let the 25th of March, 1799, be fixed upon by a refolution of the Houfe as the day when at any rate the proprietor muft decide ; and if the fyftem is to be carried through, not an hour will be loft. For my part, were I a friend to the meafure, I certainly would infift upon this delay as the moft likely means of making the public feel any zeal or anxiety in its favour ; and, if it were to pafs, of rendering it ultimately fuccefsful ; whereas if we now rafhly give it our fanction, the mifchief is done, and never can be repaired.''

The act having paffed, notwithftanding every oppofition that could be made to it, infinuations were thrown out in paragraphs and anonymous
letters

letters in the newspapers, that a redemption of tithes, on similar principles, was next in contemplation. That certainly would have been one of the most beneficial measures that could possibly have been adopted. It is to be hoped, therefore, that some public spirited minister will embrace the first favourable opportunity that may occur of carrying it into effect [b].

In regard to the land tax redeemed, notwithstanding every exertion that could be made, and though powers were given to individuals, and to corporate bodies, for selling a part of their property, of which no precedent is extant, yet, instead of from sixty to seventy millions of stock being purchased, as was expected, the total, on the 1st day of February 1802, only amounted to £. 18,001,148, and on 1st February 1803, to £. 19,180,587.

During the American war, the money borrowed

8 System of competition in subscribing to public loans.

[b] On this subject I think it proper particularly to refer to a pamphlet, intitled, " Short observations on a Commutation of " Tithes for Government Annuities," printed at Hull, anno 1798. This tract discusses, 1. The advantages the clergy would derive from a commutation of tithes for government annuities. 2. The inconvenience of tithes to the clergy and the laity. 3. The nature of the payment of tithes in Scotland, and whence it arises that they are not so oppressive there as in England. 4. Answers to the objections which may be made to a commutation of tithes for government annuities; and concludes with an estimate of the probable value of the tithes in England and Wales, which he calculates, will amount to the sum of full 50 millions sterling, the interest of which, invested in government stock, would furnish an ample income to the clergy.

by

by the public, was raifed through the means either
of *open*, or what were called *clofe*, *loans*.   In the
former cafe, any perfon might fubfcribe: according to the latter plan the loan was confined to a
few individuals.   As during that war, the ftocks
fluctuated much more than during the late conteft,
the minifter was under the neceffity of allowing
a confiderable profit to the fubfcribers, generally
from 3 to 4 *per cent.* when the bargain was made ;
and fome fortunate events having happened, after
fome of thefe loans had been negociated, the premium fometimes rofe to 8 or 10 *per cent.* and
even more.   The chance of fuch profit was much
in favour of new loans, as a fhare in them was
fuppofed to be attended with certain gain, and the
public having once been impreffed with that idea,
it materially contributed to keep up a fpirit for
lending money to the treafury ever fince.

The profit attending the loans during the
American war, excited great clamour, as furnifhing the minifter with an eafy means of corrupting
the reprefentatives of the people ; and the enormous advantages attending them, feemed to in-
dicate, that the intereft of the nation had not been
fufficiently attended to in the negociating thofe
bargains.   The late minifter of finance therefore,
refolved to try a different fyftem, namely, that of
endeavouring to excite a competition among different parties of the monied intereft, with a view
of obtaining the loan on as favourable terms for
the

the public as poffible. The attempt was certainly well intended, and to do juftice to the minifter, it is proper to ftate, that he is entirely exempted from all fufpicion of having made thefe loans the means either of perfonal advantage, or of political corruption. At the fame time it is queftionable, whether fuch competitions may not be productive of great inconveniences, and whether a better fyftem may not be fuggefted.

The inconveniences attending fuch a plan are three. 1. That it may be impoffible to excite a competition at the time, (which was actually the cafe in the year 1793,) or what is much the fame thing, that any apparent competition may be fictitious and ideal, as feems to have been the cafe regarding the loan of 1800, when three of the parties agreed to offer the fame terms, and to divide the amount between them. 2. The fecond difadvantage is, that this fyftem of competition is only calculated for perfons of a fpeculative turn, and confequently does not fuit the character and bufinefs of old, refpectable, and eftablifhed houfes. The confequence of which is, that fuch fpeculators muft bring great quantities of ftock fpeedily to the market, which diminifhes the value of the new loan, as well as of the old funds, injures the credit of the country, and confequently, though the plan may furnifh fome temporary advantage, yet ultimately it lowers the price of the funds, and renders it neceffary to raife fucceeding loans on more difadvantageous

advantageous terms.   3. But the principal difadvantage of this fyftem is, that if by competition you
enhance the rifk, and diminifh the profit of lending
money to the public, you may actually difcourage
the plan fo much, that nobody would think of
engaging in fuch a hazardous and unprofitable
fpeculation; and indeed to this circumftance may
in a great meafure be attributed the difficulty of
raifing money, which the minifter experienced in
the year 1797, which rendered it neceffary for
him to try what was called the loyalty loan, and
other meafures already difcuffed for propping up
the funding fyftem.   Whereas had the preceding
loans been given to old eftablifhed houfes, who
would have divided it in proportion among their
opulent cuftomers, the ftock would have been ab-
forbed by perfons of real property, the new
ftock, if fold, would gradually have been brought
to market; it would have fetched of courfe a
handfome profit, the knowledge of which would
have enabled government to raife, without difficulty, any fum of money the public had occafion
for during the following year.

In regard to the beft plan for raifing public
loans, the proper channel feems to me, the
bankers of the metropolis, and their correfpon-
dence at home and abroad.   There are at prefent above feventy bankers in London, to each
of whom, previous to any loan, a letter to the
following effect might be addreffed, by the Chancellor

cellor of the Exchequer, or the Secretary to the
Treafury.

" GENTLEMEN,

" I beg to inform you, that it is propofed, in the
courfe of this feffion of parliament, to raife the
fum of   for the fervice of the enfuing
year.

" As it is intended to diftribute the whole fubfcription among the different banking houfes in
London, (the ufual proportion to the bank, and
other great corporate bodies always excepted,) it
would be proper for you to inform your friends
and cuftomers, both at home and abroad, of this
intention, and to affure them that every poffible
impartiality will be obferved in diftributing the
loan.

" It is propofed, that the fubfcribers to the
new loan, for every £. 100 they fubfcribe, fhall
have $\frac{2}{3}$ in the 3 per cents. confolidated annuities,
and $\frac{1}{3}$ in the 3 per cents. reduced.   The difcount
on prompt payment fhall be   the inftalments to be paid as follows:

" In regard to the terms, it is propofed that they
fhall be 1 per cent. (in critical times it may be
found neceffary to offer 2 even 3 per cent.),
under the average market price of the ftocks
for the month preceding the day when the loan
is ftated to parliament.

" The only preference that will be given is, to
thofe who offer to depofit the largeft fum with
the firft inftalment, &c. &c."

I have

I have little doubt, if fuch a plan were once put into a fair train, that it would be the means of infuring a fupply of money, by loans, for the public fervice, in a manner perfectly unexceptionable, and by fpreading the loan over fo large a furface, it would prevent the country from being diftreffed by collecting large fums into few hands.   In fact, though a large fum is nominally borrowed at once, yet being paid by inftalments, it is properly a feries of monthly or periodical loans, the nature of which it may be proper to explain.   Let us fuppofe that twelve millions are borrowed in a year, that is at the rate of one million payable monthly.   If the loan is taken by feventy bankers in London, they would only have to pay on an average at the rate of £.14,285 for each houfe and its cuftomers, *per* month; and fo on in proportion to the quantity borrowed.   It is hardly poffible to fuppofe, that the bankers of London and their correfpondents and friends, would hefitate a moment to undertake to fupply the public, not only with that fum, but even at the rate of from £.20,000 to £.30,000 *per* month, (if the loan was made fufficiently profitable;) and the great object which every prudent minifter would naturally keep in view is, not a faving of one, or even two *per cent.* upon any particular loan, (more efpecially if that faving could not be obtained without a rifk of depreciating the price of the funds, from the quantity of ftock that might be brought to market), but that of fecuring, in all fituations and circumftances, a fupply of money

money to the Exchequer without which the public
service might not only suffer, but the very exiltence
of the country might be endangered.

And here it may be proper to mention an idea,
which may be entitled to some consideration.

In the former edition of the History of the Revenue, part 3. p. 272, it was stated, that however
dreadful such a heavy load of national debt might
appear, yet that it ought to be considered in this
respect as beneficial, namely, that it furnished us
with the means of amassing a national treasure,
preferable to any other mode that could be suggested; for it was evident, that to the utmost extent of that burthen which had been already borne
without difficulty, the nation might be safely trusted.
Every shilling therefore that could be deducted
from that sum was so much treasure gained; and
indeed that is the principal source of benefit to be
derived from any reduction of the national debt
by means of a sinking fund, which must, to a certain extent, oppress the people at present, for the
sake of a remote advantage. If this idea is well
founded, as soon as any considerable part of the
national debt is paid off, say two or three hundred
millions, the government of the country, instead of
creating new capitals, should sell off, from time to
time, as occasion might require, a part of the old
debt which it had already redeemed. This seems
to me a much simpler and better plan, than that of
creating a new capital through the medium of one
set of men, and at the same time paying off old
capitals

capitals through another channel. It would be unneceffary however to begin that plan, until fuch a quantity of ftock was accumulated by the commiffioners for difcharging the national debt, as would probably be fufficient for defraying the expences of any war in which the nation might be engaged.

Among the extraordinary events which took place, connected with the finances of the country, during the courfe of the late war, there is nothing that will probably appear more aftonifhing in after-times, than the affiftance given by government, amidft the preffure of an expenfive conteft, to the commercial and colonial interefts; and it is fortunately in my power, from the concern I had in thofe important tranfactions, to give a more complete account of their nature and origin, than has hitherto been communicated to the public.

9. Loan of Exchequer bills, and affiftance given the mercantile and colonial interefts.

From the hazard attending mercantile operations at the commencement of a new war, from the difficulty that muft be experienced in finding fafe and profitable markets for goods, during the courfe of a general convulfion ; and above all, from the univerfal terror and alarm which fpread over Europe, in confequence of the dreadful revolutionary fcenes exhibited in France, and fome of the adjoining ftates, fuch a decay of trade had taken place, and fuch a want of confidence had arifen, as had hardly ever been felt, in any former period of our hiftory.

The ftate of the metropolis, in regard to thefe important particulars, was thus defcribed by a refpectable spectable banker in Westminster, in a letter to the author, immediately before the effect of that great operation, (the issue of the Exchequer bills,) was experienced.

" The late precarious and uncommon situation
" of confidence and circulation, hath obliged every
" individual connected with trade and money
" transactions, to call forth every resource, and
" to keep ready unusual means of answering all
" demands; and of course he must look to him-
" self, and his partners, with all that care and
" anxiety, which the unfortunate state of public
" credit requires.   And the misfortune at this
" juncture is, that every man of money or re-
" sources, has been straining every nerve for six
" weeks past, to support himself or friends, and
" cannot therefore come forward, and lend that
" support to others, which their public spirit would
" prompt them to do, on so critical an occasion."

From the very general acquaintance, which, in consequence of various circumstances, the author was led to cultivate, it was probable that he had more accurate information regarding the distress which was felt in every part of the kingdom, than could fall to the lot of almost any other private individual.   An idea therefore had occurred to him, of proposing in parliament, the appointment of a select committee, to take into its consideration the causes of the commercial failures which had already taken place, and the measures which it would be expedient to adopt to prevent their farther exten-
sion.

fion. But upon communicating this plan to one
of his Majefty's confidential minifters, (the prefent
Lord Vifcount Melville,) the author was informed,
" that unlefs fomething fpecific was previoufly ar-
" ranged, the appointment of any committee, to
" take up the fubjeâ loofely, might produce mif-
" chief, with very little profpeâ of good, but that
" if he had any fpecific ideas to ftate, government
" would be glad to receive them."

In confequence of this information, I tranfmitted to the Chancellor of the Exchequer, on the
16th of April 1793, a paper, of which the following is a copy.

*Thoughts on the Means of reftoring the Commercial
Credit of the Country.*

" The caufes of the prefent miferable ftate of
commercial credit are two : 1. that formerly there
was an unbounded licenfe of iffuing paper currency,
whilft at prefent, there is a difficulty in paffing it,
and of difcriminating between thofe who have a
capital adequate to the demands upon them, and
thofe who have not: and, 2. it may be afcribed to
the diminution of the fpecie of the country, partly
owing to the fwindling praâices of the French,
who, by the moft dexterous manœuvre ever in-
vented, contrived to get the hard guineas of Enland exchanged for their paper affignats[c]. Thefe
caufes

* In a recent publication, the following account is given of
this artful manœuvre.

caufes mutually act upon each other, and their force is neceffarily augmented by the circumftance of a foreign war."

" 1. Paper circulation, kept within due bounds, is undoubtedly a bleffing to a country. If Great Britain, for inftance, requires a circulation of eighty millions, if fpecie alone could be employed as the medium of commerce, having no gold or filver of

---

" In the year 1792, the Briffotine party then ufurping the government of France, formed a confpiracy to drain Great Britain of fpecie ; perfuaded that a fufpenfion of cafh payments at the Bank, would produce univerfal bankruptcy, and ruin of our commerce.   To this end they authorifed agents in London to draw on the caiffe d'efcompte, for whatever fums and at whatever exchange it might be poffible to negociate their bills, and immediately inveft the produce thereof in gold and filver, and fend the fame to France, taking care at the fame time to raife the value of the precious metals at Paris, fo as to tempt to the utmoft the *fraudulent melting and fmuggling of guineas*.   Our minifters foon caught the alarm, and ufed every method to ftop this mifchievous traffic, but the evil had already proceeded to an extent, which in a great meafure produced the multitude of bankruptcies of 1793, with all their concomitant misfortunes. And there is little reafon to doubt the full effect of the confpiracy, had not Claviere and the reft of his gang been counteracted by others of the party, who did not well underftand the bufinefs ; and had not the monfter Roberfpierre done us one unintentional fervice, by deftroying the party.   The truth of this may be feen in Barrere's declarations when in prifon next year, accufing the Jacobins of fruftrating this great project, and refufing Claviere the fum (about £. 40,000 fterling), which he had ftipulated as the price of his agency."   See a tract entitled, Guineas an unneceffary and expenfive Incumbrance on Commerce.   Printed *anno* 1802. Appendix, p 22.

its

its own, it muſt have begun with exporting eighty millions worth of goods, in order to get the valuable metals it wanted.   Whereas fortunately, it has been diſcovered, that thirty millions of ſpecie and fifty of paper anſwers exactly the ſame purpoſe.   Thus Great Britain is in regard to capital, fifty millions richer than otherwiſe it would be, and ſaves, at the rate of *5 per cent.* on that capital, £. 2,500,000 *per annum* of intereſt.   Beſides, it would ſometimes be difficult to get additional ſpecie adequate to the increaſe of commerce, conſequently, the commercial proſperity of the country, would be limited according to the quantity of ſpecie that could be procured.   No ſuch boundary, however, to commerce does exiſt, where paper circulation is eſtabliſhed."

" It is not eaſy to aſcertain the extent of paper circulation in Great Britain.   In Scotland, according to the beſt information that can be procured, it amounts to about three millions.   In England, the notes payable to bearer, may probably be about ten times as much, and ſtating the amount of inland bills at ſeventeen millions, it makes a total of fifty millions of paper currency.   Perhaps, however, the amount might be calculated by the tax on notes."

" It is unfortunate for the country, that the importance of paper coinage, *as a national reſource,* was not better underſtood ſome time ago.   Had the coining of paper money belonged excluſively to the public, it muſt have been equal to a capital of

thirty

thirty millions sterling, the interest of which, would have rendered any other sinking fund unneceffary. As it is, the only advantage which the public derives from paper circulation, arises from the sum paid by the Bank for the privilege of iffuing notes, the stamp duties upon the notes of private bankers, and the benefit the community at large derives from facility of circulation."

" In regard to the prefent commercial distress, the great cause undoubtedly is owing to this, that persons were suffered to iffue notes, without restriction, without capital to carry on their bufinefs, or skill in the profeffion they took up; and it is rather a prepofterous idea, that a number of perfons should be suffered to coin as much paper money as they please, (because they call themfelves bankers,) whilft in the same country, so many unhappy wretches should suffer the severeft punifhments of the law, for coining a few halfpence."

" To remedy the prefent commercial diftrefs, it seems to be neceffary, in the firft place, to check that unlimited power of iffuing notes, and to diftinguish as much as poffible (to make ufe of a figurative expreffion), *the found sheep from the rotten.* Commiffioners should be appointed, without a licenfe from whom, no perfon should be allowed to fet up as a banker. The commiffioners might be the same with thofe appointed to redeem the national debt. Let every banking-houfe place £. 10,000 worth of ftock for every partner in it, in the names of thofe commiffioners, as a fecurity

for

for their commercial dealings. The principal only
to remain as a pledge, the intereſt being annually
paid to them. It is needleſs to enter into the
minute regulations of this plan, unleſs the general
idea were approved of. It is only neceſſary to
add, that landed ſecurity ought not to be received
by the commiſſioners, not being of ſo ſaleable a
nature, and at any rate, ſubject to ſo many drawbacks by ſettlements and intails. Beſides, the
proprietor can mortgage his landed property if he
chooſe it, and purchaſe into the funds."

 " If this idea were adopted, not only might an
act be paſſed for licenſing bankers, but in ſix weeks
time, every one intitled to that privilege might obtain a licenſe, which would re-eſtabliſh the currency
of their notes, and prevent the diſtreſſes which muſt
neceſſarily enſue if the credit of country banks is
totally annihilated. Indeed as ſoon as ſuch li-
cenſes are granted, the notes of ſuch bankers
ought to be received in payment of taxes, and aſ-
ſociations ought to be encouraged, for the purpoſe of giving them all poſſible currency and
credit."

 " In regard to the idea of the Bank of England
eſtabliſhing branches in the country, it requires very
ſerious conſideration. 1. The Bank at preſent ſeems
to have as much buſineſs as it can well manage.
2. Monopolies ought to be avoided as much as
poſſible on all occaſions. 3. The country ſtands
a chance of being better ſerved by the competition
of a number of private bankers, than if all its paper
circulation

circulation and commerce in money were ingroffed
by any particular fet of men."

" 2. The diminution of the fpecie of the country
is a ferious evil, particularly as in confequence
of the difcredit into which paper has got, it is
more neceffary than ever to have fpecie in abundance. Some means muft however be fallen upon
to fupply the demands of circulation, with fome
medium of commerce that will be accepted of,
otherwife the moft ferious confequences may be
expected. Already, in fome places in the country,
have the farmers taken back the cattle they have
brought to market, having nothing offered for
them but the notes of country bankers. The fame
may happen with regard to grain, &c. which may
occafion the greateft diftrefs. The want of circulation, and the deficiency of confumption, will probably diminifh the public revenue, by, from one
to two millions, and the prefent fcarcity of fpecie
will probably be much augmented, by the paying
of a confiderable body of troops on the continent."

" The diftrefs which at prefent exifts, feems to
refemble that which took place in the year 1696-7,
when exchequer bills were originally iffued. They
are, firft mentioned in 8 and 9 Will. 3. cap. 6.
The act is not printed; but it appears from the
life of Hallifax, who was Chancellor of the Exchequer at the time, and who had the merit of the
invention (p. 43), that exchequer bills were iffued
as a fubftitute for money, which was extremely
fcarce at the time, owing to the re-coinage. To
render

render thefe bills more convenient for that purpofe, fome were iffued for £. 10, others only for £. 5; and in fact this feems to be the beft expedient that can now be adopted to remedy the prefent diftrefs; and being thus fanctioned by precedent, it renders the plan lefs alarming and exceptionable."

" It is almoft unneceffary to add, that the public would gain confiderably by fuch a meafure, as no intereft need to be paid on fuch bills, at leaft for the firft year; if afterwards 3 *per cent.* were allowed on them, it would always keep them at or above par. But unlefs the general idea were approved of, it feems to be unneceffary to detail the further particulars refpecting that part of the plan."

" Thefe thoughts are haftily thrown together, with a view of giving rife to difcuffion, rather than as containing a complete fyftem, to be immediately adopted to the full extent that is propofed. Sir John Sinclair was thence induced to fuggeft the propriety of appointing a committee to take the fubject into confideration, that thefe ideas might be brought to maturity before they were communicated to government."

It was on the 24th day of April that Mr. Pitt informed me in the Houfe, that the meafure I had recommended, that of nominating a felect committee, to take into its confideration the ftate of the commercial credit of the country, had been approved of by his Majefty's government, that he

was

was to give notice on that day of his intention to move for its appointment, and that he particularly wifhed me to be one of the number. A committee was accordingly appointed on the 25th; a report was made from the committee on the 29th of April; an act paffed both Houfes and received the royal affent upon the 8th of May following [d], and the whole was carried through with a degree of celerity and judgment, which did infinite credit to the minifter, by whom the bufinefs was conducted.

The commiffioners met and commenced their proceedings, on the very day after the paffing of the act; and fome progrefs was made on that and the two following days, in receiving and determining applications, but after preparing every ftep in order to carry on the bufinefs with the greateft expedition, we were informed that the exchequer bills, on the credit of which the whole operation depended, could not be iffued till Thurfday the 16th of May.

Alarmed leaft a favourite meafure, by this unforefeen delay, might be either difappointed altogether, or at leaft rendered lefs efficient than otherwife it would have been, I was induced to try an expedient which, fortunately, was completely fuccefsful. It was an application to fome of the moft refpectable banking houfes in the metropolis, to the following effect.

" Sir John Sinclair prefents his compliments to Meffrs. ———. By the information received from

[d] 33 Geo. 3. c. 29.

Man-

Manchefter and Glafgow, there is every reafon to apprehend the moft ferious confequences, unlefs fome pecuniary affiftance is *immediately* fent to thofe places.   On fuch an occafion, every individual of public fpirit, will naturally be anxious to ftep forward, to prevent the peace of the country from being difturbed by tumults, which, if once begun, it is impoffible to fay to what length they may be carried.   An idea has occurred to Sir John Sinclair, for fending immediate relief to thofe towns, in perfecting which, he will be happy to be favoured with your affiftance.   The exchequer bills to be iffued under the late act, will not be ready for iffuing before Thurfday next, but the board of commiffioners can, on Monday, grant certificates, directing the exchequer to deliver the exchequer bills to the bearer thereof, to the amount fpecified ; the certificate therefore, is as good a fecurity as the bills themfelves. If you could conveniently advance from £. 5000 to £. 20,000 on fuch certificates, at a difcount, call it of 1 *per cent.*, you will have the fatisfaction of doing a confiderable fervice to the public, without, it is to be hoped, any material lofs or inconvenience."

" The favour of an anfwer is requefted before 12 on Monday.   It may be directed either at Whitehall before 10, or at Mercer's Hall from 10 to 12. If you approve of this meafure, the perfons to whom the exchequer bills are granted, will call at your houfe at one, with a certificate adequate to the fum you agree to take.   The produce

will

will be immediately carried down to Manchefter and Glafgow, and will be received at both thofe places before the bills are iffued from the exchequer, a point of great importance, when even a fingle hour is of confequence."

" Whitehall, Sunday, 12th May 1793."

Nothing could be more fatisfactory than the refult of this application; notwithftanding the terror and alarm which had not as yet fubfided, thefe public fpirited gentlemen, at the fuggeftion and requeft of a private individual, advanced no lefs a fum than £. 70,000 on a few hours notice[c], and the money reached Manchefter and even Glafgow, before the bills, on the fecurity of which the money was advanced, were iffued out of the exchequer. This unexpected fupply, coming fo much earlier than was at all looked for, operated like magic, and had a greater effect in reftoring confidence, than ten times the fum could have had at a later period.

Indeed nothing could turn out more complete and fatisfactory than the whole tranfaction[f]. In a report to the treafury, drawn up when the bufinefs was concluded, (which was fubfcribed by Lord

[c] I have unfortunately loft a note of the names and fums advanced by each banking houfe, but I recollect that Meffrs. Drummond of Charing Crofs, Coutts and Co., and Smith Payne and Smith, were of the number.

[f] It was the fuccefs which had attended this great operation, and the concern which the author had in the formation and conduct, which principally induced the minifter to fupport his plan for the eftablifhment of a Board of Agriculture.

Sheffield,

Sheffield, as chairman, and the other commiffioners), the advantages which had refulted from the
meafure is ftated in the following terms:—" That
" the knowledge that loans might have been ob-
" tained, fufficed in feveral inftances to render
" them unneceffary, that the whole number of
" applications was 332, for fums amounting to
" £. 3,855,624; of which, 238 were granted,
" amounting to £. 2,202,000; 45, for fums to the
" amount of £. 1,215,100 were withdrawn; and
" 49 were rejected for various reafons. The whole
" fum advanced on loans was paid; a confiderable
" part before it became due, and the remainder
" regularly at the ftated periods, without apparent
" difficulty or diftrefs. With the exception of two
" only, who became bankrupts, the parties affifted
" were ultimately folvent, and in many inftances
" poffeffed of great property.

   " The advantages of this well-timed meafure
" were evinced by a fpeedy reftoration of confi-
" dence in mercantile tranfactions, which produced
" a facility in raifing money that was prefently felt,
" not only in the metropolis, but through the whole
" extent of Great Britain.

   " The difficulties in which many confiderable
" commercial houfes were involved were thus re-
" moved, and the fatal effects of thofe difficulties,
" in other houfes who were dependent on them,
" were prevented; nor was the operation of the
" act lefs beneficial, with refpect to a variety of
" eminent manufactures, in different parts of thefe
                                          " king-

" kingdoms, who, having in a great degree fuf-
" pended their works, were enabled to refume
" them, and to afford employment to a number
" of workmen, who muft otherwife have been
" thrown on the public for fupport—and per-
" haps, in fome cafes, with the lofs of the manu-
" facture."

The commiffioners then referred to the anxious
care they had taken to preferve the moft fcrupulous
fecrecy, which fucceeded fo well, that the names
of thofe, who applied for relief, are not known to
this hour, except to the commiffioners and the fure-
ties for the refpective debts.

On this fubject Mr. Rofe very juftly remarks,
" We doubt if any inftance is to be met with,
" where fuch effential benefit has been rendered to
" the commerce and manufactures of a country, in
" a manner fo fudden, fo eafy in execution, and
" (what is perhaps the leaft important confidera-
" tion, compared with the magnitude of the object,)
" at no expence to the public.   It was fo managed,
" that the difference between the intereft paid by
" the borrowers at 5 per cent., and on the exche-
" quer bills lent to them, for which the public paid
" twopence halfpenny a day, fatisfied all the ex-
" pences of the commiffion, and left a profit of
" upwards of £. 4000 which was paid into the ex-
" chequer."

The uncommon fuccefs which had attended this
operation, induced Government to fupport a fimilar application in the year 1797, when, in confequence

quence of the devaftations which had been committed in the iflands of Grenada and St. Vincent's, not only the planters in thofe colonies, but alfo their correfpondents at home, and all thofe either directly or indirectly connected with them, were labouring under great diftrefs. Having taken fo active a part on the former occafion, I was prevailed upon to be a member of the felect committee, and a commiffioner in this fecond tranfaction. It muft be admitted, however, that this fecond attempt has not proved fo fuccefsful. Various acts have been found neceffary for prolonging the payment of the different inftalments, after they became refpectively due ; and though no ultimate lofs will probably be fuftained, yet it evidently appears, that fuch meafures ought not to be too frequently adopted, and when they are, ought to be carried on with the utmoft impartiality, and the ftricteft attention to the public intereft.

In afcertaining the caufes which contributed to the commercial failures in 1793, and which nothing but the meafure above defcribed, (namely, the iffue of exchequer bills) prevented from becoming univerfal over the whole kingdom ; there was one circumftance, which I felt it my duty ftrongly to recommend to the particular attention of the minifter, namely, that merchants importing goods from abroad, were put to the inconvenience, and fometimes to the heavy lofs, of advancing to government the duties to which fuch goods were liable

10. The bonding fyftem.

liable at the moment of importation, confequently long before the articles themfelves were generally fold. This was attended with the following dif-advantages to the merchant. 1. He was under the neceffity either of borrowing money to pay thofe duties, or of confining his trade withing narrower bounds, in order that he might be enabled to pay fuch demands out of his own capital. 2. He evidently loft the intereft of the money thus paid for duties long before the fale, unlefs he raifed the price proportionably, which was not always prac-ticable; and 3. When the duties were very heavy, and money was difficult to borrow, he was often under the neceffity of felling a part of his goods, at an inferior price, in order to clear off the demands of the cuftom houfe.

Thefe circumftances, and a wifh to promote as much as poffible the foreign commerce of the coun-try, induced the late minifter to propofe to Parlia-ment, the eftablifhment of the warehoufing or bonding fyftem, which, to a certain extent, was carried into effect by that minifter, and which is likely to be extended much further under the ad-miniftration of his fucceffor. By the propofed re-gulations, the goods of the merchant will be kept under fafe cuftody, without the neceffity of paying any duty until there is an opportunity, either of felling them at home, or of fending them to fome foreign market. By this plan the payment of drawbacks, (or the repayment of cuftom houfe du-

ties

ties formerly paid), will, in a great meafure, be prevented ; a fortunate circumftance, as the public was often defrauded in the courfe of fuch tranfactions.

Nothing can be more fatisfactory to any friend to the public intereft, who endeavours to give a general view of the progrefs of our financial hiftory, than to record tranfactions, creditable to the minifters who bring them forward, and advantageous to the country.

The fituation of thefe kingdoms, at the commencement of the year 1797, was in the higheft degree alarming.   The war was carried on without fuccefs, the finances of the country were in the greateft diforder, the enemy threatened us with invafion, and there was no profpect of peace.   At that critical emergency, feveral members of Parliament affembled together on the 26th February 1797, and came to the following refolutions.

11. The Finacial Committee of 1797.

" 1. To propofe a parliamentary inquiry into the real ftate of our finances, as the only meafure that can fave the country from bankruptcy.   It is evident, that palliatives and concealment will avail no longer; that we muft know the truth; and the fpirit and the refources of England, we have no caufe to doubt, will then be found equal to the emergency."

" 2. To inquire into the meafures that have been, or might ftill be taken, to preferve this country from invafion, againft which there cannot be too

many

many precautions, as it affects the lives and fortunes of all, and, if fuccefsful, muft end in the
overthrow of that conftitution, which it is the pride
and glory of every Britifh fubject to protect."

" 3. To afcertain, whether peace on honourable
terms, might not ftill be obtained, before another
campaign commences: for there is reafon to believe, that France, at this moment, would agree to
peace, on terms which a large majority of the
people in this country would not confider as in-
admiffible."

Though the party by whom thefe fentiments
were adopted, did not continue long united together, nor perfevere in carrying them through,
yet the public declaration of a powerful body of
men, had a proper influence on the government of
the country. The minifter announced in Parliament that a perfon was empowered to negociate
with the French Republic, which rendered it unneceffary to prefs the third refolution. Meafures
were alfo taken for putting the nation in a better
ftate of fecurity againft invafion, and it was in confequence to the firft refolution above mentioned,
that the moft efficient committee, that had hitherto
taken the finances of this country under its confideration, was appointed [g].

The

g In the Journals of the Houfe of Commons (vol. 29. p. 452.
462. 491, and 527. anno 1763,) there are fome proceedings
regarding the appointment of a felect Committee of Finance,
which

The committee concluded its labours, the firſt ſeſſion of its appointment, on the 20th of July 1797; having laid before the Houſe twenty-two reports, which filled two volumes folio; but as the ſubject of their inquiries was far from being exhauſted, (and indeed the ſucceeding reports filled two volumes folio more), I could not avoid expreſſing my aſtoniſhment in the Houſe, that the committee was not re-appointed early in the ſucceeding ſeſſion. The miniſter ſtated that he did not ſee any particular occaſion for it, but being convinced that the additional inquiries of the committee would throw conſiderable light on the ſtate of our revenue, and would in various reſpects promote the public ſervice, I perſevered in recom-

---

which is there declared to be, " *the moſt proper and effectual* " *method of examining, taking, and ſtating the publick accounts of* " *the kingdom;*" and various other committees have at different times been nominated for the ſame important purpoſe; but their reports have ſeldom given much ſatisfaction, being indiſtinct and voluminous, and generally calculated more with a view of gaining ſome particular point, than for the purpoſe of communicating to the Houſe and to the public, juſt and accurate information reſpecting the matters referred to them. Such committees ought to conſiſt, not of men in office, to report upon their own conduct, but of independant and unconnected members of the Houſe, who would not be afraid of probing matters to the bottom, or of reporting the circumſtances of the country as it appeared to them, after a full and minute examination of the papers laid before them, or, of thoſe which they might think it neceſſary to ca'l for.

mending

mending the meafure, until at laft the minifter agreed to move for the re-appointment.

It cannot be fuppofed, that in a work of this nature, it would be poffible to give even an abftract of thirty-fix reports, comprehending four volumes folio. It may be fufficient to obferve, that they contain much information no where elfe to be met with, and which had not been previoufly known: a plan for annually ftating the public accounts of the kingdom, is there exemplified, which though not perfect, yet is certainly preferable to any that had been formerly adopted, and the fame mode of ftating the public accounts has fince been purfued. Many judicious fuggeftions were made in thofe reports, fome of which have been already carried into execution, and others will probably yet take place ; and on the whole the appointment of that committee, is an event, with which both thofe who had any hand in promoting it, and ftill more, thofe who actually carried it into effect, have every reafon to be fatisfied.

But notwithftanding the labours of this, and of former committees, including alfo the reports of the various boards of commiffioners for ftating the public accounts of the kingdom, for inquiring into the ftate of the woods and forefts, and for afcertaining the fees exacted at the different offices, yet there ftill remains an ample field for inquiry and retrenchment ; a field however, which will probably remain neglected, until the neceffities of another war will render farther inveftigations effential.

tial.   Such inquiries might certainly be carried on
to more advantage in time of peace, than in time
of war; but unfortunately minifters will never take
the trouble of anticipating evils, but prefer the
odious tafk of endeavouring to remedy them, after
the mifchief has been accomplifhed.

The reader has already feen, the material affiftance which it was fortunately in my power to contribute, towards promoting the reftoration of commercial credit, in the year 1793.   I wifh moft fin-
cerely, that my fuggeftions had met with the fame
attention in 1796 and 1797, in which cafe, that
difgraceful flur on our national pecuniary refources,
the ftoppage of payment in cafh at the Bank of
England on the 26th February 1797, either would
never have happened, or would have been immediately remedied.   Indeed when I confider the
many unfuccefsful attempts which were made to
avert that national calamity, by various communications both to the minifter, and to the directors
of the bank, I am much inclined to agree in opinion with an intelligent author on this fubject, who
ftates, " that the conduct purfued by the Bank of
" England, for a confiderable time previous to the
" fufpenfion of the payment of its notes, almoft
" warrant the fufpicion, that inftead of really dread-
" ing that fufpenfion as an evil, they rather looked
" to it as an advantage [h]."   There hangs fome

Margin note: 12. The fufpenfion of payments in cafh at the Bank, and thoughts on circulation and paper currency.

[h] See Boyd's Letter to the Right Hon. William Pitt on the
ftoppage of iffues in fpecie at the Bank of England, 2d edit.
p. 70.

dark

dark myftery regarding this great event, which remains ftill to be developed.

In the paper communicated to government, on
the means of reftoring the commercial credit of
the country, in 1793, it was diftinctly ftated that
the diftrefs at that time was owing to two caufes.
1. The number of country bankers, who carried
on their bufinefs without fkill or capital; and, 2.
to the want of a fufficient quantity of fpecie or
fome other fafe and undoubted medium of circulation, for carrying on the general tranfactions of the
nation.

In regard to the firft point, it was fuggefted that
all bankers fhould be required to take out a licence, and to give fuch unqueftioned fecurity to
the public, as would prevent any rifk of their notes
falling into difcredit. It was impoffible however
to prevail upon the minifter to take any meafures
for that purpofe. The confequence was, the fatal
event now under confideration. For in the words
of the fecretary to the treafury, " whatever might
" have been the remote caufes, it feems perfectly
" clear, that the ftopping payment in cafh of two
" great banks at Newcaftle, owing to a local alarm,
" which fpread rapidly, *was the immediate occafion*
" *of the evil* [1] "

But even the neglect of this fuggeftion, would
not have occafioned the difafter, had another mea-

[1] See Rofe's Brief Examination, p. 65. alfo Third Report of
the Committee of the Houfe of Commons, p. 526. A full
fourth of the country bankers had failed. See Chalmer's Eftimate, edit. 1794. Dedication, p. 67.

fure communicated by the author both to the minifter, and to the directors of the bank, been properly attended to, namely, the iffuing of fmall
notes.   The following is a copy of the paper
tranfmitted to Mr. Pitt upon this fubject, on the
29th of April 1796.

" The increafed revenue, confumption, and
commerce of the country, undoubtedly require a
greater quantity of reprefentative figns, or circulating medium, than was neceffary three years ago;
inftead of which, there is reafon to believe, that a
decreafe has taken place, and hence the prefent
embarraffments both at the Exchange and at the
Exchequer."

" To remedy this evil, there ought to be, an
increafe either of fpecie or paper."

" Having none of the precious metals within
ourfelves, an immediate increafe of fpecie is impoffible.   It is neceffary therefore to confider
whether an increafe of paper money is not practicable."

" Perhaps the beft mode of attaining that object would be, for the bank to iffue *three* pound
and *two* pound bank notes."

" At prefent, if a perfon wants a guinea, he is
often under the neceffity of changing a ten pound,
or at leaft a five pound note.   This makes a
greater call for fpecie than is really neceffary, as
the bank, and even bankers, muft be ready to furnifh not only fuch a quantity of fpecie as is really
wanted,

wanted, but muſt alſo be prepared for demands not abſolutely neceſſary."

" It is probable that the bank might ſafely iſſue a million or two more of paper, if, to that amount, two and three pound notes were put in circulation, the effect of which would ſoon be felt in every corner of the kingdom."

" The only objection ſeems to be, the trouble of fabricating ſuch a number of ſmall notes; but if it is likely to be of public ſervice, there is every reaſon to believe that ſo public ſpirited a body as the bank, will not on that account heſitate to endeavour to remove an evil, which in a great meaſure originates from the proſperity of the country, and which it is in their power to alleviate, at leaſt with ſafety, if not with profit."

This communication unfortunately proved unſucceſsful, which I flattered myſelf was owing to the certain knowledge poſſeſſed by the miniſter, that no danger was to be apprehended. But happening to be accidentally in London in September 1796, I found the ſtate of the country, in regard to its pecuniary concerns, more alarming than ever, and that all the apprehenſions I had ſo long entertained upon the ſubject, were likely to be verified. I was thence induced to write a letter to the governor and directors of the Bank of England, of which the following is a copy.

" Gentlemen,

" Gentlemen,

" I learn, with infinite regret, the very general diftrefs, which prevails in the commercial world, from the fcarcity of money [k], and the diminution of credit ; and it would give me much, pleafure, could I furnifh any hints, which, improved on by your judgment and experience, could in the fmalleft degree tend to alleviate fuch preffing evils. For if they are not checked in time, there is too much reafon to apprehend, that they muft ultimately be productive of confequences truly ferious and alarming.

" There is certainly more wealth than ever in the country, of a folid and fubftantial nature. Our lands—our houfes—our fhipping—our manufactures—our goods of every fort, are greater in quantity, and more valuable in amount, than ever they were before. But our diftreffes are owing to the want of a fufficient quantity of a circulating medium, either of paper or of fpecie, adequate to the increafed commerce, and the increafed revenue of the country ; and alfo adequate to fupply the vacuum occafioned by that exportation of money

[k] The fcarcity of money was eafily accounted for, when the real ftate of the circulation of the bank was explained to the public. It then appeared that the average number of notes circulated in September, 1795, was £. 11;034,790 and in September, 1796, only £. 9,720,440, making a difference in fo fhort a period as one year of £. 1,314,350, the want of which, confidering the total fum circulated, muft have been feverely felt in the money market.

to

to foreign countries, which has taken place in the
courfe of the war.

" For remedying the evils in queftion, I take
the liberty of fubmitting to your confideration, the
following hints.

" I. Would not an increafe of the capital of the
Bank, enable it to ferve more effectually, both the
merchant and the public ; and would not public
credit be much improved, if a certain proportion
of the Exchequer Bills, now outftanding, were to
be fubfcribed into the new ftock ? On various occafions, the capital of the Bank of England has
been increafed, for the purpofe of relieving the
country ; and by giving the holders of Bank ftock,
the preference in the new fubfcription, they would
have no juft caufe for complaint.

" II. I am perfuaded, were the Bank to iffue *two
pound* and *three pound* Bank notes, that it would be
a great public convenience, and that very few of
them would be exchanged into fpecie. Indeed lefs
gold would be required for changing even ten
pound notes, which is often done for the fake of
getting two or three guineas, the whole fum in
coin that may be actually wanted by the holder of
the note.

" III. The increafed commerce and revenue of
the country, certainly demand a greater increafe
of a circulating medium. That increafe can only
take place either in fpecie, or in Bank paper.
Specie, however, cannot be commanded when
wanted; and if paper were to be iffued by the
Bank,

Bank, *in the usual form*, it might be immediately
converted into specie, and exported out of the
country. Might not, however, the Bank obtain
authority from Parliament, to issue a million in
notes, neither bearing interest, nor convertible into
specie, until twelve months after the date[1]; or
might there not be a particular sort of note, which,
though *issued* on the 1st of January 1796, might
be *dated* on the 1st of January 1797, and so on?
in which case it could not, till the day of its
date, be convertible into specie. Such notes would
at once pass, *by consent*, without discount. A union,
or understanding, for that purpose, among the
merchants and bankers of London, might be established in a very short space of time. The merchants might be told, that the Bank would discount
their bills, to any specified amount, for the accommodation of the public, partly payable in notes
dated 1st of January 1798, and partly in common
convertible notes; and, if the due proportion were
not exceeded, such is the want of money at the
time, that the one kind of note would pass as readily as the other. If the Bank were *applied to by*
the merchants to issue such notes, where could there
be an objection to try such a plan, at least during
the war?

" IV. The last point I shall take the liberty of
alluding to, relates to the state of the coinage; that

---

[1] Some, who startled at the idea of issuing a million of such
notes, think nothing now of the idea of having fifteen millions
not convertible into specie.

of gold in particular.   While we continue to make our gold coin so much finer than that of other nations, and almost give *a bonus* to the smelter, by demanding nothing for the expence of the manufacture, it is impossible that our coin should not either be exported abroad, or smelted down at home ; and we must, of consequence, experience all the evils resulting from a diminished currency.   Has the bank ever seriously taken that point into its consideration, and represented it to his Majesty's government ?

" I thought it my duty to trouble you with these hasty observations, on subjects deeply interesting to us all, and should be happy were these hints to prove in any respect useful for obviating evils, of a nature so likely to prove in the highest degree prejudicial to the interests of the country.

" I have the honour to be,
with great respect,
Gentlemen,
Your faithful and obedient servant,
JOHN SINCLAIR."
" Whitehall, 15th September 1796."

The reader will make every necessary allowance for a letter, written without any intention of publication, and drawn up, rather with a view of suggesting hints for the consideration of the Bank, than of recommending any particular line of conduct to be pursued.   Indeed he flattered himself, that the hints thus thrown out would have induced the
directors,

directors, if they did not approve of his ideas upon the subject, to have fallen upon some other means more likely to answer the purpose, unless there was the deepest conviction in the minds of those to whom he had addressed himself, that the evils he had apprehended were not likely to take place.

It is singular that the measure proposed thus early, though seemingly despised at the moment, yet should afterwards be adopted as soon as the mischief was done; and it is some satisfaction to the author to find, that in the opinion of intelligent men, " *if the Bank had issued these small notes in* " *time, there would have been no occasion for the* " *suspension of payment in specie*[m]."

But as no immediate mischief followed this great catastrophe, the public at large soon became extremely indifferent to the event, and the circumstances which led to it. A plan was proposed, which was sanctioned by the approbation of some of the best informed individuals connected with the monied interest, by which the suspension might have been removed in the space of a few weeks. But as that would not suit the views of the minister it met with no attention. The plan was to the following effect.

" The necessity of suspending the payment of

[m] See Address to the Proprietors of the Bank of England, by Alexander Allardyce, Esq. M. P. 3d edit. p. 153 and 154, printed *anno* 1798. The same opinion is also supported by a most respectable merchant in the city of London, who transmitted a long letter to the author on the subject of the suspension.

cash

cafh at the Bank can only be attributed to its
having too large a proportion of paper in circulation compared to the amount of its fpecie. The
notes in circulation, let us ftate, for the fake of
round numbers, at ten millions. Let us fuppofe
that the Bank could be re-opened, if inflead of
ten, it had only five millions of notes in circulation.
It has been propofed that government fhould repay
the Bank its advances to that amount: but from
the fituation of the public, the payment of fo large
a fum, in addition to all the other demands upon
it, cannot be expected; though the more it can
pay, the more it will enable the Bank to affift the
merchants with difcounts. But it will anfwer
exactly the fame purpofe, if the Bank were to add
ten millions to its prefent capital, to be paid one
half in bank-notes, which would thus be taken out
of circulation, and the other half, in exchequer
bills, and other government fecurities. The fum
would be fubfcribed in one day, as Bank ftock
bears an intereft of feven *per cent. This dividend
the public ought to guarantee, during the continuance
of its charter, as its advances to the public have undoubtedly occafioned its prefent difficulties.* It would
alfo be neceffary to give the proprietors of the old
ftock, in proportion to their refpective intereft, a
fhare in the new fubfcriptions. By adopting this
plan, the Bank of England might be opened in the
fpace of a few weeks [n]."

                                                    " The

[n] As a proof that this plan was not only practicable, but that
its effects might have been depended upon, the reader is re-
                                                    ferred

" The only objection to this measure is, that five millions of paper, representing property, being thus taken out of the market, some means must be contrived to fill up the vacuum. One mode might be to procure an additional quantity of specie, which however cannot at once be obtained; another, to issue *state notes*, or exchequer bills, on an improved plan, to that amount; but though that would be a productive resource to the government, yet such is the risk of entrusting ministers with the power of coining paper, that hardly any advantage can compensate for the mischiefs it might occasion. It would soon be found, that state notes would be rapidly multiplied beyond all reasonable bounds. The plan, therefore, that I would prefer, would be, that of licensing the bankers of London, and other large towns, to issue notes to that amount, finding proper security to commissioners appointed by the public, like the exchequer bill commissioners, and permitting the notes issued by such licensed bankers to be received in the payment of taxes during the war. This, with the credit to be derived from the security given, would enable them to discount the bills of the merchants, and to keep up the pecuniary circulation of the country."

---

ferred to the result of an operation on similar principles, which took place about a century ago, (in consequence of 8 Will. c. 20.) an account of which will be given in the farther progress of this work, when the history of the bank is detailed.

" In

" In regard to the third point, that of preventing the rifk of fuch calamities in future, the only
mode is, by altering the principles on which our
coinage has been conducted, fo as to check its being either fmelted at home, or exported to other
countries."

The fufpenfion ° having unfortunately taken

° The order of council was iffued on Sunday, February 26,
1797, and was conceived in the following terms : " Upon the
" reprefentation of the Chancellor of the Exchequer to the
" Council, ftating that, from the refult of the information
" which he had received, and of the inquiries which it has
" been his duty to make, refpecting the effect of the unufual
" demands for fpecie that have been made upon the metro-
" polis, in confequence of ill-founded or exaggerated alarms
" in different parts of the country, it appears, that unlefs fome
" meafure is immediately taken, there may be reafon to ap-
" prehend a want of a fufficient fupply of cafh, to anfwer the
" exigencies of the public fervice, it is the unanimous opinion
" of the Board, that it is indifpenfably neceffary, for the public
" fervice, that the directors of the Bank of England fhould
" forbear iffuing any cafh in payment until the fenfe of Par-
" liament can be taken on that fubject, and the proper mea-
" fures adopted thereupon, for maintaining the means of circu-
" lation and fupporting the public and commercial credit of
" the kingdom at this important conjuncture.   And it is
" ordered, that a copy of this minute be tranfmitted to the
" directors of the Bank of England ; and they are hereby re-
" quired, on the grounds of the exigency of the cafe to con-
" form thereto, until the fenfe of Parliament can be taken as
" aforefaid."   The members prefent on this memorable
occafion were : The Lord Chancellor, (Wedderburn)—the
Lord Prefident, (Earl of Chatham)—Duke of Portland,—
Marquis Cornwallis—Earl Spencer—Earl of Liverpool—Lord
Grenville—and the Right Hon. W. Pitt, (Chancellor of the
Exchequer.)

place,

place, notwithftanding every exertion in my power to prevent it, and no meafures having fince been adopted for the purpofe of removing the evil, it has been found neceffary to continue the reftriction by reiterated acts of parliament, and it is hardly poffible to fuppofe, that the Bank of England, as at prefent conftituted, can ever again open to any effective purpofe, as the leaft rumour of war, or any continuance of an unfavourable ftate of Exchange, muft always compel it to fhut again its coffers, and to fufpend its payment in cafh. In fuch a fituation, it is furely a fubject of the moft effential importance, to confider what means are the moft likely to place our pecuniary refources on the fureft and beft foundation. Previoufly however to any attempt to explain the meafures that ought now to be purfued, it will be proper to confider the nature of circulation and of paper currency, the principles of which ftill require additional explanation, notwithftanding the many volumes which have been written upon the fubject.

THOUGHTS ON CIRCULATION AND PAPER CURRENCY.

GENERAL PRINCIPLES.

The wealth of a nation properly confifts in the goods or merchandize it poffeffes, whether arifing from the produce of the foil, from manufactures or internal induftry,—or from foreign commerce.

Coin

Coin or metals may be defcribed as an article of merchandize, which, by common confent, is effential for three important purpofes.

1. For enabling individuals to barter the value of their labour for an article univerfally exchangeable.

2. For the purpofe of transferring property in goods from one individual to another, or from one nation to another, without the trouble of actual barter; and

3. For enabling the government of a country to obtain a revenue: for if the Exchequer were under the neceffity of levying its taxes in kind, how could it fit out a fleet, or maintain an army, or defray the various other expences of a ftate.

Money being the medium of barter, both for labour and goods, and in a manner the fource or bafis of public revenue, it is neceffary to preferve a due proportion between its amount, and 1. The quantity of labour that muft be paid for: 2. The quantity of goods or merchandize, the property of which muft be transferred; and 3. The total amount of the demands of the Exchequer, whether arifing from taxes or loans, or any extraordinary fpecies of contribution.

The quantity of money however inftead of being ftationary, ought always to be on the increafe.

1. To promote a greater quantum of labour, on the increafe of which the wealth and profperity of a country fo much depends.

2. To

2. To facilitate the transfer of a greater quantity of goods, among a greater body of people, as the commerce and population of a prosperous country is always augmenting; and

3. To enable the people, should it be necessary, to furnish, without inconvenience, greater supplies to the Exchequer.

We shall proceed to apply these general principles. 1. To the case of an increased quantum of labour or industry: 2. To an increased commerce in, or transfer of, goods: 3. To an increased revenue: and 4. Shall conclude with a general system for establishing the paper circulation of this country on the surest and best foundation.

I. *Increased Quantum of Labour.*

An increased medium of circulation is of more consequence, with a view of facilitating the exchange of labour, and accumulating an extent of capital necessary for that purpose, than perhaps in any other respect. It is certain that labour, properly applied, is the basis of national prosperity; but who will labour, unless by his exertions he can be furnished with the means of subsistence. The wants of every individual, more especially if incumbered with a large family, are, in civilized periods of society, extremely numerous. They cannot therefore be supplied, without being paid at least partly in coin, or in some article equally transferable. If the industry of a nation therefore is on the increase, how can

it

it be carried on without an increase of that medium of circulation, on the quantum of which it
neceſſarily depends.

Nor is this all ; induſtry muſt often be carried
on by borrowing capital, and if the medium of
circulation is limited, or leſs than the demand,
the intereſt paid for the uſe of it muſt be extremely high, which damps the ſpirit of exertion.
But if by prudent meaſures, what paſſes for money becomes abundant, the intereſt of money di-
miniſhes. Many branches of induſtry therefore,
yielding perhaps but moderate profit, may then be
carried on with advantage, and the proſperity of
the country increaſes with almoſt incredible rapidity.

Nor is this all ; the improvement of a country,
by the labour of its induſtrious inhabitants, can
never be carried to its utmoſt extent, unleſs money
can be procured, not only at a low intereſt, but
even ſinking the capital. A temporary command
of money may anſwer for common commercial
purpoſes ; but with a view of effecting *laſting improvements*, as roads, bridges, canals, harbours,
mines, buildings, together with various branches
of agricultural improvement, as draining, watering, encloſing, &c., money ought to be pro-
curable, for a long period of time, on the payment of a moderate intereſt, otherwiſe ſuch improvements will not be carried on to the extent
that might otherwiſe be expected.

There cannot therefore be a more miſtaken
opinion

opinion than this, that the profperity of a country depends but little on the quantum of its medium of circulation. In fact, an induftrious nation muft profper in proportion to the quantity it poffeffes or circulates. Let us fuppofe the total circulation of Great Britain to be 40 millions fterling in coin and in paper, bearing an intereft of *5 per cent.*, if it were reduced to 30 millions, bearing an intereft of *6 per cent.* how much would not the induftry of the nation be cramped; whereas were it raifed to 50 millions, bearing an intereft of *4 per cent.* and the whole of it actively employed in carrying on laborious occupations, it cannot be doubted, that the profperity of the country would increafe with a rapidity, and be carried to a height, which would not otherwife have been practicable.

II. *Increafed Commerce.*

Nothing can be more evident than this, that an increafed commerce, or the transfer of an increafed quantity of goods, cannot be carried on to advantage, without an increafed medium of barter. This, to a certain extent, commerce itfelf furnifhes by means of Bills of Exchange, and the rapid circulation of money which they occafion, more efpecially where it is the ufual practice to difcount fuch bills only for two or three months. But ftill that accommodation is not fufficient, and cannot always be obtained. Hence commerce has experienced, and muft always experience frequent checks, unlefs there is at all times plenty of money

in

in circulation, in proportion to its increafe or extent.

But we are told, that no increafe of circulation is neceffary for the merchant. Let him fell his goods cheaper, and he will always find a market. Unlefs the fale however, is attended, not only with indemnification, but with profit, there muft be an end to commerce; and unlefs the merchant can procure money on loan, until a fale can be made on fair and adequate terms, he may be ruined. Nor is this obfervation confined to one article of commerce only; it is applicable to all. There is no branch carried on to any extent, or pufhed with any fpirit, that does not occafionally feel a fcarcity of money. It is faid, why fhould the public en-courage fpeculations, or intereft itfelf in their be-half. The anfwer is obvious. All trade is, pro-perly fpeaking, fpeculation, and all the encourage-ment wifhed for is, that merchants may have the command of money, at the legal intereft of 5 *per cent*. when they have occafion for it, and can pro-duce good fecurity. This however they cannot always obtain, unlefs money, the medium of barter or circulation, is increafed with the increafe of their goods or merchandize.

III. *Increafed Revenue.*

The public revenue of a country, unlefs fur-nifhed from property in land, evidently arifes from the labour or merchandize, or the value thereof, which the individuals of a nation can furnifh, after

fupplying

supplying themfelves with the neceffaries and conveniencies of life.

But after a public revenue has reached a certain
ftandard, let us fuppofe, that ten millions of additional income, is neceffary for the public exigences.   How is that fum to be raifed, without,
1. More goods and wealth; or, 2. A higher price
for them; or, 3. A greater facility of barter, by
means of an increafed medium of circulation.

1. An additional quantity of goods, to a certain
extent, may be obtained, by greater induftry, and
by improvements in agriculture, and other arts:
but unlefs there is a more extended market for
them, the price diminifhes, and the refult will prove
on the whole, rather a lofs than an advantage to
the community.

To explain this doctrine, let us fuppofe, that
the goods annually produced in the united kingdom, are worth 100 millions fterling *per annum*;
if the quantity were increafed one-fifth, and if the
price were lowered in proportion, we fhould not,
in a pecuniary point of view, be one farthing
richer; and in regard to finance, the people at
large, would in fact be lefs able than before, to
furnifh fupplies to the Exchequer. Thofe who purchafed goods cheaper, and confumed them, might,
to a certain extent, be benefited, and be enabled of
courfe to pay more to the public; but all the various claffes of the community by whofe induftry
the goods were made and brought to market,
                                            would

would not be able to pay near so much as they did before, and would necessarily be impoverished.

2. Let us next suppose, that the quantity of goods remains the same, but that the price increases one-fifth. The amount of the annual income of the nation, would then rise from 100 to 120 millions in value, and there would be a much larger fund for paying the demands of the public.

3. Let us, in the last place suppose, that the price not only increases, but that there is also an additional quantity of the medium of transfer, by which a good market or rapid sale is secured. The country is then in the highest possible state of public prosperity. *Abundance of merchandize, at a high price, and a rapid sale, constitutes the summit of national felicity, in so far as regards income or revenue, and a nation enjoying such advantages, can pay, without difficulty, taxes to an amount, that seems hardly to be credited by nations who have not been placed in the same situation.* Those with fixed incomes, may, in some respects, suffer, but they are sufficiently indemnified, by the certainty and the regularity with which their incomes are paid, and the easiness with which they can obtain credit, or capital, to increase their incomes by industry.

Three things then are essential for public prosperity; namely,

1. An additional quantity of labour or goods, in so far as may be necessary, for internal consumption or foreign export.

2. An

2. An increaſed price of goods, ſo as not to hinder conſumption at home or exportation abroad; and,

3. An increaſed medium of barter, ſo as to ſecure a rapid ſale and a certain market.

Let us conſider therefore, how the laſt, which is by far the moſt material, can be obtained, for plenty of money will always ſecure a good price, and good prices will neceſſarily promote the raiſing a greater quantity of goods.

4. General ſyſtem, for eſtabliſhing the paper circulation of the country on a ſure foundation.

In countries where mines do not exiſt, if the if the precious metals alone are the medium of circulation, an increaſe of coin or ſpecie cannot be obtained, except by means of commerce ; but in that caſe, goods muſt be exported to purchaſe bullion for the purpoſe of coinage, and the nation is, to that extent, impoveriſhed, merely to procure a medium of barter.

For inſtance, if in conſequence of additional taxes, ten millions of money ſhould be wanted for additional circulation, were gold and ſilver neceſſary for that purpoſe, ten millions worth of goods muſt be exported, merely to procure the repreſentative of circulating wealth [p].

Hence therefore the advantages of paper money. Gold and ſilver repreſent property actually

[p] In the ſtate of coin, it is at firſt more valuable than in the ſhape of goods, on account of its transferable nature, but its value is conſtantly diminiſhing by wear.

ſent

sent abroad, and in the possession of foreign nations: *whereas paper money, when issued on proper principles, represents property at home and in our possession.* Were it possible to keep up a proper proportion between the two, so that the paper issued could always be converted into coin, as foreign or domestic commerce required it, the state of a country, in so far as regards its circulation, must be in the highest degree prosperous.

Paper currency, by which I mean any security payable to the bearer on demand, is of three sorts. The first, issued by the Government of a country; the second, by private individuals; and the third, by corporations erected for that special purpose.

1. To a certain extent paper money might be circulated by the Government of a country, but such a plan is liable to much abuse. When issued like exchequer bills in England, bearing interest, it does not answer the purpose of money, from the uncertainty of its value, varying according to the amount of the interest due. If issued, not as a loan bearing interest, but as actual coin, like the assignats of France, the Government, from the facility of coining it, soon exceeds all bounds; its value rapidly depreciates, and ultimately is reduced to nothing.

2. It has hitherto been the policy of this country, to permit individuals to issue paper money, without any restriction, and it cannot be denied, that this liberty, immediately previous to the commencement of the late war, was attended with useful consequences. Every town in the kingdom
became

became the centre of a paper mint, and what paſſed currently for money abounded. The reſult was highly ſatisfactory. The intereſt of money fell, that ſure teſt of public proſperity. Improvements of every kind were rapidly carried on. The cultivation of a common, the formation of a new canal, the conſtruction of a new harbour, the eſtabliſhment of a new manufacture, or of a new branch of foreign trade, never ſtopped for want of capital. The prices of every ſpecies of agricultural produce increaſed, which gave a new fillip to the art of huſbandry. The revenue roſe to an amount which equalled the expectations of the moſt ſanguine, and the country exhibited the delightful ſpectacle of comfort, induſtry, and wealth.

But this pleaſing, though baſeleſs fabric, being built on falſe credit, and defective principles, in a great meaſure fell to the ground. No ſooner was the confidence which the public had given to private banks deſtroyed, than the abſurdity was generally acknowledged, of giving to every individual, who choſe to aſſume it, the privilege of coining paper money. At firſt, only ſome of private banks, who traded without ſufficient capital, gave way; this threw diſcredit upon others, however ſubſtantial, and the ſtorm at laſt affected the bank of England itſelf, in a manner too recent, and too well known, to render any account of it here neceſſary.

That paper money might be iſſued by country banks, with much public advantage, if they were

put

put under a proper fyftem of regulation, can hardly be queftioned ; but that, without giving any fecurity for the notes they circulate, or obtaining any licence for that purpofe, any individual, or any fet of men, fhould be permitted to coin paper, and iffue it as money, can hardly be juftified on any found principle of policy.

With a view of laying the foundation of a plan for licenfing country bankers to iffue notes, which feemed to me fo effential for the public intereft, I drew up the following outlines of the regulations that might be adopted.

Plan for li-
cenfing
country
bankers.

1. That no individual or company be permitted to iffue engraved notes, payable to bearer on demand, without having obtained a licence for that purpofe.

2. That fuch licence be granted by a Board of Commiffioners eftablifhed for that fole object, refembling the one by which exchequer bills were iffued for the relief of the commercial intereft ; and that fimilar fecurities be required either perfonal, funded, or landed, as may be thought moft advifable ; and,

3. That a licence be granted for iffuing notes, to double the amount of the fum for which fecurity is given ; fuch notes either to be fubfcribed by fome perfons authorifed by the commiffioners, or ftamped under their authority [q].

[q] Proper ftamps would be a great fecurity againft forgery.

The

Obfervations on the above Syftem.

The nature of fuch proceedings, is now fo well afcertained by the experience of two commiffioners, that no difficulty would be found, in carrying the above plan into effect, both with refpect to the granting a licence, and afcertaining the fecurity to be required.

The whole may be done by one commiffion affembled in the city of London, for the Exchequer Bill Commiffioners, found no difficulty in examining applications from every part of the kingdom.

The licence for iffuing notes may be fafely granted for double the value of the fecurity given, becaufe there is every reafon to fuppofe that fuch notes never could be circulated, without receiving for them what was prefumed, at the time, to be equivalent to their full value. Indeed a banker muft be extremely unfkilful, if the effects which he holds in fecurity for the notes he iffues, would not produce at leaft 10*s*. in the pound, and for the other 10*s*., the fecurity given to the commiffioners would be fufficient. The public therefore, would, on the whole, be completely fafe, even though the banker had liberty to iffue double the extent of the fum for which fecurity was given, and it certainly would be a great accommodation to him.

If this plan were to be adopted, the ftamp now applicable to notes payable to bearer on demand, ought to be repealed, and a new ftamp, under the authority of the new Board of Commiffioners, fubftituted in its room. In that cafe indeed, even a
higher

higher ftamp duty might be impofed, which would
defray the expence of the new Board, and which
the bankers could well afford to pay, as the additional credit they would derive, when trading under the fanction of fuch a licence, would be of infinite fervice to them.

Indeed how can this plan be objected to in regard to private bankers, when the fame principles
have been already carried into effect, to a greater
extent, in the cafe of the Bank of England. The
liberty which that corporation enjoys of iffuing
notes, is in confequence of a licence granted to it,
in confideration of its having advanced to the public a confiderable fum, which is refponfible for the
notes it circulates. Befides which, the bank has
occafionally given fome premiums to the public,
for the renewal of the privileges it has obtained;
and as the money it has advanced has, for feveral
years paft, remained at a low intereft, confequently
the public circuitoufly derives fome fhare of the
profits arifing from its paper circulation.

It is not propofed, however, that private bankers
fhould be liable to the fame burdens, or to the fame
extent, but it is certainly defirable that none but fubftantial men fhould be permitted to iffue notes, and
that the number of fuch notes fhould be afcertained.
By adopting that plan, we fhould enjoy all the advantages of paper circulation, without its concomitant evils. It would be for the intereft of the
bankers to make the circulation as extenfive as
poffible, and to infure to the public all the benefits
to be derived from extent; whilft, at the fame
time,

time, it would be in the power of parliament, if it were found too extenſive, to check the evil, by reducing the quantity of paper permitted to be circulated, within proper bounds.

Corporations for circulating paper, money may be of two deſcriptions, namely, for iſſuing either great or ſmall notes. *On corporations iſſuing notes.*

The bank of England was, till the ſtoppage of payments in caſh, *anno* 1797, a corporation of the firſt deſcription ; and indeed, inſtead of its iſſuing ſmall notes, perhaps it would have been better that another corporation had been erected with that ſpecial privilege.   From the immenſity of its tranſactions, it cannot poſſibly do juſtice, in its preſent ſtate, to the plan of iſſuing ſmall notes.   Such notes, though leſs in point of value, muſt always become more in regard to number, than large ones [r].   This leads me therefore to mention a plan, which would probably be acceptable to the Bank of England, and which at the ſame time would, in various reſpects, moſt eſſentially promote the public intereſt.

The Bank of England has ſo long poſſeſſed its monopoly, and has been of ſuch important ſervice to the public [s], that any attempt to eſtabliſh another

[r] This was actually the caſe on the 25th of January 1803, when the value of the large notes iſſued by the bank was £. 13,404,190, and of the ſmall ones, £. 3,280,870, conſequently there muſt have been a greater number of ſmall notes.

[s] Sir Francis Baring thus ſtates the importance of the bank of England. " It has hitherto been beyond the power of hu-

other bank would not probably be fuccefsful, I would therefore recommend an increafe of two millions to the capital of the bank, and the eftablifhment of two branches, one to remain where it is fituated at prefent, and to carry on the iffuing of large notes, and all the other bufinefs to which it was accuftomed, prior to the fufpenfion in 1797; and the fecond branch to be eftablifhed at Weft-minfter [t], and to have the fole privilege, in fo far as regards the metropolis, of iffuing notes under £. 5. Each branch to have a feparate body of directors, but the profits of both to be confolidated

---

" man refearch to afcertain correctly the caufes and mode in
" which the immenfe machine of circulation moves, and yet
" the fact is beyond a doubt, that the paper circulation of
" fifteen millions and a half helps to move with a facility which
" nothing but long experience can reconcile to our belief.
" 1. The national income, loans, &c. fuppofe fifty millions.
" 2. The exports. 3. The imports. 4. Internal or domeftic
" trade. 5. Private circulations to an enormous amount. 6.
" Agriculture, fhipping, mines, &c. We may confider with
" wonder and aftonifhment the fmall fpace which the fun ap-
" pears to fill in the firmament, while we know and feel that
" every part of our globe benefits by the vivifying effects of
" its rays. The Bank of England is, to the agriculture, com-
" merce, and finance of Great Britain, its fun: and the circu-
" lation of fifteen millions and a half of its paper is the bafis
" on which its convenience, property, and fafety have hither-
" to refted." See Sir Francis Baring's anfwer to Mr. Boyd
on the influence of the ftoppage of iffues in fpecie at the bank
of England, printed anno 1801, p. 14.
    [t] The King's Mews would be a proper fituation for the propofed eftablifhment.

together,

together, and to be divided amongft the proprietors of bank ftock.

If this plan were adopted, even if the fufpenfion
of payments in cafh, were to be continued, in fo
far as regards the city branch, and the notes iffued
there; yet there would be no reafon for extending
it to the Weftminfter department. For the whole
capital vefted in the Weftminfter branch, ought to
be employed in the difcounting of bills at two or
three months date, by which means the branch
would always have the command of its capital; as
fuch bills might be made payable, either in the
fmall notes which it iffued, or in fpecie. Were
fuch a branch alfo eftablifhed, there would be no
difficulty in pointing out a mode of fabricating its
notes, by which all rifk of forgery would be prevented.

Such a plan would be attended with a variety
of public advantages. It is probable, that inftead
of three millions of fmall notes, the bank might increafe the quantity, through the medium of its new
eftablifhment, to at leaft five or fix millions, without exceeding the demand or overloading the market. Can any means be thought of, that would
enable the public better to bear up under any
preffure, than fuch an addition to the circulating
medium of the country, when it can be done with
perfeft fafety. What is the foundation of the
taxable income of the nation, but the annual fale
of goods; and if, by plenty of money, you facilitate the fale of goods or increafe their price, do

you

you not augment the income of the people, and
confequently enable them, with infinite more eafe
than otherwife could be the cafe, to pay their taxes,
and to carry on their induftry. Let us take, for
example, a landed gentleman of £. 5000 a year.
His tenants, from a fcarcity of money, may not be
able to fell their produce, or may be obliged to
take an inferior price, or to agree to a diftant payment. In that cafe, how can he receive his rents
punctually, or pay regularly the demands of the
Exchequer ? Increafe the circulating medium, and
thefe difficulties will vanifh.   By an increafed
price, and readier market, he may be enabled to
increafe his rents, and to pay even the additional
demands of the Exchequer, without materially diminifhing his own expenditure, and confequently
without much inconvenience. Let us next take
perfons connected with trade, whofe fuccefs entirely depends on a command of capital or on credit. Open a fhop where the manufacturer, or the
merchant, can difcount their bills with certainty,
when the fecurity is good, and they will find no
difficulty in paying the taxes to which they are
fubject, and extending their commerce. The fame
obfervations are applicable to almoft all the various
other claffes of fociety.

And here it may be proper to remark, that for
increafing the income of the people at large, for
augmenting their induftry and commerce, and enabling them to pay their taxes, the iffuing of fmall
notes is to the full as neceffary as large ones. The
objest

object that ought to be kept in view, is, to facilitate, as much as poffible, the immenfe mafs of daily and hourly tranfactions, for many of which fmall notes are much better calculated than large ones. But the fummit of policy would be, to have one great corporation erected for the **purpofe of** iffuing large notes, applicable to great tranfactions, and another for iffuing fmall notes, with a view of facilitating the multiplied bufinefs of common life. It would anfwer however, much the fame purpofe, if two feparate branches of the fame corporation were eftablifhed, each having a diftinct department to carry on.

I fhall now briefly ftate the general refults to be drawn from the preceding obfervations.

General Deductions.

1. That an increafe of labour, a more extended commerce, and an increafed revenue, require an addition to the circulating medium of a country.

2. That fuch an increafe is beft obtained, by means of a well regulated paper circulation.

3. That fuch a paper circulation is beft conducted, when private individuals are prohibited from iffuing notes, unlefs when duly licenfed for that purpofe, and when either two diftinct corporations, or two branches of the fame corporation, are eftablifhed, one for circulating large notes, and the other for fmall ones.

And, 4. That if the paper circulation of a country is properly regulated, the periodical returns of

com-

commercial diftreffes, will in a great meafure be prevented, and the demands of the Exchequer, however great, will be paid without difficulty or murmur.

I have thus fhortly explained the principles of a plan, for placing the paper circulation of this country on the fureft and beft foundation, which I have no doubt is perfectly practicable, and every objection to which might be eafily removed. It would require however, a wife, intelligent, and upright government to carry it into full effect, or even to lay the foundation of fo great a fyftem. Were it once fairly eftablifhed, I truft that it would prove the moft important fource of wealth, profperity, and happinefs to the people of Great Britain, that had hitherto been brought forward.

CONCLUSION.

Little did I imagine, when this chapter was originally fketched out, that it could poffibly have extended to fo great a length. I truft however, that any impartial reader, who favours this work with a perufal, will not confider his time and labour mifapplied. The author has endeavoured to difcufs, the various topics therein treated of, in fuch a manner, as to enable any perfon, converfant in fuch queftions, to judge for himfelf. Much has he to lament, that the want of health, and the impoffibility of procuring all the information neceffary for the complete elucidation of fo many fubjects, fhould have rendered it greatly more defective

tive than otherwife it would have been.   At the
fame time he flatters himfelf, that, even the greateft
political cynic, would prefer feeing the obfervations
and ftatements contained in this chapter, in their
prefent ftate, however imperfect, than altogether
buried in oblivion.

C H A P. IV.

*Of the prefent State of the public Revenue, and of
the different Branches of which it confifts.*

THE taxes levied in this country at prefent, are
either temporary, or perpetual.   The firft are
annually voted by parliament, or have been impofed for a limited time; the fecond having been
granted in perpetuity, may be legally exacted until annulled by the legiflature.   Previoufly to the
Revolution, the people of this country had been
accuftomed to give only occafional aids to the fovereign in times of difficulty and war.   The fame
fyftem it was imagined would have been prefevered
in, after that event took place.   Little was it apprehended, that fo many perpetual taxes would
have been neceffary, and far lefs that the land and
malt taxes, though annually voted, would ever
have become in fome meafure, a part of the permanent income of the crown : nay, that the land

tax

tax fhould not only be rendered perpetual, but that
the proprietors of the landed property in the kingdom, fhould be required to buy up this tax, at the
higheft rate, at which it had ever been impofed.

1. Temporary taxes.

The temporary taxes which formerly exifted
were thofe on land and malt, and though the former is commuted, and in part redeemed, yet I
propofe ftill to continue it under its old head, as
the progrefs made in its redemption has not yet
been confiderable, as the taxes fubftituted in its
room require no particular explanation, and as the
old tax, in fo far as regards the tax of four fhillings
in the pound on penfions and offices, ftill remains
a temporary duty.

1. Land
tax.

That branch of the revenue, now known under
the name of the land tax, originated, as has already
been obferved, from thofe monthly affeffments firft
impofed in the time of the commonwealth. They
were likewife occafionally levied in the reign of
Charles the Second, and when it became neceffary,
after the Revolution, to raife confiderable fums of
money in order to maintain William the Third upon
the throne, and to carry on the war againft France,
this fource of national income, being deemed peculiarly productive and efficient, was continued.

The prefent land tax, though unqueftionably a
moft important branch of the revenue, is never-
thelefs liable to fome objections.

It was originally intended merely as a temporary
regulation ; but it has continued, fo far as regards
the

the rate impofed upon each diftrict, uniformly the fame. So that in places which, from various circumftances, have rifen to a flourifhing ftate, (for inftance the parifh of Marybone in London), when the tax is at the rate of four fhillings in the pound, the inhabitants do not pay perhaps fixpence. Whereas in other diftricts, which have not been equally profperous, when the tax is at four fhillings, perhaps fix fhillings is demanded by the collector [u].

Nay, the tax is not only now unequal, but was fo from the beginning; every city and county being in a great meafure allowed to affefs itfelf, without almoft any check or control upon their proceedings. Hence thofe who wifhed well to the revolution, and the government that was then eftablifhed, gave in a fair ftate of the property they poffeffed; whilft others were happy to fhow their zeal for the exiled family, and to gratify their felfifhnefs at the fame time, by reducing their income to as low a rate as could poffibly be ftated.

The land tax, as it is now called, was alfo originally intended to be a tax upon income, whether it proceeded from land, or fome profeffional profits. But inftead of taxing the real profits of profeffional men, the duty was impofed on their ftocks

[u] This fubject is ably difcuffed, in a work intituled, " The " alteration of the conftitution of the Houfe of Commons, and " the inequality of the land tax confidered jointly," by J. Brand, C. L. M. A. 1 vol. octavo, printed *anno* 1793.

in

in trade only : a regulation in the higheſt degree
unequal, as ſome profeſſions are very productive
where little ſtock is required; whereas others with
a great ſtock are far from being lucrative. Attempts have been fruitleſsly made to remedy ſo
great a ſource of inequality [x].

As it was propoſed to lay a tax of four ſhillings
in the pound on the income of every individual;
it was thought very abſurd to exempt thoſe from
the tax, who, by the offices they held, enjoyed
their income from the public. But this well-de-
ſigned regulation, from the manner in which it has
been executed, has been another ſource of inequality. For the advantage ariſing from the tax on
public officers has been given, not to the nation at
large, but to the particular place in which they are
ſituated. This is a circumſtance peculiarly favourable to the capital, the great emporium of
office, and to other diſtricts, particularly Cheſhire,
where there are now many officers in the ſalt department, a duty that did not exiſt at the revolution. Nay, it is attended with an additional unfortunate circumſtance : for when the ſalary of the
officer is ſmall, though he muſt pay the land tax
duty of four ſhillings in the pound, yet, in ſome
caſes, he is repaid that very duty out of the revenue of the department to which he belongs.
Thus the public treaſury relieves diſtricts from the
payment of certain taxes which they were not only

---

[x] See part iii. chap. i. p. 18.

bound,

bound, but, which it is more than probable, they were able to defray.

But the circumftance the moft to be regretted is, that though the land-tax was fuppofed to produce, at the rate of four fhillings in the pound, a certain income of £.1,989,673 : 7 : 10¼ for England, and £.47,954 : 1 : 2 for Scotland, making in all £.2,037,627 : 9 : 0¼, yet it was uniformly deficient, to the amount, at an average, of about £.235,000 *per annum*, varying according to the regularity with which the tax was collected, and the amount of the different charges to which it was liable.

The caufes of this deficiency are next to be explained.

The expence of the collection in England (for Scotland muft pay its proportion free of all charges into the Exchequer) muft firft be deducted.

Collectors poundage at 3*d. per* pound
   on £.1,989,973   £.24,870
Clerks ditto, at 1½*d. per* pound   12,435
                                       ‾‾‾‾‾‾‾
                                          37,305
Receivers poundage on the balance, (after
   deducting the above fum,) at the rate
   of 2*d.* in the pound, on £.1,952,368.   16,269
                                       ‾‾‾‾‾‾‾
                                       £.53,574

Thus the expence of collection cannot be complained of, as it is below even three *per cent.*

There is alfo allowed, under the name of conduct money, a fum of about £.1,260 *per annum* to
                                              the

the receivers of the land-tax in Wales, who complain of the great difficulty which they find in remitting the money to London.

The only part of England which claims any relief from this tax is the borough of Lyme Regis in Dorfet ; to which a deduction of £. 140 : 19 : 6 is annually granted by the treafury, on the footing that the lands on which that fum was affeffed have been wafhed away by the fea.

Before the land-tax is paid into the Exchequer, the expence of the militia, and of apprehending deferters from the army, and conveying them to fome place of fecurity, falls alfo to be deducted, which was calculated by the committee of finance at £. 91,000 *per annum*; but which, by the eftimates for the years 1787 and 1788, amounts to £. 116,137.

By 21 Geo. III. cap. 58. claufe 8. the bounties payable for the encouragement of raifing hemp and flax in England, are directed to be paid by the receivers of the land-tax in the feveral counties within which the fame has been raifed. This may occafion a deduction of from £. 10 to £. 15,000 *per annum.*

But the principal caufe of the deficiency of the land-tax is, the practice, which has arifen from the public neceffities, of empowering government to borrow two millions upon the credit of the tax as foon as it is voted. Exchequer bills are iffued for that purpofe, upon the fecurity of which the Bank advances the money, which is gradually paid off,

as

as the produce of the tax is tranfmitted to the treafury. On fome occafions very confiderable fums
were due by the public, on Exchequer bills ftanding out undifcharged; and large fums, unneceffarily detained in the hands of the different receivers, are fometimes loft by their failure and
bankruptcy. Such loffes might be prevented in
future, if proper attention were paid to the fecurity
given by the receivers; if by defraying the expence of the militia, and of the bounties above
mentioned, from fome other fund, no apology was
given for any detention of the public money; and
if the Bank were to undertake the remittance of
the money, upon the payment of a certain moderate
poundage from the receivers.

But fome have fuggefted, that inftead of attempt- Equaliza-
ing to improve the prefent land tax, or to make tion of the
any partial regulations refpecting it, it would be land-tax.
better to have a new valuation, and to levy an
equal rate over the whole ifland. Unfortunately,
the treaty of union with Scotland is in a great degree an infuperable bar, (unlefs the confent of that
part of the kingdom could be obtained), to any
propofition of this nature, at leaft to a general
equalization of the land-tax; and if Scotland were
to be exempted, the remote diftricts of England
would have reafon to complain. So ufeful, however, would fuch a regulation be, that it might be
advifable to give to Scotland, for a renunciation of
that ftipulation, fuch advantages in regard to
the duties of the cuftoms, as, by encouraging its
trade,

trade, might prove ftill more beneficial to that country.

But were this objection removed, a propofal for an equal land-tax might not perhaps be perfectly relifhed by every individual in England, and might with fome appearance of juftice be objected to by thofe, who have lately purchafed eftates with an idea, that the faith of the public was pledged to admit of no alteration in the rate of affeffment.

This objection, however, will not ftand the teft of a ftrict examination. It is well known that parliament has never given any real foundation for fuch an idea. On the contrary, by frequently varying the amount of the tax from one to four fhillings in the pound, it evidently referved to itfelf a complete power over that important branch of the national revenue.

Befides, this objection can only be made by thofe who have recently purchafed eftates, which upon a re-valuation would be found liable to an additional burden : and as every recent purchafe is not of that defcription, the rule would not univerfally hold good.

Indeed, fuch is the evident juftice of the meafure, and the neceffity of it has become fo very apparent, that perhaps any oppofition that is apprehended to fuch a plan is more imaginary than real ; and a point fo material to the general interefts of the country, might be gained without much unpopularity or clamour, were the new affeffment not to take effect immediately, but to commence at
any

any future period; for inftance, ten years after the paffing of the act.

Others have recommended to leave the prefent land-tax as it is. Let it be a perpetual rent-charge, they fay, at the rate of four fhillings, or of two fhillings in the pound, and impofe an additional fhilling upon land in general on a new valuation. Even this plan, though lefs exceptionable, is ftill hardly confiftent with the articles of the union.

If ever an equalization is brought about, it has been much difputed at what time it fhould be carried into execution, and how long it ought to remain unaltered. To continue a tax on landed property at one rate for fome time, is undoubtedly not a little favourable to agriculture; and to that circumftance the great improvement of England is partly owing. For furely if individuals are obliged to pay, for having, at a great expence, made fome addition to their annual income, the prudent and the cautious, who are the moft likely to improve and better their eftates, will not be very apt to expend their money in a manner fo unprofitable. Some admirable ideas have been thrown out upon that fubject, by a modern political writer [y]. Perhaps, on the whole, the beft plan would be, to have a new valuation every fifty years; to allow deductions where the rents had really fallen; and where they had rifen, in confequence of real and expenfive improvements, to lay a tax on only one-half of the additional income for a certain number of

[y] See Smith's Wealth of Nations, vol. ii. p. 426.

years.

years. It would not be difficult to form a plan upon such principles, that might be productive of the happieft confequences.

Of a landed revenue.
    It would be improper to quit this fubject, without mentioning an idea which fome have contended for; namely, that as the real income of every country originates from the land, all taxes therefore fhould be at once impofed on that fpecies of property. The faying of Artaxerxes, an ancient king of Perfia, is recorded by a great hiftorian as difcovering a deep infight into the conftitution of government: "The authority of the prince," he faid, "muft be defended by a military force, "that force can only be maintained by taxes, and "all taxes muft at laft fall upon agriculture [z]." The fame fentiment has fince been enforced by the celebrated Locke [a], and has lately been revived in France, and maintained by feveral ingenious men.

    Notwithftanding fuch great and refpectable authorities, both of theoretical and of practical ftatefmen, the fallacy of fuch a pofition can no longer

[z] Gibbon's Hiftory, vol. i. p. 215.

[a] See Locke's Confideration of the lowering the Intereft and raifing the Value of Money; (Works, 2d edit. 3 vol. fo. 1722.) where he contends that taxes, however contrived, and out of whofe hands foever immediately taken, do, in a country where their great fund is in land, for the moft part terminate upon land: nay perhaps it will be found that thofe taxes which feem leaft to affect land, will moft furely of all other fall upon the rent. He fuppofed the rent of England, *an.* 1691, only twelve millions.

be

be queſtioned.   In an inland country like Perſia, or in a ſtate where induſtry does not flouriſh, as was the caſe even in England, previouſly to the revolution, ſuch an idea may, to a certain degree, be well founded.   But it can hardly be diſputed, that the manufacturer, who by his labour improves the value of the productions of the ſoil, and hence procures a ſubſiſtence for himſelf and family, and the merchant who raiſes an income from the profits of exporting thoſe commodities to other nations, depend for their means of livelihood, not upon the produce of the land, but upon the profits of their labour; and from thoſe profits alone are enabled to pay their taxes to the public.   Indeed, were it admitted, (though it can hardly be ſeriouſly maintained in a commercial country), that the whole income of the nation aroſe from the cultivation of the ſoil, yet ſtill by impoſing duties upon conſumption, a greater revenue may be raiſed than by a direct tax upon land.   By the latter method you only tax the proprietor of the ſoil, who has only a certain portion of the produce, and a conſiderable part of which is neceſſarily taken from him for the ſubſiſtence of others.   Whereas by the former method, the public ſhares in the profits of thoſe individuals, who derive any benefit from the ſoil, by any means, whether directly or indirectly: and hence, whilſt the tax of four ſhillings in the pound on land was ſeverely felt by many individuals in Great Britain, though it yielded only at the rate of two millions *per annum*, a tax on barley,

ley, in all its various ftages and modes of confumption, to the amount of about fix millions, is levied
without difficulty, or any material oppreffion[b].

Another theory of nearly the fame nature, it may
be proper briefly to mention.

By the principles of the feudal fyftem, the
holders and poffeffors of land, claimed an exemption from all pecuniary taxes, being bound to perfonal fervices in war, and obliged to appear when
called upon, either to oppofe or to attack the enemies of their country. A modern author has, with
great ingenuity, reverfed this propofition, and
contends, that as the landholders are no longer the
defenders of the ftate, and if they appear in that
capacity, are paid for their fervices like others, they
ought therefore to be accounted an *uneffential clafs*
in the community, and that the whole pecuniary
burdens ought to be impofed upon them[c].

There is undoubtedly much plaufibility in this
idea. Such expences, it is true, as are neceffary to

[b] This fubject would have required a fuller difcuffion, had
not M. Necker, in his treatife on the adminiftration of the
finances of France, vol. i. chap. 6. proved the utter impracticability of converting all the taxes of that country into one
land-tax, and affigned reafons for it, applicable to every nation,
and which cannot be overturned.

[c] See a plan for finally fettling the government of Ireland
upon conftitutional principles. Printed for Stockdale, *anno*
1785 ; written by John Gray, Efq. Perhaps the time will foon
come when either the landed or the monied intereft muft be
facrificed ; in which event it is not difficult to forefee who will
be confidered the *uneffential clafs* in this commercial country.

defend

defend our foreign commerce, and the settlements connected with it, that commerce ought to defray, since those by whom our trade is carried on, are principally benefited by it. But nothing would be more politic than to instil it into the minds of our possessors' of land, that they are the natural defenders of the country at home, that it is necessary for them to acquire a knowledge in the art of war, and to encourage a military spirit ; and that if they become languid and effeminate, and abandon the posts which it is their duty to maintain, they will become an unnecessary and uselefs class, and ought alone to defray those public charges which their own degeneracy may occasion.

Such were the observations which had occurred to me regarding this subject, *anno* 1790, when the preceding edition of this work was printed; since which period the plan of endeavouring to procure a redemption of the land-tax has been attempted. The general principles of that great alteration in our financial system, have been already discussed in the preceding chapter. Nothing therefore remains, but to state, 1. The progress that has been made in carrying through the plan. 2. The nature of the taxes which are annually imposed in room of the land-tax; and 3. to consider whether some measure might not be pointed out, by which the whole of the old land-tax might be gradually redeemed and extinguished.

The nature of this plan was first announced to the public in an anonymous pamphlet, but supposed to

1.Origin and progress of the land-tax redemption.

to come from a respectable quarter, printed in November 1797 [d] : and considering the low state of publick credit at the time, when with £.49 in money, you could purchase £.100 of 3 *per cent.* stock, it is not to be wondered at, that it should attract the attention of the minister, who could hardly be aware, till the experiment was fairly tried, of the difficulties attending it, or the slow progress it would make.

The first act for the redemption of the land-tax, received the royal assent on the 21st June 1798; but though that law was sufficiently voluminous, it has since been found requisite to pass eight acts additional, (some of them of considerable length), and more will still be necessary. After all, the progress made in the sale has fallen far short of the expectations originally entertained of it. Instead of £.66,666,666 of stock being purchased, the amount on the 1st February 1803, was only £.19,180,587 : 5 : 2, with very little prospect of any material addition.

2. Substitutes for the land-tax.

As the frequent calling of parliaments, was supposed to depend much, upon the necessity the crown was under, of assembling the two houses for granting the annual taxes on land and malt, (on the produce of which the maintenance of the civil government depended,) when the land-tax was

[d] See a proposal for liquidating £.66,666,666 of the 3 *per cents.* by converting the land-tax into a permanent annuity, with cursory observations humbly submitted to both Houses of Parliament. Octavo, Nov. 10, 1797.

rendered

rendered perpetual, it was thought neceffary to
convert fome of the taxes formerly perpetually impofed into annual grants, and the following branches
were pitched upon ; namely, the duties on malt,
impofed by 27th of Geo. 3. on fugar by 27, 34,
and 37 Geo. 3, and on tobacco and fnuff, by 29th
Geo. 3, the produce of which at the time exceeded
that of the land-tax to the amount of about
£. 400,000 *per annum*. It certainly would have
anfwered the object better in a conftitutional point
of view, to have had the taxes on houfes and windows, and the affeffed taxes in general, appropriated
for that purpofe, rather than duties of a precarious
and fluctuating nature. Befides, merchants importing tobacco or fugar, or perfons employed in
the manufacturing of malt, might be compelled, by
a bold and tyrannical government, to pay any demands made upon them, more efpecially as they
might expect to be indemnified by the fale of the
article at a price proportionally augmented. But any
tax that was only to be annually granted, as a check
upon the power of the crown, and as a fecurity to
the conftitutional rights and privileges of the people, ought to be impofed upon the property of that
people at large, and not upon any fmall number of
them, fo that the government, if it attempted any
illegal exaction, would have the great body of the
nation to contend with, or at leaft a number of its
moft powerful and opulent fubjects. The land-
tax was certainly the beft article that could have
been pitched upon, and the duties on houfes and

windows,

windows, and other branches of the affeffed taxes, would have been the fitteft fubftitute.

3 Plan for buying up the land-tax remaining unredeemed.
It is evident that there is little chance of the land-tax being ever redeemed, according to the prefent fyftem.   At the fame time, fo much progrefs has been already made, that it is impoffible to overturn what has been done, and to eftablifh this tax on its old foundation. As matters therefore have gone fo far, and as preferving the remains of this tax, would occafion confufion in our publick accounts, and be attended with other unpleafant confequences, as jealoufy between thofe who are and are not liable to a land-tax, it certainly would be defirable, to get rid of it as foon as circumftances would permit.   Perhaps the beft plan for that purpofe would be, to enact, that all thofe who did not redeem their land-tax before a given day (fay the 1ft of January 1804), or at leaft enter into a contract for that purpofe, fhall be fubject to an additional land-tax, for the purpofe of completing the redemption within a given time, according to one or other of the following calculations, giving the parties interefted the choice of any of them they might prefer.

When the redemption was originally propofed on the 2d of April, 1798, it was calculated that a transfer of £.40 of 3 per cent. ftock fhould redeem £.1 of land-tax, confequently £.100 of land-tax will require £.4000 ftock, or ftating the 3 per cents at an average price of 75, it would amount to £.3000 in money.   In order to raife
that

that fum, according to the calculations made by Mr. Morgan, perfons liable in the land-tax, paying £. 14 : 6 : 8 *per annum* of addition *per* £. 100, would have their land tax-redeemed, (calculating intereft at 5 *per cent.*) in 50 years, or an annual payment of £. 24 : 17 will redeem their land-tax in 40 years, or £. 45 : 3 *per annum* in 30 years.

The public-purchafing the ftock at 75, would only receive 4 *per cent.* for its money, but if it were made compulfitory, it would be right to give the parties taxed the advantage of an additional 1 *per cent.* in the accumulation; and as proprietors are authorifed, even in the cafe of entailed eftates, to fell a part of their property, in order to get rid of the tax entirely, fuch an additional tax as a fund for redemption, can be lefs objected to.

On the fuppofition that at an average, an annual payment of £. 20 for every £. 100 of old land-tax, would be the amount of the redemption fund, and that £. 1,400,000 in all would be redeemed by that means, the total fund for redemption would amount to £. 280,000 *per annum*, which fum, properly applied, would redeem the whole of the old land-tax, (according to the price of ftocks) in a period of from 30 to 40 years.

The revolution had taken place fome time, and the public had experienced the greateft difficulties in raifing the fupplies, before parliament could be prevailed upon to impofe a duty upon malt; together with a proportionable rate on cyder and perry,

4. Old annual malt tax.

perry, and other liquors, the ufe of which might diminifh the confumption of that article.

It was firft granted *anno* 1697[e], and it was always fuppofed would be only a temporary impoft. By the treaty of union with Scotland[f], it was agreed, that during the continuance of the duty on malt, which then exifted in England, (but which expired on the 4th of June 1707,) Scotland fhould not be charged with it. Indeed that country was not included in the malt act until the year 1713, and even then it was thought advifable for government to affume a fort of difpenfing power, and to give directions that it fhould not be levied. Nay, the Scots were fo impreffed with an idea, that they were in a manner for ever exempted from fuch a duty, by the treaty of union, that when the tax was firft enforced in that country, *anno* 1725, it occafioned confiderable riots, which were with difficulty fuppreffed.

The income of this tax for England alone, exclufively of Scotland, at the rate of 6*d. per* bufhel, was originally calculated at £.750,000 a-year, a fum which was far from being exaggerated; for, on the average of eight years, ending midfummer 1724, it produced at the rate of £.755,000 *per annum.*—It fell off, however, during the American war; and its amount during the year, ending 5th

[e] By 8 and 9 Will. III. cap. 22. It had formerly been attempted during the commonwealth.

[f] Art. xiii.

January,

January, 1803, deducting the expences of management and collection, was only as follows:

State of the Net Produce of the Annual Malt Tax for one Year, ending 5th January, 1803.

	Net Produce.
England - - - - - -	£. 679,322
Scotland - - - - -	23,571
Total - - - -	£. 702,893

If the plan above alluded to of making the affeffed taxes annual, inftead of the duties on fugars, tobacco, and malt, were to be adopted, the taxes on malt might alfo be confolidated, including the old annual malt tax, (which would tend to fimplify our financial accounts,) and the affeffed taxes, producing above three millions *per annum*, would do more than cover the whole.

2. Perpetual Taxes.

For fome years after the revolution, when any duty was laid on, it was only granted until the money borrowed upon the credit of the tax was paid off, and then it ceafed of courfe. About the year 1710 a very different fyftem was adopted: perpetual taxes were impofed, and the duty was continued, though the loan borrowed fhould be repaid. The furpluffes, it is true, were referved for the difpofal of parliament; but in a conftitutional view, that is far from being a fufficient check. The crown being thus legally invefted

with

with the power of drawing money from the property of its subjects, when once that money is
placed in the Exchequer, there must be much less
difficulty in prevailing upon parliament to agree
to any mode of expenditure which the sovereign
may incline to prefer, or to lay it out without the
consent of that assembly if it should prove re-
fractory [g].

The perpetual taxes now levied in this country,
may be considered under four general heads:—
1. Customs.—2. Excise.—3. Stamps.—4. Miscellaneous Taxes.

1. Customs.   It is the opinion of many able men, that the
imposing of duties upon the importation or exportation of goods, is incompatible with the real
interests of a commercial country. Where such a
system is adopted, a great increase of capital becomes necessary; because the merchant must advance the duty immediately on the goods being
landed, which in fact is locking up so much of his
stock that would otherwise be employed in trade,
until he is reimbursed [h]. Besides, he considers
himself as intitled to charge in the price of the
commodity not only the tax itself, but also a commercial profit thereon, which increases in all the
various hands through which it passes, until the
article arrives at the ultimate stage of consumption,
whereby the interest and accumulated profits on

[g] History of our National Debts, Part iv. p. 8, 9.

[h] The warehousing or bonding system, when carried to its
full extent, will in a great measure obviate this objection.

the

the tax, often exceed the amount of the tax itfelf. This is a ftrong argument for levying all duties as near the ftage of confumption as may be found confiftent with the fafety of the revenue. The great trade which is carried on by the Dutch, not-withftanding many natural difadvantages, is not a little attributed to the inconfiderable duties that are levied at their ports. It is farther to be ob-ferved, that high duties, by holding out a premium to the clandeftine trader, encourage fmuggling, with all its pernicious confequences. At the fame time it is fo difficult to raife a great revenue upon principles perfectly unexceptionable, and mankind are fo apt to confider taxes levied on confumption as a part of the price, and confequently no tax at all, that I am not furprifed to find in almoft every country fuch duties have exifted.

The cuftoms may be divided into four branches : cuftoms on goods imported, exported, or carried coaftways, and the tonnage duty lately impofed.

Cuftoms on goods imported.

Duties on goods imported into a country, were originally laid upon the fubjects of the realm, under the pretence of defraying the charges of guard-ing the coafts from pirates ; and upon foreign mer-chants, for the liberty given them by the fovereign, of trading in his dominions.

Of all the branches of the cuftoms, this is un-queftionably the leaft exceptionable. The duties, however, fhould be at fo low a rate, as to dif-courage, if not totally prevent, all contraband trade ; and taxes upon articles neceffary for the

manufactures

manufactures of the country, or raw materials, the
value of which may be greatly improved by the
labour of the people, ought to be avoided.

Were it possible consistently with the interests
of the revenue, to carry these principles into
practice in this country, the wealth and commerce
of Great Britain would soon receive very material
additions.

Cuftoms on goods exported.

Formerly duties were impofed on the exportation of almoft every commodity that was fent
out of this country. It was contended, that fuch
duties were not paid by the natives, but came out
of the pockets of foreigners. Such ideas, however, are now exploded. Experience has afcertained, that foreign nations will not give beyond a
certain price for any commodity whatever, and
that by taxing goods exported, you either force
them to give up the confumption, or to trade with
other places for a fupply.

The principal tax of that nature ftill remaining,
is the duty upon coals; but fuch is the fuperior
quality of that article in this country, that it is
fully able to bear it. Indeed coals are fuch a neceffary of life, and though abundant, yet undoubtedly capable of being exhaufted, that inftead
of a duty, fome have propofed a total prohibition
of exportation: a plan which muft be adopted,
fhould there ever arife the leaft well founded apprehenfions of a fcarcity of that commodity.

Lead, tin, and alum, are alfo liable to certain
duties on exportation. As lead mines are in general

neral found in wafte and barren foils, which, were it not for their mineral wealth, would be utterly abandoned, it is queftionable how far fuch a duty ought to be continued.

The other taxes upon goods exported, are not liable to much objection, being principally impofed on raw materials, and intended to give our manufacturers an advantage over rival nations in their refpective branches of induftry.

But of all the cuftom-houfe duties now exacted in Great Britain, there is none fo truly exceptionable as that upon coals carried coaftways; the tax being equally injurious to the navigation and maritime ftrength, to the manufactures, the agriculture, and the fifheries of this country.

Cuftoms on goods carried coaft-ways.

The coal trade, it is well known, is the beft nurfery for Britifh feamen. Sailors bred up in that trade, can hardly be equalled for fkill, fpirit, and hardinefs in their profeffion. By taking off the duties upon coals carried coaftways, an invaluable treafure of perhaps 10,000 feamen, would be added to the maritime force of the country. Nor would the number of fhipwrights, neceffary for building the veffels, in confequence of fuch an additional demand for fhipping, be an unimportant circumftance.

It is commonly remarked, that manufactures flourifh beft wherever coals are the cheapeft and moft abundant. In fo cold a country as Great Britain fuel is a real neceffary of life, and is required in fabricating almoft all our manufactures.

Whilft

Whilſt this tax continues, the various manufacturing advantages reſulting from the cheapneſs of that article, are confined to particular diſtricts. Whereas, by aboliſhing that duty, all places would be more nearly on a footing; hence induſtry and commerce would ſpread over the whole face of the country.

Nor is the duty upon coals leſs pernicious to agriculture. It renders it neceſſary, in many parts of the kingdom, to devote conſiderable quantities of improveable ground to rear wood for the purpoſe of firing. And in thoſe parts, of the iſland, particularly in the more remote parts of Scotland, where peat and turf can be had, the ſummer is not ſpent by the farmer, in procuring manure, in fallowing his fields, or in raiſing crops to enrich and fertilize the ſoil, but is principally waſted in collecting firing for the winter ſeaſon [i].

If any ſet of men are entitled to public encouragement, ſurely thoſe who maintain themſelves by fiſhing only, who procure a ſubſiſtence in a manner ſo truly precarious, who run ſuch perpetual hazard of being loſt in the little boats in which they truſt themſelves, and who form a ſpecies of naval militia, whoſe ſervices the public can at any time command, have by far the beſt founded pretenſions; and of all the encouragements that could be given to them, that of enabling

[i] The tax on coal carried coaſtways, in ſo far as regards Scotland, has been fortunately commuted.

them

them to fupply themfelves with firing at an eafy rate would perhaps be the moft acceptable. Their whole labour might then be devoted to their own profeffion; nor would the miferable neceffity of procuring a fcantity fupply of fuel tempt them to wafte fo confiderable a portion of their time in any other occupation.

It is hoped that thefe confiderations will, fome time or other, occafion a commutation of this duty, fince there is hardly any other tax that could poffibly prove equally detrimental; and as, without fome fubftitute, fo important a branch of the revenue, producing about £. 600,000 *per annum*, cannot be difpenfed with.

In the former edition of this work it was re- *Tonnage* marked, that the cuftom-houfe duties at that time *duty.* were principally levied either according to the fuppofed value of the different commodities conformably to particular rates, or in proportion to the fize, weight, and meafurement of the articles, making fome difference according to the country whence the goods were brought; and giving advantages to the fhips belonging to and manned by Britifh fubjects, over thofe of a different defcription. A hint was then thrown out of levying in part thofe duties on the tonnage, preferving always fome diftinction between natives and aliens, and giving the former a preference. So great an alteration certainly could not be hazarded at once, or to any great extent; but, perhaps, it might not be impolitic, to lay a fmall tonnage duty

duty according to the place whence the veffel
came, or to which it was going, and the cargo with
which it was loaded, and to levy the reft by a rate
ad valorem. Such a regulation might contribute
to check fmuggling by diminifhing the temptation,
as a tonnage duty could not well be evaded, as
other duties are, and by a late act it has been carried into effect, though perhaps on a fcale too burthenfome on the merchant.

Amount of the Cuf-toms. A particular account of this great branch of the
revenue, for one year ending the 5th of January
1803, will be found in the Appendix; the grofs
receipt is as follows.

1. Grofs receipt to be accounted for in England	-	-	£. 9,682,336 14 8¼
2. Do. in Scotland	-	-	837,583 18 10½
	Total	-	£. 10,519,920 13 7¼

In regard to the branches whence thefe fums
were received, the following ftatement contains the
moft important.

1. Net produce of the tax on imports	£. 7,722,677	3 5¼
2. Net produce of the tax on exports	262,381	0 0½
3. Net produce of the duties coaftways	702,186 12	1¼
	£. 8,687,244	15 7

The above includes the new tonnage duty both
outwards and inwards.

In the cuftom houfe accounts detailed in the
Appendix, will alfo be found, a fum to the amount
of

of £. 26,825 : 17 : 8¼, remitted from the plantations. In confequence, however, of various de-
duétions from the grofs receipt on account of
difcounts, drawbacks, &c. the total net produce
applicable to national objeéts, was reduced to the
fum of £. 7,415,726 : 19 : 3¾.

It is impoffible to read the particular detail of
the articles yielding a revenue to the cuftoms,
(which will be found in the Appendix), without
being ftruck with the variety of petty objeéts; as
briftles, cork, feathers, human hair, chip hats, le-
mons and oranges, mats, mitts, bees wax, tapes,
&c. which, however trifling in themfelves, yet
produce a confiderable revenue when accumulated
together, clearly proving that, in order to raife a
great income, the fmalleft artiċle ought not be
overlooked.

It is alfo proper to remark, that the mercantile
principle of raifing every article within ourfelves
we can either manufaéture or produce, is not per-
feétly compatible with the interefts of at leaft this
branch of the revenue. For inftance, were all the
linens, iron, and hemp we confume, produced at
home, which is far from being impraéticable, our
cuftoms would diminifh to the amount of about
£. 460,000 *per annum*, and we might lofe the exportation of goods of equal value, in which our
countrymen are as beneficially employed as they
would be in any other mode.

Laftly, when the aftonifhing revenue raifed from
fugar, groceries, oils, filk, tea, muflins, tobacco,

wines,

wines, foreign spirituous liquors, drugs, &c. is considered, we cannot but perceive how much a nation is benefited by foreign commerce, which is
not only the source of industry at home, in order
to produce the fittest articles for foreign markets,
but which also furnishes the means of raising, without difficulty or complaint, a great income, to be
applied in any manner the best calculated for the
interests of the nation.

2. Excise.   The learned commentator on the Laws of England, (Sir W. Blackstone), has given so full, and
at the same time so concise an account of the origin and progress of the excise, and of the principles
on which it is founded, that it may be sufficient to
refer the reader to his popular and admirable work
for information upon the subject. Notwithstanding the plausible objections that may be urged
against this tax, particularly on account of the en-
croachments which it necessarily occasions on the
rights and liberties of no inconsiderable body of
the people ; yet since the necessities of the state require a great revenue, it may be considered on the
whole " as the most easy and indifferent levy that
" could be made upon the public [k]." But, as an
explanation of the whole system of the excise laws,
and the various regulations which they contain,
would require a volume of itself, it is proposed at
present merely to give a general view of the sum
which the excise produced for the year ending 5th

[k] See Scobell, p. 72. and 452.

January

January 1803, (the particular detail of which will be found in the Appendix,) and to add such observations upon the different branches of that revenue as may occur to the author.

STATE of the Revenue of the Excise, for one year ending the 5th January 1803.

1. Total gross receipt in England, to be accounted for within the year, including the annual malt   -   £. 15,526,408 18 7¼
2. Do. in Scotland   -   -   1,307,377 7 3¾

£. 16,833,786 5 11

The net produce applicable to national objects, and to payments into the Exchequer, was as follows.

1. England   -   -   £. 13,832,086 2 4
2. Scotland   -   -   1,095,452 1 8¼

£. 14,927,538 4 0¼

To the principal branches of the revenue of excise, namely, the duties upon malt and malt liquors of every kind, including the distillery, there can be no objection, except upon the idea that they have been carried to too great a height, and that the rate ought be diminished. But some have contended, that duties upon the necessaries of life are peculiarly pernicious to a manufacturing country; and others assert, and are perhaps better

founded

founded in their opinion, that all duties upon manufactures themselves ought to be abolished.

The excifes levied on what may be called the
neceffaries of life, exclufively of coals, which has
been already taken notice of, and falt, to be afterwards mentioned, but including candles, leather,
foap, and ftarch, are on an average above a million.

It is faid that the levying of thefe duties, fo confiderable a part of which muft neceffarily fall upon
the poor, has the effect of raifing the price of labour, and enables other ftates, where fuch taxes
do not exift, to fell their goods at a lower rate, and
confequently to fecure the confumption and market of foreign nations; and it is commonly afferted, that the excifes which are levied in Holland
proved the means of ruining the manufactures for
which that country was once fo famous.

Such reafoning, however plaufible, may be con-
troverted.

Mankind are far from being naturally fond of
laborious occupations; and there are few who, if
left to their own inclinations, would not wifh to
pafs away their time in floth and eafe, did not neceffity compel them to induftry and exertion.

In manufactures alfo, perfection cannot be acquired or retained without perpetual attention; and
if manufacturers, from the cheapnefs of living, and
by being exempted from taxes, could maintain
themfelves and their families by the labour of only
three days in the week, few could refift the temptation,

tion, though in confequence of being idle for the other four, they would become lefs expert in their profeffion.

It is remarked in manufacturing towns, that their commerce never flourifhes fo much, and is never carried on to fuch advantage, as when, from the high price of provifions, the workmen are compelled to labour with uncommon affiduity.

Though a confiderable part of the above taxes is paid by the poor, yet the rich are far from being exempted ; and with thefe taxes, the wages of the former have in fome degree increafed, though it muft be acknowledged in a very unequal proportion.

A total exemption from taxes in favour of the poor, is a fyftem impracticable in a country fo loaded as we are at prefent; and, in a free ftate, perhaps would be unjuft : for there the poor have rights to which they are entitled as well as the rich ; and they ought to pay for the privileges they enjoy.

On the whole, though an idea of fo humane and beneficent a nature, as that of relieving the burdens of the poor, ought to be attended to, if a proper fyftem for that purpofe could be formed; yet I queftion much, were it practicable, whether it would add in any great extent to their comfort and happinefs. I fhould imagine indeed, could the abolition be afforded, that it were better to continue thefe taxes as they are, however they may affect the lower ranks of the people, and to divide

what

what they pay into two parts; appropriating the one to bounties upon exported manufactures, and annually diftributing the other among fuch of the married poor as have families to maintain, in proportion to the number of their children, and giving fmall annuities to thofe who, after a life fpent in laborious induftry, are unable, from ficknefs or age, to maintain themfelves; that thus the fituation of that valuable clafs of men might be rendered as comfortable as the defective ftate of human nature will admit of.

Confe-
quences of
taxing ma-
nufactures.

The different manufactures on which excife duties are levied, namely, paper, glafs, wire, and printed linens, have produced of late above a million.

Important as fuch a fum undoubtedly is, in the. prefent circumftances of this country, yet the propriety of at leaft attempting to raife it in fome other mode can hardly be queftioned.

I can conceive that a duty, without rifk of lofs to the public, might be laid upon a manufacture, with which other nations could not fupply us, and with which we cannot properly fupply other nations. But taxing manufactures of a different defcription, ought on no account to be adopted; a greater variety of inconveniencies arifing from it than can well be imagined.

The tax upon paper, for inftance, not only affects that particular manufacture, but has alfo occafioned important confequences with regard to the art of printing, which, in regard to beauty at

leaft,

leaft, is falling off in this country ; a circumftance partly at leaft, to be attributed to the high price of that material[1]. Indeed of late the duty has been raifed to a height, which tends to injure not only the literature, but the morals of the nation[m].

Such are the natural advantages which this country enjoys for carrying the glafs manufacture to perfection, that, perhaps, nothing but the high duties that are impofed upon it, prevents our fupplying the greateft part of Europe with almoft every fpecies of that article.

The duty upon printed linens might furely be commuted, and levied through the medium of thofe by whom they are made up. In the prefent mode, they difcourage a very elegant and important manufacture.

It is faid that the duties are drawn back upon exportation; and confequently, that they only affect the home confumption. But a drawback can never compenfate for the trouble and vexation refulting from the infpection of public officers, who will only attend at times fuitable and convenient

[1] Alderman Boydell, in his catalogue of the pictures in the Shakfpeare Gallery (Preface, p. 15.) makes the fame obfervation, and flatters himfelf, by his new edition of our immortal poet, to reftore the reputation of this country in regard to the art of printing, " in which," he fays, " to our difgrace be it " fpoken, we are behind every neighbouring nation."

[m] See the Report from the committee on the bookfellers' and printers' petition, printed 22d March 1802, which ftates this matter in a very ftrong light, and proves the neceffity of lowering the duty confiderably.

to themfelves; for the heavy lofs which the manufacturer feels from being compelled to advance
the money for payment of the duties long before
he is reimburfed; and ftill more from being
obliged to pay taxes on goods which are damaged,
and confequently unfaleable. Befides, if the ufual
profit of the manufacturer is 20 *per cent.* he muft
charge 20 *per cent.* on the duty he advances.
Whereas the merchant, who receives the drawback, will only make a deduction in proportion to
the fum he receives, and the legal intereft. This
muft render the price of our manufactures much
higher, (even when exported, with all the advantages of a drawback), than would otherwife be
the cafe. In manufactures alfo where great art and
fkill are neceffary, where much depends upon the
genius and fancy of the artift, where machinery
is perhaps of great importance, and in which the
artift has made difcoveries he is defirous of keeping to himfelf, and does not wifh that even a hint
of them fhould be communicated to others, any
tax, however infignificant, may be productive of
the greateft inconveniences to the manufacturer,
and may damp his fpirit and exertions, without
yielding much income to the ftate [n].

If circumftances, therefore, would admit of fuch
taxes being abolifhed, or if proper commutations
could be contrived, nothing would probably prove

---

[n] The tax on cottons, fuftians, &c. impofed by Mr. Pitt, on
thefe grounds, after fome ftruggle was given up.

of

of more real fervice to the public.   Indeed, if manufacturing induftry is at all to be loaded, it would
be fair and equitable to make no exception, and
inftead of taxing particular manufactures, to impofe
duties upon fuch articles as all manufactures muft
confume.

The duty laid on goods fold by auction is ano- Tax on
ther branch of the excife that may be objected to. auctions.
It is a plan borrowed from the Dutch, like many
of our recent taxes.   The difficulties to which thefe
people were reduced might juftify almoft any impofition.   But if ever the fituation of this country
would admit of taxes being abolifhed, the duty on
auctions ought unqueftionably to be included in the
number, unlefs fome means could be contrived to
take it out of the pocket of the rich purchafer,
inftead of the needy feller.   At prefent it has rather
a tendency to increafe the mifery of thofe who, in
all probability, are already fufficiently reduced, than
to diminifh the riches of the opulent.

Various fteps were taken, in the reign of queen Brick tax.
Anne, for the purpofe of impofing a duty upon the
bricks, tiles, flate, lime, and ftones, made ufe of
within the limits of the bills of mortality; and it
was afterwards propofed to extend the tax to all
places within ten miles of the cities of London and
Weftminfter[o].   But fuch a plan, though reftricted
to the neighbourhood of a wealthy, and, in the opinion of many, an overgrown metropolis, whofe

[o] Comm. Journ. vol. xvii. p. 131. 157. 159. 173. 197.

increafe

increafe ought, on that idea, to be checked, was rejected, and certain branches of the ftamp duties were fubftituted in its room [p].   As fuch a tax certainly has a tendency to check the population and improvement of the country, the fooner the nation can be relieved from it, in many refpects the more defirable, more efpecially in fo far as regards bricks neceffary for draining land, that effential agricultural improvement.

Licences.   In the farther progrefs of this work it will appear, that meafures might be adopted, to render duties in the fhape of licences lefs exceptionable. At prefent, by confounding the new beginner and the veteran in trade, and by making no diftinction between them in regard to the duties they are refpectively charged with, competition is neceffarily diminifhed, bufinefs naturally falls into a few hands, and confequently the public can never expect to be equally well ferved.

Salt tax.   I fhall now proceed to lay before the reader, fome obfervations on a moft important branch of our revenue, namely, the falt tax, which is at prefent under the management of the excife, the board, to whofe care it was formerly entrufted, having been abolifhed.

The duty levied upon falt took its rife in the Roman republic, where the principles of commerce were far from being underftood, and where no attention was paid to its encouragement.   Such a tax

[p] Comm. Journ, vol. xvii, p. 203.

might

might be confiftent with the nature of that government, and the fituation of that empire : but in Britain, the cafe is materially different, and it is difficult
to eftimate the magnitude of the loffes which it has
occafioned.

It appears from the important and laborious inveftigation that has been made into the ftate of the
Britifh fifheries, that nothing has had fuch a tendency to prevent their rifing to the height to which
it is fo defirable they fhould attain, as the tax upon
falt : for without that material the commodity cannot be made fit for exportation ; nor can the home
confumption become fo general and extenfive, as
otherwife it would prove.

It is a tax that deeply affects the poor, who are
obliged, from their fituation in life, to confume a
greater quantity of falted provifions than their richer
neighbours.

It is univerfally acknowledged, that every plan
which tends to augment the price of navigation
ought to be avoided ; and yet we continue a tax
which renders the fubfiftance of our feamen dearer,
and compels not only our merchants, but even the
public itfelf, to procure immenfe quantities of falted
provifions from Ireland, with which we might otherwife fupply ourfelves.

The rock falt with which Chefhire abounds,
joined to the cheapnefs and abundance of coal,
would enable this country to underfell its commercial rivals, and to fupply the greater part of Europe with that neceffary article, to the amount perhaps

haps of a million *per annum*, were it not for this unfortunate duty; and hence, inſtead of our being able to import ſalt into other countries, in the manner we might do, France and Ireland at this time contribute to ſupply our conſumption.

The article of barilla, a ſpecies of ſalt made uſe of in ſome of our manufactures, is imported into Great Britain to the amount of at leaſt three hundred and fifty thouſand pounds *per annum*. Whereas if the duty on ſalt were aboliſhed, there would be no occaſion to apply to any country for that commodity [q].

To many ſoils, ſalt is a manure, which might be applied with advantage; but whilſt the duty continues, it is impoſſible to make uſe of it, at leaſt to any extent.

Theſe circumſtances being conſidered, it cannot well be accounted an exaggerated calculation, that it occaſions the introduction of commodities into this country, which would not otherwiſe be neceſſary, and prevents the creation of wealth, which might otherwiſe be acquired, to the amount of at leaſt three millions *per annum*, which are thus ſacrificed for the ſake of the income derived from this branch of our finances.

[q] Barilla is made from the aſhes of an herb that grows on the coaſts of the Mediterranean, particularly in Spain. It is made uſe of in making glaſs and ſoap, and in bleaching. A preparation from ſea ſalt, if duty free, would be cheaper, and would anſwer the ſame purpoſes.

The

The objections to the falt tax being very generally felt and acknowledged, an application was made, by a number of refpectable gentlemen, to the Right Honourable Henry Addington, foon after he was appointed Chancellor of the Exchequer, requefting him to take the fubject into confideration and, if poffible, to have fome other tax fubftituted in its room. In confequence of that application, the minifter, on the 14th May 1801, moved for the appointment of a felect committee to enquire into the laws regarding the duties on falt, and the inconveniences arifing therefrom, and to report the fame, with their opinions thereupon, to the Houfe. The reports of that committee contain much interefting information upon the fubject, and the advantages of repealing this tax are clearly pointed out. It is to be hoped, therefore, that the firft favourable opportunity will be embraced for that purpofe. In the interim, it would be defirable to have a diftinct treatife on the fubject, under the following general heads. 1. What is the grofs produce of the falt tax in England, Scotland, and Ireland? 2. What is the net produce in each kingdom refpectively, and the nature and caufes of any deduction from the grofs receipt? 3. What is the effect of the tax on the price of the article itfelf, and the probable amount of the additional price paid by the public in confequence of its being taxed? 4. What are its effects in regard to the price of provifions, as bread, cheefe, butter, falted

meat,

meat, fish, &c. ; and does it not particularly affect
the food of the middling and lower orders of society ?   5. What are its effects on the fisheries ?
6. What on the commerce of the country, occa-
sioning the importation of barilla and potash, and
preventing the exportation of salt and many other
articles connected therewith ?   7. What are its
effects on our manufactures, as leather, bleaching,
paints, &c. ?   8. What are its effects on agriculture, in regard to manure, the feeding of cattle,
&c. ?   9. What are its effects on the revenue, and
has it not a tendency to promote smuggling ?
10. What are its effects on the public expenditure,
and to wh   extent does it encrease the price of
provisions for the army and navy, the expence of
transports, &c. ?   11. Is it not probable, that the
art of manufacturing salt would be greatly improved, if no such tax existed ?   12. Would it not
tend to promote the health of the people, if abundance of salt could be had at a reasonable price,
and of a superior quality ?   Lastly, What would be
the best means of commuting this tax in England,
Scotland, and Ireland ?

A work that would fully explain all these particulars, would be an inestimable present to the
public.

§. Stamps.   The origin of the mode of raising a revenue
by means of stamps is not a little singular.

In the wars which the Dutch carried on for
maintaining their rights and privileges against the
house

houfe of Auftria, they were reduced, as might naturally be expected in fo unequal a conteft, to the
greateft difficulties and diftrefs.   Not knowing in
what manner to raife money, they offered, by
public edict, a confiderable fum to any one, who
fhould difcover the moft ufeful and the leaft burdenfome mode of adding to the revenue.   Such
an offer naturally produced many propofals.
Among the reft the *vectigal chartæ*, in the Dutch
language called *Impoft van befegelde Brieven*, was
fuggefted, and the idea being approved of, the individual by whom it was propofed received the reward due to his talents and invention[r].

As the hiftory of this tax is far from being generally known, it may not be improper to give
fome account of the arguments made ufe of on
each fide relative to it, when originally impofed.

The firft idea included every thing that has fince
been fuggefted upon the fubject.   It was propofed,
that no petitions fhould be received by the ftates,
by the magiftrates of any city or diftrict, or by the
judge of any court, unlefs they were ftamped; that
no proceedings in law, that no receipts or acquittances, no deeds written by notaries, attornies,

[r] Others trace this tax to a period ftill more remote. See
Bibliotheque Hiftorique de la France, par Jacques Le Long,
tome fecond. Liv. 3. Article 5. No. 28,145. A Paris, an.
1769. Differtation fur l'Origine du Papier et Parchemin
Timbre.   Elle eft imprimee dans les varietes hiftoriques.
L'Auteur y fait voir, que cette nftitution, recente parmi nous,
etoit connue, et en ufage chez l s Romains, fous l'empire de
Conftantine.

scriveners,

fcriveners, lawyers, and the like ; and that no inftrument of any kind fhould be received as evidence, or in any manner fuftained by a court of
juftice, unlefs a certain fum had been paid, under
the name of ftamp duty, in proportion to the nature, quality, and value of the matters therein
contained.

The propofal was fupported by the following
arguments :

1. That the burden was in itfelf but fmall and
inconfiderable : 2. That the poor and lower ranks
of people, having little or no occafion for fuch
writings, would be almoft totally exempted : 3.
That the wealthier citizens, having many contracts
to make, and many law fuits depending, would
have frequent occafion for ftampt paper; and confequently the tax would yield a confiderable revenue to the public.

Thofe who oppofed the project faid, that fuch
ftamps might eafily be counterfeited by private
perfons, and that it would be difficult to detect the
fraud : to which it was anfwered, that this would
unqueftionably be prevented, if public officers
were appointed to fubfcribe their names to the
ftamps, it being much eafier to counterfeit a feal
or ftamp, than the hand of any one. And when
it was objected, that public ftamps might be procured even to counterfeited deeds, and thereby
confirm their authority ; it was anfwered, that by
putting the ftamp at the fide, and not at the bottom, of the page, it would denote, that the public,

by

by such a mark, did not authenticate the instru-
ment, but merely demonstrated, that the parties
had fulfilled the orders of the legiflature, in making
ufe of fuch a material [s].

Such was the origin of ftamp duties in Holland.
They were firft eftablifhed in this country *anno*
1671 [t]. But fo many acts have fince been paffed
upon the fubject, that a mere enumeration of the
duties fills a volume [u]. It cannot therefore be
expected that they fhould be fpecified in this work.
It will be fufficient to give a ftatement of the income arifing from this branch of the revenue, for

[s] See Difquifitiones Politicæ, Hagæ Comitis *anno* 1651, ca-
fus 50. This work was tranflated into Englifh, under the title
of *Arcana Imperii Detecta*, printed at London *anno* 1701. The
tranflation (which was faid to have been executed by the famous
D'Avenant) is hardly to be met with, and the original is ftill
fcarcer..

Another account is given of the origin of ftamps, which de-
duces them from the protocolæ of the Roman notaries, whofe
example was imitated in France, and became, in the year 1655,
a fource of revenue in that country. Perhaps the perfon who
propofed this tax in Holland, might have taken the hint from
fome of the legal proceedings of the Roman law. But it is to
be obferved, that the book whence the above account is drawn
up, was printed *anno* 16,1, and that this mode of raifing a revenue did not exift in France until four years afterwards. It is
more than probable, therefore, that in fo far as refpects modern Europe, the merit of this tax may be given to the Dutch,
to whom indeed many other financial difcoveries ought to be
attributed.

[t] By 22 Car. II. cap. iii. See part i. p. 191.

[u] See a complete abridgment of the ftatutes relative to the
ftamp duties, in one volume octavo. Printed *anno* 1783.

the

he year ending 5th January 1803, (being the lateſt account extant,) together with ſuch obſervations as may occur regarding any particular article in the account.

Produce of the Duty on Stamps for one Year, ending 5th January 1803.

1. Total groſs receipt in England to be
   accounted for,   —   £.3,192,052 1 3¼
2. Ditto Scotland,   —   202,265 8 9

£.3,394,317 10 c¾

More particular information regarding this branch of the revenue will be found in the Appendix.

Tax on receipts.   It appears from the preceding account of the origin of ſtamps, that a duty upon receipts or acquittances, was recommended by the inventor of this mode of taxation ; and ſuch a tax has been long eſtabliſhed in different parts-of the continent, without being productive of any great inconvenience [x] ; but when it came to be propoſed in this country, it encountered a very formidable oppoſition. That oppoſition was fortunately refiſted, and the tax is now paid without furniſhing much cauſe for complaint. The only well-founded objection

[x] In Denmark, all kinds of receipts muſt be written upon ſtamped paper; the ſmalleſt ſtamp for this purpoſe is of the value of two pence Engliſh, and the higheſt two pounds eight ſhillings. See Williams's State of the Northern Governments, vol. i. p. 399.

to

to it feems to be, that the original idea, by which
the duty was proportioned to the greater or fmaller
value of the articles to which it related, has not
been adhered to.   Perhaps, if the mode of levying
the tax were altered, and if the duty were impofed
upon the perfon who receives the money, and not
upon the perfon who pays it; and if no receipt
were to be valid that was not written upon ftamped
paper, there are few branches of this department
that would prove more productive.

It is an unfortunate circumftance for a commer- Poft horfe
cial nation, that the neceffities of the ftate fhould ^{tax.}
have given rife to a tax on the intercourfe that
takes place between one part of the country and
another; fince there is nothing that tends fo much
to fpread induftry, wealth, and civilization, and in
fhort all the pleafures and advantages of fociety, as
an eafy and quick conveyance.   By fuch a communication between the capital and the country,
the whole fociety becomes, in a manner, one firm
and compacted body, impreffed with the fame
ideas, actuated by the fame principles, fpeaking
the fame language, animated by the fame fpirit,
and in every refpect refembling the fellow-citizens
of the fame town.   The remoteft parts of a kingdom, are thus gradually brought to be nearly as
valuable and important as thofe fituated in the
neighbourhood of the metropolis.   The health of
the inhabitants alfo is preferved by travelling about,
in furveying and vifiting their own country; and
improvements

improvements and information of every kind are more rapidly and more eafily communicated [r].

But unfortunately a tax on the internal communication of the country has not only been impofed, but a new plan of levying it has been adopted, by farming the tax to publicans [z] : a mode which has long been defervedly exploded at home; is univerfally condemned in every part of Europe where the fubject of finances is at all known or confidered; and has ever been held peculiarly inconfiftent with the principles of a free conftitution.

It is hardly poffible to difcover even a plaufible reafon for fo impolitic a regulation. This tax had yielded, at the rate of one penny *per* horfe for each mile, the fum of £.140,000 of grofs, and £.125,000 of net income. In the budget of 1785, it was ftated, that an additional halfpenny *per* mile, would produce £.50,000 *per annum,* and an act for levying that duty was accordingly paffed [a]. Inftead of fo confiderable an addition, however, the grofs produce *anno* 1786 amounted only to £.166,199, and the nett to £.148,820. It now produces only

[r] It may be curious to calculate the fum which is annually laid out on pofting in England. The grofs produce of the tax is about £.220,000. The farmers of the duty probably have £.30,000 of profit; total, £.250,000: and as the tax is at the rate of 3 *d. per* mile, or one-fourth of the rate charged for poft-horfes, the people of Great Britain muft pay on the whole about a million *per annum* for pofting.

[z] By 27 Geo. III. cap. 26.   [a] 25 Geo. III. cap. 51.

at

at the rate of £.217,657 of net profit. Surely, for such a difference, the principles of our financial fyftem ought never to have been violated; and if it is intended merely as an experiment how far the farming of certain other branches of the revenue can anfwer, there is no faying to what a noxious extent it may be carried.

Befides, other plans to prevent frauds ought to have been tried, before fo pernicious a principle was adopted. A duty to a certain amount, (fup-pofe equal to the produce of one half of the tax), might have been laid on every horfe kept for the purpofe of being hired for pofting, (which could not have eafily been evaded, as the ftables of an inn-keeper are neceffarily open to the infpection of the public,) and the other half might have been levied at the gates. Or the commiffioners for hackney coaches might have been entrufted with the charge of levying this duty, giving them a *per centage* on the additional income they were enabled to raife, by their zeal and fuccefs in difcovering the beft mode of checking evafion.

The income derived from the remaining fources of the public revenue, both in England and Scotland, from the 5th January 1802, to ditto 1803, was as follows.

4. Mifcellaneous taxes.

Heads

Heads of Revenue.	Grofs Receipt to be accounted for.			Net Produce.		
	£.			£.		
1. Land and Affeffed Taxes -	5,535,348	13	7$\frac{1}{2}$	5,318,126	13	3$\frac{3}{4}$
2. Poft Office -	1,423,370	4	3$\frac{3}{4}$	1,095,353	11	3$\frac{1}{4}$
3. One Shilling *per* Pound on Penfions and Salaries	66,102	3	6$\frac{3}{4}$	65,557	18	9$\frac{3}{4}$
4. Sixpence *per* Pound on Penfions and Salaries -	61,820	3	10	60,728	15	11
5. Hackney Coaches	27,697	10	10$\frac{1}{4}$	25,109	10	5$\frac{1}{4}$
6. Hawkers and Pedlars -	8,600	19	7$\frac{1}{2}$	5,725	19	7$\frac{1}{2}$
	7,122,939	15	9$\frac{3}{4}$	6,570,602	9	4$\frac{1}{2}$
Small Branches of the hereditary Revenue of the Crown.						
7. Alienation Fines	12,166	7	4	10,643	10	6
8. Poft Fines -	2,737	6	6^3	2,737	6	6$\frac{3}{4}$
9. Seizures -	62,073	3	7$\frac{1}{2}$	62,073	3	7$\frac{1}{2}$
10. Compofitions	1	13	4	1	13	4
11. Proffers -	640	0	0	640	0	0
12. Crown Lands	47,505	5	10$\frac{1}{4}$	41,812	18	9$\frac{1}{2}$
Total -	7,248,063	12	6$\frac{1}{2}$	6,688,511	2	2$\frac{1}{4}$

Commutation tax.

In the former edition of this work, I gave a very particular account of the origin of the celebrated commutation tax, the fubftance of which it may not be improper to preferve in this part of the prefent impreffion.

The duty of hearth-money had not long been abolifhed after the revolution, before it was found neceffary to levy another tax on houfes, in proportion to the number of windows they contained, fo that in the language of the time it was faid, " that
" the

" the country had got nothing by the fwap." Vari us other taxes have fince been impofed on houfes and windows, none of which however occafioned fuch a diverfity of opinion, or gave rife to fo much difcuffion, as the one diftinguifhed by the name of the commutation tax.

It is well known that the great difadvantage attending duties upon confumption is this, that the payment of thofe duties may be evaded by the introduction of contraband articles, and that the higher the duty, the greater is the temptation to fmuggle. An increafe in fuch taxes, therefore, has often occafioned a decreafe in the revenue; and Swift's farcaftic remark upon fuch projects of finance has often been verified; " that in the arith-" metic of the cuftom-houfe, two and two, inftead " of making four, fometimes amounts only to " one."

But of all the articles on which too high a duty was dangerous, perhaps that on tea ought to have been peculiarly avoided; fince, notwithftanding the diftance whence it was brought, it was impoffible to prevent neighbouring and rival nations from importing it any quantity they might incline; and no commodity could be better adapted for an illicit trader, on account of the certainty of a demand, and the fmall bulk in which confiderable value could be carried. Impreffed with thefe ideas, Sir Matthew Decker, one of the moft intelligent and public-fpirited mercantile characters of his time, ftrongly urged the neceffity of

making

making fome regulation that would check the contraband commerce in tea, fince it was the profits
upon that article, that enabled the fmuggler to
carry on a trade of the fame kind in other commodities.

The plan he fuggefted was, to impofe a duty on
every family in England that drank tea, the
higheft at the rate of twenty fhillings, and the
loweft at the rate of five, in proportion to the
number of perfons in each family; and that all
public houfes felling tea, fhould pay £.5 in London and Weftminfter, and forty fhillings in every
other part of England [b]. But this propofal, according to the confeffion of the author, was only
intended to raife £.130,000 a-year, which was
then the amount of the excife duties paid upon
that commodity.

The meafure propofed by Decker was borrowed
from the regulations which ftill exift in fome of
the provinces in Holland: but every perfon in the
leaft acquainted with the government of the two
countries will eafily perceive, that a fyftem calculated for the one, cannot always be adopted by the
other. The ftrict police and rigid laws eftablifhed
in the United Provinces, would be accounted here
the height of tyranny and oppreffion [c]. In Hol-

[b] Serious Confiderations on the feveral high duties which
the nation in general labours under; third edition, printed *anno*
1744.

[c] A general account of the mode of levying the inland taxes
of Holland will be given in the third volume, affording a better
view of that important fubject than any hitherto known.

land.

land, any perfon who attempts to evade the public taxes is punifhed with the utmoft feverity; whereas in Britain, it is unfortunately accounted rather a venial trefpafs.

But though fo bold a meafure as that of taking off the duties upon tea entirely, could not be adopted, yet the neceffity of fome regulation, that would check the fmuggling of that article, was univerfally acknowledged. A committee was appointed by the houfe of commons on the 6th of February 1745, to take this important fubject into confideration[d]: by whom two reports were drawn up and prefented to the houfe, containing much curious information, and hints which proved not a little ferviceable to the revenue at the time[e].

The duties to which teas were then liable were about 14 *per cent. ad valorem*, payable to the cuftoms, and an inland duty of four fhillings *per* pound to the excife. On an average of five years (ending Midfummer 1745), only 768,520 pounds of tea had paid duty, and the medium produce of the revenue was at the rate of £.175,222 *per annum*. Such was the fituation of this branch of our commerce and revenue, when, *anno* 1745, an act was paffed by which the inland duty was re-

[d] Commons Journals, vol. xxv. p. 57.
[e] The firft is printed in Commons Journals, vol. xxv. p. 161. The other report was not fuffered then to be read or printed (fee p. 180); but was publifhed *anno* 1763 by Sir Stephen Theodore Janffen, in the volume intitled, " fmuggling laid open."

duced

duced to one shilling in the pound, and an additional excise duty of 25 *per cent. ad valorem* was imposed, according to the price at which teas were purchased at the public sales of the East India company . In regard to the custom-house duty of 14 *per cent.*, it continued at the same rate.

The advantages of this judicious measure, originally proposed by Sir Stephen Theodore Janssen, were soon perceived. The average consumption of the commodity, at a medium of seventeen years and a half, subsequent to the reduction, amounted to 3,957,634 pounds; and the income arising from thence came to £.490,553, being an addition to the revenue of £315,331 *per annum.* This was the first experiment, of any material consequence, in the financial history of this country, which established' the important principle, that the lowering of a high duty, upon an article of consumption, might very considerably advance the produce of the public revenue [g].

Unfortunately, however, the plan of retaining only a moderate duty upon teas was not adhered

---

[f] 18 Geo. II. cap. 26.

[g] See " Smuggling laid open in all its extensive and destructive Branches, with Proposals for the effectual Remedy of that most iniquitous Practice ; by Sir Stephen Theodore Janssen." 1 vol. octavo, printed *anno* 1763.   Postlethwayt also, in his Commercial Dictionary (*voce* Tea) has given us the tables of the consumption of tea from 1734 to 1763, copied from that work.   It is hardly necessary to add, that the pretensions of modern statesmen, to the merit of discovering that a reduction of duty may increase the revenue, is not perfectly well founded.

to ; for, *anno* 1748, a tax of 5 *per cent.* took place upon dry goods, including teas, and other additions were afterwards made both to the excife and cuftoms, infomuch that, *anno* 1783, the duties upon tea were as follows :

Cuftoms £.27 : 10 *per cent.* paid by the company.
Excife £.28 : 15 *per cent.* } paid by the con_
And 1*s.* 1*d.* $\frac{80}{100}$ *per* grofs pound } fumer.

It might naturally be expected, that fuch heavy duties would increafe the contraband trade of an article fo peculiarly well calculated for the purpofes of the fmuggler. And a variety of other frauds being known to exift in other branches of the revenue, a felect committee of the houfe of commons was appointed to inquire into the illicit practices fo prevalent at that time. The valuable reports drawn up by that committee, are well entitled to the reader's attention ; but the only part of them to which it is propofed at prefent to refer, relates to the article of tea [h].

In the third report of the committee, prefented the 23d of March 1784, a plan is mentioned (originally fuggefted by an active and intelligent officer of the Eaft India company [i]), the object of which was, a very confiderable reduction in the tea duties ; and as the plan would naturally occafion

[h] In the Parliamentary Regifter for 1783, vol. xiv. the three reports prefented by this committee are publifhed.
[i] The late William Richardfon, Efq. accountant-general of the company.

a dimia diminution of revenue, calculations were drawn up, stating the principles on which such deficiency might be made up, by a tax upon windows. The committee, however, instead of enforcing the idea, very cautiously remarked, that they thought it their duty to suggest the plan to the house, as deserving a serious discussion : and when the subject was first proposed in parliament by the minister, the chairman of the committee stated, " That the " plan, though possibly not impracticable, was " full of difficulties, liable to create much public " fermentation, and certain to be the subject of " many long debates in that house [k]."

The public were prepared for some regulations of that nature, by a paragraph in his majesty's speech on the 19th of May 1784, which recommended the alarming progress of frauds in the revenue, accompanied in so many instances with violence, as a matter which could not fail, on every account, to excite the attention of parliament ; and the system formed for that purpose, was stated to the house on the 21st of June following.

The grounds on which this measure was proposed were shortly these : That tea was the staple of smuggling, insomuch that though the East India company sold only 5,500,000 pounds weight for home consumption, there were from twelve to thirteen millions of pounds consumed in the kingdom. That to remove this evil, the best possible

[k] Speech of the Right Hon. William Eden, Parliamentary Register, vol. xv. p. 230.

plan

plan was, to lower the duty upon tea in such a degree as to take away from the smuggler the temptation to carry on an illegal trade: but as the revenue could not afford any material diminution at present, that it would be neceſſary to propoſe a new tax, as a ſubſtitute in its room. The ſum required would be from £. 700,000 to £. 800,000 per annum, £. 169,000 of which was propoſed to be raiſed by a duty of 12½ per cent. on the price paid by the purchaſer at the public ſales of the company[1], and the remaining £. 600,000 by an additional duty upon windows. The happy conſequences which were to reſult from the adoption of this meaſure, were repreſented in the moſt flattering colours: " The public revenue," it was ſaid, " would be conſiderably a gainer, and yet " the people would have no reaſon to complain " of additional burdens, *as they would be ſavers by* " *the plan* [m]."

It would require a volume to give a hiſtory of the various debates which have taken place upon this ſubject, or an account of the arguments for and againſt the meaſure which have at different times been urged [n]. The miniſter who propoſed

it

[1] The miniſter at firſt propoſed a duty of 12½ per cent. on bohea, 25 per cent. on ſouchong, 30 per cent. on ſinglo, 40 per cent. on congo, &c. ; but, ultimately the ſame ad valorem duty of 12½ per cent. was impoſed on teas indiſcriminately.

[m] Mr. Pitt's ſpeech, Parl. Regiſter, vol. x. p. 230.

[n] See particularly Parl. Regiſter, vol. xv. p. 230. vol. xvi. p. 377,

it has termed the commutation act " *glorioufly fuc-*
" *cefsful* [o]," whereas his opponents have held it
forth as abfurd, extravagant, and pernicious [p].
The beft mode of forming an impartial opinion
upon the fubject will be, to confider the confequences refulting from it, whether of a commercial,
financial, or political nature.

Confidered merely as a commercial regulation,
many plaufible arguments may be urged in its fa-
four. It has certainly increafed, in a very confiderable degree, the commerce of this country
with China, augmented our fhipping and feamen
in that trade, and produced all the other advantages refulting from a more extended navigation.

Confidered alfo merely as a matter of finance,
the exchequer is no material lofer by the bargain.
It appears from the commutation act [q], that the
cuftoms on tea, at an average of five years,

---

p. 377, and p. 90 in the Debates of the Houfe of Lords in the
fame volume; alfo, vol xx. p. 156. 161. 354, &c.   Some
very able pamphlets have likewife been written upon the fubject,
more particularly, Obfervations on the Commutation Project,
by Thomas Bates Rous, Efq.; Mr. Baring's Principles of the
Commutation Act eftablifhed by Facts; Obfervations relative
to the Taxes upon Windows or Lights, by M. de Lolme;
Mr. Twining's Obfervations on the Tea and Window Act,
&c. &c.

   [o] Parl. Regifter, vol. xx. p. 354.
   [p] Ditto, p. 158.
   [q] 24 Geo. 3. c. 28.

amounted

amounted to £. 348,547 : 6 : 9 and the excife to
£. 555,917 : 3 : 6 making in all £. 904,464 : 10 : 3
which was a larger fum than had been originally
fuppofed. The whole commutation fund for
the year, ending Michaelmas, 1788, produced
£. 781,657 : 9 : 5. The difference is confiderable, amounting to £. 122,807 but muft, in fome
degree, be made up to the public, by additional
duties received on other articles ; the checking of
fmuggling in tea having operated beneficially in
preventing illicit practices in other branches of the
revenue.

The arguments which have been urged againft
this meafure, confidered as a great political operation, are fhortly as follows : " That it en-
" courages an enormous confumption of a foreign
" commodity, in no refpect neceffary or ufeful :—
" That it encourages the confumption of a com-
" modity which there is reafon to believe is far
" from being favourable to the health of the
" people :—That it encourages commerce with a
" country but little difpofed to take our goods and
" manufactures in return, but which requires pay-
" ment in bullion, and thereby diminifhes our do-
" meftic wealth and circulation :—That it en-
" courages an article which prevents the con-
" fumption of the wholefome beverages of our own
" country, which in every point of view ought to
" be preferred, more efpecially as fo large a por-
" tion of our revenue is derived from them ; and
" that for the purpofe of obtaining this pernicious
                                        " article,

" article, at an eafy rate, we impofe a tax which
" materially tends to decreafe the number of
" houfes, and confequently the population of the
" country, or at leaft to render the dwellings of
" the people uncomfortable, if not unhealthy '."
In addition to thefe arguments, it is urged, that
by encouraging the confumption of the higher
priced teas, we double, and may treble the coft of
the article in the market of China, which may totally
reverfe the balance of our trade, were it ever fo
much in our favour; and that for fupplying the
extraordinary demand occafioned by the project,
we were obliged to purchafe from the companies
eftablifhed by rival nations, no lefs a quantity than
17,009,877 lb. weigh, which coft us the enormous
fum of £. 2,048,797 : 18 : 2.

The injuftice of the commutation tax, in many
inftances, can hardly be difputed; individuals being compelled to pay the tax who confume no tea,
and thofe who do confume it, not paying in any
adequate proportion.

The bargain between the public and the Eaft
India Company alfo has not been adhered to. The
tax on windows is regularly exacted, whilft the
price of tea continues nearly as high as formerly.

'. Windows were originally intended for the free admiffion of
air, which our anceftors wifely thought might not a little contribute to the health of the people. Window is in fact a corruption of *windoor*, and this tallies very well with Johnfon's
explanation of the word, " An aperture in a building by which
" air and light are intromitted."

Did

Did this profit go into the exchequer, it might be paid without murmur; but enriching, as it does, the speculators and dealers in that commodity, it is naturally complained of.

But the strongest argument against the commutation tax was, that the experiment was unnecessary. It had formerly been ascertained, that the duties, as they stood *anno* 1750, were sufficient to check smuggling, for the consumption regularly increased from that period[s]. At the duties of the year 1750, 2,700,000*lb.* weight of tea produced £. 372,600. Had the duties been reduced to the same standard (by which smuggling would have been effectually prevented), when the consumption in this country rose to 16,200,000*lb.* weight of tea, (which was under the quantity sold in the year ending September 1787), the income produced would have amounted to the enormous sum of two millions two hundred and thirty-five thousand six hundred pounds, *and no commutation tax could have been necessary*[t].

This

---

[s] The consumption would never have increased so regularly as it did, had it been impeded by smuggling. But it rose gradually from 2,700,000*lb.* its amount in 1750, to 4,393,983*lb.* the quantity consumed *anno* 1762.

[t] If by reducing the tax on teas to the standard of the year 1750, there was the least apprehension of smuggling, the custom-house duty of 14 *per cent.* which then existed, might be given up, and the following plan might be adopted:

Let there be a separate department at the India house under the management of three or more directors appointed for that
special

Taxes on horfes em- p'oyed in hufbandry.

This perhaps, on the whole, is the moſt im-politic of all our taxes. To impoſe a duty upon the inſtruments by which the food of the people is raiſed, cannot be juſtified on any ſound principle of policy: and it would be much better to levy ten times the ſum in any other way. When the

ſpecial purpoſe.—Let theſe directors be impowered to diſpoſe of the company's teas *by private ſale,* and not by public auction, as by act of parliament muſt be done at preſent.—Let certain agents be appointed in all the principal towns in the kingdom, for the purpoſe of retailing teas for the behoof of the company, at a certain moderate profit; but if any tea is purchaſed by a licenſed retailer, a reaſonable diſcount to be given.—No quan-tity to be ſold by the directors or their agents under half a cheſt. —The books of the company to be open to the inſpection of the treaſury, and a duty of one ſhilling *per lb.* and 25 *per cent. ad valorem,* to be charged to the company for the public behoof. During the ſpace of one year ending September 1787, 16,692,427 *lb.* weight of tea were ſold by the India company, and the duty at 12½ *per cent.* came to £.336,095. A ſhilling *per lb.* upon that quantity would have produced £.834,621 and 25 *per cent. ad valorem* £.672,190 making in all £.1,506,811 which is the loweſt ſum at which the revenue to be drawn from tea, with any tolerable management, ought to be calculated. The public ſales, by affording the means of ſpeculation and mo-nopoly, encourage ſmuggling. No contraband trade could exiſt, were the company permitted to enter into a fair conteſt with the illicit trader at his own home, even loaded with theſe duties; and whoever conſiders the immenſe buſineſs carried on under the management of the commiſſioners of the exciſe and of the cuſtoms, will ſee little difficulty in a board of reſpectable directors conducting the ſale of teas conſumed in this country, in a manner uſeful to the company, and *very profitable indeed* to the ſtate.

cultivation

cultivation of the ground is made fubject to fuch
impofitions, the farmer muft either convert his
ground to grafs, or raife the price of grain, either
of which tends to promote the importation of
foreign grain, and all the fatal confequences refulting therefrom. Inftead of difcouraging, every
means ought to be thought of, to promote the
agriculture of the country, as the beft foundation
of national ftrength, and the moft likely means of
fecuring every other defcription of public profperity.

The miferable ftate to which the domains of The royal
the crown are reduced, (which at one period or domains.
another comprehended fo confiderable a part of
the land in England), is a fufficient proof how little
territorial poffeffions are calculated for being the
fource of national income. No property could be
better guarded, than thefe poffeffions were, by in-
numerable laws againft invafion. Yet art and
avarice burft through every reftraint, and have
rendered them fo very infignificant in regard to
the income they produce, that until their real value was lat ly made known, they were hardly confidered , a part of the revenue of the country intitled to any particular attention. During the
thirty-three years of the reign of George the Second, the income they yielded, was, at an average,
only £. 5641 *per annum* [u]. Their amount during
this reign has been equally contemptible. In re-

[u] Their produce during the whole reign was only £.186,263.

gard

gard to their ftate at prefent, it is fufficiently explained in the reports of the commiffioners appointed to inquire into the condition of the woods,
forefts, and land revenues of the crown, where the
reader·will be furnifhed with ample information on
the fubject.

The landed poffeffions of the crown, it is remarked by the commiffioners, confift of three
diftinct branches:—1. Of fee farm and other un-
improvable rents.   2. Of landed poffeffions held
of the crown by leafe.   3. The woods, forefts,
parks, and chafes.

The fee-farm rents are certain fums paid annually to the crown for lands held in perpetuity
by their prefent poffeffors, and confequently can
never be increafed or improved.   The following
is a ftate of their amount:

Vifcontiel rents and feifures - - -	£. 831 16 5¼
Rents in South and North Wales - -	6342 1 2¼
Rents in feveral divifions of the counties of England - - - - - - - -	5462 1 5¾
Total - £.	12,635 19 2¼

Thefe are the fums, the receipt of which is
actually acknowledged by the different officers.
But various other claims are annually made to the
amount of £.14,877 : 9 : 8¼ with fo little juftice
or attention, that the very arrears on that flender
revenue have accumulated to the enormous fum
of £.437,555 : 7 : 4.   Several fee-farm rents have
been

been fold in confequence of an act paffed for that purpofe [x]. The money which the fale produced has purchafed a capital, in the 3 *per cent.* confolidated annuities, to the amount of £.122,351 : 17 : 3 the intereft on which is £.3671 : 11.

The lands held by leafes under the crown are an object of greater importance. The old rents are eftimated at £.10,563 : 12 : 1. New or additional rents are commencing at different periods to the amount of £.6221 : 0 : 2¼. The fines paid at an average of 22 . years, are about £.7410 *per annum,* and the real improved value of thefe eftates, at a very moderate eftimate, has been calculated at £.102,626 : 14 : 1⅛ *per annum.*

It is not propofed, however, to enter farther into the difcuffion of this fubject at this time, as in fact this branch of the royal domains, together with the third branch, namely, the woods and forefts [y], are rather to be confidered as a foundation for future hopes, than as producing an income at prefent of any material confequence. They will naturally fall to be confidered therefore in a fubfequent part of this work, in which fome account will be given of the national refources. It will be fufficient for our prefent purpofe to give the following abftract of this branch of the public

[x] 26 Geo. 3. cap. 87.

[y] There is every reafon to hope, that the royal woods and forefts, under Lord Glenbervie's management, will, in due time, furnifh a valuable fupply of timber to the Britifh navy.

revenue,

revenue, drawn up by an author, who had official access to information respecting it.

Gross amount of rents - - - -	£.36,720	7 1
Fines for leases on an average of ten years	7700	0 0
	44,420	7 1

To be deducted.

Rents granted away, or usually left in arrear - - -	17,530 15 10		
Land-tax allowed and deducted from rents received -	3505 12 7		
		21,036	8 5
Total annual receipt		£.23,883	18 8

Other deductions.

Charges of management - -	3999 8 3		
Perpetual pensions and grants to individuals - - - -	4794 17 7		
Salaries to the keepers of prisons, castles, &c. - - -	991 0 7		
Salaries to the judges and other officers in Wales -	1446 10 9		
Commissioners of taxes and incidents in their office -	1322 0 0		
		12,553	17 2
Net produce		£.10,830	1 6[z]

Such is the whole income drawn from 130 manors, about 52,000 acres of arable, meadow, and pasture land, about 1880 houses in London and Westminster, and about 450 houses, mills, and cottages,

[z] Observations on the Land Revenue of the Crown, by the Hon. John St. John.

in various other parts of England. It is a fortunate circumftance however for the public intereft, that the land revenue of the crown, is at prefent under the care of a moft active and intelligent officer, (John Fordyce, Efq. furveyor-general of crown lands,) who labours with unceafing folicitude, to augment the income of that branch of the revenue, and to furmount thofe difficulties, which former inattention and mifmanagement have placed in his way.

As far back as the year 1662, four hundred hackney coaches were licenfed in the cities of London and Weftminfter[a]; but the fum exacted from them, was then appropriated for the purpofe of repairing the highways and fewers, and of paving and cleaning the ftreets of the metropolis; nor was it difcovered, until the year 1694, that this might become a branch of the public revenue. Hackney coaches.

By the firft act paffed for that purpofe[b], permiffion was given to licenfe a number not exceeding 700 hackney coaches; each licence to continue for 21 years, upon payment of the fine of £.50 and giving fecurity for the additional fum of £.4 per annum; and a board of commiffioners was appointed for granting licences, and for executing the different powers contained in the act. The number was increafed in the reign of Queen Anne, to 800 coaches[c], and the commiffioners were alfo invefted with authority to licenfe hackney

[a] By 3 and 4 Car. 2. cap. 2.
[b] 5 and 6 Will. and Mary, cap. 22.
[c] 9 Anne, cap. 23.

chairs,

chairs, not exceeding 200, at the rate of 10 shillings *per annum*, which number was increased first to 300, and afterwards to 400[d]. *Anno* 1770, a thousand hackney coaches were permitted to be licensed, and the sum of 5*s. per* week, or £.13 *per annum*, was imposed upon them. That duty has since been doubled, consequently they now pay at the rate of £.26 each *per annum*[e].

It is difficult to comprehend, how so large a sum can be afforded for such a permission. Certain however it is, that there is no want of applications for licences, and consequently the trade must be sufficiently profitable. It furnishes a satisfactory answer to those who complain of the sums in which they are taxed by government for the liberty of carrying on their different professions (as attorneys, dealers in exciseable commodities, &c.;) for here so high a duty as £.26 a year is paid, after deducting which, the profits of the business must maintain a coachman and two horses, and must contribute to the repairs of the carriage and the maintenance of its owner.

But the principal cause for taking any particular notice of this branch of the revenue, is an idea that has often occurred to the author of this work; that

---

[d] See 9 Anne, cap. 19.   Also, 12 Geo. 1. cap. 12 and 16. Geo. 2. cap. 26.   The number of chairs have since been again reduced to 200.

[e] 24 Geo. 3. cap. 27.

a transfa transference of the duties upon fervants to this office, and intrufting to this board powers over domeftic fervants, fimilar to thofe which they now enjoy in regard to hackney coachmen, would, in various points of view, be an advantageous regulation.   The want of police, in regard to fervants, is a great public difadvantage.   If they knew that there exifted a fummary jurifdiction, with power fufficient to punifh thofe petty frauds, (which with them is the commencement of every fpecies of crime,) they would be lefs apt to give way to temptations, which at prefent they find it difficult to refift.   And the good confequences which have refulted from intrufting thefe commiffioners with authority over hackney coachmen, (who would otherwife have been a race of men totally ungovernable), tend to juftify the idea, that intrufting the fame board with fuch powers over fervants, as might be neceffary for their regulation, would be an advantageous meafure both to them and to the public[f].

Itinerant retailers, known under the name of hawkers, pedlars, or petty chapmen, have long been an object of taxation, partly for the fake of revenue, but perhaps principally for the purpofes

Hawkers and pedlars.

---

[f] If domeftic fervants could not be put under the control of this board, it would at leaft be ufeful to inveft them with fome authority over the porters in the city of London, particularly thofe who carry parcels from inns, who have no bounds in the exorbitancy of their demands.

of police [g]. It was *anno* 1697 that a licence duty was firſt impoſed upon them. Perſons travelling on foot, were charged with a duty of £ 4, and £.4 additional were impoſed on ſuch as made uſe of horſes for tranſporting their merchandiſe. Theſe duties were doubled by an act paſſed *anno* 1785 [h], by way of a boon to the ſhopkeepers, and a re-compence to them for the burdens to which they were then ſubjected. But when the tax upon ſhops came to be repealed, theſe additional duties tell of courſe. Ideas were thrown out, when the ſhop-tax was paſſed, that the hawkers and pedlars ought to be totally aboliſhed. It was contended that they were a vagrant, and even pernicious race of people, of no poſſible advantage to the commu-nity. It was natural for the ſhopkeepers to wiſh for the annihilation of the only ſet of perſons who enter into any competition with them. But how-ever obnoxious the rivalſhip might be to thoſe who have a permanent reſidence in towns, whoſe profits however by this rivalſhip are reſtrained within proper bounds, yet ſtill there are many parts of the country, at a diſtance from market towns, that could not well be ſupplied with many articles neceſſary for them, without the aſſiſtance of theſe itinerant dealers, who are thus the means of ex-tending the conſumption of our own manufactures, and the ſale of goods that might otherwiſe periſh

[g] They were firſt put under the control of the commiſſioners for tranſportation.

[h] 25 Geo. 3. cap. 78

in

in the warehoufes of our merchants, or in the fhops
of the retailer. This tax however is falling off in
produce, and as the country improves, and new
towns or villages are built, will naturally diminifh
every year. *Anno* 1723 it yielded £.10,773 of
grofs, and £.8604 of net income; whereas *anno*
1788, in confequence of the exorbitant taxes demanded from the hawkers and pedlars, and the
harfh and cruel regulations to which they were
fubjected, it fell off to £.2170 of net produce. It
yielded in the year ending 5th January 1803,
£.5279 of profit to the Exchequer.

The following account will then give a general
view of the income of Great Britain, for the year
ending 5th January 1803.

Heads of Revenue.	Total Receipt to be ac-counted for within the Year.			Total Payments appli-cable to national Ob-jects.		
	£.	s.	d.	£.	s.	d.
1. Cuftoms - -	10,519,920	13	7¾	7,415,726	19	3¼
2. Excife - -	16,833,786	5	11	14,927,538	4	0¼
3. Stamps - -	3,394,317	10	0¾	3,169,363	12	3¼
4. Mifcellaneous taxes - -	7,248,063	12	6¼	6,688,511	2	2¼
Total -	37,996,088	2	1¾	32,201,139	17	9¼

The lottery, an extraordinary but precarious
fource of revenue, produced laft year no lefs a fum
than £.525,458 of net profit.

It muft appear almoft incredible, to any perfon
who has not traced the fources of public revenue

in

in general, and more efpecially the peculiar advantages, of a financial nature, which this country poffeffes, that it fhould be competent to the production of fo enormous a fum, and that the profpect fhould be rather in favour of an increafe than a diminution.

But the above fum, great as it may appear, is far from being the total amount of burdens to which this country is fubjected. A variety of other articles muft be ftated, in order to give a complete view of the fums levied in thefe kingdoms for public purpofes.

Additional
burdens
upon the
public. The poor's rates, from the reports of the committee appointed by parliament to confider the returns made by the overfeers in regard to the ftate of the poor, were calculated on a medium of three years, ending *anno* 1785, at £.2,100,587[1], to which there was to be added £.258,710 *per annum* of charitable donations, making in all at that time £.2,359,297. But the amount now, cannot be lefs than four millions.

The annual income of the public hofpitals in England and Scotland, may be ftated at £350,000. Greenwich hofpital alone receives from 60 to £.70,000 a-year, without fharing in any part of the public income: the fixpenny tax upon feamen, its landed eftates and property in the funds, producing that fum.

The money arifing from turnpikes in England and Scotland muft be very great, amounting to at

---

[1] This includes certain fums levied for county purpofes.

leaft

leaft £.600,000 *per annum* ; and as many roads are made by affeffment, for the benefit of particular diftricts, for which no toll is demanded, and in fome places ftatute labour is exacted in kind, it is probable that £.100,000 additional is annually expended for fimilar purpofes.

An immenfe income is enjoyed by the different towns and corporations in England. London alone poffeffes a revenue of £.120,000 *per annum*. The whole cannot be calculated at lefs than £.500,000 a year in England, and £.100,000 in Scotland.

A variety of taxes are levied upon the people on navigable rivers, canals, and the ferries, amounting perhaps to £.250,000 a-year.

The expence of lighting and watching the different towns in the kingdom, and the roads in the neighbourhood of the capital, and in making and repairing the ftreets, is greater in this country than in any other part of Europe, and may fafely be calculated at £.300,000 a-year.

The money levied in Ireland, including the charges of collection, the bounties payable in that country, the tolls therein exacted, the eftates of the different corporations, and the expence of the poor, of lighting their towns, the public hofpitals, &c. will amount to at leaft £.400,000 *per annum.*

The revenues of the churches of England, Scotland, and Ireland, cannot be ftated at lefs than three millions more.

Hence

Hence the money levied for public purpofes, in the European part of his Britannic majefty's dominions, may be ftated as follows:

CALCULATION of the Sums of Money levied within the Year, for public Purpofes, in Great Britain and Ireland.

1. Grofs Receipt of all the taxes to be accounted for within the year - - £.	37,996,088
2. Profit of the lottery - -	525,458
3. Poor's rates and county expences -	4,000,000
4. Public hofpitals, including that of Greenwich[k]	350,000
5. Turnpikes in England and Scotland -	600,000
6. Parochial road affeffments and ftatute labour	100,000
7. Income of towns and corporations in England	500,000
8. Ditto in Scotland - -	100,000
9. Navigable rivers, canals, &c. -	250,000
10. Lighting, watching, and paving ftreets -	300,000
11. Public taxes, and other burdens payable in Ireland - -	4,000,000
12. Revenue of the churches of England, Scotland, and Ireland - -	3,000,000
Grand total £.	51,721,546

Let it not be imagined, that the author has any defire, to exaggerate, in the above ftatement, the burdens with which thefe kingdoms are loaded. No man would wifh to do fo, who has any feeling for his fellow fubjects, or any tincture of humanity. On the contrary, by ftating how much is already exacted, it will be apparent, that lefs can

[k] Chelfea Hofpital is paid out of the public revenue; Greenwich out of its own peculiar funds.

be

be afforded for the future. The more the people are loaded, the lefs they can bear an addition. The ftruggle therefore between rival nations, and the boaft and glory of their ftatefmen, ought to be, not who pays the moft, but from whom the leaft is exacted. May fuch be the great fource of competition between France and England! may the rulers of both countries contend for the future, whofe adminiftration fhall prove the lighteft and leaft burthenfome! and may the rivalfhip never ceafe, until both nations attain fuch eafe and abundance, that in the memorable words of Henry 4th of France, " Le plus pauvre pût tous les di- " manches, mettre une poule au pot ;" or, in the words of a Britifh fentiment, " *May the pooreft labourer enjoy, not only a comfortable dinner with his family on Sunday, but the real neceffaries of life, during every other day of the week.*"

APPEN.

APPENDIX.

No. I.

STATE of the Revenue of Great Britain for One Year, ending 5th January 1803.

CUSTOMS.

SPECIES OF GOODS.	NET PRODUCE.		
	England.	Scotland.	Great Britain.
	£. s. d.	£. s. d.	£. s. d.
Afhes, Pearl	5,859 14 8	465 1 4	6,324 16 —
———— Pot	2,248 6 7	2,146 14 9	4,395 1 4
Barilla	44,465 16 4	775 17 —	45,241 13 4
Beads, Coral	1,799 14 10	— —	1,799 14 10
Beer, Spruce	2,489 19 2	— —	2,489 19 2
Books, bound	2,662 10 5	26 19 3	2,689 9 8
———— unbound	4,661 1 7	136 15 8	4,797 17 3
Bottles, Glafs	5,189 19 1	120 12 3	5,310 11 4
Boxes, Pill	1,237 3 1	— —	1,237 3 1
Brimftone	2,759 12 2	— —	2,706 12 2
Briftles, undreft	9,460 15 11	393 13 7	9,854 9 6
Bugle, Great	1,456 17 10	— —	1,456 17 10
Carpets, Turkey	1,757 18 4	— —	1,757 18 4
China Ware	1,921 3 4.	— —	1,921 3 4
Copper, unwrought	3,215 18 4	— —	3,215 18 4
Cordage	2,406 — 6	286 13 8	2,692 14 2
Cork	6,019 7 5	387 15 5	6,407 2 10
DRUGS. { Borax, refined	1,129 19 —	— —	1,129 19 —
Camphire, unrefined	1,142 16 8	— —	1,142 16 8
Caffia Lignea	1,745 9 11	— —	1,745 9 11
Cortex, Peru	3,237 12 1	— —	3,237 12 1
Cream of Tartar	2,063 1 11	12 7 7	2,075 9 6
Ginfang	466 3 6	— —	466 3 6
Gum Guiaçi	1,271 7 —	— —	1,271 7 —
Jalop	1,671 4 10	— —	1,671 4 10

CUSTOMS—*continued.*

SPECIES OF GOODS.	England.			Scotland.			Great Britain.		
	£.	s.	d.	£.	s.	d.	£.	s.	d.
DRUGS									
Juniper Berries	2,901	1	8	3	14	—	2,904	15	8
Oil, Palm	3,425	18	6	—	—		3,425	18	6
—— Turpentine	3,743	6	6	27	19	2	3,771	5	8
Opium	2,148	3	10	—	—		2,148	3	10
Quickfilver	23,895	11	4	130	10	—	24,026	1	4
Rhubarb	3,021	17	2	—	10	5	3,022	7	7
Saccarum Saturni	2,030	19	2	248	3	8	2,279	2	10
Senna	2 395	15	10	—	—		2,395	15	10
Succus Liquoritiæ	6,974	5	4	391	7	5	7,366	12	9
Verdigreafe	1,892	15	9	20	19	—	1,913	14	9
DYE STUFFS									
Berries	2,010	—	6	—	—		2,010	—	6
Cochineal	8,073	9	8	—	—		8,073	9	8
Indigo	24,356	3	8	78	16	6	24,435	—	2
Logwood	1,260	5	8	42	4	11	1,302	10	7
Maddar	3,434	1	8	3 4	9	1	3,758	10	9
—— Roots	1,783	7	5	—	—		1,783	7	5
Redwood	1,367	14	9	—	—		1,367	14	9
Shumack	2,570	14	5	121	6	5	2,692	—	10
Smalts	17,160	11	4	651	8	3	17,811	19	7
Earthenware, unrated	2,100	9	7	—	—		2,100	9	
Elephants Teeth	6,822	13	6	76	7	11	6,899	6	
Feathers for Beds	7,380	1	10	541	7	6	7,921	9	4
Fifh, Oyfters	2,613	9	—	—	—		2,613	9	—
Fruit, Lemons and Oranges	19,671	13	11	588	6	2	20,260	—	
—— Nuts, fmall	2,572	19	11	2	2	3	2,575	2	2
Glafs Plates	8,845	8	3	8	10	2	8,853	18	5
GROCERY									
Almonds, Jordan	2,547	15	6	435	19	1	2,983	14	7
—— not Jordan	1,731	11	4	272	18	7	2,004	9	11
Annifeeds	376	15	9	40	5	3	417	1	—
Cloves	4 097	8	5	—	—		4,097	8	5
Cocoa	1,912	3	8	7	16	3	1,919	19	11
Coffee	17,461	11	1	428	5	1	17,889	16	2
Currants	122,888	16	2	101	18	1	122,990	14	3
Figs	5,575	5	11	667	11	9	6,242	17	8
Mace	987	—	4	—	—		987	—	4
Nutmegs	4,570	—	—	—	—		4,570	—	—
Pepper	48,183	8	—	—	—		48,183	8	—
Prunes	11,394	16	6	1,453	14	2	12,848	10	8
Raifins, Denia	24,241	16	—	1	19	4	24,243	15	4
—— Lexia	22,031	7	3	2,032	2	11	24,063	10	2
—— Lipari	3,343	4	7	31	19	7	3,375	4	2
—— Smyrna	8,276	10	1	—	—		8,276	10	1
—— Solis	32,856	15	—	4,048	9	5	36,905	4	5

CUSTOMS—*continued.*

SPECIES OF GOODS.	NET PRODUCE.		
	England.	Scotland.	Great Britain.
	£. s d.	£. s. d.	£. s. d.
GROCERY. Rice - -	599 11 11	413 11 7	1,013 3 6
Succads - -	1,386 1 11	73 14 5	1,459 16 4
Sugar, Brown -	2,878,649 5 9	234,263 4 10	3,112,912 10 7
Tamarinds - ' -	822 15 4	84 10 5	907 5 9
Tea - - -	144,758 13 8	— —	144,758 13 8
Turmeric - -	804 — 1	14 14 10	818 14 11
Hair, Horfe - -	1,946 12 9	195 12 —	2,142 4 9
Hats, Chip - -	4,505 9 6	— —	2,505 9 6
—— Straw - -	1,557 5 9	— —	2,557 5 9
Hemp, rough - -	96,694 16 5	19,149 — 5	115,843 16 10
Hides, Horfe - -	2,074 15 8	295 12 —	2,370 7 8
—— Indian - -	2,465 12 2	— —	2,465 12 2
—— Lofh - -	2,995 12 9	— —	2,995 12 9
—— Ox or Cow -	3,387 7 6	1,303 8 7	4,690 16 1
—— —— Tanned	1,422 1 7	193 16 5	1,615 18 —
Incle, wrought - -	2,119 1 11	2 — 10	2,121 2 9
Iron, Bar - -	168,185 9 10	21,542 1 —	189,727 10 10
—— Caft - - -	3,780 16 —	400 6 5 8	4,181 2 5
Kelp - - -	949 4 9	— —	949 4 9
Lace bone - - -	2,659 6 7	— —	2,659 6 7
LINEN. Cambrics - -	13,599 3 2	— —	13,599 3 2
Canvas, Heffens -	17,388 16 3	— —	17,388 16 3
—— Spruce -	2,994 12 3	4 2 8	2,998 14 11
Damafk Napking Silefia -	983 1 3	— 12 6	983 13 9
Damafk Tabling Silefia -	4,135 9 2	15 3 10	4,150 13 —
Drilling - -	3,688 8 6	4 13 10	3,693 2 4
Germany, above 36 Inches broad	382 13 9	— —	324 14 8
Germany, under 36 Inches -	343 5 7	— —	212 16 2
Germany, Narrow	41,306 17 6	294 9 5	41,601 6 11
Ruffia, Broad, above 22½ Inch.	38,459 19 7	482 13 3	38,942 12 10
Ruffia, Broad, above 31½ Inch.	2,641 4 6	46 13 9	2,687 18 3
Ruffia, Broad, above 36 Inch.	11,534 13 9	1,334 7 10	12,869 1 7
Ruffia, Narrow -	13,309 8 1	6 18 3	13,316 6 4
—— Towelling and Napke -	1,441 2 3	62, 13 11	1,503 16 2

CUSTOMS—*continued.*

SPECIES OF GOODS.	NET PRODUCE.		
	England.	Scotland.	Great Britain.
	£. s. d.	£. s. d.	£. s. d.
Manufactured and Un- manufactured Arti- cles of India	7,999 5 4	— —	7,999 5 4
Mats, Ruffia - -	3,612 1 2	379 13 3	3,991 14 5
Oil, Ordinary - -	20,101 9 10	157 15 11	20,259 5 9
—— Sallad - -	4,787 5 6	93 — 5	4,880 5 11
—— Train - -	10,216 7 7	1,022 15 10	11,239 3 5
Paper - - -	4,376 17 7	43 12 10	4,420 10 5
Pictures - - -	5,300 1 3	34 8 8	5,334 9 11
Piece Goods of India. { Callicoes - -	17,571 1 6	— —	17,571 1 6
Muflins - -	77,003 9 4	— —	77,003 9 4
Nankeens - -	17,293 4 11	— —	17,293 4 11
Prohibited - -	11,395 2 6	— —	11,395 2 6
Rags - - -	1,333 11 1	174 17 —	1,508 8 1
Salt - - -	1,034 13 6	179 16 10	1,214 10 4
Seeds, Clover - -	11,155 11 6	376 4 —	11,531 15 6
—— Linseed - -	11,474 9 9	398 11 10	11,873 1 7
—— Rape or Cole -	4,896 — —	— —	4,896 — —
Shells, Mother of Pearl	3,594 6 7	— —	3,594 6 7
Ships Hulls and Mate- rials - -	2,785 3 9	— —	2,785 3 9
SILK. { Bengal, raw -	76,642 6 9	— —	76,642 6 9
China, raw -	19,626 3 10	— —	19,626 3 10
Italian, raw -	71,648 12 5	12 7 6	71,660 19 11
Thrown -	156,401 4 4	— —	156,401 4 4
SKINS. { Bear, Black - -	8,220 9 6	71 7 9	8,291 16 11
Beaver - -	980 7 10	9 13 9	990 1 7
Calf, raw -	2,009 4 4	196 17 11	2,206 2 3
—— tanned -	22,101 13 7	149 11 10	22,251 5 5
Deer, in Hair -	5,360 13 2	38 3 3	5,398 16 5
Fox, Ordinary -	107 6 —	26 1 2	133 7 2
Goat, raw -	2,130 6 10	— —	2,130 6 10
Kid, dreffed -	4,591 2 9	— —	4,591 2 9
—— undreffed -	3,547 9 4	— —	3,547 9 4
Lamb in Wool -	2,269 18 —	— 11 7	2,270 9 7
Martin - -	367 18 3	174 1 6	541 19 9
Mink - -	1,107 3 11	69 8 4	1,176 12 3
Otter - -	620 12 3	32 10 5	653 2 8
Raccoon - -	672 10 6	— 2 4	672 12 10
Seal - -	620 8 8	115 7 8	735 16 4
Wolf - -	1,471 9 8	— —	1,471 9 8

CUSTOMS—*continued.*

SPECIES OF GOODS.	NET PRODUCE.		
	England.	Scotland.	Great Britain.
	£. s. d.	£. s. d.	£. s. d.
Soap, Hard - -	2,288 — 3	·11 5 11	2,299 6 2
Spirits, Brandy - -	81,900 15 4	1,883 11 3	83,784 6 7
———— Cordial Water -	1,121 1 7	11 15 7	1,132 17 2
———— Geneva - -	34,065 12 5	8,437 1 10	42,502 14 3
———— Rum - -	89,946 3 4	22,301 3 10	112,247 7 2
Stones, Blocks of } Marble - - }	1,910 6 4	98 10 —	2,008 16 4
Tallow - - -	38,879 13 1	4,536 8 9	43,416 1 10
Tar - - -	5 048 — 4	919 5 5	5,967 5 9
Thread, Sifters - -	2 001 17 11	6 — 3	2,007 18 2
Tobacco - - -	284.156 18 1	43,465 2 9	327,622 — 10
Tortoisefhell - -	1,065 6 2	44 6 4	1,109 12 6
Tow - - -	3,216 15 3	2,096 3 10	5,312 19 1
Turpentine - -	9 309 16 10	1,378 5 —	10,688 1 10
Wax, Bees - -	10,275 9 1	146 7 7	10,421 16 8
WINE. ⎰ Canary - -	4,126 7 4	— —	4,126 7 4
Cape - - -	304 — 1	— —	304 — 1
French - -	30,084 3 10	4,579 16 8	34,664 — 6
Madeira - -	56,924 5 6	912 3 10	57,836 9 4
Portugal - -	780,667 18 7	49,659 — 4	830,326 18 11
Rhenifh - -	4,344 15 10	149 10 11	4,494 6 9
Spanifh - -	167,913 13 2	18,457 8 5	186,371 1 7
Other Wines -	1,942 7 9	— —	1,942 7 9
WOOD. ⎰ Balks - -	4,292 1 6	5,325 — 5	9,617 1 11
Battens - -	16,897 7 6	2,187 16 11	19,085 4 5
Boards, Paling -	2,107 3 10	97 6 11	2,204 10 9
———— Scale -	1,760 2 2	— —	1,760 2 2
———— Wainfcot -	908 15 —	21 8 6	930 3 6
Deals - -	241,439 5 6	20,441 9 1	261,880 14 7
———— Ends - -	8,316 16 10	1,703 14 2	10,020 11 —
Lathwood - -	7,291 9 4	990 15 8	8,282 5 —
Mahogany - -	18,984 7 9	1,645 16 11	20,630 4 8
Mafts - - -	10,722 11 1	762 17 11	11,535 9 —
Oars - - -	1,248 1 —	— —	1,248 1 —
Plank, Oak - -	8,598 5 11	1,977 10 6	10,575 16 5
Staves - - -	23,754 6 8	728 9 1	24 482 15 9
Timber, Fir - -	156,750 12 11	30,451 17 6	187,202 10 5
———— Oak -	3,232 2 10	607 7 6	3,839 10 4
Uphers - -	1,933 12 11	63 7 7	1,997 — 6
Wainfcot Logs -	4,039 10 6	163 15 3	4,203 5 9
Wool, Cotton - -	152,081 12 3	23,976 10 3	176,058 2 6
Yarn, Cotton - -	855 12 10	— 6 —	855 18 10
———— Mohair - -	4,023 2 5	— —	4,023 2 5

CUSTOMS—*continued.*

SPECIES OF GOODS.	NET PRODUCE.								
	England.			Scotland.			Great Britain.		
	£.	s.	d.	£.	s.	d.	£.	s.	d.
Zaffar - - -	1,887	17	—	—	—		1,887	17	—
Duty by the Act 42d of the King, Cap. 43, on Tonnage of Shipping Inwards -	56,090	11	9¾	7,354	4	2¾	63 444	16	—½
Sundry small Articles, the Duties on which have not amounted to £. 1,000 each -	154,759	12	5¼	22,899	13	7½	177,659	6	—¾
£.	7,153,187	17	4	581,968	13	7¼	7,734,915	2	5¼
Deduct the Amount of those Sums where the Drawback exceeds the Gross Receipt -	9,222	6	5	3,257	1	1	12,237	19	—
Total Duties Inwards	7,143,965	10	11	578,711	12	6¼	7,763,444	16	—½
Subsidies collected on: Alum - -	2,578	18	7	93	8	7	2,672	7	2
Coals - -	97,527	14	2½	7,578	8	2	105,106	2	4½
Lead - -	34,930	12	8½	1,291	6	5¾	36,221	19	2¼
Tin - -	4,419	10	6	—	12	6¼	4,420	3	—¼
Indigo - -	4,062	12	8	17	16	10	4,080	9	6
Skins, Beaver -	599	4	9	—	—		599	4	9
Other Articles -	13,744	12	8¾	154	9	6¼	13,899	2	3
Duty by the Act 42d of the King, Chap. 43d on Goods Exported	51,558	1	5¼	4,710	7	—½	56,268	8	5¾
——— on Tonnage of Shipping Outwards -	36,630	16	3¾	2,482	7	—	39,113	3	3¾
Total Duties Outwards	246,052	3	10¾	16,328	16	1¾	262,381	—	—½
Carried Coastways: Coals - -	655,277	1	11	—	—		655,277	1	11
Stones & Slates	17,468	6	1¾	3,275	17	—½	20,744	3	2¼
Wine - -	1,153	19	4¾	126	—	7¼	1,280	—	—
One Shilling per Chaldron on Newcastle Coals - -	24,885	7	—	—	—		24,885	7	—
Total Duties Coastways	698,784	14	5½	3,401	17	7¾	702,186	12	1¼

CUSTOMS—*continued.*

SPECIES OF GOODS.	NET PRODUCE.								
	England.			Scotland.			Great Britain.		
	£.	s.	d.	£.	s.	d.	£.	s.	d.
Remittances from the Plantations -	26,825	17	8¼	—	—		26,825	17	8¼
Received From the Receiver of Fines and Forfeitures for the King's Share of condemned Tobacco -	4,810	11	6¼	1	3	6½	4,811	15	—¾
Received From the Inspector of Corn Returns	1,022	17	—	—	—		1,022	17	—
Received From the Receiver General of the Counties on Account of Windows, by the Act 24th Geo. III.	856	5	11¼	—	—		856	5	11¼
Received From the Receiver General of Excise, for Wine sold - -	4,111	13	5½	—	—		4,111	13	5½
Arrear of Duty by Act 38th of the King, Cap. 76. on Goods and Shipping - -	79,715	1	9¾	4,072	8	1½	83,787	9	11¼
Quarantine Duty on Tonnage 1800 -	7,083	17	—½	245	1	—¼	7,328	18	—¾
Grand Total - £.	8,213,228	13	8¾	602,760	19	—	8,815,989	12	8¾

CHARGE.

	England.			Scotland.			Great Britain.		
	£.	s.	d.	£.	s.	d.	£.	s.	d.
Balance in the Hands of the different Collectors, on 5th January 1802 - -	18,673	15	9½	19,768	14	4¼	38,442	10	1¾
Balance in the Hands of the Receiver General of Scotland, on 5th January 1802	—	—		28,830	6	5¾	28,830	6	5¾
Bills arising and remitted out of the Revenue of 1801, but which were not brought to Account until 1802 - -	86,337	4	3½	9,866	15	10¾	96,204	—	2¼
Amount of Net Produce brought forward - - -	8,213,228	13	¾	602,760	19	—	8,815,989	12	8¼
£.	8,318,239	13	9¾	661,226	15	8¾	8,979,466	9	6½

DISCHARGE.

		England.			Scotland.			Great Britain.		
		£.	s.	d.	£.	s.	d.	£.	s.	d.
By Bounties - -		1,790,359	2	3¾	136,761	15	9¼	1,927,120	18	1
— Repayments on Over Entries and damaged Goods - -		64,244	11	11¼	14,651	10	7¾	78,896	2	7
Money impressed in the Hands of different Out Port Collectors		—	—		360	—	—	360	—	—
Paid towards the Support of His Majesty's Civil Government in Scotland -		—	—		56,789	1	4½	56,789	1	4½
Charges of Management		490,028	7	3¼	59,586	3	6¼	549,614	10	9½
Payments into the Exchequer.	Consolidated Customs - -	935,528	7	1	39,306	—	—	974,834	7	1
	Bricks and Tiles 1794	35	2	9½	—	—		35	2	9½
	Paper - 1794	3,727	18	2½	—	—		3,727	18	2½
	Slates & Stones 1794	14,621	11	3¾	1,470	—	—	16,091	11	3¾
	Wood, Fruit, and Oil 1795	104,981	6	10¾	9,410	—	—	114,391	6	10¾
	Coals and Salt 1795	17,099	3	10½	1,030	—	—	18,129	3	10½
	Wine - 1796	470,709	4	2	32,970	—	—	503,679	4	2
	Sugar and Bricks, including £.5 and £.10 per Cent. 1796	108,512	4	6½	8,548	—	—	117,060	4	6½
	Pepper, &c. 1797	120,558	18	6	5,817	—	—	126,375	18	6
	Plate imported 1797	6	11	2¼	—	—		6	11	2¼
	Goods and Shipping 1798	66,513	8	3¼	3,580	—	—	70,093	8	3¼
	Sugar & Coffee 1799	95,530	16	2¾	9,198	—	—	104,728	16	2¾
	Sugar and Malt 1800	407	8	8¼	—	—		407	8	8¼
	Do. Do. - 1801	491,074	7	—	—	—		491,074	7	—
	Wood, Sugar, &c. 1801	244,188	—	9	30,606	—	—	274,794	—	9
	Paper, &c. - 1801	3,697	15	6¼	—	—		3,697	15	6¼
	Sugar and Malt 1802	2,314,866	14	9¼	110,670	—	—	2,425,536	14	9¼
	Goods and Shipping 1802	738,267	14	2¼	75,695	—	—	813,962	14	2¼
Balance in the Hands of the different Collectors, on the 5th January 1803 -		22,671	4	8	17,715	5	7¼	40,386	10	3¼
Balance in the Hands of the Receiver General of Scotland, on the 5th January 1803		—	—		42,093	13	—¼	42,093	13	—¼
Bills arising out of the Revenue of 1802, but which were not brought to Account until the Year 1803		220,609	13	7¾	4,969	5	9½	225,578	19	5¼
£.		8,318,239	13	9¾	661,226	15	8¾	8,979,466	9	6½

GENERAL STATEMENT

CHARGE.

	England.			Scotland.			Great Britain.		
	£.	s.	d.	£.	s.	d.	£.	s.	d.
Balance in the Hands of the different Collectors, on the 5th January 1802 -	18,673	15	9½	19,768	14	4¼	38,442	10	1¾
Balance in the Hands of the Receiver General of Scotland, on 5th January 1802	—	—		28,830	6	5¾	28,830	6	5¾
Bills arifing and remitted out of the Revenue of 1801, but which were not brought to Account until 1802. - -	86,337	4	3½	9,866	15	10¾	96,204	—	2¼
Grofs Receipt within the Year - -	9,577,325	14	7¼	779,118	2	1¾	10,356,443	16	9½
£.	9,682,336	14	8¼	837,583	18	10½	10,519,920	13	7¼

OF THE PRECEDING ACCOUNT.

DISCHARGE.

	England.			Scotland.			Great Britain.		
	£.	s.	d.	£.	s.	d.	£.	s.	d.
By Drawbacks, Repayments and Bounties of the Nature of Drawbacks -	2,326,352	14	11½	228,226	8	6½	2,554,579	3	6
Bounties for promoting National Objects	892,348	—	2½	99,544	1	—¼	991,892	1	2¾
By Money impressed in the Hands of different Out Port Collectors -	—	—		360	—	—	360	—	—
Paid towards the Support of His Majesty's Civil Government in Scotland -	—	—		56,789	1	4½	56,789	1	4½
Charges of Management -	490,028	7	3¼	59,586	3	6¼	549,614	10	9½
Payments into the Exchequer -	5,730,326	13	11¾	328,300	—	—	6,058,626	13	11
Balance in the Hands of the different Collectors	22,671	4	8	17,715	5	7¼	40,386	10	3¼
Balance in the Hands of the Receiver General of Scotland, on 5th January 1803	—	—		42,093	13	—¼	42,093	13	—¼
Bills arising out of the Revenue of 1802, but which were not brought to Account until the Year 1803	220,609	13	7¾	4,969	5	9½	225,578	19	5¼
£.	9,682,336	14	8¾	837,583	18	10½	10,519,920	13	7¼

EXCISE IN ENGLAND.

DUTIES.	Gross Actual Receipt in Money. £.	s	d.	Net Produce of each Article. £.	s.	d.
Auctions - Duty and Licences	149,027	6	$3\frac{1}{2}$	144,049	1	$2\frac{1}{2}$
Beer - - - - -	2,147,037	2	$0\frac{3}{4}$	1,927,267	8	10
Bricks and Tiles - - -	114,865	10	$2\frac{1}{2}$	110,799	16	$0\frac{1}{2}$
Candles - Duty and Licences	278,548	7	$5\frac{1}{4}$	231,797	3	$9\frac{1}{2}$
Coaches - Duty and Licences	2,279	0	0	2,212	10	$10\frac{1}{4}$
Cocoa Nuts and Coffee - -	40,744	9	$1\frac{1}{4}$	35,274	15	$1\frac{3}{4}$
Cyder, Perry, and Verjuice -	40,162	18	$0\frac{1}{2}$	37,287	19	$8\frac{3}{4}$
Glass - - - - -	209,515	7	$2\frac{1}{2}$	139,507	4	5
Hides, Skins, Vellum, and Parchment	279,359	15	$10\frac{1}{2}$	251,391	8	$7\frac{1}{4}$
Hops - - - - -	246,215	11	1	227,350	18	$9\frac{1}{4}$
Metheglin or Mead, and Vinegar -	26,039	8	$7\frac{3}{4}$	26,020	7	$11\frac{3}{4}$
Printed Goods - -	612,910	1	2	285,629	5	$11\frac{1}{4}$
Sope - - - - -	488,163	7	$5\frac{1}{2}$	417,768	17	11
Spirits British - - -	671,556	11	$3\frac{1}{2}$	658,918	4	$8\frac{1}{4}$
Spirits Foreign - - -	1,023,757	18	$8\frac{3}{4}$	975,231	14	$11\frac{1}{4}$
Starch - - - - -	55,581	7	$8\frac{1}{2}$	49,733	15	8
Sweets - - - -	12,188	17	$9\frac{3}{4}$	12,065	7	$8\frac{1}{4}$
Tea - - - -	240,367	6	$\frac{1}{4}$	210,461	4	$2\frac{1}{4}$
Wine - - - -	348,592	13	$3\frac{3}{4}$	301,789	6	$3\frac{1}{4}$
Wire - - - -	4,359	7	$3\frac{1}{4}$	3,173	11	8
Licences to Dealers in Coffee, Chocolate, and Tea - -	15,996	2	$0\frac{3}{4}$	15,708	19	$0\frac{3}{4}$
Licences to Makers of, and Dealers in Exciseable Commodities -	44,794	6	10	43,979	17	$9\frac{3}{4}$
Licences to Retailers of Spirituous Liquors	170,331	6	$8\frac{3}{4}$	168,401	4	$1\frac{1}{2}$
Licences to Retailers Do. - of Wine - -	32,574	2	$11\frac{1}{2}$	31,884	18	$4\frac{3}{4}$
Licences to Sellers of Gold and Silver Plate	9,968	4	$2\frac{3}{4}$	9,484	9	$7\frac{1}{4}$
33 Geo. 3. Ch. 28 British Spirits -	108,129	15	$6\frac{1}{4}$	108,039	11	2
34 Geo. 3. Ch. 2 British ditto -	109,887	14	$5\frac{1}{4}$	109,797	15	1
34 Geo. 3. Ch. 3 Foreign ditto -	194,279	11	$8\frac{1}{4}$	194,243	7	$8\frac{1}{4}$
34 Geo. 3. Ch. 4 Foreign ditto -	194,461	13	$10\frac{1}{4}$	194,425	9	$10\frac{1}{4}$
34 Geo. 3. Ch. 15 Bricks and Tiles	68,087	9	5	66,976	18	$6\frac{3}{4}$
34 Geo. 3. Ch. 20 Paper, see below.						
34 Geo. 3. Ch. 27 Glass - -	76,755	19	$4\frac{3}{4}$	55,739	0	$5\frac{3}{4}$
35 Geo. 3. Ch. 10 Wine - -	582,415	18	2	526 515	12	$1\frac{1}{4}$
35 Geo. 3. Ch. 10 Sweets - -	7,489	1	$5\frac{3}{4}$	7,469	10	$9\frac{3}{4}$
35 Geo. 3. Ch. 11 British Spirits -	81,292	7	3	81,244	6	3
35 Geo. 3. Ch. 12 Foreign ditto -	192,361	10	0	192,325	9	0
35 Geo. 3. Ch. 13 Tea - -	240,059	6	$10\frac{1}{2}$	235,390	1	$0\frac{1}{4}$
35 Geo. 3. Ch. 13 Coffee and Cocoa Nuts	28,420	15	$0\frac{1}{2}$	28,392	2	$8\frac{1}{2}$
36 Geo. 3. Ch. 13 Tobacco & Snuff	191,241	7	$1\frac{1}{4}$	172,798	16	$6\frac{1}{4}$
36 Geo. 3. Ch. 123 Sweets - -	7,745	4	$5\frac{1}{4}$	7,726	0	9
37 Geo. 3. Ch 14 Bricks - -	38,002	6	$3\frac{1}{2}$	37,558	3	$11\frac{1}{4}$
37 Geo. 3. Ch 14 Cocoa Nuts and Coffee -	7 890	15	0	7,889	5	0
37 Geo. 3. Ch 14 Tea - - -	308,614	13	1	304,822	5	$2\frac{3}{4}$
37 Geo. 3. Ch 14 British Spirits -	108,500	14	$0\frac{1}{4}$	108,410	9	8
37 Geo. 3. Ch 14 Foreign ditto -	194,066	15	$6\frac{1}{4}$	194,030	11	$6\frac{1}{4}$
37 Geo. 3. Ch 14 Auctions - -	84,462	11	$2\frac{3}{4}$	83,147	2	$11\frac{1}{2}$

EXCISE IN ENGLAND—*continued.*

DUTIES.	Grofs Actual Receipt in Money.			Net Produce of each Article.		
	£.	s.	d.	£.	s.	d.
38 Geo. 3. Ch. { 42 Tea - -	154,307	6	6½	151,693	4	2½
{ 89 Salt - -	974,417	19	3¾	875,684	12	6¼
40 Geo. 3. Ch. 23 { Spirits } Britifh	111,341	15	0	111,250	5	7¼
{ Spirits } Foreign	194,543	10	9¾	194,507	4	9¼
{ Tea - -	154,307	6	6½	152,443	18	2¾
41 Geo. 3. Ch. 8 Tea - -	308,614	13	1	303,741	12	6¼
Paper, fee below,						
{ 38 Beer - -	160,543	12	0⅓	160,168	0	1
{ Hops -	21	9	0¼	21	9	0¼
42 Geo. 3. Ch. { Malt - -	633,187	3	1¾	632,575	16	8
{ Irifh Spirits -	8,837	8	0	8,836	18	0
{ 94 Paper -	289,118	18	4½	253,774	2	8¼
ANNUAL DUTIES.						
Tobacco and Snuff - - -	452,553	19	10	389,922	12	6½
Malt Comm^d. 26th March - -	1,219,284	6	10	836,816	7	7
Old Malt, Mum, Cyder, and Perry	767,108	8	9½	679,321	2	5¼
£.	15,517,290	16	8	13,784,889	0	8¼

ABSTRACT OF THE ACCOUNT.

	£.	s.	d.
CASH refting on 5th January 1802, brought from laft Year's Account - - - - - }	9,118	1	11¼
RECEIVED between the 5th January 1802 and 5th January 1803 - - - - }	15,517,290	16	8
£.	15,526,408	18	7¼
PAID Charges of Management - - -	520,022	13	8
Taxes - - - - -	31,012	3	1¾
Exports - - - - -	682,166	5	1¼
Bounties - - - - -	24,078	19	8½
Allowances - - - - -	461,121	1	4¼
Penfions - - - - -	14,000	0	0
Exchequer Payments - - -	13,774,158	8	10¼
Cafh refting on 5th January 1803, transferred to next Account - - - }	19,848	13	9¼
£.	15,526,408	18	7¼

EXCISE IN NORTH BRITAIN.

DUTIES.		Gross Actual Receipt. £.	s.	d.	NET PRODUCE. £.	s.	d.	Remitted to the Commissioners of Excise, London. £.	s.	d.
Auctions	Consold	7,956	0	7¾	7,670	18	7	7,500	0	0
	1796	4,408	6	10¼	4,384	8	4¼	4,500	0	0
Beer, &c.	Consold	61,002	18	8¼	21,147	6	5¾	7,000	0	0
	1802	10,098	14	2½	7,472	10	10½	7,000	0	0
Bricks & Tiles	Consold	3,442	10	8	3,313	9	5	3,250	0	0
	1794	1,999	10	9½	1,935	12	7¾	2,000	0	0
	1796	844	6	9¾	815	8	4	1,000	0	0
Candles		17,107	13	0¼	13,263	1	5¾	10,000	0	0
Coaches		59	0	0	59	0	0			
Coffee & Cocoa	Consold.	282	1	8½	271	1	9¼	250	0	0
	1795	282	1	8½	271	1	9¼	250	0	0
	1796	13	0	3	13	0	3			
Glass	Consold.	29,449	12	6¼	10,739	12	10½	4,250	0	0
	1794	6,514	1	4½						
Hides		23,058	14	10	18,823	3	2	13,000	0	0
Paper	Consold	10,953	19	4¼	9,880	1	7¾	10,250	0	0
	1801	10,977	19	3¾	10,419	13	5¾	10,750	0	0
	1802	9,861	15	11	9,849	16	11	8,750	0	0
Printed Goods		103,550	13	7	66,707	0	3¼	50,500	0	0
Sope		76,201	15	10¾	64,413	12	5½	49,250	0	0
Starch		4,347	5	10½	1,860	4	0	500	0	0
Salt		57,655	8	9	49,946	19	1¼	52,000	0	0
Malt, Additional	1802	30,354	3	5½	30,354	3	5½	30,000	0	0
Do Consolidated		14	18	5	10	18	3	500	0	0
Distillery	1800	256,268	8	6½	249,026	4	5	250,250	0	0
Foreign Spirits	Consolidated & 1791	160,651	5	10¾	130,036	18	1¼	55,000	0	0
								35,000	0	0
								25,750	0	0
	1794	25,679	16	4½	25,667	4	4½	25,750	0	0
	1795	25,679	16	4½	25,667	4	4½	25,750	0	0
	1796	25,679	16	4½	25,667	4	4½	25,000	0	0
	1800	25,679	16	4½	25,667	4	4½			
Wine	Consold	26,843	14	2¼	22,795	16	9¼	22,000	0	0
	1795	45,038	2	0¾	36,808	0	2½	37,250	0	0
	1796	134	12	9½						
Tobacco	Old Consold	—	—		—	—		510	0	0
	1795	26,603	18	0	26,525	15	3	24,740	0	0
Plate	Licences	350	7	0	333	5	0	250	0	0
Spirit	Licences	24,160	12	8	23,182	13	11½	22,500	0	0
Tea	Licences	1,513	1	0	1,407	19	0	500	0	0
General	Licences	2,476	0	0	2,435	10	0	1,750	0	0
Fines, &c.		13,163	7	10¼	9,968	16	6¼			
TOTAL Excise		1,130,339	19	1¾	938,673	16	1¼	824,500	0	0

EXCISE IN NORTH BRITAIN—*continued.*

DUTIES.	Grofs Actual Receipt.			NET PRODUCE.			Remitted to the Commiffioners of Excife, London.		
	£.	s.	d.	£.	s.	d.	£.	s.	d.
Malt, 23 June - - -	22,461	14	4	10,389	5	8¾	6,250	0	0
D° 25 March -	30,847	6	7	23,571	18	9¾	24,250	0	0
Tobacco, 25 March - -	62,871	8	1¼	61,960	1	10¾	59,000	0	0
TOTAL Malt & Tobacco Ann^l	116,180	9	0¼	95,921	6	5¼	89,500	0	0
GRAND TOTAL - -	1,246,520	8	2	1,034,595	2	6½	914,000	0	0

A GENERAL STATE of the foregoing ACCOUNT.

	£.	s.	d.	£.	s.	d.	£.	s.	d.
Cafh remaining to be accounted for, on 5th January 1802	60,856	19	1¾						
Grofs Receipt, from 5th January 1802 to 5th January 1803	1,246,520	8	2	1,307,377	7	3¾			
Charges of Management	117,980	13	10						
Exports - - -	75,208	13	11						
Allowances - -	18,735	17	10½	211,925	5	7½			
ACCUMULATED NET PRODUCE - -	—	—		—			1,095,452	1	8¼
DISPOSAL of the NET PRODUCE:									
Bounties on Fifh exported - -	1,423	7	5						
Bufs and Barrel Bounties paid on Deficiency of Money in the Cuftoms -	40,543	5	4						

‑EXCISE IN NORTH BRITAIN—*continued.*

	£. s. d.	£. s. d.	£. s. d.
Paid per Trea-sury Warrant. To (Mr. A. Monro 'for behoof of) Dr. Jᵃˢ Jaffray, 'for Enquiries into Diftilleries & Salt Works -	1,338 10 4		
Paid per Exchequer Precepts. To the Agent for the Equivalent Company -	5,300 0 0		
To the Receiver General of the Crown Rents,&c.	68,915 15 0½		
		117,520 18 1½	
Remitted to the Commiffioners of Excife, London - -	914,000 0 0		
Refting to be accounted for, on 5th Jan. 1803 -	63,931 3 6¾		
		977,931 3 6¾	
			1,095,452 1 8¼
ABSTRACT: Cafh refting to be accounted for, on 5th January 1802 -	— —	60,856 19 1¼	
Grofs Receipt, from 5th January 1802 to 5th January 1803 -	— —	1,246,520 8 2	
CHARGE - -	— —		1,307,377 7 3¾
Charges of Management, Exports, and Allowances -	— —	211,925 5 7½	
Difburfements out of the Net Produce -	— —	117,520 18 1½	
Remittances to London	— —	914,000 0 0	
Refting to be accounted for, on 5th Jan. 1803 - -	— —	63,931 3 6¾	
DISCHARGE -	— —		1,307,377 7 3¾

3. STAMPS. ENGLAND.

HEADS OF DUTY.		GROSS PRODUCE.			NET PRODUCE.		
		£.	s.	d.	£.	s.	d.
Confolidated Stamp Duties - -		624,468	18	4	525,826	3	—½
Infurance - -	1782	169,136	19	4¾	160,015	17	4
Gold and Silver Plate -	1784	29,611	17	10¼	24,620	17	1
Race Horfe - -	1784	739	1	—½	673	12	2
Poft Horfe - -	1785	217,926	1	2½	215,304	14	10
Medicine - -	1785	11,070	7	7	9,293	17	9
Game - - -	1785	56,049	—	11¾	52,060	18	3
Attornies Licences -	1785	34,885	8	5	34,354	9	1
Pawnbrokers Do. - -	1785	4,695	9	9	4,480	13	4
Perfumery - -	1786	52	18	9	50	16	11
Lottery Stamps and Licences -		6,748	2	10	997	8	8
Additional Game -	1791	27,339	6	11	26,140	4	7
Bills of Exchange - -	1791	142,279	3	8½	137,844	12	2
Receipts - -	1791	58,070	2	6½	51,814	2	5
Attornies Articles -	1794	26,347	19	6½	25,659	6	—
Additional Duties - -	1795	37,093	17	9	36,231	3	9
Hair Powder Certificates -	1795	1,208	11	6¾	1,153	16	9
Additional Receipts - -	1795	10,750	15	3½	9,978	16	1
Sea Infurance - -	1795	105,381	9	3½	100,701	9	4
Horfe Dealers Licences -	1795	261	9	11½	225	—	1
Legacy Duty - -	1796	128,518	5	9½	125,306	10	5
Hat Duty - -	1796	41,862	18	5¾	36,401	16	6
Additional Stage Coach -	1797	56,666	16	2½	56,075	1	7
Deeds, &c. - -	1797	727,765	5	7¼	684,567	5	8
Armorial Bearing Certificates	1798	591	13	3½	563	16	6
Small Notes - -	1799	14,288	3	10	14,054	16	1
Duties - -	1801	489,242	10	5	475,232	7	6
Medicine - -	1802	16,243	3	7½	14,051	2	10
	£.	3,039,295	19	11½	2,823,680	16	8½

GENERAL STATEMENT.

CHARGE.

	£.	s.	d.
1802. Jan. 5th.			
Balance in Bills outstanding	3,126	9	8
Do - - of Cash in the Hands of the several present Distributors in England	103,910	2	6¼
Do - - of Cash due from sundry Distributors who have died or gone out of Office since January 5th, 1800			
Do - - of Cash in the Hands of the Receiver General, as per Lottery Account of January 5th, 1802	21,628	7	11½
	91	1	
Gross Produce	3,039,295	19	11¼
	£ 3,168,052	1	3¾

DISCHARGE.

	£.	s.	d.
1802. Jan. 5th.			
Parliamentary Allowances	80,118	3	1¾
Debentures	6,458	4	3
The Two Universities for Almanacks	1,250	—	—
Charges of Management	74,792	17	3¾
Incidents	32,230	8	—
Imprest	5,335	—	—
Parchment, Paper, and Blanks, for the Use of the Country	15,370	10	7
Exchequer Payments	2,836,139	16	5
1803. Jan 5th.			
Balance in Bills outstanding	3,815	19	5
Do - - of Cash in the Hands of the several present Distributors in England	94,977	10	5
Do - - of Cash due from sundry Distributors who have died or gone out of Office since January 5th, 1800	174,412	10	6¼
Do - - of Cash in the Hands of the Receiver General	91	1	8
	£ 3,168,052	1	3¾

SCOTLAND.

HEADS OF DUTY.	GROSS PRODUCE.			NET PRODUCE.			Remittances paid into the EXCHEQUER.		
	£.	s.	d	£.	s.	d.	£.	s.	d.
Confolidated Stamp Duties	35,486	12	8¼	30,459	15	6½	30,939	16	6
Infurance - 1782	2,886	—	10	2,712	7	6	2,715	—	—
Gold & Silver Plate 1784	1,141	18	5	1,077	8	2½	1,297	—	—
Race Horfe - 1784	20	6	—	20	5	7	37	—	—
Poft Horfe - 1785	2,:34	1	10	2,353	10	3¼	2,357	15	7
Medicine - - 1785	6	13	9	—	2	4	117	—	—
Game - - 1785	3,585	1	6	3,372	11	5	3,339	—	—
Attornies Licences 1785	3,711	12	—	3,549	5	4	2,534	—	—
Pawnbrokers - 1785	5	—	—	4	7	3	19	—	—
Additional Duty in Scotland 1786	1,635	7	11	1,563	8	2	1,666	—	—
Ditto - - - Game 1791	1,866	19	6	1,820	6	5	1,797	—	—
Bills of Exchange 1791	20,648	1	5	19,303	12	9	18,881	—	—
Receipts - - 1791	3,814	14	1	3,631	4	8	3,442	—	—
Additional Duties 1795	125	11	6	124	14	7	134	—	—
Ditto - - - Receipts 1795	566	3	—	565	8	9	558	—	—
Sea Infurance - 1795	8,163	8	9	7,881	14	—	7,467	—	—
Legacy Duty - 1796	6,683	1	11¾	6,049	17	2	5,883	—	—
Hat Duty - - 1796	971	—	6	833	12	4	877	—	—
Additional Stage Coach - 1797	2.574	1	10	2 353	10	3¼	2,357	15	7
Deeds, &c. - 1797	48,324	8	10	44,690	14	5½	44,099	—	—
Small Notes - 1799	3,303	16	8	2,907	4	11	2,906	—	—
Additional Duties 1801	33,381	7	6	31 891	14	—	31,710	—	—
Medicine Duty 1802	204	9	9	204	9	9	50	—	—
	182,100	—	3	167,376	5	8¼	165,183	7	8

GENERAL STATENENT OF THE ACCOUNT, INCLUDING
THE BALANCES.

CHARGE.		DISCHARGE.	
	£. s. d.		£. s. d.
Balance in the Hands of Alexr Menzies, Receiver General for Scotland, Jan. 5th 1802 - -	20,165 8 6	Parliamentary Allowances - -	3,111 9 3
		Debentures - -	5 19 5
Grofs Receipt within the Year -	182,100 — 3	Incidents - -	2,650 — 3½
		Charges of Management - -	8,956 5 7
		Remittances paid into the Exchequer -	165,183 7 8
		Balance of Cafh in the Hands of Alxr Mac Lean, Receiver General for Scotland, Jan. 5th 1803 -	22,358 6 6½
	£.202,265 8 9		£.202,265 8 9

4. LAND and ASSESSED TAXES ENGLAND.

GROSS PRODUCE, being the Grofs Receipt An. 1802.				NET PRODUCE, being the Payments into Exchequer and Receiver General of the Cuftoms.			
	£.	s.	d.		£.	s.	d.
Land Tax -	1,548,574	18	5½	Land Tax -	1,378,771	5	8½
Affeffed Taxes -	3,372,882	19	8	Affeffed Taxes -	3,221,275	4	—¼
Income Duty -	2,977,161	8	2¾	Income Duty -	2,893,855	15	7½
Aid and Contribu-tion Tax -	44,989	4	3	Aid and Contribu-tion Tax -	44,125	11	7¼
Commutation (Cuftoms) -	276	14	11¼	Commutation (Cuftoms) -	276	14	11¼
	£.7,943,885	5	6½		£.7,538,306	11	11¼

SCOTLAND.

GROSS PRODUCE, being the Grofs Receipt An. 1802.				NET PRODUCE, being the Payments into Exchequer and to Receiver General of Cuftoms.			
	£.	s.	d.		£.	s.	d.
Land Tax -	32,312	18	—	Land Tax -	36,000	—	—
Affeffed Taxes -	163,784	19	5	Affeffed Taxes	147,000	—	—
Income Duty -	256,405	15	5	Income Duty -	339,000	—	—
Aid and Contribu-tion Tax -	3,917	—	8	Aid and Contribu-tion Tax -	3,000	—	—
Commutation (Cuftoms) -	—	—	—	Commutation (Cuftoms) -	—	—	—
	£.456,420	13	6		£.525,000	—	—

5. POST OFFICE.

	Grofs Produce.	Management.	Returns.	Packet Eſtabliſhment.	Captured and Extra Packets.	Iriſh, with £4,000 per Annum.	Iriſh Inland Poſtage.	NET.
	£. s. d.	£. s. d.	£. s. d.	£. s. d.	£. s. d.	£. s. d.	£. s. d.	£. s. d.
Inland Letters	9,45,168 6 5	188,322 7 4	33,195 4 6	22,650 11 3	17,779 8 1	—	—	683,270 15 3
Foreign ditto	153,747 12 3	22,709 1 6	487 5 8	10,289 — —	6,898 13 7	—	—	113,363 11 6
Twopenny Poſt	58,909 10 1	23,892 3 8	—	—	—	—	—	35,017 6 5
Scotland	121,700 13 6	18,692 19 4½	7,610 9 —½	—	—	—	—	95,397 5 1
Ireland	859 1 8	—	2,798 — 5	—	—	9,138 12 10	7,693 15 5	19,961 13 —
	1,319,118 3 11	253,616 11 10½	44,090 19 7½	32,949 11 3	24,618 1 8	9,138 12 10	7,693 15 5	947,010 11 3

6. DUTIES ON SALARIES AND PENSIONS.

ENGLAND.

	£.	s.	d.
Grofs Produce of the One Shilling per £. Duty on Salaries and Penfions from 5th January 1802 to ditto 1803 -	47,457	10	6
Declared Balance on 5th January 1802 - - -	—	6	10¼
Total Charge - - £.	47,457	17	4¼

DISCHARGE.

				£.	s.	d.
By Cafh paid into the Exchequer during the Period of the Account - - - £.47,156 — —						
By Poundage on £.47,457. 10. 6. at 1¼ per £. 2 6 12 2						
By Fees paid at the Exchequer, and on attefting the Account - - - 4 13 6				47,457	5	8
Balance due by Mr. Lane on the 5th January 1803 - - - - - - £.				—	11	8½

SCOTLAND.

	£.	s.	d.
Balance in the Hands of the Receiver General on the 5th January 1802 - - - - - -	11,983	1	5
Grofs Produce, Year ended 5th January 1803 £.3,163 16 3			
Payments thereout on Account of Management 213 6 9			
Net Produce Year ended 5th January 1803 —— ——	2,950	9	6
Payments into the Exchequer - - -	14,933	10	11
	14,900	0	5
Balance in the Hands of the Receiver General on the 5th January 1803 - - - - - £.	33	4	6

SIXPENNY DUTY.

	£.	s.	d.
ENGLAND—Grofs Produce of the Sixpenny Duty on Salaries, Penfions, and Incidents, from 5th January 1802 to 5th January 1803 - - - - - -	59,264	17	6¼
SCOTLAND—Dᵒ - - - Dᵒ - - Dᵒ - - - - -	2,554	9	9
	61,819	7	3½
Declared Balance of the Account, ended the 5th January 1802 - - - - - -	— 16		6¼
Total Charge - - - £.	61,820	3	10

DISCHARGE.

	£.	s.	d.
By Cafh paid into the Exchequer during the Period of the Account - - -	60,728	—	—
By Poundage on £.61,819 7s. 3d½ at 1½ per £.	386	7	5
By Fees pa d at the Exchequer, and on attefting the Account - - - -	5	—	6
By One Years Compenfation paid to Thoˢ Aftle Efq. late Receiver General of the Sixpenny Deductions, per Treafury Warant -	700	—	—
	61,819	7	11
Balance due by Mr. Lane, on the 5th January 1803 - - - - - - - £.	—	15	11

7. HACKNEY COACH OFFICE.

Actual Receipt in Money.	Net Produce.	Payments into the Exchequer.	Charges of Management.	Balance in Hand, 5th January 1803.
£. s. d. 27,697 10 10¾ 325 — 10¾	£. s. d 25,109 10 5¼	£. s. d. 24,975 — —	£. s. d 2 588 — 5½	£. s. d. 134 10 5¼
27,372 10 —				

8. HAWKERS and PEDLARS.

	Grofs Receipt.	Net Produce.	Net Payments into the Exchequer.	Charges of Management.
Year ending 5th January 1803 - -	£. s. d. 8,500 19 7½	£. s. d. 5,725 19 7½	£. s. d. 5,279 — —	£. s. d. 2,875 — —

9. ALIENATION OFFICE, 22d February 1803.

				£.	s.	d.
Remaining in the Hands of the Receiver General at the End of Hilary Term 1802 - - - £5,709 — 8						
Paid into the Receipt of His Majesty's Exchequer in the above Year - - - - 2,941 5 4						
				2,767	15	4

Received on Writs of Covenant and Writs of
Entry, to the End of Easter
Term 1802 - - - £2,120 3 4
- - - - - on the like, to End of Trinity Term
following - - - - 909 10 —
- - - - - on the like, to End of Michaelmas
Term following - - - 2,028 6 8
- - - - - on the like, to End of Hilary Term
1803 - - - - - 1,399 6 8

Gross Produce - - - - £6,457 6 8

Paid Charges of
Management, for
Easter Term 1802 £.313 5 5
- - - the like, for
Trinity Term
following - 317 2 —
- - - the like, for
Michaelmas
Term following - - 289 1 3
- - - the like, for
Hilary Term
1803 - - 295 6 8
- - - the Amount
of a Treasury
Warrant for
an Allowance
to G. Courthope and C.
Luxmore,
Esquires - 308 1 6
——————— 1,522 16 10

Paid the Clerk of the Hanaper,
at the End of Easter, Trinity,
Michaelmas, and Hilary Terms
—£.500. per Term - - - 2,000 — —
——————— 3,522 16 10

		£.	s.	d.
		2,934	9	10
Net Produce - - -				
Remaining in the Hands of the Receiver General at the End of Hilary Term 1803 - - - - - - £		5,702	5	2

10. POST FINES.

	£.	s.	d.
Balance in the Hands of the Receiver General on the 5th of January 1802 - - - - - - - -	2,535	10	6¼
Receipt within the Year ending the 5th of January 1803 -	201	16	—
Balance in the Hands of the Receiver General on the 5th of January 1803 - - - - - - - -	£.2,737	6	6¼

11. ALUM MINES and other INCIDENTS.

	£.	s.	d.
Rent of Alum Mines - - - - -	960	—	—
Rent of Light Houses - .. - - -	6	13	4
Seizures of Uncustomed and Prohibited Goods - -	62,073	3	7¼
Compositions - - - - - -	1	13	4
Profers - - - - - - -	640	—	—
£	63,681	10	3½

12. LOTTERIES An. 1801 and 1802.

	LOTTERY, A° 1801.		LOTTERY, 1802.	
	£. s. d.	£. s. d.	£. s. d.	£. s. d.
The Lotteries were granted for raising the Sum of		701,250 —		1,455,000 —
To the Chief Cashier of the Governor and Company of the Bank of England, for Prizes	500,000 —		900,000 —	
D° - for receiving Subscriptions	1,000 —		3,000 —	
Discounts on Prompt Payment	620 13 11		1,541 14 11	
To the Commissioners for drawing and managing the Lottery, and for Expences attending the same	12,400 —	514,020 13 11	25,000 —	929,541 14 11
Net Profit to the Public		187,229 6 1		525,458 5 1

APPENDIX.

No. II.

ACCOUNT of the Prices of the different Stocks from the 1ſt January 1731, to the 1ſt January 1803.

The following Abſtract is drawn up in order to give a general View of the Variations in the Price of the different Funds, and confequently of the State of our public Credit, fince the Year 1730. Thoſe who are defirous of procuring more accurate Information upon the Subject, may have their Curiofity gratified by confulting the different periodical Publications, and the Books kept at the Stock Exchange, whence this Account is taken. The Reader will pleafe to obferve, that where a Blank is left it denotes that there is no Variation from the preceding Month; and that the Price is in general ftated at a medium Rate, neither the higheſt nor the loweſt.

Year.		India Stock.	Bank Stock.	S. S. Stock.	S. S. Ann.	3 per Cents.
1731.	January	189	144	103	106	95
	February	190	145	101	107	94
	March	198	147	103	108	96
	April	194	——	104	106	——
	May	196	145	102	——	——
	June	——	146	103	107	99
	July	194	147	——	108	95
	Auguſt	——	146	——	——	96
	September	——	148	——	——	——
	October	174	145	102	109	94
	November	175	146	103	110	95
	December	181	148	——	108	97
1732.	January	178	149	101	110	96
	February	177	——	98	——	97
	March	175	150	99	——	——
	April	178	148	98	108	——
	May	177	147	——	——	——
	June	168	148	97	109	——
	July	163	150	98	110	98
	Auguſt	157	152	104	111	99
	September	——	——	——	——	——
	October	155	149	——	——	——
	November	154	——	——	109	101
	December	156	——	——	——	——

Year.		India Stock.	Bank Stock.	S S.Stock.	S.S.Ann.	3 per Cents.
1733.	January	159	150	105	110	100
	February	—	151	102	—	—
	March	158	150	—	—	—
	April	—	—	—	111	102
	May	162	—	103	110	—
	June	163	—	106	—	103
	July	160	—	105	109	100
	August	152	145	104	105	97
				Trading Stock.		
	September	151	143	80	—	97
	October	140	132	73	101	92
	November	136	130	72	—	—
	December	141	137	81	102	—
1734.	January	136	133	75	100	92
	February	135	132	76	99	—
	March	136	—	75	—	90
	April	—	—	74	100	—
	May	142	134	76	—	—
	June	146	137	80	104	94
	July	141	136	79	104	92
	August	142	—	78	105	93
	September	146	140	81	106	94
	October	141	135	79	104	92
	November	—	—	81	105	—
	December	149	139	83	106	94
1735.	January	149	139	83	105	94
	February	147	140	82	106	92
	March	149	141	—	107	94
	April	148	—	—	—	—
	May	—	138	83	105	—
	June	—	—	—	—	—
	July	146	—	82	106	97
	August	145	140	80	—	94
	September	147	—	82	107	—
	October	—	—	—	106	—
	November	167	146	90	108	98
	December	169	145	93	109	93
1736.	January	169	147	95	109	100
	February	174	149	99	111	102
	March	176	150	98	—	104
	April	—	—	—	—	—
	May	—	—	—	—	—
	June	—	149	99	112	105
	July	172	—	—	114	113
	August	176	151	—	—	105
	September	—	—	—	—	—
	October	178	143	100	113	—
	November	—	149	—	111	—
	December	—	148	—	—	—
1737.	January	177	149	111	—	—
	February	179	151	—	112	—
	March	181	147	101	107	—

Year.	India Stock.	Bank Stock.	S.S. Stock.	S.S. Ann.	3 per Cents.
April	180	145	102	108	105
May	181	147	103	110	——
June	182	146	——	111	107
July	174	143	——	110	105
August	176	145	101	111	106
September	——	——	——	——	——
October	——	142	——	——	——
November	——	——	——	——	——
December	——	143	——	110	——
1738 January	174	140	1··(	110	106
February	176	141	——	112	——
March	174	——	100	111	105
April	——	——	——	——	——
May	173	142	101	110	——
June	——	——	——	——	——
July	162	140	99	109	102
August	170	143	101	111	105
September	171	145	103	113	——
October	173	142	——	111	——
November	——	141	——	——	——
December	121	142	104	112	106
1739. January	121	143	103	112	104
February	168	——	97	111	——
March	——	144	100	112	105
April	——	142	——	113	——
May	169	——	——	111	——
June	159	138	95	109	100
July	153	137	94	108	98
August	154	139	93	——	99
September	155	134	94	——	93
October	——	135	—	106	97
November	157	138	96	109	93
December	159	139	97	110	100
1740. January	154	138	96	109	98
February	——	139	95	——	99
March	——	141	98	111	100
April	——	139	—	——	101
May	162	141	100	——	——
June	164	140	101	112	100
July	159	142	——	——	— ··
August	104	144	——	——	101
September	——	——	98	——	100
October	153	——	—	108	99
November	——	——	98	110	—
December	——	138	—	109	—
1741. January	157	140	102	111	98
February	——	142	101	112	99
March	——	——	102	——	——
April	164	143	104	113	101
May	159	140	103	111	——
June	160	141	——	——	——

Year.	India Stock.	Bank Stock.	S.S.Stock.	S.S.Ann.	3 per Cents.
July	155	141	103	111	99
Auguſt	——	——	101	——	98
September	157	——	103	112	99
October	159	140	104	111	89
November	161	138	105	112	101
December	——	135	104	111	100
1742. January	——	136	——	112	98
February	157	——	105	111	99
March	——	139	105	113	100
April	159	137	——	111	101
May	161	——	106	113	——
June	172	142	109	114	102
July	174	——	111	——	100
Auguſt	173	143	109	——	101
September	172	——	——	——	100
October	174	140	110	113	——
November	178	143	111	——	101
December	——	——	——	114	102
1743. January	——	145	112	114	101
February	——	——	110	——	100
March	——	——	——	——	——
April	186	146	111	113	101
May	195	148	115	114	103
June	——	147	114	103	102
July	189	——	——	105	103
Auguſt	——	——	110	115	102
September	——	148	111	115	101
October	194	146	113	114	102
November	——	——	——	——	——
December	——	147	——	——	——
1744. January	194	148	——	113	99
February	182	145	——	110	96
March	18	142	103	108	90
April	——	——	105	——	93
May	172	——	——	——	——
June	178	144	108	111	—
July	176	146	109	112	—
Auguſt	——	147	——	110	—
September	178	——	——	——	—
October	——	144	109	——	—
November	——	——	105	111	—
December	——	146	——	——	—
1745. January	180	145	109	110	89
February	182	——	106	——	—
March	——	147	107	——	—
April	——	——	——	——	92
May	187	146	109	——	93
June	186	——	——	111	92
July	181	——	——	——	90
Auguſt	174	143	103	108	87
September	170	141	——	102	85

Year.	India Stock.	Bank Stock.	S.S.Stock.	S.S.Ann.	3 per Cents.
October	172	138	100	105	86
November	169	133	98	103	—
December	163	127	——	100	—
1746. January	176	125	94	97	76
February	154	——	—	93	75
March	156	——	—	—	—
April	167	124	97	97	82
May	——	——	—	96	—
June	174	127	—	97	83
July	178	133	105	102	85
August	—	136	106	106	89
September	184	135	——	——	88
October	180	131	——	104	85
November	——	126	103	101	83
December	——	128	104	——	84

Bank 4 per Cents.*

Year.	India Stock.	Bank Stock.	S.S.Stock.	S.S.Ann.	3 per Cents.
1747. January	180	127	103	95	83
February	177	128	99	97	84
March	175	129	102	96	86
April	157	128	104	97	85
May	151	126	103	96	86
June	155	125	102	97	—
July	156	122	103	95	—
August	161	125	104	93	82
September	160	126	100	—	—
October	——	121	99	—	—
November	162	119	100	—	—
December	161	120	99	—	81
1748. January	160	118	100	91	79
February	157	119	94	90	82
March	156	120	92	89	76
April	157	122	105	93	80
May	170	124	106	96	88
June	176	126	110	100	90
July	184	127	107	97	89
August	178	——	106	—	90
September	180	128	——	98	88
October	183	129	107	99	91
November	178	——	——	97	90
December	175	126	106	96	89
1749. January	176	127	107	98	91
February	174	129	106	101	94
March	175	131	107	102	95
April	177	128	——	——	—
May	179	134	114	105	100
June	185	136	115	106	99
July	186	137	116	105	100

This Stock is now known under the Name of the 3 per Cent Reduced, in confequence of the reduction of interest, from 4 to 3½, and afterwards to 3 per Cent, during the Adminiftration of Mr. Pelham.

Year.	India Stock.	Bank Stock.	S.S. Stock.	Bank 4 per C.	3 per C.
August	189	140	115	104	100
September	191	139	117	——	101
October	190	138	115	105	102
November	189	135	112	104	99
December	188	133	111	——	100
1750. January	186	134	110	102	98
February	187	132	111	100	99
March	188	134	109	102	—
April	185	131	110	103	100
May	184	133	——	104	——
June	188	134	112	105	101
July	187	132	——	102	——
August	186	135	111	103	100
September	184	——	113	104	——
October	185	133	112	——	101
November	187	134	——	——	——
December	188	136	113	103	99
1751. January	185	135	112	100	97
February	186	136	110	101	98
March	187	139	112	102	99
April	189	137	113	103	100
May	192	138	114	104	99
June	195	141	115	——	101
July	190	140	116	103	103
August	184	139	113	104	100
September	187	142	1'5	105	99
October	188	140	117	104	100
November	190	142	113	——	101
December	189	143	117	103	102
1752. January	187	141	118	104	101
February	188	144	116	105	102
March	187	145	117	104	——
April	189	143	118	——	103
May	190	146	120	107	104
June	192	147	121	106	105
July	186	148	——	109	106
August	188	147	120	108	105
September	191	144	119	107	——
October	192	143	121	106	104
November	194	142	122	107	——
December(13)	195	143	123	108	106⅜
				Reduced to 3½.	
1753. January	191	144	122	107	106
February	192	143	121	——	104
March	193	141	120	106	——
April	194 *	140	——	——	105
May	195	138	——	——	——
June	197	137	121	——	——
July	193	——	122	107	——
August	192	138	120	——	103

* Dividend reduced to 4½ per Cent.

Year.		India Stock.	Bank Stock.	S.S.Stock.	Bank 4 per C.	3 per C.
	September	191	137	120	107	104
	October	193	136	119	105	——
	November	194	135	120	——	——
	December	193	136	121	104	105
1754.	January	187	135	——	103	104
	February	188	134	118	104	102
	March	186	133	117	——	——
	April	189	132	118	105	103
	May	190	133	119	104	——
	June	102	134	——	105	104
	July	187	133	——	——	——
	Au. uſt	188	130	118	——	——
	September	187	132	——	——	——
	October	185	133	116	104	103
	November	183	132	——	103	102
	December	182	129	117	101	——
1755.	January	180	130	114	102	100
	February	176	129	113	100	101
	March	173	131	112	99	99
	April	171	129	109	98	98
	May	172	126	111	99	97
	June	174	127	112	93	99
	July	167	126	104	92	—
	Auguſt	165	127	103	93	92
	September	166	123	104	—	90
	October	148	122	103	92	93
	November	149	123	104	93	91
	December	150	120	105	—	92

					Bank 3½ per Cent.	
1756	January	145	121	104	92	89
	February	143	119	101	91	—
	March	142	120	100	90	—
	April	141	118	102	—	90
	May	140	117	101	89	89
	June	135	116	100	—	—
	July	133	117	——	—	87
	Auguſt	134	116	99	88	80
	September	133	117	100	89	88
	October	——	115	99	90	—
	November	135	116	—	88	89
	December	136	115	100	87	88
1757.	January	133	116	101	88	86
	February	135	117	100	89	87
	March	137	119	99	91	89
	April	139	116	101	90	88
	May	142	119	——	89	89
	June	140	113	102	—	90
	July	133	119	——	—	88
	Auguſt	130	120	——	90	89
	September	138	——	100	—	91
	October	141	119	——	89	—

Year.		India Stock.	Bank Stock.	S.S Stock.	Bank 4 per C.	3 per C.
	November	142	117	104	90	89
	December	140	118	—	—	90
1758.	January	141	119	103	—	91
	February	145	121	104	92	94
	March	146	122	106	93	—

3 per C. Confol.

Year.		India Stock.	Bank Stock.	S.S Stock.	Bank 4 per C.	3 per C.
	April	147	119	105	—	93
	May	148	121	—	—	94
	June	146	122	106	—	95
	July	140	120	107	—	97
	Auguft	132	118	108	—	90
	September	135	—	101	—	89
	October	134	117	102	—	90
	November	136	—	100	—	91
	December	137	—	—	—	98
1759.	January	133	116	98	—	88
	February	135	117	97	—	86
	March	134	—	95	—	82
	April	129	—	93	—	80
	May	128	113	92	—	—
	June	126	114	—	—	79
	July	123	111	—	—	—
	Auguft	125	110	94	—	82
	September	126	112	—	—	81
	October	130	—	95	—	—
	November	134	111	96	—	84
	December	141	113	97	—	—
1760.	January	134	114	96	—	82
	February	—	112	90	—	81
	March	135	110	—	—	82
	April	137	—	92	—	—
	May	136	109	94	—	—
	June	138	110	—	—	—
	July	140	111	93	—	83
	Auguft	139	—	—	—	—
	September	141	—	—	—	82
	October	142	110	—	—	83
	November	139	107	90	—	80
	December	140	106	88	—	76
1761.	January	137	105	86	88	74
	February	136	104	—	89	73
	March	135	107	87	90	76
	April	143	115	88	100	88
	May	144	114	96	102	87
	June	143	—	—	101	86
	July	141	115	—	—	81
	Auguft	134	112	90	94	76
	September	133	111	88	92	74
	October	128	—	84	88	72

Year.	India Stock.	Bank Stock.	S S. Stock.	Bank 4 per Cents.	3 per Cent. Confol.
November	127	103	83	86	71
December	123	98	81	81	66
1762. January	115	94	76	74	63
February	114	95	75	78	68
March	115	96	78	77	67
April	117	97	79	81	70
May	118	98	81	85	73
June	—	—	—	83	72
July	116	100	84	84	75
Auguft	134	108	95	95	79
September	145	102	91	91	81
October	139	109	94	92	80
November	153	110	98	100	86
December	157	119	101	97	87
1763. January	158	120	102	100	90
February	169	126	105	105	93
March	170	131	106	108	96
April	172	126	—	107	92
May	170	123	—	105	91
June	171	122	104	106	—
July	165	118	—	100	89
Auguft	162	114	95	97	87
September	159	116	94	95	84
October	154	111	92	94	—
November	155	112	94	96	83
December	157	113	93	—	—
1764. January	158	114	94	95	82
February	159	116	93	—	84
March	152	117	95	97	86
April	154	115	—	98	83
May	149	114	—	99	—
June	145	113	—	—	—
July	147	—	93	94	81
Auguft	146	—	92	—	82
September	148	122	—	—	83
October	150	123	95	93	80
November	153	127	—	94	82
December	151	122	—	98	83
1765. January	152	126	96	97	85
February	—	130	—	98	87
March	—	—	—	—	—
April	154	—	—	—	—
May	—	—	—	97	—
June	—	129	—	98	86
July	156	133	102	100	—
Auguft	—	136	—	101	87
September	163	—	—	—	89

* On the 29th January 1762, Bank Stock was as low as 91, the loweft Price known.

Year.		India Stock.	Bank Stock.	S.S. Stock.	Bank 4 per Cents.	3 per Cent. Confol.
	October	163	136	102	99	91
	November	——	——	——	102	92
	December	——	135	——	104	90
1766.	January	162	134	101	102	89
	February	——	——	——	100	87
	March	——	——	102	103	88
	April	178	——	——	101	89
	May	189	135	——	102	90½
	June	——	——	——	——	—
	July	——	——	——	——	88
	Auguſt	207	139	——	103	90
	September	223	——	——	——	87
	October	218	——	——	101	89
	November	217	136	——	——	—
	December	——	140	——	——	—
1767.	January	220	141	101	102	88
	February	234	143	——	——	89
	March	246	——	——	——	88
	April	254	——	——	100	—
	May	248	144	104	101	——
	June	250	147	102	103	87
	July	253	148	104	102	—
	Auguſt	267	150	105	——	—
	September	270	152	107	——	88
	October	273	158	108	101	90
	November	268	155	——	——	91
	December	265	158	109	102	90
1768.	January	260	161	108	103	91
	February	261	163	106	104	92
	March	262	165	107	108	93
	April	272	166	108	103	—
	May	271	167	110	104	—
	June	269	168	——	101	92
	July	275	164	——	103	90
	Auguſt	276	166	105	99	89
	September (6)	276¼	167	——	100	—
	October	275	162	——	——	—
	November	271	160	104	101	88
	December	272	161	——	——	89
1769.	January	275	162	103	102	88
	February	276	163	——	——	—
	March	275	165	——	——	—
	April	273	164	106	——	—
	May	264*	166	105	99	89

* India Stock on the 1ſt of May was 273¾ but unfavourable accounts from the Eaſt Indies cauſed a remarkable fall in the courſe of the month ; on the 27th it was 250, and on the 31ſt 230. In conſequence of the alarm a General Court was held 1ſt June, when extracts from the laſt advices from India being read, the

Year.	India Stock.	Bank Stock.	S.S. Stock.	Bank 4 per Cents.	3 per Cent. Consol.
June	237	166	105	100	89
July	225	—	—	—	—
Auguft	228	168	104	—	—
September (5)	227	168½	—	101	88
October	226	160	—	98	—
November	224	159	102	93	84
December	220	150	—	94	—
1770. January	217	152	—	96	85
February	218	153	—	95	87
March	227	151	—	—	—
April	—	154	—	—	—
May	—	148	—	96	86
June	220	150	—	—	84
July	217	145	—	—	83
Auguft	219	138	—	94	78
September	196	137	—	95	—
October	197	133	—	96	—
November	181	132	—	88	—
December	—	134	—	—	84
1771. January	214	148	—	87	86
February	213	—	—	93	85
March	216	146	—	97	87
April	223	155	—	98	88
May	228.	153	—	95	81
June	—	155	—	—	86
July	—	—	—	96	—
Auguft	217	—	—	—	—
September	218	154	—	—	87
October	216	149	—	—	—
November	217	148	—	93	—
December	—	150	—	—	86
1772. January	219	152	—	—	87
February	215	—	—	—	—
March	—	153	—	—	—
April	213	149	—	—	88
May	213	150	—	—	—
June	224	151	—	—	—
July	223	—	—	—	95
Auguft	208	149	—	—	89
September	194	148	—	—	—
October	181	147	—	—	88
November	165	144	—	—	—
December	167	145	—	—	—

Court, to quiet the minds of the Proprietors, ordered a paragraph to be inferted in the public papers, ftating, " that the affairs of the Company were in a flourifhing fituation, and that there was no real caufe for the alarm which had lately happened." This produced a temporary rife of the Stock, but it foon declined again.

Year.		India Stock.	Bank Stock.	S.S Stock.	Bank 4 per Cents.	3 per Cent. Consols.
1773.	January	160	143	102	93	87
	February	162	142	—	—	—
	March	153	143	—	—	—
	April	14?	139	—	—	86
	May	142	140	—	—	—
	June	143	—	—	—	87
	July	1?1	—	—	—	—
	August	152	142	—	—	—
	September	154	143	94	92	—
	October	149	—	—	90	86
	November	144	141	—	—	—
	December	140	—	—	91	—
1774.	January	139	140	93	90	87
	February	140	1?9	—	91	86
	March	141	141	—	—	—
	April	1?7	139	—	—	—
	May	152	—	94	—	87
	June	151	145	—	—	—
	July	150	143	—	—	88
	August	148	141	—	—	—
	September	147	142	—	93	—
	October	149	—	96	—	—
	November	150	143	—	—	89
	December	152	145	—	—	—
1775.	January	153	146	98	92	90
	February	155	142	—	—	—
	March	159	144	—	—	87
	April	157	142	99	—	88
	May	156	—	—	9?	—
	June	151	—	—	—	—
	July	—	—	—	—	—
	August	153	—	—	90	89
	September	156	141	—	—	—
	October	155	144	98	—	—
	November	165	140	97	91	88
	December	164	142	—	—	—
1776.	January	163	143	96	90	90
	February	165	142	95	—	89
	March	162	141	—	—	87
	April	155	—	—	—	86
	May	—	—	—	—	85
	June	160	138	—	—	84
	July	—	—	94	88	82
	August	—	137	—	87	—
	September	—	—	—	—	83
	October	163	134	—	83	81
	November	167	135	—	—	—
	December	—	—	—	—	82

Year		India Stock.	Bank Stock.	S S. Stock.	Bank 4 per Cents.	3 per Cent. Confol.
1777.	January	169	136	93	84	80
	February	——	138	——	——	78
	March	——	——	——	——	79
	April	165	——	——	——	——
	May	——	134	——	——	——
	June	——	132	——	——	76
	July	——	——	——	——	——
	Auguft	158	130	——	——	——
	September	——	——	——	——	78
	October	163	129	——	——	——
	November	165	130	——	——	——
	December	167	——	——	——	76
1778.	January	164	120	——	——	72
	February	158	117	——	——	70
	March	144	113	——	——	64
	April	137	107	——	——	61
	May	129	109	——	——	——
	June	——	——	——	——	62
	July	134	——	——	——	61
	Auguft	136	115	——	——	63
	September	——	114	——	——	64
	October	——	113	——	——	66
	November	139	110	——	——	63
	December	141	——	——	——	62
1779.	January	140	107	——	——	60
	February	148	109	——	——	59
	March	——	——	——	——	61
	April	155	——	——	——	64
	May	151	——	——	——	63
	June	——	112	——	——	60
	July	——	——	——	——	59
	Auguft	——	108	——	——	61
	September	——	111	——	——	——
	October	144	——	——	——	——
	November	——	——	——	——	——
	December	——	——	——	——	60
1780.	January	150	113	——	——	61
	February	——	114	——	——	——
	March	——	——	——	——	——
	April	156	112	——	——	60
	May	157	——	——	——	——
	June	150	113	——	——	——
	July	——	116	——	——	63
	Auguft	——	114	——	——	——
	September	——	——	——	——	——
	October	——	——	——	——	61
	November	——	111	——	——	——
	December	——	——	——	——	——

Year.		India Stock.	Bank Stock.	S.S. Stock.	4 per Cents	3 per Cents.
1781.	January	146	108	—	—	57
	February(1)	148	105⅝	—	—	58
	March	—	112	—	—	59
	April	—	—	—	—	—
	May	—	113	—	—	—
	June	—	116	—	—	57
	July	—	—	—	—	—
	Auguſt	—	114	—	—	—
	September	140	110	—	—	56
	October	139	111	—	—	—
	November	—	—	—	—	—
	December	—	—	—	—	—
1782.	January	130	110	—	—	—
	February(27)	—	—	—	—	53¾
	March	—	112	—	—	54
	April	—	114	—	—	57
	May	—	115	—	—	59
	June	—	—	—	—	60
	July	—	114	—	—	53
	Auguſt	—	—	—	—	56
	September	—	—	—	—	57
	October	134	115	—	—	55
	November	—	—	—	—	59
	December	—	—	—	—	61
1783.	January	140	117	76	—	64
	February	145	126	—	85	66
	March	141	134	—	—	68
	April	138	135	—	—	—
	May	—	133	—	—	—
	June	—	131	—	86	66
	July	—	126	—	84	67
	Auguſt	—	127	—	83	—
	September	141	—	—	—	66
	October	125	118	—	—	63
	November	120	115	—	—	62
	December	119	112	—	—	58
1784.	January(14)	118½	113	—	75	57
	February	123	116	—	76	56
	March	124	118	—	74	55
	April	—	115	—	—	56
	May	—	114	—	75	57
	June	122	—	—	73	—
	July	—	116	64	74	55
	Auguſt	125	117	—	—	54
	September	126	111	—	—	—
	October	—	112	—	70	—
	November	—	110	—	—	55
	December	128	112	—	—	—
1785.	January	132	116	—	71	56
	February	130	115	—	—	55

Year		India Stock.	Bank Stock.	S.S.Stock.	4 per Cents	3 per Cents.
	March	131	117	—	—	57
	April	133	112	—	73	58
	May	135	115	—	—	—
	June	136	117	—	—	—
	July	140	118	—	74	—
	Auguſt	142	120	—	—	59
	September	147	122	66	75	95
	October	149	129	—	76	66
	November	——	130	—	82	70
	December	156	129	—	87	72
1786.	January	155	140	70	83	73
	February	156	139	—	89	69
	March	158	140	—	—	—
	April	159	138	78	—	—
	May	161	137	—	87	70
	June	162	143	—	90	71
	July	161	146	81	—	72
	Auguſt	166	149	—	91	73
	September	168	151	—	92	74
	October	165	158	—	96	76
	November	166	150	—	98	78
	December	——	148	—	95	74
1787.	January	163	149	—	92	73
	February	164	150	—	93	70
	March	166	152	—	95	74
	April	168	153	—	96	76
	May	169	154	—	92	77
	June	171	156	—	93	73
	July	169	150	—	94	70
	Auguſt	159	147	80	91	72
	September	163	148	—	88	69
	October	169	146	—	95	70
	November	173	149	—	96	72
	December	175	154	—	95	75
1788.	January	174	156	84	97	76
	February	176	158	—	—	75
	March	175	160	—	96	—
	April	——	166	—	94	—
	May	——	172	—	—	—
	June	170	173	—	—	76
	July	169	171	—	—	—
	Auguſt	——	178	—	96	74
	September	167	172	—	—	—
	October	170	173	—	94	—
	November	169	172	—	—	—
	December	168	171	83	93	73

* The above is copied from the former edition. During the remaining four-teen years, it is thought moſt expedient to alter the arrangement, beginning with the loweſt rate of intereſt, namely the 3 per Cents. and inferting the price of the 5 per Cents. inſtead of the South Sea Stock. The averages are calculated by Mr. Grellier of the Royal Exchange Aſſuiance Office.

Year.		3 per Cent. Confols.	4 per Cent. Confols.	5 per Cents.	Bank Stock.	India Stock.
1789.	January	72	93	110	170	—
	February	73	94	111	172	163
	March	74	96	113	175	167
	April	—	94	—	173	168
	May	75	95	115	175	169
	June	77	97	116	178	170
	July	—	91	115	181	172
	Auguft	78	99	116	187	176
	September	80	101	119	189	177
	October	—	99	118	187	—
	November	78	97	117	182	176
	December	—	98	118	—	173
1790.	January	78	100	117	186	171
	February	—	—	—	—	—
	March	—	—	118	185	—
	April	80	—	119	186	173
	May *	73	94	112	170	155
	June	—	—	114	172	157
	July	—	95	111	171	156
	Auguft	77	99	116	183	164
	September	—	98	—	181	165
	October	74	93	111	173	154
	November	79	99	118	183	168
	December	80	100	120	185	169
1791.	January	80	102	119	188	170
	February	—	—	118	—	169
	March†	81	103	119	188	168
	April	78	99	117	182	162
	May	81	100	119	184	164
	June	82	101	120	186	166
	July	81	102	119	187	165
	Auguft	86	105	120	196	180
	September	89	104	118	200	190
	October	88	—	116	201	192
	November	87	101	118	195	186
	December	89	102	119	199	—
1792.	January	50	102	116	202	186
	February	94	104	119	213	200
	March	96	—	—	216	211
	April	95	102	—	210	210
	May	92	99	118	202	207

* The probability of a rupture with Spain in confequence of the tranfactions at Nootka Sound, caufed a confiderable depreffion of the Stocks; 3 per Cent. Confols which on the 30th April were 80¾, had fallen on the 11th May to 70, but foon recovered a little, the average of the month being not lefs than above ftated

† Towards the end of March when the fubject of the claim of Government to the ufe of the unreceived Dividends was in difcuffion, Stocks declined confider-ably, 3 per Cent. Confols. being on the 26th March at 75¾, but foon after re-covered a little.

Year.		3 per Cent. Consols.	4 per Cent. Consols.	5 per Cents.	Bank Stock.	India Stock.
	June	91	100	119	205	208
	July	92	101	118	204	209
	August	91	102	117	206	206
	September	90	101	——	200	204
	October	—	100	——	——	210
	November	88	98	116	195	205
	December*	76	90	110	175	——
1793.	January	77	91	106	175	181
	February†	72	87	101	166	176
	March ‡	75	88	105	170	200
	April	78	89	109	175	212
	May	76	—	107	165	211
	June	77	90	109	168	210
	July	—	92	107	176	213
	August	—	94	108	177	210
	September	74	92	106	172	206
	October	75	90	——	168	——
	November	74	88	107	165	207
	December	—	89	108	167	209
1794.	January	70	86	101	161	202
	February	67	83	——	157	200
	March	—	—	——	161	201
	April	69	84	103	163	203
	May	70	—	——	167	207
	June	—	—	104	166	——
	July	67	83	101	164	199
	August	—	84	——	——	198
	September	66	85	——	——	195
	October	64	80	100	152	188
	November	67	84	103	157	191
	December	65	82	102	155	189
1795.	January	63	80	97	153	187
	February	62	79	96	152	183
	March	—	—	94	153	182
	April	63	77	96	154	187
	May	65	79	97	159	192
	June	67	80	—	166	199
	July	68	82	—	169	197
	August	—	84	99	170	2 0
	September	69	85	100	169	199

* The probability of war, caufed a rapid fall of the Stocks; 3 per Cent. Confols which on the 12th November were 90¼, had fallen on the 3d December to 74.

† 3 per Cent. Confols, which on the 15th January were 78⅜ declined with the other Funds, as the proceedings in France appeared to render war certain, and on the 11th of February were at 71.

‡ The great rife of India Stock was occafioned by the agreement with government for the renewal of the Charter, which arrangement included an increafe of the Dividend.

Year.		3 per Cent. Conſols.	4 per Cent. Conſols.	5 5 Cents.	Bank Stock.	India Stock.
	October	68	82	100	167	198
	November	68	84	102	166	200
	December	70	86	102	173	205
1796.	January	69	85	100	177	216
	February	68	84	—	175	212
	March	—	85	—	174	212
	April	67	82		174	214
	May	65	81	99	167	210
	June	63	79	97	160	205
	July	60	78	95	154	194
	Auguſt	59	—	89	152	185
	September	56		88	151	182
	October	58	74	83	139	176
	November	56	75	87	146	178
	December	57	73	85	144	175
			74	87		176
1797.	January	54	73	81	140	167
	February*	53	70	79	139	160
	March	50	—	75	139	152
	April	—	63	—	136	152
	May	48	61	—	124	150
	June	50	62	—	119	149
	July	53	65		123	—
	Auguſt	52	64	77	130	160
	September†	50	—	76	—	159
	October	49	59	74	—	156
	November	48	58	72	118	151
	December	49	59	73	—	149
					117	176
1798.	January	48	59	69	118	146
	February	49	60	70	121	—
	March	50	62	73	122	148
	April	49	59	72	117	—
	May	48	—	74	118	—
	June	49	61	76	119	150
	July	48	62	74	123	144
	Auguſt	49	65	76	128	150
	September	50	—	77	131	148
	October	51	66	80	130	153
	November	55	69	85	137	167
	December	52	66	82	136	161
1799.	January	53	67	81	138	161
	February	—	69	82		161
	March	54	71	83	140	165
						166

* On the ſtoppage of caſh payments at the Bank 27th February 3 per Cents. roſe from 50⅝ to 52½ ; 4 per Cents. from 66 to 67¼ ; and 5 per Cents. from 76¼ to 77⅞, this was the natural conſequence of the inability to procure *Caſh* for Bank paper, which put a ſtop to ſelling out for that purpoſe.

† On the 20th September the day of Lord Malmſbury's arrival from Liſle, 3 per Cent. Conſols fell to 47⅜ which was a lower price than they had ever been at before.

Year.		3 per Cent. Confols.	4 per Cent. Confols	5 per Cents.	Bank Stock.	India Stock
	April	54	69	84	135	168
	May	55	—	86	138	169
	June	59	74	88	143	172
	July	62	79	93	160	183
	Auguft	65	83	96	170	199
	September	64	84	—	171	200
	October .	60	74	90	156	190
	November*	61	75	91	158	191
	December	62	77	54	156	198
1800.	January	61	77	90	155	195
	February	—	78	91	156	200
	March	62	81	94	162	202
	April	63	—	97	161	208
	May	—	80	98	162	210
	June	62	81	—	161	—
	July	63	82	97	163	206
	Auguft	64	84	—	167	203
	September	65	85	98	171	207
	October	64	82	99	167	206
	November	—	81	—	165	205
	December	63	79	98	161	203
1801.	January	60	79	93	159	192
	February	57	77	91	152	187
	March	56	75	91	153	—
	April	59	77	95	163	193
	May	60	78	96	163	200
	June	61	79	—	167	201
	July	60	80	95	168	195
	Auguft	—	—	—	—	—
	September	—	81	—	—	—
	October†	67	86	101	182	212
	November	68	84	100	189	215
	December	67	—	98	187	216
1802.	January	68	85	98	189	213
	February	69	86	100	191	214
	March	—	—	101	181	213
	April	76	92	105	195	226
	May	75	90	102	190	220
	June	—	88	103	183	212
	July	73	89	101	190	215
	Auguft	69	87	100	185	207
	September	—	—	101	183	203
	October	68	85	100	186	205
	November	—	83	101	180	202
	December	—	86	102	187	—

* In confequence of the change that had taken place in the French government and their fuppofed pacific intentions, 3 per Cents rofe on 18th November from 61 to 64½, but foon declined again.

* The figning of Preliminaries of Peace was made known on 2d October, and naturally caufed a great rife of the Stocks; 3 per Cent. Confols which the preceding day were 59⅝ got up to 67½, and on the 5th to 69¼.

The reader will pleafe to obferve, that the Dividend on India Stock at prefent is at the rate of $7\frac{1}{2}$, on Bank Stock at the rate of 7, and on South Sea Stock at the rate of $3\frac{1}{2}$ per Cent. The accounts that will be given of thefe different Companies will explain what was the amount of former Dividends.

The above abftract may be of fome ufe to fuch perfons as may be defirous of making calculations refpecting the real or comparative value of the different funds. But it would be worthy the attention of government, in a country like this, whofe profperity and power depend fo much upon the wifdom with which it raifes the fupplies for public purpofes, to have a complete and regular account drawn up and publifhed, of the prices of every fpecies of funded property, as far back as they can now be traced. It would furnifh the means of afcertaining in future times, which is the moft eligible mode of borrowing money, whether perpetual or temporary Annuities—whether annuities for one or for more lives, whether borrowing from Companies and bodies corporate, or from unconnected individuals—and whether a great capital with a lower intereft, or a low capital with a higher intereft, ought to be preferred. Nor is this a trifling object; for even a fmall faving upon fo enormous a debt as that to which we are now fubject, is not beneath the attention of the wealthieft and moft powerful nation.

From an attentive examination of the preceding tables, the following obfervations may be deduced:

1. That as the 3 per Cents. bore on the 18th of December, 1752, the higheft price known in this country (namely $106\frac{3}{4}$ per Cent.); whereas on the 27th February, 178?, the credit of Great Britain was confequently then at its greateft height: the fame ftock bore little more than one half of that price (namely $53\frac{3}{8}$). An amazingly rapid decline in the value of the fame property, in the fhort fpace of about thirty years; and tends to prove how much the public creditors are interefted iu promoting wife and judicious plans for redeeming the national debt; fince in the fame proportion, their property, if in three per cent. ftock, in thirty years more, might have fold at little more than 26 per Cent. whereas were the public burdens put in a fair way of being gradually diminifhed and paid off, they might have rifen, in the very fame fpace of time, to 106 per Cent. again. During the courfe of the late war, the 3 per Cents. were ftill lower than $53\frac{3}{8}$, for on the 20th September, 1797, they fell to $47\frac{3}{4}$.

2. The higheft price which the ftocks have borne fince the year 1730, has been as follows:

India Stock	-	6th September, 1768,	$276\frac{1}{4}$
Bank Stock	-	5th September, 1769,	$168\frac{3}{4}$
South Sea Stock	-	20th May, 1768,	111
Bank 4 per Cents.	-	16th March, 1768,	$105\frac{3}{8}$
Three per Cents.	-	18th December, 1752,	$106\frac{3}{4}$

The loweft prices were alfo as follow:

India Stock	-	14th January, 1784,	$118\frac{1}{2}$
Bank Stock	-	29th January, 1762,	91
South Sea Stock	-	22d February, 1782,	$62\frac{1}{4}$
Bank 4 per Cents.	-	8th March, 1782,	$68\frac{1}{2}$
Three per Cents.	-	27th February, 1782,	$53\frac{3}{4}$
Ditto	-	20th September, 1797,	$47\frac{3}{4}$

And the following feems to have been the greateft fall in the Price of any Stock during that period:

India Stock, 30th of May, 1772, was fold for - 226
On the 21ft of January, 1774, fetched only $137\frac{1}{4}$

Total difference in eighteen months $88\frac{3}{4}$

It is farther evident, from comparing the prices of the different Stocks in the years 1768 and 1769, with the years immediately preceding, that property in the funds then reached its higheſt price, or, at leaſt, its ſteadieſt level; and hence that it requires ſeven or eight years of profound peace, before the public credit of the country naturally arrives at the greateſt pitch of which it is capable

N.B. The reader whò may wiſh to know the real quantum of Intereſt that is drawn according to the prices of the different Stocks, may conſult the table of equatiòn in Mortimer's Every Man his own broker, and the compartive view of the funds, ſubjoined to Blewert's tables for calculating the value of Stocks and Annuities. It is ſufficient at preſent to remark, that the ſame intereſt, to wit, £ 5 per centum per annum is received, if £ 60, in money, is paid for One hundred pounds of 3 per cent. Stock ; or 80, in money, for £ 100 4 per cents ; or £ 100, in money, for £100 5 per cents ; or £120, in money, for £ 100 6 per cents; or £ 140, in money, for £100 7 per cents; or £ 160, in money, for £ 100 8 per cents.

APPENDIX.

No. III.

Hints regarding the Value of Money at different Periods, and the Depreciation thereof.

———

IT is not proposed here to discuss the advantages or inconveniencies attending the depreciation of money, respecting which I have already stated the result of my reflections; but it is not only a curious, but an important subject of enquiry, to ascertain what has been the real progress and extent of that depreciation in the successive periods of our history.

It is with much pleasure that I mention upon this occasion, first, the valuable and laborious researches of one of the most respectable members that has ever sat in parliament (Sir George Shuckburgh Evelyn, Bart. Member for Warwick-shire), and next, the work of an ingenious author, (John Wheatley, Esq.) who has lately printed his remarks on Currency and Commerce *. The former has published in the Philosophical Transactions, (1798, part i. p. 176), a table, which exhibits, in a comprehensive view, the value of money, in arithmetical proportions, from the Conquest to the present time, of which the following is a copy.

Proportion of the Value of Money from the Conquest to the present Time.

Year.								Rate.
1050	-	-	-	-	-	-	-	26
1100	-	-	-	-	-	-	-	34
1150	-	-	-	-	-	-	-	43
1200	-	-	-	-	-	-	-	51
1250	-	-	-	-	-	-	-	60
1300	-	-	-	-	-	-	-	68
1350	-	-	-	-	-	-	-	77
1400	-	-	-	-	-	-	-	83
1450	-	-	-	-	-	-	-	88
1500	-	-	-	-	-	-	-	94
1550	-	-	-	-	-	-	-	100
1600	-	-	-	-	-	-	-	144
1650	-	-	-	-	-	-	-	188
1675	-	-	-	-	-	-	-	210
1700	-	-	-	-	-	-	-	238
1720	-	-	-	-	-	-	-	257
1740	-	-	-	-	-	-	-	287

* In one volume 8vo. printed by Cadell and Davies. An. 1803.

Year.								Rate.
1750	-	-	-	-	-	-	-	314
1760	-	-	-	-	-	-	-	342
1770	-	-	-	-	-	-	-	384
1780	-	-	-	-	-	-	-	427
1790	-	-	-	-	-	-	-	496
1795	-	-	-	-	-	-	-	531
1800	-	-	-	-	-	-	-	562

The latter (Mr. Wheatley) has drawn up various calculations, founded on the principle of the above table, giving an account of the comparative value of the revenue during the 18th century. For thefe the reader is referred to the work itfelf, but, as a fpecimen of them, there is herewith fubjoined an efti- mate of the value of a pound fterling, during every ten years of the preceding century.

In	1700	-	-	-	0	8	$5\frac{1}{4}$	
	1710	-	-	-	0	8	$9\frac{1}{2}$	
	1720	-	-	-	0	9	$1\frac{1}{4}$	
	1730	-	-	-	0	9	8	
	1740	-	-	-	0	10	$2\frac{1}{2}$	Were equal to a Pound Sterling of 1800.
	1750	-	-	-	0	11	2	
	1760	-	-	-	0	12	2	
	1770	-	-	-	0	13	$7\frac{3}{4}$	
	1780	-	-	-	0	15	$2\frac{1}{2}$	
	1790	-	-	-	0	17	$7\frac{3}{4}$	
	1800	-	-	-	1	0	0	

APPENDIX.

No. IV.

An Antidote to Defpondency ; or, Progreffive Affertions from refpectable
Authority, tending to prove that the Nation was ACTUALLY UNDONE,
prior to the Revolution in 1688 ; and that it has remained in a continued
State of Ruin, or Decay, ever fince that memorable Era.

IT has often been remarked, that the Englifh are more inclined than any other
nation to view the dark fide of the profpect ; to fear every thing, and to
hope for nothing. In the month of November in particular the fta e fuffers
exceedingly ; and whoever ferioufly fits down to confider, in that gloomy feafon of the year, the fituation of the country, concludes, after mature reflection, *that the country is undone* ; or that matters are fo bad, that the bufinefs of
government cannot poffibly be carried through another Seffion *.

As any ideas of that nature are, in a particular manner, contrary to the
interefts of a ftate that depends upon credit for fupplying the means of defending itfelf, or of annoying its enemies, it is thought that a greater benefit
cannot be conferred upon the public, than by proving how groundlefs fuch
opinions are, in the firft place, from the infinite refources of which the nation
is actually poffeffed, which, it is hoped, are not eafily to be exhaufted, and
which have hitherto ftood many a fevere trial : and fecondly, from its ap-
pearing to be an indifputable fact, that fimilar defponding apprehenfions have
been publicly avowed by perfons of refpectable authority for above a century
paft, during which period it is well known that the nation has enjoyed no inconfiderable degree of happinefs and profperity.

It is, therefore, propofed to lay before the reader fome extracts from works
of authority in political queftions, containing progreffive affertions of the miferable ftate of the nation for above a century paft, though the event has proved
that it has continued to profper, notwithftanding the melancholy apprehenfions which many able and intelligent individuals entertained of a very oppofite
nature.

Anno   I. " It may be undeniably and uncomfortably obferved, that
1680. whilft every one hath eagerly purfued his private intereft, *a kind
of common confumption hath crawled upon us* ; fince our land rents
are generally much fallen, and our home commodities funk from
their late price and value ; our poor are vaftly increafed, and the
reft of the people generally more and more feel the want of money.

* See the World, No 99, 21ft of November, 1754.

This

This difeafe, having grown upon us in times of peace, when no foreigners have exhaufted us by warlike depredations, may very juftly
amaze us; and the more, when at the fame time we obferve that fome
of our neighbouring nations, lately our equals, or much our inferiors
(I mean the French and Dutch), are become fo prodigioufly rich and
powerful on a fudden. Certainly thefe mighty productions muft have
fome great and vigorous caufes, which have been very furioufly working of late years, and fuch as have not fallen under common obfervation."
—*Britannia Languens*; or, *a Difcourfe of Trade.* Printed An. 168c. Introduction, p. 1.

1689. " I fear the author doth too truly tell us, that the trades of tillage, graz-
ing, dairy, clothing, fulling, &c. that formerly enriched the occupiers
of them, have in thefe latter years been the ufual fhipwrecks of men's
ftocks and eftates; that we have in a manner loft the Eaft-land and
the Northern Trades; that the cheapnefs of intereft d th not proceed
from the plenty of money, but the fcarcenefs of fecurity; and that
no new improving manufacture is to be heard of in England, *but that
of Perriwigs.*"—*A difcourfe of the Growth of England,* &c. *by way of
letter to a perfon of honour.* Printed An. 1689. P. 184.

1694. II. " I think it paft difpute, that there is not one man of an hundred
who would in any manner have contributed to this revolution (Anno
1688), if they could have forefeen that thereby we fhould have been
engaged in fo durable, expenfive, and deftructive a war, in defence of
the Dutch and other confederates; not only to the eternal fcandal of
our loyalty, religion, honefty, juftice, honour, and morality, but to the
wafte and confumption of our ftores of arms and ammunition, the lofs
of our fhips and men, the inundation of foreign force, to the very in-
flaving the nation to their intereft, councils, and conduct, *and the utter
beggaring of ourfelves, by the decay of traffick and unfupportable taxes.*"—
England muft pay the piper. By Sir R. W. Printed Anno 1694.

1699. III. " Unlefs this can be compaffed (namely, reducing the revenue of the
crown to the fum of £ 2,300,000 per annum), it will be found that,
in no long courfe of time, we fhall languifh and decay every year, by
fteps eafy enough to be perceived by fuch as confider of thefe matters.
Our gold and filver will be carried off by degrees, rents will fall,
the purchafe of land will decreafe, wool will fink in its price, our ftock
of fhipping will be diminifhed, farm-houfes will go to ruin, induftry will
decay, *and we fhall have upon us all the vifible marks of a declining people.*"
—*An Effay upon the probable methods of making a People Gainers in the
Balance of Trade.* By Dr. D'Avenant. Originally printed Anno 1699.
See alfo his Effay on the Balance of Power, " I will venture to fay, from
the time of the Norman invafion we never had a more difmal view
before us." Originally publifhed An. 1701 : printed in his works
vol. iii. p. 302.

1710. IV. " *Are we not almoft driven to the very brink of deftruction?* Our treafures are riotoufly wafted, our conftitution in danger of being fubvert-
ed, and the nation almoft in general corrupted ! Yet is it not a ftrange
and wonderful thing, that while the nation is almoft bankrupt, wealthy
men fhould fhoot up in feveral offices like mufhrooms ; and while the
Government was endangered to be beggared, that all its fervants fhould
riot in fuch wealth and plenty, that the bare handling of a brufh in any
office was the ready way to a plentiful fortune, as if the public treafury
had

had been thrown in there only for the officers to brush it into their own pockets ?—*A Letter touching the Rise of all the Embezzlements and Mismanagements of the Kingdom's Treasure, from the Revolution to the present Parliament.* Printed Anno 1710.

1720. V. " It is evident from the immediately preceding state, that near one moiety of the duties therein mentioned ariseth from the customs ; *and it is too well known, and a sad truth it is, that the balance of trade has been for some time past considerably against us.* That our silver coin, is grown very scarce ; and that it is impossible our gold can stay at home, till an advantageous turn is given to our trade. And under these unhappy circumstances, and that of our public debts, the nation, I think, can never be justified to run into any new expence for a reason of less importance than that of an immediate preservation of the religion and liberties thereof.—*A Collection of Treatises.* By Archibald Hutcheson, Esq. Printed Anno 1721.

1722 VI. " Can it be proved that a free people can taste the high enjoyments that flow from property and liberty, when loaded with numerous duties and immersed in debts of such a magnitude, that the discharging thereof is almost impracticable with the safety of the nation ? And that our credit and reputation is growing and increasing, notwithstanding we are likely to be driven to the unavoidable choice of two melancholy extremes, *viz.* The blotting out of our books, and an effacing, as irretrievable, an infinite number of creditors, who have lawful and just claims upon us ; or, the paying off debts by the virtue of wild schemes, and by that means to sink under a final bankruptcy. Ought not such a people to reflect with horror and anguish of heart at any who either by mismanagement or villainy have reduced them *to so terrible an ebb.*" —*The nature and weight of the national taxes.* By T. Gordon, Esq. In the Collection of Trenchard and Gordon's tracts, printed Anno 1751. Vol. I. p. 366.—Originally printed Anno 1722.

1727. VII. " Is there not already a land-tax upon our estates as large as can be reasonably desired in time of peace ? Are not all our ordinary expences burthened with duties ; or, is there any considerable branch of commerce which does not pay its custom ? Is there scarce any thing that we eat, drink, wear, or in any manner use, which does not contribute to the necessities of the Government ? Are not many things doubly, trebly, and even quadruply laden ? Is not this generally lamented by all people ? What, therefore, shall we say to a man who lays plans for future ministers to oppress his fellow-subjects with such grievous burthens, *as neither we nor our children shall be able to bear* !" —*Remarks on a late book, entitled, An Essay on the public Debts of this Kingdom.* Printed An. 1727.

1736. VIII. " The vast load of debt under which the nation still groans, *is the true source of all those calamities and gloomy prospects of which we have so much reason to complain.* To this has been owing that multiplicity of burthensome taxes, which have more than doubled the price of the common necessaries of life within a few years past ; and thereby distressed the poor labourer and manufacturer ; disabled the farmer to pay his rent ; and put even gentlemen of plentiful estates under the greatest difficulties to make a tolerable provision for their families. From this have proceeded those infinite swarms of locusts and caterpillars in office, who not only prey on the vitals of industry, but render even

even our liberties precarious, and dependent on the will of thofe, who have the fole nomination and direction of them. And to this we muft likewife afcribe that ruinous fpirit of luxury, corruption, and venality, which hath infected the whole nation, and almoft effaced the very marks of frugality and public virtue amongft us."—*The Craftfman*, No. 502, 14th of February, 1736.

1737. IX. " For my part I do not know any one neceffary of life upon which we have not fome tax or another, except water ; and we can put no ingredient I know of into water, in order to make it palatable and cheerful, without paying a tax. We pay a tax for air, and for the light and heat of the fun in the day-time, by means of our tax upon windows ; and for light and heat in the night-time, by means of our duties upon coals and candles; we pay a tax upon bread, meat, roots and herbs of all kinds, by means of our falt duty ; we pay a tax upon fmall-beer, by means of the malt tax; and a heavy additional tax upon ftrong-beer, by way of excife. Nay, we cannot have any clean thing to put upon our backs, either of woollen or linen, without paying a tax, by means of the duty on foap, &c.— See *Torbuck's Debates*, Vol. XV. p. 209.

1739. X. " What are then the circumftances of this kingdom and of France ? —On one fide mortgaged revenues, credit funk at home and abroad, an exhaufted, difpirited, difcontented people. On the other, a rich and popular government, ftrong in alliances, in reputation, in the confidence and affection of its fubjects.—Our well-equipt fleets and well-dreft troops give, to be fure, an air of magnificence ; but then it is well known *that we owe almoft Fifty Millions*, and have been forced to apply the Sinking Fund, not to difcharge that debt, *but to furnifh out thefe Shows*; whilft in moft parts of England gentlemen's rents are fo ill paid, and the weight of taxes lies fo heavy upon them, that thofe who have nothing from the court can fcarce fupport their families.— *Confiderations upon the prefent State of our Affairs at Home and Abroad. In a Letter from a Member of Parliament to a Friend in the Country.* By George Lord Lyttelton. See his Works, Edition 1774, Vol. I. p. 64 and 65.

1745. XI. " I fhall conclude with afking this queftion—Whether we think ourfelves able, under a great load of annual taxes, increafing debts, mortgaged and anticipated funds, a vifible decay of both trade and money, to continue for any foreign intereft whatfoever, either the bullies or paymafters of all the other powers in Europe ? And whether it would not better demonftrate our wifdom and economy, and that love we profefs to our country and pofterity, if we confined our quarrels more to that element on which our infular fituation gives us an advantage, and to that meafure of expence *which fuits our prefent declining cir umftances.*—*A Survey of the National Debt.* Infcribed to Sir John Phillips. Printed Anno 1745.

1749. XII. " Our parliamentary aids from the year 1740, exclufively, to the year 1748, inclufively, amount to £ 55,522,159 16s. 3d. a fum, that will appear *incredible to future generations*, and is fo almoft to the prefent —'Till we have paid a good part of our debt, and reftored our country in fome meafure to her former wealth and power, it will be difficult to maintain the dignity of Great Britain, to make her refpected abroad, and fecure from injuries, or even affronts on the part of her neighbours."

neighbours."—*Some Reflections on the present State of the Nation.* By Henry St. John, Lord Viscount Bolingbroke. Edition 1773. Vol. IV. p 137 and 147.

1756. XIII. " It has been a general received notion, among Political Arithmeticians, that we may increase our national debt to *One Hundred Millions ;* but they acknowledge that it muft then ceafe, by the debtor becoming bankrupt.—But it is very difficult to comprehend, if we do not ftop at *Seventy-five Millions,* where we fhall ftop.—*A Journal of Eight Days Journey,* &c. *in Letters.* By Samuel Hannay, Efq. Printed An. 1756, in one Volume Quarto, p. 318.

1757. XIV. " The great bane of our trade is the high price of our commodities. And muft not the augmentation of our debts and taxes ftill enhance their price ? And muft not this at length prove the ruin of our whole commerce ? In order to eafe our trade, and to prevent its total deftruction, muft we not at any rate get rid of our debts and taxes ? Since the more we run in debt, the lefs able fhall we be to pay them, can we get rid of them without the abfolute ruin of all the public creditors ? And what a fcene of confufion and horror muft this produce in the kingdom ?"—*Great Britain's True Syftem.* By Malachy Poftlethwayt, Efq. p. 48

1761. XV. " The firft inftance of a debt contracted upon parliamentary fecurity occurs in the reign of Henry the Sixth.—The commencement of this pernicious practice deferves to be noted ; a practice the more likely to become pernicious the more a nation advances in opulence and credit. The ruinous effects of it are now become apparent, *and threaten the very exiftence of the nation.*"—*Hume's Hiftory of England.* Octavo Edition of 1778, Vol. III p. 215.—But originally printed Anno 1761.

1765. XVI. " Thus much is indifputably certain, that the prefent magnitude of our national incumbrances very far exceeds all calculations of commercial benefit, and is productive of the greateft inconveniences, by the enormous taxes that are raifed upon the neceffaries of life, for the payment of the intereft of this debt, &c. &c.—And laftly, they weaken the internal ftrength of a ftate, by anticipating thofe refources which fhould be referved to defend it in cafe of neceffity."—*Blackftone's Commentaries,* Vol. I. p. 328. Edition 1775. *.

1774. XVII. " I am grieved to obferve, that we have many taxes more hurtful to individuals, than advantageous to the public revenue. Multiplied taxes on the neceffaries of life, candles, foap, leather, ale, falt, &c. raife the price of labour, and confequently of manufactures. If they fhall have the effect to deprive us of foreign markets, *which we have reafon to dread,* Depopulation and Poverty muft enfue."—*Kaim's Sketches of the Hiftory of Man.* Firft Edition, Vol. I. p. 484.

1776. XVIII. " I fuppofe there is no mathematical, ftill lefs an arithmetical demonftration, that the road to the Holy Land was not the road to Paradife, as there is, that the endlefs increafe of National Debts is the direct road to National Ruin. *But having now completely reached that goal,* it is needlefs at prefent to reflect on the paft. It will be found in the

* See alfo Preliminary Difcourfe to Poftlethwayte's Dict. on the wretched ftate of our Finances. 3d Edit. An. 1766.

prefent

prefent year 1776, that all the revenues of this ifland, North of Trent,
and Weft of Reading, are mortgaged or anticipated for ever. Could the
fmall remainder be in a worfe condition were thofe Provinces feized by
Auftria and Prufia ? There is only this difference, that fome event
might happen in Europe which would oblige thefe great Monarchs to
difgorge their acquifitions. But no imagination can figure a fituation
which will induce our creditors to relinquifh their claims, or the public
to feize their revenues. So egregious indeed has been our folly, that
we have even loft all title to compaffion in the numberlefs calamities
that are waiting us."—*Hume's Hiftory of England.* Vol. V. p. 475.
Note B.

1776. XIX. " Great Britain feems to fupport with eafe a burden, which half a
century ago nobody believed her capable of fupporting. Let us not,
however, upon this account rafhly conclude, that fhe is capable of fupporting any burden; nor even be too confident that fhe could fupport, without great diftrefs, a burden *a little greater* than what has been
laid upon her "—*An Enquiry into the Nature and Caufe of the Wealth of
Nations.* By Adam Smith, &c. Vol. II. p 363.

1777. XX. " We are now involved in another war, and the public debts are
increafing again faft ; the prefent year (1777) muft make another great
addition to them ; and what they will be at the end of thefe troubles,
no one can tell.—The union of a foreign war to the prefent civil
war might perhaps raife them to *Two Hundred Millions*, but more probably it would fink them to *Nothing* —*Additional Obfervations on the
Nature and Value of Civil Liberty,* &c. By Richard Price, D.D. Third
Edition. P. 148.

1783. XXI. " If the premifes are juft, or nearly juft, and nothing effectual is
done to prevent their confequences, the infallible, inevitable conclufion
that follows, is, That the ftate is a bankrupt, and that thofe who have
trufted their All to the public faith, are in very imminent danger of
becoming (I die pronouncing it) Beggars." *An Argument to prove that it
is the indifpenfable Duty of the Creditors of the Public to infift that Government do forthwith bring forward the confideration of the State of the Nation.*
By John Earl of Stair. Printed An. 1783.

It would not be difficult to make confiderable additions to the above extracts, were it neceffary to adduce any farther proof, that even the ableft men
may entertain ill-founded and groundlefs apprehenfions refpecting the Political
Strength and Financial Refources of the Nation. The fentiments of the Author, upon thefe points, have ever been very different. Even as early as the
year 1783, in the midft of much terror and defpondency, he hefitated not to
affert, " That our diftreffes were too deeply coloured, that our financial re-
" fources were not totally deftroyed, and that Britain might ftill retain *its ele-
" vated rank* among the Potentates of Europe." However vifionary fuch ideas
were confidered at the time, they have fince been amply verified : a circumftance which muft prove the fource of pride and exultation to every real friend
to the happinefs of his country. Indeed, nothing but the groffeft mifmanagement, or the vileft degeneracy and corruption, can poffibly effect the ruin of fo
powerful an empire, inhabited by a race of people, diftinguifhed for ftrength,
for courage, and for ability.

APPENDIX.

No. V.

General View of a propofed Analyfis of the Sources of Public
Revenue.

THE Author of this publication has it in contemplation, as foon as other
avocations will admit of it, to fubmit to the confideration of the public, a
general and fyftematic Analyfis, of the Sources of Public Revenue, and the
Principles on which they are refpectively founded : and a variety of materials
for that extenfive undertaking are already collected. But an attempt of that
nature cannot be haftily completed ; for it requires a thorough inveftigation
into the revenues of every nation both ancient and modern, and an attentive
confideration of the various works which have been written in the different
languages of Europe upon the fubject of Finance : and as many circumftances
may occur, which may prevent him, for a confiderable fpace of time, from
carrying into full effect an object requiring fuch labour and refearches, he muft
content himfelf, for the prefent, with publifhing an Abftract of his intended
Analyfis, and with requefting that the Reader, who may be converfant in fuch
enquiries, would favour him with any obfervations which may occur upon an
attentive perufal of it, either refpecting the Table itfelf, or the manner in
which the particular Sources of Public Revenue are therein arranged.

T A B L E

OF THE

SOURCES OF PUBLIC REVENUE.

I. *Property vested in the Public.*

1. Lands - - - - -	1. Forests. 2. Pasture lands. 3. Arable lands. 4. Gardens and vineyards.
2. Buildings - - - -	1. For private habitation. 2. For public entertainments. 3. Public baths.
3. Fishings - - - -	1. In fresh water. 2. In salt water. 3. Of pearls.
4. Mines - - - -	1. Of metals. 2. Of salt and minerals. 3. Of precious stones.
5. Peculiar Productions - -	1. Bitumen. 2. Balm of Gilead. 3. Alum. 4. Terra Sigillata. 5. Mineral waters.

II. *Rights or public lucrative Prerogatives intrusted to the Government of a Country.*

1. Right of Seignory - - -	1. Non entry. 2. Relief. 3. Wardship. 4. Marriage. 5. Fine of alienation. 6. Aids. 7. Escheat. 8. Purveyance. 9. Pre-emption.

2. Right to unappropriated Property - - - -
{
1. Bona vacantia.
2. Treasure trove.
3. Waifs.
4. Estrays.
5. Goods wrecked.
6. Goods not inherited.
7. Goods of deceased foreigners.
}

3. Right of declaring Peace or War.
{
1. Plunder in War - { 1. At sea. 2. On land. }
2. Tributes from other nations.
3. Subsidies.
}

4. Judicial Rights - - -
{
1. Judging and determining causes.
2. Fines and pecuniary punishments.
3. Confiscation.
4. Registers.
5. Stamps.
}

5. Rights as the Fountain of Honour of Office, &c. - - -
{
1. Sale of honours.
2. Sale of offices.
3. Sale of franchises, &c.
}

6. Rights as the Arbiter of Commerce - - - -
{
1. Commerce carried on by agents.
2. Monopolies farmed out.
3. Monopolies granted.
4. Lotteries.
5. Post-office.
6. Monopoly of posting.
7. Coinage { 1. Of metals. 2. Of paper. }
8. Tolls and passage taxes { 1. At sea. 2. On land. }
9. Port duties.
}

7. Rights as the Guardian of Morals - - - -
{
1. Sumptuary taxes.
2. Taxes on public amusements.
}

8. Rights as the Head of the church
{
1. Custody of temporalities.
2. Right of corody.
3. Extra parochial tithes.
4. First fruits and tenths.
5. Religious revenues belonging to the church.
6. Religious revenues belonging to laymen.
}

III. *Voluntary Contributions.*

1. Voluntary Contributions by Citizens - - - -
{
1. In time of peace.
2. In time of war.
}

2. Gifts from Strangers - -
{
1. In cases of unforeseen disaster, as an earthquake, &c.
2. In time of war.
}

IV. *Involuntary Contributions or Taxes on Individuals.*

1. Of personal Services - -
{
1. In peace.
2. In war.
}

2. Of Taxes paid in Kind   -   - { 1. Of grain.
                                   2. Of cattle, &c.
                                   3. Of manufactures.

3. Of taxes o n Perfons   -   - { 1. On perfons in general.
                                   2. On women.
                                   3. On Bachelors.
                                   4. On ftrangers.
                                   5. On obnoxious perfons.
                                   6. On flaves.
                                   7. On abfentees.

4. Of taxes on real Property   -   { 1. On lands.
                                     2. On buildings { 1. Hearth money.
                                                       2. Window lights.
                                                       3. On tiles.
                                                       4. On gates.
                                     3. On fifheries.
                                     4. On mines.

5. Of Taxes on perfonal Property   { 1. On the Intereft of money.
                                     2. On plate.
                                     3. On carriages.

6. Of Taxes on Property when
   transferred   -   -   -   { 1. By auction.
                               2. By private fale.
                               3. By will.

7. Of Taxes on Income   -   - { 1. From different profeffions.
                                 2. From the public.

8. Of Taxes on Confumption   - - { 1. Cuftoms.
                                    2. Excife.

V. *Public Loans.*

1. Compulfive Loans   -   - { 1. Of provifions, carriages, &c.
                              2. Of money.

2. Voluntary Loans   -   -   - { 1. On valuable pledges.
                                 2. On the perfonal credit of the govern-
                                    ment.
                                 3. On the fecurity of the public do-
                                    mains.
                                 4. On the produce of particular taxes.
                                 5. By granting—temporary annuities.
                                 6. —————annuities on lives.
                                 7. —————contingent annuities.
                                 8. —————perpetual annuities.

Which laft is the climax of Financial Invention.

APPENDIX.

No. VI.

On the Bankruptcies which have taken place fince the Year 1748, and more efpecially of the Country Bankers An. 1793.

———

IN the third chapter of this work, a variety of obfervations were made on the failure of credit and the number of Bankruptcies in the year 1793 : in order to enable the reader to form a more perfeċt idea of this fubjeċt, it is propofed to give 1, A Lift of Bankruptcies, from the year 1748 to the year 1797 ; and, 2. A Lift of the Country Bankers that ftopt in the year 1793.

A LIST OF BANKRUPTCIES,
From the Year 1748 to the End of the Year 1797.

Year.	No.	Year.	No.	Year.	No.
1748	130	1765	239	1782	558
1749	91	1766	342	1783	532
1750	169	1767	360	1784	521
1751	172	1768	351	1785	502
1752	153	1769	344	1786	510
1753	242	1770	397	1787	509
1754	238	1771	433	1788	707
1755	213	1772	523	1789	502
1756	279	1773	507	1790	585
1757	274	1774	337	1791	583
1758	315	1775	350	1792	636
1759	254	1776	435	1793	1802
1760	221	1777	535	1794	816
1761	182	1778	656	1795	708
1762	230	1779	522	1796	760
1763	243	1780	458	1797	869
1764	322	1781	458		

Total Amount from 1748 to 1797 - - - - - 21,645

This Table shews the dreadful pre-eminence, in point of Bankruptcies, of the year 1793, above every other.

The following is the Lift of the Country Bankers that ftopt in the Year 1793 ; drawn up by Mr. Chalmers*.

County.	No.	County.	No.
In Yorkfhire	12	In Kent	2
Northumberland	7	Nottingham	1
Lincoln	7	Hereford	1
Suffex	6	Effex	1
Lancafhire	5	Buckingham	1
Northampton	4	Hants	1
Somerfet	4	Berkfhire	1
Warwick	3	Cornwall	1
Stafford	2	Durham	1
Worcefter	2	Carmarthen	1
Shropfhire	2	Dorfet	1
Chefhire	2	Wilts	1
Monmouth	2		
			71

Is it not to be lamented, after fo decifive a proof of the difadvantages and dangers attending the unreftrained privilege of Country Banking, that no proper fyftem fhould have been formed for its future regulation, which expofes the nation to another return of fimilar calamities.

* " An Eftimate of the Comparative State of Great Britain," by Geo. Chalmers, Efq. edit. 1794; Dedication, p. 67.

END OF THE SECOND VOLUME.

THE ADAM SMITH LIBRARY

Works by Adam Smith

AN INQUIRY INTO THE NATURE AND CAUSES OF THE WEALTH OF NATIONS
[1776]

2 volumes, medium quarto

The first facsimile of the original edition of the most famous book in economics. In two bindings: *de luxe*, bound in full antiqued calf, stamped in gold, with a slip case; library, bound in sturdiest buckram.

THE THEORY OF MORAL SENTIMENTS
[1759]

Adam Smith's first major work; indispensable for an understanding of the basic philosophy underlying *The Wealth of Nations*. A reprint of the latest Bohn Library issue of 1892. x, 506 pp.

LECTURES ON JUSTICE, POLICE, REVENUE AND ARMS
[1763]

Edited with an introduction and notes by EDWIN CANNAN
[1898]

Student notes of Adam Smith's course at the University of Glasgow; his early work on economics. xli, 293 pp.

THE EARLY WRITINGS OF ADAM SMITH
Edited with an introduction by J. RALPH LINDGREN

This volume includes: Preface to William Hamilton's *Poems*, writings in *The Edinburgh Review* of 1755, *Essays on Philosophical Subjects*, *Considerations Concerning the First Formation of Languages*.

The first complete collection of Adam Smith's early writings. 255 pp.

Books on The Life of Adam Smith

THE LIFE OF ADAM SMITH
[1895]
By JOHN RAE

With an Introduction
"Guide to John Rae's *Life of Adam Smith*" by Jacob Viner

A handsome reprint of the most important *Life*, with an introduction which appraises the present state of knowledge about the life of Adam Smith, written by the leading contemporary authority. 146, xv, 449 pp.

ADAM SMITH, AS STUDENT AND PROFESSOR
[1937]
By WILLIAM R. SCOTT

Second in importance ony to John Rae's *Life*, this book, illustrated with pictures and facsimiles of documents, preserves a wide variety of source material concerning Adam Smith's life and work chiefly at the University of Glasgow. Crown octavo, xxv, 445 pp.

BIOGRAPHICAL MEMOIRS OF ADAM SMITH
By DUGALD STEWART

Written in 1793, Dugald Stewart's *Memoir* is the first biography of Adam Smith, and the only one by a contemporary, friend and fellow student of economics and philosophy. Reprinted from Volume X of Stewart's *Collected Works*, with about 30 pages of notes added in 1811 and further material added in 1858. The complete volume which includes *Memoirs* of William Robertson, Thomas Reid and Dugald Stewart himself is reprinted. clxxvii, 338 pp.

Adam Smith's Own Library

A CATALOGUE OF THE LIBRARY OF ADAM SMITH
By JAMES BONAR
2nd edition, 1932   xxiv, 218 pp.

A FULL AND DETAILED CATALOGUE OF BOOKS
WHICH BELONGED TO ADAM SMITH
[1951]
By YADAO YANAIHARA
ix, 126 pp. and plates

These two volumes list most of the books known to have belonged to Adam Smith. A most detailed account of Adam Smith's library appears in Jacob Viner's introduction to John Rae's *Life of Adam Smith*.

Contemporary Discussions of
The Wealth of Nations

A LETTER FROM GOVERNOR POWNALL TO ADAM SMITH
[1776]

By THOMAS POWNALL

This comment on *The Wealth of Nations*, published in the same year, is one of the first and is particularly interesting since it was written by a governor of the colony of Massachusetts. 48 pp., 8½ x 11.

THE STATE OF THE POOR
Or, A History of the Labouring Classes in England, from the Conquest to the present period . . .
[1797]

By SIR FREDERIC MORTON EDEN

3 vols.   Crown quarto

This great collection of information about the working classes of England in the 18th century forms a valuable background to the ideas of Adam Smith.

AN INQUIRY INTO THE NATURE AND ORIGIN OF PUBLIC WEALTH—AND INTO THE MEANS OF ITS INCREASE
[1804]

By JAMES MAITLAND, 8th Earl of Lauderdale

An early major critique of *The Wealth of Nations*. 500 pp.

OBSERVATONS ON THE SUBJECTS TREATED IN DR. SMITH'S INQUIRY . . . 2nd EDITION
[1817]

By DAVID BUCHANAN

A volume of essays added to Buchanan's edition of *The Wealth of Nations* which was the first annotated edition. Comments from what became the Malthusian point of view. xvi, 316, 88 pp.

A TREATISE ON POLITICAL ECONOMY
[1821]

By JEAN-BAPTISTE SAY

Say's work, written in 1803, translated into English in 1821, is credited with putting Adam Smith's views in a more logical form. It is in this form that Smith's views were widely propagated throughout the nineteenth century and even in our day. lx, 488 pp.

NEW PRINCIPLES ON THE SUBJECT OF POLITICAL ECONOMY
[1834]
By JOHN RAE

A major critique of *The Wealth of Nations*, based on experience of life in the United States and Canada; attacks free trade, emphasizes sociological factors in capital formation; pioneer study of economc development. xvi, 414 pp.

Modern Comment on Adam Smith's Work

MONETARY THEORY BEFORE ADAM SMITH
[1923]
By ARTHUR E. MONROE

The outstanding modern treatise on monetary theory before Adam Smith, with special emphasis on the eighteenth century. xi, 312 pp.

THE SPIRIT OF '76 AND OTHER ESSAYS
[1927]
By CARL BECKER, J. M. CLARK, WILLIAM E. DODD

Lectures in commemoration of the 150th anniversary of *The Wealth of Nations* and *The Declaration of Independence*. 135 pp.

ADAM SMITH 1776-1926
[1928]
By J. M. CLARK, PAUL H. DOUGLAS, JACOB H. HOLLANDER, GLENN R. MORROW, MELCHIOR PALYI, and JACOB VINER

Comments on various aspects of Adam Smith's work and significance 150 years after the publication of *The Wealth of Nations*. ix, 241 pp.

PREDECESSORS OF ADAM SMITH
[1937]
By E. A. J. JOHNSON

The growth of British economic thought before Adam Smith, with an exposition of the ideas of the leading British mercantilist writers, xiii, 423 pp.

For additional information about *The Adam Smith Library*, its privileges and conditions of membership, please write the publisher:

AUGUSTUS M. KELLEY · *Publishers*
24 East 22nd Street, New York, New York 10010